Marx, Engels, and Marxisms

Series Editors
Marcello Musto
York University
Toronto, ON, Canada

Terrell Carver
University of Bristol
Bristol, UK

The Marx renaissance is underway on a global scale. Wherever the critique of capitalism re-emerges, there is an intellectual and political demand for new, critical engagements with Marxism. The peer-reviewed series Marx, Engels and Marxisms (edited by Marcello Musto & Terrell Carver, with Babak Amini, Francesca Antonini, Paula Rauhala & Kohei Saito as Assistant Editors) publishes monographs, edited volumes, critical editions, reprints of old texts, as well as translations of books already published in other languages. Our volumes come from a wide range of political perspectives, subject matters, academic disciplines and geographical areas, producing an eclectic and informative collection that appeals to a diverse and international audience. Our main areas of focus include: the oeuvre of Marx and Engels, Marxist authors and traditions of the 19th and 20th centuries, labour and social movements, Marxist analyses of contemporary issues, and reception of Marxism in the world.

More information about this series at
http://www.palgrave.com/gp/series/14812

Kevin B. Anderson · Kieran Durkin ·
Heather A. Brown
Editors

Raya Dunayevskaya's Intersectional Marxism

Race, Class, Gender, and the Dialectics of
Liberation

Editors
Kevin B. Anderson
Department of Sociology
University of California, Santa Barbara
Santa Barbara, CA, USA

Kieran Durkin
Department of Politics
University of York
York, UK

Heather A. Brown
Department of Political Science
Westfield State University
Westfield, MA, USA

ISSN 2524-7123   ISSN 2524-7131   (electronic)
Marx, Engels, and Marxisms
ISBN 978-3-030-53716-6   ISBN 978-3-030-53717-3   (eBook)
https://doi.org/10.1007/978-3-030-53717-3

Cover image: Rendering by Palestinian artist Maliha Maslamani of Alaa Salah leading a rally during the 2020 Revolution in Sudan

This Palgrave Macmillan imprint is published by the registered company Springer Nature Switzerland AG
The registered company address is: Gewerbestrasse 11, 6330 Cham, Switzerland

Titles Published

1. Terrell Carver & Daniel Blank, *A Political History of the Editions of Marx and Engels's "German Ideology" Manuscripts*, 2014.
2. Terrell Carver & Daniel Blank, *Marx and Engels's "German Ideology" Manuscripts: Presentation and Analysis of the "Feuerbach chapter,"* 2014.
3. Alfonso Maurizio Iacono, *The History and Theory of Fetishism*, 2015.
4. Paresh Chattopadhyay, *Marx's Associated Mode of Production: A Critique of Marxism*, 2016.
5. Domenico Losurdo, *Class Struggle: A Political and Philosophical History*, 2016.
6. Frederick Harry Pitts, *Critiquing Capitalism Today: New Ways to Read Marx*, 2017.
7. Ranabir Samaddar, *Karl Marx and the Postcolonial Age*, 2017.
8. George Comninel, *Alienation and Emancipation in the Work of Karl Marx*, 2018.
9. Jean-Numa Ducange & Razmig Keucheyan (Eds.), *The End of the Democratic State: Nicos Poulantzas, a Marxism for the 21st Century*, 2018.
10. Robert X. Ware, *Marx on Emancipation and Socialist Goals: Retrieving Marx for the Future*, 2018.
11. Xavier LaFrance & Charles Post (Eds.), *Case Studies in the Origins of Capitalism*, 2018.

TITLES FORTHCOMING

George C. Comninel, *The Feudal Foundations of Modern Europe*

James Steinhoff, *Critiquing the New Autonomy of Immaterial Labour: A Marxist Study of Work in the Artificial Intelligence Industry*

Spencer A. Leonard, *Marx, the India Question, and the Crisis of Cosmopolitanism*

Joe Collins, *Applying Marx's Capital to the 21st century*

Levy del Aguila Marchena, *Communism, Political Power and Personal Freedom in Marx*

Jeong Seongjin, *Korean Capitalism in the 21st Century: Marxist Analysis and Alternatives*

Marcello Mustè, *Marxism and Philosophy of Praxis: An Italian Perspective from Labriola to Gramsci*

Satoshi Matsui, *Normative Theories of Liberalism and Socialism: Marxist Analysis of Values*

Shannon Brincat, *Dialectical Dialogues in Contemporary World Politics: A Meeting of Traditions in Global Comparative Philosophy*

Stefano Petrucciani, *Theodor W. Adorno's Philosophy, Society, and Aesthetics*

Francesca Antonini, *Reassessing Marx's Eighteenth Brumaire: Dictatorship, State, and Revolution*

Thomas Kemple, *Capital after Classical Sociology: The Faustian Lives of Social Theory*

Tsuyoshi Yuki, *Socialism, Markets and the Critique of Money: The Theory of "Labour Note"*

V Geetha, *Bhimrao Ramji Ambedkar and the Question of Socialism in India*

Xavier Vigna, *A Political History of Factories in France: The Workers' Insubordination of 1968*

Atila Melegh, *Anti-Migrant Populism in Eastern Europe and Hungary: A Marxist Analysis*

Marie-Cecile Bouju, *A Political History of the Publishing Houses of the French Communist Party*

Gustavo Moura de Cavalcanti Mello & Henrique Pereira Braga (Eds.), *Wealth and Poverty in Contemporary Brazilian Capitalism*

Peter McMylor, Graeme Kirkpatrick & Simin Fadaee (Eds.), *Marxism, Religion, and Emancipatory Politics*

Mauro Buccheri, *Radical Humanism for the Left: The Quest for Meaning in Late Capitalism*

Rémy Herrera, *Confronting Mainstream Economics to Overcome Capitalism*

Acknowledgments

The editors would like to thank the following publishers for permission to reprint from their publications:

Lexington Books, for "Introduction: Raya Dunayevskaya's Concept of the Dialectic," in *The Power of Negativity: Selected Writings on The Dialectic in Hegel and Marx*, edited by Peter Hudis and Kevin B. Anderson.

W. W. Norton & Company for "Raya Dunayevskaya's Marx," from *Arts of the Possible: Essays and Conversations*, by Adrienne Rich, 2001.

The New Statesman for "Why Marx is More Relevant than Ever in the Age of Automation," by Paul Mason, May 7, 2018.

Il Ponte Editore, "*Marxismo e libertà:* a proposito del libro di Raya Dunayevskaya", by Rodolfo Mondolfo, in *Il Ponte* (Florence), Vol. XIX, Number 10, October 1963.

Éditions Syllepse for "Une Marxisme de la libération," Preface to Raya Dunayevskaya, Marxisme et Liberté, by Frédéric Monferrand, 2016.

New Politics for parts of Kevin B. Anderson, "*Marxism and Freedom* after Sixty Years, for Yesterday and Today," No. 65 (Summer), July 2018.

In addition, Kieran Durkin would like to acknowledge funding from the European Union's Horizon 2020 research and innovation program under the Marie Sklodowska-Curie grant agreement No 794656.

PRAISE FOR *RAYA DUNAYEVSKAYA'S INTERSECTIONAL MARXISM*

"This is an important collection of essays appraising the legacy of an underappreciated Marxist philosopher, Raya Dunayevskaya. Perhaps her underappreciation was rooted in the philosopher's own gender, or perhaps in her stunning recasting of Marxism itself through an early and avid commitment to frameworks of gender and race. Now as mass antiracist protests redefine the horizons of human freedom on our streets, Raya Dunayevskaya's writing can do the work it was always meant to do, provide a theoretical grounding to the cry for freedom of the oppressed."
—Tithi Bhattacharya, *co-author of* Feminism for the 99% (2019)

"The essays in this collection explore Raya Dunayevskaya's revolutionary humanism, which extends class analysis to race, gender, and other dimensions of dominance, and insists that theory does not stand above practice but shapes and is shaped by the experience of liberatory social movements. Dunayevskaya's work highlights and develops the humanism at the center of Marx's thought and makes Marx relevant to our time."
—Barbara Epstein, *Professor of the History of Consciousness Studies, University of California, Santa Cruz, USA, and author of* Political Protest and Cultural Revolution (1993)

"Too many intellectuals fail to see that dialectical studies and innovations on revolutionary practice are not exclusively men's work. As ideas of women ranging from those of Rosa Luxemburg, Emma Goldman, and

He-Yin Zhen to Grace Lee Boggs have been receiving increased attention, it is clear that their critical challenge is to think human transformation and flourishing through what everyone has to offer. Kevin B. Anderson, Kieran Durkin, and Heather A. Brown, and the community of scholars they assembled to explore the thought of Raya Dunayevskaya make it clear that her ideas were no less than revolutionary. Offering analyses beyond the reduction of class versus race and gender, the humanist logic of both-and and openness is brought forth with breathtaking clarity. This book pays proper respect to the ideas of this great revolutionary thinker through pushing aside fetish and ushering forth, through eyes wide open to contemporary pandemics and uprisings, the ongoing power and beauty of living thought."

—Lewis R. Gordon, *University of Connecticut, USA, and author of* Freedom, Justice, and Decolonization (2020)

"*Raya Dunayevskaya's Intersectional Marxism* truly addresses Race, Gender, Class and the Dialectics of Liberation, and the excellent book edited by Kevin B. Anderson, Kieran Durkin, and Heather A. Brown demonstrates the relevancy of Dunayesvskaya's work for this era of crisis and tumultuous struggle and upheaval. The book engages both scholars and activists, and demonstrates how revolutionary theory can become a weapon of transformational practice."

—Douglas Kellner, *Distinguished Professor, UCLA, USA and author of* Herbert Marcuse and the Crisis of Marxism (1984)

"Periodically the world is in flames and those who would topple not just statues but the whole exploitative order begin to dream again of what might be. New times overlay on old ones. Raya Dunayevskaya's remarkable achievement is to be in her time and outside of it—to see so clearly, practically, philosophically, what steers the world, and to see what is suppressed within this, what distorts and what is emergent, ready to activate another time and be activated once new times constellate. Dunayevskaya imagines and works towards times to come—but also anticipates a faceting of Marxism to account for the many-threaded nature of the present world, with its skirmishes around multiple points of oppression and social division. Dunayevskaya's analyses relay, agilely, between the pressure points of class, race, sex, gender, the discordant effects of colonialism, war and nationalism, but they stand also, insistently, at the intersection of philosophy and politics, transforming and elaborating each in the process. So persuasive are her accounts of Marxist Humanism, one wonders how any Marxism could shed such a qualifier that makes all sense of the project. This volume appraises not just a legacy but the potential for current and future liberatory struggles, grounded by philosophical rigour and oriented towards a practical sense of a limitless creativity."

—Esther Leslie, *Professor of Political Aesthetics, Birkbeck College, University of London, UK, and author of* Walter Benjamin (2000)

"At such a turbulent historical moment in which armed white militia cosplay their favorite action stars on the steps of our statehouses, and Nazi ideology is disinterred from the blood-stained soil of history, *Raya Dunayevskaya's Intersectional Marxism* could not come at a more urgent time, offering revolutionary praxis informed by intersectionality as means of shifting the tectonic plates of our contemporary political landscape. Rejecting the tepid liberalism claiming the mantle of democracy as incapable of providing an answer to the rise of neofascism, this outstanding collection of essays offers lucid and provocative Marxist-Humanist interpretations of the contemporary political scene, emphasizing the intersectional experiences of people of color and recognizing that these experiences, marked by systems of mediation linked to race, gender, colonialism, class and globalization, when placed against the backdrop of the movement towards freedom from oppression, are always lived in ways that make them greater than the sum of their parts."

—Peter McLaren, *author of* Che Guevara, Paulo Freire, and the Pedagogy of Revolution (1999)

CONTENTS

Part IV   Freedom and Liberation

NOTES ON CONTRIBUTORS

Kevin B. Anderson is Professor of Sociology at University of California, Santa Barbara, with courtesy appointments in Feminist Studies and Political Science. He is the author of *Lenin, Hegel, and Western Marxism* (1995), *Foucault and the Iranian Revolution* (with Janet Afary, 2005), and *Marx at the Margins* (2010/2016). Among his edited volumes are the *Rosa Luxemburg Reader* (with Peter Hudis, 2004) and the *Dunayevskaya-Marcuse-Fromm Correspondence* (with Russell Rockwell, 2012). He also writes regularly for *New Politics*, *The International Marxist-Humanist*, and *Jacobin* on Marxism and on international politics and radical movements in Africa, Europe, and the Middle East.

David Black born 1950 in Newcastle-Upon-Tyne, was educated at Rutherford Grammar School and Middlesex Polytechnic. Now resident in London, he works as a journalist, author, musician and video-maker. His published books include, (co-authored with Chris Ford) *1839: The Chartist Insurrection*; *The Philosophical Roots of Anti-Capitalism: Essays on History, Culture, and Dialectical Thought*; (as editor) *Red Republican: the Complete Annotated Works of Helen Macfarlane*; and *Acid Outlaws: LSD, Counter-Culture and Counter-Revolution*.

Heather A. Brown is an Associate Professor of Political Science at Westfield State University. She has written widely on Marxism, feminism, and ecology and is the author of *Marx on Gender and the Family: A Critical Study*.

Kieran Durkin is Marie Skłodowska-Curie Global Fellow at University of York, and former Visiting Scholar at University of California Santa Barbara, where he has been studying the Marxist Humanist tradition. He is author of *The Radical Humanism of Erich Fromm* and (co-edited with Joan Braune) *Erich Fromm's Critical Theory: Hope, Humanism, and the Future*.

Peter Hudis is a Professor of Humanities and Philosophy at Oakton Community College and author of *Marx's Concept of the Alternative to Capitalism* (Brill, 2012) and *Frantz Fanon: Philosopher of the Barricades* (Pluto Press, 2015), and has published in numerous journals on international politics, Latin American social movements, critical race theory, and contemporary political and social philosophy. He co-edited *The Power of Negativity: Selected Writings on the Dialectic in Hegel and Marx*, by Raya Dunayevskaya and *The Rosa Luxemburg Reader* as well as *The Letters of Rosa Luxemburg*. He currently serves as General Editor of *The Complete Works of Luxemburg*, a forthcoming 17-volume collection; he has edited Volume 1 (*Economic Writings 1*) and co-edited Volume 2 (*Economic Writings 2*) as well as Volumes 3 and 4 (*Political Writings 1 and 2*). He is a Member of the International Marxist-Humanist Organization.

Ndindi Kitonga is a Kenyan-American educator, long-time organizer, and activist in Los Angeles who has written on revolutionary critical pedagogy and democratic education.

Karel Ludenhoff is an Amsterdam-based labor activist and a writer on Marx's critique of political economy whose essays have appeared in *Logos* and other journals.

Paul Mason is an award-winning journalist, writer, filmmaker and public speaker. He has written a number of books, including *Postcapitalism, Why It's Kicking Off Everywhere* and *Clear Bright Future: A Radical Defence of the Human Being*. Current work in development includes a short book about Karl Marx, a drama-documentary about the Spanish Civil War, and the play *Feel My Pulse*.

Rodolfo Mondolfo (1877–1976) was a prominent Italian philosopher and socialist humanist. Forced into exile under Mussolini's fascist regime, he lived subsequently in Argentina, where he continued to teach at the university level despite difficulties under the Peronist regime. He was the author of several books on Marx, Engels, and Gramsci, as well as ones on ancient Greek philosophy and on Rousseau, Hobbes, and Spinoza.

Frédéric Monferrand holds a Ph.D. in Philosophy from Nanterre University, France and is currently a post-doctoral researcher at the University of Namur, Belgium. He wrote various articles on Hegel, Marx, Marxism, and Critical Theory. With Vincent Chanson and Alexis Cukier, he co-edited 'La réification. Histoire et actualité d'un concept critique' (La Dispute, 2014), with Félix Boggio-Ewanjée Epée, Stella Magliani Belkacem and Morgane Merteuil, he co-edited "Pour un féminisme de la totalité" (Amsterdam, 2017). He also co-wrote a *Dictionnaire Marx* with Juliette Farjat (Ellipse, 2020) and is currently preparing a book on the Young Marx's critical ontology.

Lilia D. Monzó is Associate Professor of Education in the College of Educational Studies at Chapman University. She engages a Marxist-humanist, revolutionary critical pedagogy to develop a praxis for class struggle and the struggle against racism, sexism and all forms of oppression that could lead to a socialist alternative and a "new humanism." She is an active member of the International Marxist-Humanist Organization and teaches classes on social movements. She has published significantly in academic journals including in *Policy Futures in Education, Journal of Critical Education Policy Studies, Anthropology and Education Quarterly, Postcolonial Directions in Education,* and in alternative public pedagogy sources *IMHO Journal* and *Truthout.* Her latest book is *A Revolutionary Subject: Pedagogy of Women of Color and Indigeneity.*

Adrienne Rich (1929–2012) was an American poet, essayist and feminist.

Alessandra Spano is a Ph.D. candidate in Political Philosophy at the Department of Political and Social Sciences of Catania. She received an M.A. in Philosophy at the University of Bologna with a thesis focused on the political thought of Raya Dunayevskaya. This research was the inspiration for her focus on Marxist-Feminism and critical theory, the concentration for her doctoral investigation, particularly looking at the United States as a political space that is simultaneously imperialist, 'colonized', and global. Her interests include: Marxism, feminist theory, African-American studies, German idealism, psychoanalysis, and radicalism in the United States.

CHAPTER 1

Introduction

Kevin B. Anderson, Kieran Durkin, and Heather A. Brown

Our present societal and intellectual landscape is marked by fear, disruption, and radical change. The political sinews that regulated and managed the global capitalist system after 1945, and which at first seemed to have been reinvigorated by the collapse of the Soviet bloc in 1989–1991, are fraying, from NATO to the EU, in no small part the result of disastrous wars in the Middle East. At an economic level, the Great Recession of 2007–2008 wiped away the neoliberal claims to have solved the problems of stagnation that had doomed the earlier Keynesian economics, as the new economy revealed itself to be a house of cards. A decade

K. B. Anderson (✉)
Department of Sociology, University of California, Santa Barbara, Santa Barbara, CA, USA
e-mail: kanderson@soc.ucsb.edu

K. Durkin
Department of Politics, University of York, York, UK
e-mail: kieran.durkin@york.ac.uk

H. A. Brown
Department of Political Science, Westfield State University, Westfield, MA, USA
e-mail: hbrown@westfield.ma.edu

© The Author(s) 2021
K. B. Anderson et al. (eds.), *Raya Dunayevskaya's Intersectional Marxism, Marx, Engels, and Marxisms*,
https://doi.org/10.1007/978-3-030-53717-3_1

later, the COVID-19 epidemic triggered an even deeper economic crisis while laying bare as never before the dehumanization of contemporary capitalism. Even in developed countries like the U.S. and the UK, central governments floundered in early 2020 while medical, delivery, food, grocery, janitorial, and other workers performed the dangerous labor that is really basic to social existence. Across the globe, hundreds of thousands of people lost their lives to the pandemic, while billions suffered wrenching economic privation. This was both a healthcare and an economic crisis, deeper than anything since the Great Depression.

By late spring 2020, as society began to awaken from the first phase of COVID-19, the greatest mass movement in the U.S. since the 1960s broke out over the police murder of George Floyd, a semi-employed Black man in Minneapolis. During this Black Lives Matter uprising, which spread across the country and internationally, hundreds of thousands of mainly young people demonstrated, occupied highways and streets, toppled statues of prominent racists, attacked and looted luxury goods stores, burned at least one police station and surrounded another, while occupying the surrounding streets. The Trump administration met demonstrators outside the White House with repression so forceful that it backfired, with even military leaders being forced to distance themselves publicly from Trump, the most openly racist president in a century. Rubbed raw by mass unemployment, indebtedness, and lack of affordable housing, the new generation of youth faces a world it did not make, in a stance of resistance and of idealism in the finest sense of the word. More sensitive to sexism, heterosexism, and, above all, racism, than any previous generation, they have followed the lead of Black youth, swelling the Black Lives Matter movement into a massive challenge to the social order that shows no sign of abating. As Ndindi Kitonga, one of the contributors to this volume intoned, after participating in the first weeks of the uprising in Los Angeles:

> What we call for with regard to these curfews and the harassment is a questioning of where the money is coming from to fund this. The City does not run out of rubber bullets or tear gas. Yet, as someone who does outreach to our unhoused people, I beg the City for personal protective equipment (PPE) and shelter. I beg for food and unemployment compensation to help our people. There seems to be no resources to help people, but there are always resources to brutalize people. Something else I want to emphasize is that while this is of course an anti-racist protest, it is *also* a

working class uprising of people of all colors. This is also an anti-capitalist uprising. It is a demand for people to stop being overcome by capital. The graffiti in Beverly Hills is not just "fuck the police," but it is also down with capitalism and down with white supremacy. We witness people connecting the dots, you see.

These are exactly the connections, or intersections, that were central to the life and work of Raya Dunayevskaya, and that are at the heart of this book.

Today, global capitalism is increasingly seen as the enemy of human flourishing, whether in its exploitation of labor, its environmental destruction, its virulent racism, or its continued threat of nuclear destruction. The new generation faces a life of precarity, underemployment, overwork for those employed, and indebtedness. Even strong proponents of the capitalist order see no clear way back toward the promised land of growth and prosperity.

The concomitant crisis in thought and in wider society has led to neofascist and rightwing populist and nationalist forces coming to power in a number of countries, most notably the U.S., Britain, Brazil, Hungary, Poland, Turkey, India, and the Philippines. Meanwhile, older authoritarian regimes in Russia, China, and Saudi Arabia have tightened the screws on their populations even as Australia burned and the Syrian people faced a final massacre by the Assad regime.

But the crisis in the economic, political, and ecological spheres has also led to a resurgence of the left and of revolutionary opposition to systems of global dominance, as seen most dramatically in the 2011–2013 revolutions in the Middle East/North Africa region (MENA), the 2011 Occupy movement, and early Black Lives Matter, as well as in electorally based movements like Syriza in Greece and those around Corbyn in the UK and Sanders in the U.S. In 2018–2020, grassroots radical activism returned with a vengeance, with the Yellow Vests and the pension strikes in France, and most dramatically with the outbreak of what is being called the Second Arab Spring in Sudan, Algeria, Iraq, and Lebanon. Sudan also exhibited a deeper African dimension that resonated in both North and Sub-Saharan Africa. At an intellectual level—what the socialist tradition has called "the battle of ideas"—Marxist thought has also seen a resurgence, especially in the English-speaking world, putting postmodernism and the politics of difference on the defensive.

Today's intellectual left is, broadly speaking, divided into two major streams. The first stream, often espousing some forms of Marxism, highlights capital and class, accusing the left of the 1990s and after of being stuck in what it disparages as "identity politics." The second stream holds to a focus on race, gender, and sexuality, attacking Marxists for a kind of class reductionism whose return they are shocked to see.

Can a Marxist theory and practice, albeit one that is informed by intersectionality, dialectically transcend (*aufheben*) this contradiction? More specifically, can the theory and practice of the Marxist-Humanist and feminist philosopher Raya Dunayevskaya (1910–1987) help to overcome this contradiction within today's progressive left? Those are the issues that inspired the present volume.

As someone who pioneered the rigorous class analysis of the Soviet Union as state capitalist and who early on critiqued Rosa Luxemburg's quasi-underconsumptionist economic theories as inadequate, Dunayevskaya was the rare Marxist thinker at home as easily with arguments about declining profit rates in Vol. III of *Capital* in relation to economic crisis, as she was with Hegel, dialectics, and the young Marx. From her earliest days in the Communist Party youth group in Chicago in the late 1920s, she also fought for the centrality of race to an understanding of U.S. capitalism, subsequently working with C. L. R. James and Grace Lee Boggs in the 1940s and 1950s to critique class-reductionist Marxism via a creative reading of Marx, Lenin, and Trotsky. By the 1960s, she had written profoundly on the African revolutions and their theorists, especially Frantz Fanon, also developing at this time concept of "Black masses as vanguard" of the American revolution. By the 1970s, she began to explore anew socialist feminism, here centering on a century of struggle as well as on key women Marxist theoreticians and their neglected feminist dimension, most notably Luxemburg.

Her resulting 1982 book, *Rosa Luxemburg, Women's Liberation, and Marx's Philosophy of Revolution* ran up against a certain indifference if not outright rejection in many quarters, including many feminist academics. A major exception was the acclaimed revolutionary feminist poet Adrienne Rich, who, nudged by the Black revolutionary feminist Gloria Joseph, analyzed in depth the work of Dunayevskaya in this period. In 1986, a year before Dunayevskaya's death, Rich published a major retrospective on her in the *Women's Review of Books* that we are most glad to republish in this volume. While this helped to generate a wider discussion of Dunayevskaya in the 1980s/1990s, especially in the work of Margaret

Randall on women and revolution, it did not succeed at that time in drawing the larger streams of feminist thought back to Marxism, let alone to Dunayevskaya's version of Marxist-Humanism.

That missed juncture between revolutionary feminism and Dunayevskaya's Marxist-Humanism has inspired the title of this collection, "Raya Dunayevskaya's Intersectional Marxism," which highlights the ways in which her writings intertwine issues of race, gender, and colonialism with those of capital, class, and globalization. But what was the nature of that missed juncture, in the early 1980s?

In that period, Dunayevskaya launched a multipronged effort to recast Marxism for an era that had experienced Black insurgency, antiwar activism, and revolutionary feminism on a massive scale, even as the sharp turn to the right (later understood as "neoliberalism") was beginning to form. She did so via critical analysis of these revolutionary movements, but also through newly unearthed texts of Karl Marx and Rosa Luxemburg. This led to reconsiderations of the women's movement of the time, especially its African and African-American dimensions, rethinking Marx in light of his late writings on gender and on revolution outside Europe, and a pathbreaking analysis of Luxemburg that portrayed her for the first time as a revolutionary feminist, in sharp contrast to almost all previous interpretations, which had denied the imputation of feminism. *Rosa Luxemburg, Women's Liberation, and Marx's Philosophy of Revolution* sought to bring Marxist thought alive for a new generation that had come through the defeats of the 1960s movements and that embraced a worldview in which race and gender were as important as class. While Dunayevskaya did not use the term intersectionality—a term which did not come into wide use during her lifetime—she worked with a similar concept in her 1982 book, as exemplified in this passage: "And just as the Sojourner Truths and Harriet Tubmans learned to separate from what they called their 'short-minded' leaders who would not fight for woman's suffrage in the 'Negro hour' of fighting for Black male suffrage, so the new Women's Liberation Movement arose from participation in the Black freedom struggles of the '60s, and the Black women, in turn, made their own declaration" (103).

It is this focus on both difference and commonality that is often missing in discussions of intersectionality. Certainly, the vastly different theories of intersectionality have offered important discussions of the need to take various differences in social positionality seriously as this affects the ability of successful coalitions to form and for disempowered groups to claim their own power in progressive movements. However, difference can be best understood once there is a reference to a commonality that individuals can be measured against. For Dunayevskaya, who was committed to a Marxist-Humanist position, this commonality is our striving for greater freedom—for a new society that is free of structural impediments to individual and communal flourishing. This must be worked out philosophically and politically in a world where difference abounds and serves as a means to evaluate both one's own position and that of others relative to a vision of a better future that is possible. Thus, Dunayevskaya offers a positive vision of intersectionality which takes our common humanity, worked out through philosophical and political struggle, as a basis for unity rather than asserting already ossified differences and working in coalition from those distinctions. At the same time, she saw the struggles of Black people and revolutionary feminists as sources of creative difference inside the radical movement. Black and feminist movements often constituted a real revolutionary vanguard—not only in action but also in thought—that the labor and socialist movements needed to learn from, and sometimes follow. Moreover, at a theoretical level, these kinds of experiences needed to be incorporated into Marxist, dialectical theory, as seen in the concept of "a movement from practice that is itself a form of theory" that undergirded Dunayevskaya's first book, *Marxism and Freedom*. In this sense, her notion of commonality involved facing these differences, and the tensions they created, head on. It meant developing from them a notion of Marxist-Humanist commonality that was capacious enough to incorporate all these differing strands of thought and action.

Unfortunately, *Rosa Luxemburg, Women's Liberation, and Marx's Philosophy of Revolution* appeared during the retrenchments of the 1980s, when even many radical intellectuals were seduced by the timid social democracy of Jürgen Habermas or the ultimately disempowering poststructuralism of Michel Foucault. In 1992, in the wake of the implosion of the Soviet bloc, Richard Rorty, then considered a leading radical philosopher, intoned that "large theoretical ways of finding out how to end injustice" as in Marx had failed the test of history and that the left should strive for democracy, civil society, and the creation of wealth in a free market. Rorty concluded that no "alternative to capitalism" existed, and went so far as to declare, provocatively, that "the only hope for getting the money necessary to eliminate intolerable inequities is to facilitate the activities of people like Henry Ford...and even Donald Trump"! (1992: 4).

In this period, many radical intellectuals embraced a postmodern or poststructuralist politics of difference, which also served to draw them away from Marxism of any kind, with its aspiration for class solidarities across national, gender, and racial lines. As 1960s icons Daniel Cohn-Bendit and Gilles Deleuze put it in 1987 in a classic statement of the politics of difference that pointedly left out capital and class: "The goal is...what we call a *culture of dissensus* that strives for a deepening of individual positions and a resingularization of individuals and human groups. What folly to claim that everyone – immigrants, feminists, rockers, regionalists, pacifists, ecologists, and hackers – should agree on a same vision of things! We should not be aiming for a programmatic agreement that erases their differences" (cited in Sanbonmatsu 2004: 14).

These intellectual trends were conditioned by developments in global capitalism, as Ronald Reagan, Margaret Thatcher, and Pope John Paul II—and their implicit ally, Ayatollah Ruhollah Khomeini—were in the process of rolling back many of the gains of the 1960s. The bloody defeats of the Marxist-led revolutions in Nicaragua and Grenada and the transformation of the Iranian revolution into a fundamentalist dictatorship helped to recast the 1980s as a period of retrogression. All this accompanied the ushering in of neoliberalism, which Dunayevskaya at the time castigated as "Reaganomics."

Today, the historical and intellectual landscape has changed dramatically. Neoliberalism has been called widely into question, targeted by forces further to the right, like rightwing populism and nationalism, but also by a left that has been resurgent in both political and intellectual life. The politics of difference that emerged in the era of poststructuralism has also receded. Both have been put on the defensive by the Great Recession and the rise of large global movements against economic exploitation and inequality. At the same time, a narrow politics of class and economic determinism has emerged with a vengeance on the left, seeing itself as the antidote to the politics of difference.

It is at this juncture that we invite the readers of this volume to consider Raya Dunayevskaya—philosopher, Marxist-Humanist, feminist, anti-racist activist, and revolutionary—as a thinker who was often out of joint with her times but who also speaks to ours with great resonance.

A more specific and immediate impetus for the present book on the part of its living authors and editors, most of them long familiar with

Dunayevskaya's life and work, lies in a series of talks and papers from the year 2018, the sixtieth anniversary of the publication of Dunayevskaya's most influential book, *Marxism and Freedom*. Its original 1958 edition included in the appendix the first published English translations of major parts of Marx's *Economic and Philosophical Manuscripts* and of Lenin's *Philosophical Notebooks*. The book based itself on an original reading of the work of Hegel, Marx, and Lenin, along with an analysis of the later stages of capitalism (monopoly and state capitalism), and of popular revolution and resistance, from the French revolution through the upheavals of her own day like the 1956 Hungarian Revolution, and including the epochal Montgomery Bus Boycott of 1955–1956, whose revolutionary significance she discerned early on. But the book had been preceded by—and was accompanied by—nearly two decades of serious dialogue with several other revolutionary thinkers around the dialectic, race and class, the heritage of Marxism, and the nature of contemporary capitalism, including the Stalinist, fascist, and democratic welfare state versions of state capitalism. Initially, these dialogues were with C. L. R. James and Grace Lee Boggs, her co-theorists in the Johnson-Forest (JFT) or State-Capitalist Tendency of 1941–1955. To this day, their philosophical correspondence of 1949–1951 remains unpublished, although joint works like *State-Capitalism and World Revolution* and other individual works from each author have been acclaimed for decades. This is equally true of the writings by working-class militants associated with them, as in Dunayevskaya's comrade Charles Denby's *Indignant Heart: A Black Worker's Journal*, an early edition of which appeared in 1952, or Grace Lee Boggs's comrade and spouse James Boggs's later work, *The American Revolution: Pages from a Negro Worker's Notebook*.

   Dunayevskaya's correspondence with Herbert Marcuse began in late 1954, just as the JFT was splitting apart, with Dunayevskaya and Denby on one side and C. L. R. James, Grace Lee Boggs and James Boggs on the other. Dunayevskaya's long dialogue with Marcuse—much of it over Hegel, Marx, and dialectics—took place between two kindred spirits, albeit with some major political and philosophical disagreements, while both were quite isolated during the McCarthyite 1950s. This correspondence, which dealt heavily on Dunayevskaya's side with her concept of Hegel's absolute negativity as new beginning, had grown out of her 1953 "Letters on Hegel's Absolutes," originally part of her correspondence with Grace Lee Boggs. These letters were later published numerous times in pamphlet form by Dunayevskaya, who considered this text her foundational statement on dialectics, the place where she began to make an original philosophical contribution. (For an annotated version, see Hudis and Anderson [2002: 15–32].) While she never received a real response from Grace Lee Boggs or C. L. R. James to what was one of her last philosophical dialogues with them, in a certain sense she was able to renew this dialogue with Marcuse. Here too, though, it was somewhat one-sided, with Marcuse never convinced of the revolutionary character of Hegel's absolutes. Nor did they agree on the Hungarian Revolution of 1956—which Dunayevskaya extolled as a creative form of working-class revolution while Marcuse was more reticent—or on the consequences of automation for the working class. (For an annotated edition of their correspondence, see Anderson and Rockwell [2012].) Marcuse wrote the preface to *Marxism and Freedom* and referred to the writings of Dunayevskaya's comrade Denby in his *One-Dimensional Man*. Shortly after, however, the correspondence broke off for several years after a heated dispute about Cuba's growing authoritarianism. Dunayevskaya moved in another direction, traveling to West Africa and forging ties with African socialist humanists.

For Dunayevskaya, the correspondence with Marcuse was part of the development of what was to become her deepest study of the dialectic, *Philosophy and Revolution: From Hegel to Sartre and from Marx to Mao* (1973). There, she argued that, despite their multifaceted nature and mass participation, the radical movements of the 1960s had failed because a tendency toward spontaneism had blocked efforts to form a compelling and humanist philosophical vision of the future. This also clouded their strategic perspectives on issues like race and revolution in the U.S. Thus, she chided France's Cohn-Bendit for having downplayed the importance of theory during the French uprising of 1968. She similarly criticized the U.S. white New Left for its undialectical empiricism and pragmatism at a general level. To Dunayevskaya, this kind of pragmatism was exemplified in the New Left's plunge into the much more massive anti-Vietnam War movement in 1965 in such a way that left the Black movement with the sense that their white allies had abandoned them. This was a highly original explanation of the rise of the Black Power movement and its separatist wing. It also constituted a critique of the way Marxist groups with some influence over the antiwar movement, like the Trotskyist Socialist Workers Party, had worked to keep the focus of the large, national anti-Vietnam War marches on the single issue of the immediate withdrawal of all U.S. troops, even allying with liberal pragmatists to block proposals for the demonstrations to include slogans like "End Racism Now" alongside "Bring the Troops Home Now."

As she honed *Philosophy and Revolution* during the 1960s, Dunayevskaya also examined more sympathetically the socialist humanist tendencies in Eastern Europe and Africa, visiting West Africa in 1962. (Stalinist repression did not permit a trip to Eastern Europe of this sort.) In both Eastern Europe and Africa, she found thinkers who had traveled the same road as she had, from the young Marx to a critique of contemporary forms of oppression and alienation. Among the thinkers she saw as the most creative—whom she contrasted to what she saw as the weaknesses of Adorno in his *Negative Dialectics*, which tended toward the exclusion of the subject—were the Afro-Caribbean revolutionary theorist Frantz Fanon and the Czech philosopher Karel Kosík.

It was also in this period that her correspondence with Erich Fromm commenced. This began as Fromm was at work on his *Marx's Concept of Man* (1961), the book that made the young Marx an indispensable part of the intellectual map of the English-speaking world for the first time. Fromm also invited Dunayevskaya to contribute to his widely circulated edited collection, *Socialist Humanism* (1965). This book helped to give her work wider recognition, especially at an international level, putting her in closer touch with Eastern European Marxist humanists. It speaks volumes about the obstacles women thinkers faced in this period, even on the left, that Dunayevskaya was one of only two women authors among thirty-two contributors. Eight years later, she was able to obtain a major publisher, Delacorte Press, for *Philosophy and Revolution*, for which Fromm later helped arrange the translations into Spanish (Mexico) and German (Austria).

In the 1960s, as she was finishing *Philosophy and Revolution*, Dunayevskaya deepened her critiques of some of the newer trends in revolutionary Marxism, among them Maoism and Guevarism, which she saw as having disoriented the movement and thereby abetting its defeat. Here, her principled stances cost her support on the left, especially among some of the youth she wanted to win over to Marxist-Humanism. For although many were breaking with the Soviet Union over its 1968 invasion of Czechoslovakia in order to crush a democratic government with socialist humanist tendencies, Maoism and Guevarism retained support in many sectors of the New Left. If Russian Stalinism, with its heavy-handed "dialectical materialism" and "scientific socialism" represented a kind of deterministic objectivism, Maoism and Guevarism illustrated for

Dunayevskaya an equally serious obstacle to revolutionary dialectics, a form of voluntarism and hyper-subjectivism.

Philosophy and Revolution, which appeared in 1973 as the New Left was winding down, never achieved the impact of *Marxism and Freedom*. Still, it increased Dunayevskaya's reputation as a serious dialectician and remains to this day one of the greatest contributions in this area. The book combined a deep engagement with Hegel, Marx, and Lenin with searing critiques of Trotsky, Mao, and Sartre, along with a much more sympathetic philosophical-political analysis in the final three chapters on the African revolutions, the East European anti-Stalinist ferment and revolts, and the Black, antiwar, and women's liberation movements of the 1960s in the U.S. and France. Dunayevskaya delved once again into the dialectic in her last writings in the mid-1980s as she began to research a book tentatively entitled "Dialectics of Organization and Philosophy." Some of the draft material for this book was included in a posthumously published collection of her writings on dialectics, *Power of Negativity* (Hudis and Anderson 2002).

By the late 1970s, Dunayevskaya was turning increasingly toward a critical analysis of revolutionary feminism in the U.S. Her new theorizing also took in the women's movement's emergence internationally at key junctures like the 1979 Nicaraguan revolution, or the early stages of the Iranian revolution during that same year, when feminists briefly took on the Islamists in an attempt to forestall their takeover. These radical movements and revolutions created a new context for *Rosa Luxemburg, Women's Liberation, and Marx's Philosophy of Revolution*. The book began with a strikingly new treatment of Rosa Luxemburg, placing feminist concerns at the center of her life and work for the first time, in a way that has set the tone for discussions of Luxemburg ever since. But Dunayevskaya was no Luxemburgist. To be sure, in addition to appreciating her revolutionary feminism, Dunayevskaya extolled Luxemburg's attacks on reformism, her concept of spontaneity, her refusal to separate feminism from revolutionary Marxism, her deep commitment to anti-imperialism, and her commitment to revolutionary democracy, as seen in her critique of the one-party regime Lenin and Trotsky established after the 1917 revolution. But at the same time, Dunayevskaya strongly criticized Luxemburg's moves away from Marx's concept of capitalist crises, her failure to support anti-imperialist movements, and her lack of engagement with the dialectic.

The last part of the *Rosa Luxemburg, Women's Liberation, and Marx's Philosophy of Revolution*, on Marx, contained one of the first analyses of the new turn in his last years toward the Global South and issues of gender and the family, all of it linked to his concept of "revolution in permanence." In four chapters on Marx, Dunayevskaya also elaborated a critique of Engels, not so much for the usual reason, first articulated by Georg Lukács, that his work exhibited a kind of scientistic positivism. Instead, Dunayevskaya focused more on the new critique she had developed of the unilinear determinism of Engels's *Origin of the Family, Private Property, and the State*. She contrasted Engels's treatment to the subtler dialectic she discerned in Marx's *Ethnological Notebooks* (Krader 1972). (The portion of these notebooks on anthropologist Lewis Henry Morgan had actually inspired Engels's classic book.) This critique of Engels led to the broader concept of "post-Marx Marxism as pejorative," which included not only Engels, but also Lenin, Trotsky, and Luxemburg. None of them, in Dunayevskaya's eyes, developed a fully dialectical version of Marxism.

In addition, *Rosa Luxemburg, Women's Liberation, and Marx's Philosophy of Revolution* featured two chapters on revolutionary feminism in the post-World War II period, with a focus on Black feminism and on global revolutionary movements. It was amid this discussion that Dunayevskaya also brought to a point her analysis of Luxemburg as a revolutionary feminist who had to withstand determined but covert resistance on the part of her male colleagues to her assumption of a theoretical and political leadership position in the Marxist movement of the time.

It is this book, and *Women's Liberation and the Dialectics of Revolution* (1985), a collection of her essays that Dunayevskaya assembled a few years before her death, that form the basis for our view that Dunayevskaya's Marxist-Humanism was an intersectional Marxism *avant la lettre*. But as discussed above, these two books appeared at a time when the feminist movement, whether in activist circles or academia, was turning away from Marxism and revolution. And in academia, by the 1980s, it should also be mentioned that gender studies were turning in many cases to an explicitly anti-Marxist philosophical perspective, in the form of poststructuralism.

However, as also discussed above, the worm has turned again, with the upsurge of anti-capitalist leftwing radicalism in recent years. This is why Dunayevskaya's writings have become topical in new ways today.

* * *

The present volume is divided into four parts. Part I is concerned with Dunayevskaya's engagement with Hegel and the notion of "dialectics" that stems from his philosophy. In Chapter 2, Anderson and Hudis offer an extended account of Dunayevskaya's engagement with the largely neglected Hegelian concept of *absolute* negativity. Setting Dunayevskaya's engagement in the context of other Hegelian Marxist accounts—such as those of Lukács, Marcuse, and Adorno—they demonstrate the ways in which she developed the young Marx's appropriation of absolute negativity into a new interpretation of her own, whereby a positive arises from the negation in the form of a "path to a new beginning" as a veritable force for liberation. Hudis and Anderson outline how Dunayevskaya's writings on Hegel and dialectics provide a new basis for developing a vision of the future—of totally new human relations, of an end to the division between mental and manual labor, and of alienated gender relations—which can both animate and give direction to the emerging freedom struggles of our time.

In Chapter 3, Alessandra Spano examines Dunayevskaya's development of her distinctive philosophy of Marxist-Humanism. Charting her work as part of the Johnson-Forest tendency—through her 1940s analyses of Soviet economic policy, the break with Trotsky and the Workers' Party, and the development of the critique of state capitalism and beyond—Spano pulls out the Hegelian threads that underlie Dunayevskaya's thought. Dealing also with the split with C. L. R. James, Spano documents the way in which Dunayevskaya's philosophical "breakthrough" on Hegel's notion of the Absolute paved the way for a new and distinctive dialectic of philosophy and organization that is premised upon assisting the autonomous organization of the working class against capital.

In Chapter 4, Peter Hudis explores the indispensability of philosophy in Dunayevskaya's writings, drawing out the uniqueness of her position here vis-à-vis the divergent accounts of C. L. R. James and Grace Lee. Dunayevskaya's analysis of Hegel's notion of the Absolute idea, Lenin's *Hegel Notebooks*, and Marx's 1844 *Economic and Philosophic Manuscripts* are discussed, as is the later part of her career, in which she broaches the issue of philosophy and organization in a direct sense. Philosophy, for Dunayevskaya, is shown to be needed not just in order to grasp the roots of Marx's thought but to reconstitute Marxism for realities that Marx himself never had to face, and notably for the challenge of articulating a communicable conception of a noncapitalist future that will fit the demands of the present.

Part II is concerned with the centrality of race and gender in Dunayevskaya's thought, and the revolutionary subjectivity contained therein. In Chapter 5, feminist poet Adrienne Rich explores Dunayevskaya's emphasis on the dual movement from theory to practice and from practice to theory, particularly as it relates to the Women's Liberation Movement, which Dunayevskaya saw as both "force and reason." Through a discussion of *Marxism and Freedom*, *Philosophy and Revolution*, *Rosa Luxemburg*, *Women's Liberation and Marx's Philosophy of Revolution*, and *Women's Liberation and the Dialectics of Revolution*, Rich illustrates Dunayevskaya's unique practice of truly listening to the voices within the various social movements who are calling for and working to build a new concept of freedom. These voices had a profound influence on Dunayevskaya's lifelong work of reinterpreting Marx for her own time.

In Chapter 6, Heather A. Brown offers a reading of late twentieth-century gender politics through Dunayevskaya's engagement with Marx and the historical events since his death that have demonstrated the need for an expanded and deepened understanding of the dialectics of history. Focusing particularly on Dunayevskaya's utilization of Marx's notion of a "revolution in permanence," which would abolish and transcend all exploitative relations, Brown details how women and non-traditional-gender-conforming individuals throughout the world provide new avenues for inquiry as they say "no" to many of the most oppressive aspects of patriarchal capitalism, in turn providing the basis for building a truly inclusive, non-racist, nonsexist society.

In Chapter 7, Ndindi Kitonga analyzes Dunayevskaya's theorization of "the Black dimension" in the U.S. and Africa as part of her wider framework of total liberation. As she delves deep into Dunayevskaya's engagement with the politics of racialization and the Black self-development of subjectivity (including the struggles of U.S. Blacks, the African independence movements of the late 1950s and 1960s, the Black Consciousness Movement, Abolitionist Feminism, and the writings on Frantz Fanon) Kitonga demonstrates the nuanced ways in which Dunayevskaya was able to steer a path beyond the perils of class reductionism toward the creation of truly human foundations capable of realizing the unextinguishable desire to be free.

In Chapter 8, Lilia D. Monzó explores the notion of revolutionary subjectivity as found in Dunayevskaya's writings. With reference to Dunayevskaya's extension of Marx's notion of the unity of idealism and materialism and the dialectical relationship between practice and theory, and calling upon thinkers such as Paolo Freire, Rosa Luxemburg, Frantz Fanon, and Gloria E. Anzaldúa, Monzó demonstrates how such a subjectivity is embodied in the leading role of women in movements as diverse as Black Lives Matter, the Zapatistas, Rojava, and Idle No More. These movements, with their embodiment of subjectivity and objectivity, are presented as a model of the kind of intersectional revolutionary politics that Dunayevskaya actively championed in her time.

Part III looks at the life and work of Dunayevskaya as considered in connection with notable twentieth-century figures and movements, thereby documenting the wider influence and reach of her work. In Chapter 9, Rodolfo Mondolfo places Dunayevskaya's humanist reading of Marx in the context of the Italian publication of *Marxism and Freedom* in the early 1960s, noting the thematic similarities with the writings of Marx, Rousseau, Hegel, Fromm, and Lenin, among others. On the basis of this discussion, Mondolfo proceeds to draw out the central concern with freedom that enlivened the major revolts of the time—from the workers' insurrection in East Germany in June 1953, to Russian political prisoners' revolt in the forced-labor camps of Vorkuta in July 1953, to the workers' insurrection in Budapest and in Hungary as a whole in October 1956, and the retroactive critique provided by it to the deformation of Bolshevism in the USSR—thereby showing Dunayevskaya to be keenly attuned to the pulse of history.

In Chapter 10, Paul Mason develops an account of the humanism of Marx's writings vis-à-vis the major debates of twentieth-century Marxism. Using the work of Dunayevskaya as a grounding, Mason discusses the epistemological debates that characterized the Second International, the anti-humanist debates of the postwar period, and the debates over automation that mark the present day. What results is a novel thesis whereby an appeal is made for a moral philosophy that dovetails with a reconstituted Marxist theory of knowledge and a provisional anthropology of the species to act as the basis of a projected transition beyond capitalism.

In Chapter 11, Karel Ludenhoff contrasts Dunayevskaya's and Luxemburg's respective accounts of Marx's theory of the nature of capitalist crises. Through a detailed elaboration of Dunayevskaya's interpretation of the law of the tendential decline in the rate of profit, Ludenhoff demonstrates how Marx's account—enlivened by its humanist attention to the subjectivity of the voices from below—consists of a new unity of economics, philosophy, and revolution, disclosing the different forms of revolt that reveal the logical development of the system to the point where no alteration in exchange or distribution could fundamentally change anything. Contrasted with Luxemburg's theory—whereby the cause of capitalist crisis lies in a deficiency of demand—Dunayevskaya's theory reaches beyond economic analysis to the impulse of new forces and passions in the dialectical movement of society,

In Chapter 12, David Black charts Dunayevskaya's revolutionary travels in Britain and Europe following the publication of *Marxism and Freedom*. In a revealing insight into this period in her life, and into the wider left at the time, Black draws on upon hitherto unpublished correspondence, along with reviews of her work in the period, to paint a picture of Dunayevskaya as in dialogue (at times critical) with leading Leftist figures such Tony Cliff, Onorato Damen, and Cornelius Castoriadis. Black also unearths a history of movement building, with the spread of Dunayevskaya's philosophy and practice of Marxist-Humanism in England and Scotland, via the notable worker-intellectual figures of Frank Williams and Harry McShane and the leading figures of the African Forum.

Part IV is concerned with exploring the themes of freedom and liberation that enliven Dunayevskaya's writings. In Chapter 13, Paul Mason contextualizes Dunayevskaya's Marxist-Humanism, placing it in relation to the Marxism of her contemporaries and fellow radicals, Leon Trotsky, Frieda Kahlo, and Natalia Sedova Trotsky. Mason charts the biographical and political interrelations between these four figures as set against the interpretation of Marxism that came to predominate in the century and more following Marx's death. In an account which places a central stress on the importance of Marx's 1844 *Economic and Philosophical Manuscripts* and Dunayevskaya's interpretation of them, Mason singles out Dunayevskaya, in contradistinction to Trotsky, Kahlo, and Sedova, as the only figure of the four who provides the link between classic Marxism and the only form in which it can be relevant today: namely, radical humanism.

In Chapter 14, Frédéric Monferrand delves into the heart of *Marxism and Freedom*, articulating Dunayevskaya's critique of state capitalism and the centrality of the notion of the unity of theory and practice that is found there. Dunayevskaya's account of the USSR as state capitalist is strongly defended by Monferrand on the basis of its consistent application of Marx's account of the "law of value" and the "average necessary labor time." Monferrand also delves into Dunayevskaya's account of Marxism as a theory of liberation that calls on us to reconnect with the strategic creativity that once belonged to emancipatory movements and to supplement the question "what is to be done?" with that concerning where we want to go. The hope is that through this process we can take back the historical initiative that has been ceded to capital, and which is waiting there for our repossession of it.

In Chapter 15, Kieran Durkin explores Dunayevskaya's resurrection and repurposing of the humanism of Marx's thought, which is, at the same time, the essence of her own thinking. Set against the rise of the theoretical anti-humanism of Louis Althusser that came to exercise such a dominant influence in Marxian thinking, Durkin extrapolates upon Dunayevskaya's incisive account of the fundamental thematic continuities between Marx's early and late writings—a continuity which holds while refusing to reduce the later to the former. Durkin also elaborates the ways in which Dunayevskaya goes beyond even the capacious understanding of the late Marx, in the expansion of the humanist dialectic to Blacks, women, and youth, to what she came to understand toward the end of her life as a reconfigured form of what Gramsci described as "absolute humanism."

In Chapter 16, Kevin B. Anderson discusses Dunayevskaya's distinction between two kinds of subjectivity which was announced first in the 1964 edition of *Marxism and Freedom*. Anderson's discussion here locates the origin of this distinction in Dunayevskaya's opposition to the voluntarism of Mao Zedong's "revolutionary will," a form of subjectivity which she points out has no regard for objective conditions. Contrasted to this alienated form of subjectivity, is the Marxist-Humanist subjectivity proffered by Dunayevskaya, which is rooted in the dialectical development of the ground for revolution in both its subjective and objective sense, as seen in the most creative of the grassroots movements of the time, like the Montgomery Bus Boycott. Through this discussion—which also encompasses Dunayevskaya's engagement with Marx and Lenin on these themes—Anderson places the relationship between theory and practice as at the heart of the liberation struggles of the future.

We hope that these essays will help a new generation to recapture—and to build upon for today—the writings of Raya Dunayevskaya, whose capacious, humanist form of Marxism was in constant dialogue, not only with the dialectical tradition of Marx and Hegel, but also with contemporary radical thinkers like Fromm and Marcuse, and with the living movements of her time on the part of groups like rank-and-file labor, the Black masses, and revolutionary feminists. As we have stressed, her intersectional form of Marxism can help us today to transcend the division between a class politics that sometimes tends toward class reductionism, and a politics of race, gender, or sexuality that sometimes neglects the needed critique of capital. In short, Dunayevskaya offers us dialectical universals that are *true*—pointing to a new human society while at the same time recognizing and theorizing about the multiplicity of forces and ideas of opposition to today's alienated, exploitative social reality.

REFERENCES

Anderson, Kevin B. and Russell Rockwell, eds. 2012. *The Dunayevskaya-Marcuse-Fromm Correspondence*. Lanham, MD: Lexington Books.

Boggs, James. 1963. *The American Revolution: Pages from a Negro Worker's Notebook*. New York: Monthly Review Press.

Denby, Charles. 1978. *Indignant Heart: A Black Worker's Journal*. Boston: South End Press.

Dunayevskaya, Raya. 1958, *Marxism and Freedom: From 1776 Until Today*. New York: Bookman Associates.

———. 1973. *Philosophy and Revolution: From Hegel to Sartre, and from Marx to Mao*. New York: Delacorte.

———. 1982. *Rosa Luxemburg, Women's Liberation, and Marx's Philosophy of Revolution*. Atlantic Highlands, NJ: Humanities Press.

———. 1985. *Women's Liberation and the Dialectics of Revolution: Reaching for the Future*. Atlantic Highlands, NJ: Humanities Press.

Fromm, Erich. 1961. *Marx's Concept of Man*. New York: Frederick Ungar.

———, ed. 1965. *Socialist Humanism*. New York: Doubleday.

Hudis, Peter and Kevin B. Anderson, eds. 2002. *The Power of Negativity: Selected Writings on the Dialectic in Hegel and in Marx*. Lanham: MD: Lexington Books.

James, C. L. R, Raya Dunayevskaya, and Grace Lee Boggs. [1950] 2013. *State Capitalism and World Revolution*. Oakland: PM Press.

Kitonga, Ndindi. 2020. "Black Lives Matter Uprising in Los Angeles: Working Toward a New Humanist Society." *The International Marxist-Humanist* (June 13). https://imhojournal.org/articles/black-lives-matter-uprising-in-los-angeles-working-toward-a-new-humanist-society/.

Krader, Lawrence. 1972. *The Ethnological Notebooks of Karl Marx*. Assen: Van Gorcum.

Marcuse, Herbert. 1964. *One-Dimensional Man: Studies in the Ideology of Advanced Industrial Society*. Boston: Beacon Press.

Randall, Margaret. 1992. *Gathering Rage: The Failure of Twentieth Century Revolutions to Develop a Feminist Agenda*. New York: Monthly Review Press.

Rorty, Richard. 1992. "The Intellectuals and the End of Socialism." *The Yale Review* 80, no. 1/2 (April): 1–16.

Sanbonmatsu, John. 2004. *The Postmodern Prince: Critical Theory, Left Strategy, and the Making of a New Political Subject*. New York: Monthly Review Press.

Hegel and Dialectics

CHAPTER 2

Raya Dunayevskaya's Concept of Dialectic

Peter Hudis and Kevin B. Anderson

THE PRESENT MOMENT

Marx's *oeuvre*, which many had declared obsolete, has taken on new life at the dawn of the twenty-first century because the strength of his critique of the destructive power of capital is so missed. Today's unprecedented inequities in wealth and power, accompanied by wrenching technological changes and environmental havoc, as well as monopolization and social fragmentation, are increasingly begetting the sense that the time has come to return to Marx. In a process that conjures up the spirit of the dialectic itself, the very fact which had been heralded as proving the death of Marx—the universalization of capital, as it invades every corner of the earth and all spheres of everyday life—has led workers as well as intellectuals, activists as well as academics, to look anew at what Marx's work means for today. This is reflected in everything from journalistic

P. Hudis
Oakton Community College, Des Plaines, IL, USA

K. B. Anderson (✉)
Department of Sociology, University of California, Santa Barbara, Santa Barbara, CA, USA
e-mail: kanderson@soc.ucsb.edu

© The Author(s) 2021   23
K. B. Anderson et al. (eds.), *Raya Dunayevskaya's Intersectional Marxism*, Marx, Engels, and Marxisms,
https://doi.org/10.1007/978-3-030-53717-3_2

discourses on the need to face "the specter of Marx," to theoretical analyses on the cogency of the Marxian critique of globalized capitalism.[1] The more the globalization of capital spurs social dislocation and impoverishment, the more we can expect such appraisals of Marx in the coming period.

One surprising feature of much of the current return to Marx, however, is the relative silence on Hegel and the dialectic. This attitude has developed despite Marx's insistence in *Capital* and other works that his method was at its core dialectical and that Hegel's dialectic was for him "the source of all dialectic" (Marx 1976: 102, 744). For example, in his *Specters of Marx*, Jacques Derrida on the one hand terms Marx's writings "urgent" for an understanding of today's globalized capitalism, while on the other distances himself from the Hegelian dialectic, which he calls an "onto-theology" and "anthropo-theology" (Derrida 1993: 13, 144). From the vantage point of the Frankfurt School, a tradition once rooted in a form of Hegelian Marxism, Jürgen Habermas rejects the Hegelian dialectic as the remnant of a romantic idealist philosophy of consciousness, and attacks Marx for remaining "tied to Hegelian logic" (Habermas 1987: 338) Even Moishe Postone, a Frankfurt-trained Critical Theorist who has urged a return to Marx's critique of capital in order to comprehend the present crisis, considers the Hegelian dialectic as little more than a philosophical expression of the logic of capital (Postone 1993).

At the same time, the present moment is rife with serious studies of Hegel by non-Marxists. The past decade has experienced a veritable explosion of new works on Hegel in the Anglo-American world, as seen in such recent books as H. S. Harris's *Hegel's Ladder*, a 1600-page study of Hegel's *Phenomenology of Mind*. On a more modest, and yet significant level, new studies on Hegel by feminists, especially those from a postmodernist background, have emerged.[2] Yet instead of intersecting, the ongoing discussions of Hegel and Marx often appear as two trains passing each other in the dead of night, very nearly unnoticed by one another.

Fredric Jameson has spoken to this problem:

This is a time when people no longer understand what dialectical thinking is or why the dialectic came into being in the first place, when they have abandoned the dialectical for less rewarding Nietzschean positions. So there is certainly a need today for a revitalized vision of the dialectic. There I would certainly not abandon Marx, but I would want to go back to Hegel for an enlargement of the way we have normally understood Marx. This is not any particularly new idea with me. Lenin had already said that no one could understand *Das Kapital* who had not already worked his way through Hegel's logic…. I think the coming years will show an unconscious need for the dialectic which some of us on the left ought to have the mission to satisfy. (Jameson 1997: 93)[3]

At each stage in the history of Marxism, revolutionaries and theorists have felt the need to hew a path out of the seemingly insurmountable barriers facing the radical movement by turning anew to Hegel. This was true of Lenin in 1914, when he responded to the collapse of established Marxism with the outbreak of World War I by delving into Hegel's *Science of Logic*. It was true of such diverse tendencies as the Frankfurt School and French neo-Marxists in the 1930s and 1940s, who turned to Hegel in a period defined by fascism and the rise of Stalinism. Likewise, in the 1950s, in the face of the new challenges posed by the freedom struggles of the post-World War II era, Raya Dunayevskaya (1910–1987) developed the philosophy of Marxist-Humanism through a direct encounter with Hegel's dialectic.

Dunayevskaya's life and work represent a rare combination of passionate involvement in freedom struggles and intense philosophical exploration. Born in Ukraine in 1910, she immigrated to the U.S. as a teenager, and by the mid-1920s became involved in labor, socialist, and Black liberation movements. After serving as secretary to Leon Trotsky in 1937–1938, she broke with him at the time of the Hitler-Stalin Pact in 1939, and subsequently developed a theory of state-capitalism. She argued that Roosevelt's New Deal, Hitler's Germany, and especially Stalin's Russia, represented varieties of a new stage of global capitalism, one in which the fetishism of state planning was paramount.[4] This work soon brought her into a period of close collaboration with the Trinidadian Marxist and cultural critic C. L. R. James. During the 1940s, she also engaged in dialogue with a number of intellectuals of the anti-Stalinist left, such as Meyer Schapiro, and became a sharp critic of those, such as the pragmatist Sidney Hook, who strongly rejected Hegel as a reactionary thinker.

By the mid-1950s, Dunayevskaya moved in a different direction from James, as she developed a new position, rooted in a reexamination of the Hegelian underpinnings of Marx's thought, which she soon termed

Marxist-Humanism. In the late 1950s, she engaged in an extensive correspondence on dialectics with the Critical Theorist Herbert Marcuse and, a bit later, with Erich Fromm, another former Frankfurt School member.[5] In her *Marxism and Freedom* (1958), to which Marcuse contributed a critical preface, she included as appendices the first English translations of major parts of Marx's 1844 *Economic and Philosophical Manuscripts* and of Lenin's *Philosophical Notebooks*. In rethinking and extending Marx's humanist conceptions in light of the contemporary struggles of rank-and-file labor, women's liberation, African Americans, and youth from the 1950s to the 1980s, she developed an original philosophy of liberation rooted in a continuous return to the Hegelian dialectic. On the one hand, this entailed scathing critiques of anti-Hegelian Marxists such as Louis Althusser, and on the other, more sympathetic but nonetheless probing critiques of leading dialecticians, many of them Hegelian Marxists, including Marcuse, Georg Lukács, Karl Korsch, and Theodor Adorno. In her later discussions of dialectics, she also gave prominence to what she regarded as the highly original contributions of the African liberation theorist, Frantz Fanon and also to dissident East European Marxist humanists as can especially be seen in her *Philosophy and Revolution* (1973) and *Rosa Luxemburg, Women's Liberation, and Marx's Philosophy of Revolution* (1991).

CONTEMPORARY ISSUES IN DIALECTICAL PHILOSOPHY

The need to return to the Hegelian dialectic with new eyes is no less urgent today, in light of the crisis confronting all liberation movements, whether of workers, Blacks and other minorities, women, lesbians and gays, or youth. This crisis is disclosed by the aborted and unfinished revolutions which have marked this century, from Russia 1917 to Spain 1936, China 1949, and Cuba 1959, and from Iran to Nicaragua to Grenada in the 1970s and 1980s. In particular, the experience of the Russian Revolution after 1917 suggests that even to *begin* to hew a path out of this crisis means confronting such questions as, what happens *after* the revolution? How can we ensure that a new form of totalitarianism or bureaucracy will not once again take over after the collapse of the old order? How can ending the division between mental and manual labor move from underlying concept to social practice?

Here is where Dunayevskaya's work as founder of Marxist-Humanism in the U.S. takes on special importance. Few thinkers in the revolutionary tradition have focused as exhaustively on these issues as Dunayevskaya, especially on the need to philosophically confront the question of what happens *after* the revolution. And even fewer have done so by means of a new interpretation of Hegelian dialectics. On the whole, radical interpreters of Hegel in this century have emphasized such aspects of his thought as the master–slave dialectic and the unhappy consciousness in the *Phenomenology of Mind*, or the concepts of essence, negativity, or contradiction in the *Science of Logic*. While Dunayevskaya also addresses these issues, we believe that her core contribution to dialectics centers on what many other Marxists have ignored or rejected—Hegel's concept of *absolute* negativity.[6] In Hegel, absolute negativity signifies not only the negation of external obstacles, but also the negation of the earlier negation of them. The power of negativity gets turned back upon the self, upon the internal as well as external barriers to self-movement. Such a negation of the negation is no mere nullity, for the positive is contained in the negative, which is the path to a new beginning.

One of Hegel's first references to absolute negativity in the *Science of Logic* occurs during a critique of Spinoza's notion that "every determination is a negation." Hegel considers such a stress on negativity to be a great advance over previous positions. However, this advance is not without contradiction and in Hegel's view has the drawback of dissolving into a "formless abstraction," because this type of bare negativity lacks determinateness (Hegel 1969: 113). At this point, Hegel goes beyond bare or first negativity to what he calls second or absolute negativity, with the latter containing not only a rejection of the old, but also the basis for a forward movement: "But in all this, care must be taken to distinguish between the *first* negation as negation *in general,* and the second negation, the negation of the negation: the latter is concrete, absolute negativity, just as the former on the contrary is only *abstract* negativity" (1969: 115–116).

If the question of absolute negativity were exhausted here, in a more or less formal process of the negation of the negation, there would be far less controversy among radical interpreters of Hegel. For example, writing more than a century ago, Friedrich Engels, whose studies of dialectics have formed the basis of most orthodox Marxist discussions of the topic ever since, did at least mention the negation of the negation. However, while extolling a formalized and sometimes scientistic notion of negation of the negation, Engels also attacks Hegel's Absolute Idea, which, he maintains, includes a notion of "the end of history" in which "the whole dogmatic content of the Hegelian system is declared to be absolute truth, in contradiction to his dialectical method, which dissolves all that is dogmatic" (Engels 1990: 360–361). Thus, Engels mentions the negation of the negation as a principle of the dialectic while attacking the Absolute Idea as dogmatic and even reactionary.

In contrast to Engels and most subsequent interpreters within the Marxist tradition, Dunayevskaya finds extremely important insights for a dialectics of liberation in Hegel's Absolutes, which Hegel develops in the concluding chapters of his major works. In so doing, she focuses on the chapters on Absolute Knowledge in the *Phenomenology*, the Absolute Idea in the *Science of Logic*, and the Absolute Mind in the *Philosophy of Mind*.

Hegel's Absolutes have been frequently dismissed not only as dogmatic, but also as a closed ontology. These are interpretations which, as Dunayevskaya argues, are hard to maintain once one examines Hegel's actual texts. This can be seen from a few representative passages from the chapter on the Absolute Idea with which Hegel concludes the *Science of Logic*. Hegel begins his discussion by stating that the Absolute Idea is "the identity of the theoretical and the practical idea," thereby holding to a notion of practice as well as of theory at the very point where some have seen only a flight into an abstract universal. A few lines further in this same passage, Hegel also writes that "the Absolute Idea ... contains within itself the highest degree of opposition" (1969: 824). Here, at least, Hegel rejects the notion of an oppositionless totality which has absorbed all negativity and particularity, as is so often charged. Some pages later, at the conclusion of the chapter, Hegel writes of the Absolute Idea as an "absolute liberation," as a dialectic of freedom in which "no transition takes place" (1969: 843). The human spirit now moves toward liberation, having already worked through the myriad obstacles which lay in wait for freedom in the previous 800 pages of his work.

Dunayevskaya's focus on Hegel's Absolutes countered the traditional Marxist view of them as a "closed ontology" in which all particularities and differences are effaced in the name of an abstract unity. As early as her initial studies on dialectics in the late 1940s, she emphasized "the sheer genius of [Hegel's] language which defines identity as 'unseparated difference'"(Dunayevskaya in Hudis and Anderson 2002: 350). Nor was she attracted to Hegel's Absolutes out of an affinity with Lukács's emphasis on totality. Throughout her work, from her "Letters on Hegel's Absolutes" of 1953 through *Marxism and Freedom* (1958), *Philosophy and*

Revolution (1973) and *Rosa Luxemburg, Women's Liberation and Marx's Philosophy of Revolution* (1991), she saw in Hegel's Absolutes "the categories of freedom, of subjectivity, of reason, the logic of a movement by which humanity makes itself free" (Dunayevskaya 1989: 26). As she put it in Chapter 1 of *Philosophy and Revolution*, her most sustained and important discussion of Hegel,

> Precisely where Hegel sounds most abstract, seems to close the shutters tight against the whole movement of history, there he lets the lifeblood of the dialectic—absolute negativity—pour in. It is true that Hegel writes as if the resolution of opposing live forces can be overcome by a mere thought transcendence. But he has, by bringing oppositions to their most logical extreme, opened new paths, a new relationship of theory to practice, which Marx worked out as a totally new relationship of philosophy to revolution. Today's revolutionaries turn their backs on this at their peril. (1989: 34)

This interpretation diverges in important ways from those of other Hegelian Marxists, such as Lukács and Marcuse. Dunayevskaya applauds Lukács's argument in *History and Class Consciousness* (1923) that the dialectic is the core of Marxism, but she also critiques his theory of reification. In *The Young Hegel* (1948), Lukács, like Dunayevskaya, writes with respect to Absolute Knowledge in Hegel's *Phenomenology* that "it would be quite mistaken to see the 'absolute spirit' as nothing but mysticism" (Lukács 1975: 510).[7] Here, as elsewhere in his work, Lukács connects Hegel's writings to the historical and social reality of his time. However, Lukács in the end dismisses Absolute Knowledge as a type of flight from objective reality which cannot serve as a source for the further development of Marxist dialectics: "Absolute Knowledge, Hegel's designation for the highest stage of human knowledge, has a definite idealistic significance: the reintegration of 'externalized' reality into the subject, i.e. the total supersession of the objective world" (Lukács 1975: 513).

In his *Reason and Revolution* (1941), Frankfurt School member Herbert Marcuse, also like Dunayevskaya, stresses the revolutionary character of Hegel's dialectic, especially the concept of negativity: "Hegel's philosophy is indeed what the subsequent reaction termed it, a negative philosophy. It is originally motivated by the conviction that the given facts that appear to common sense as the positive index of truth are in reality the negation of truth, so that truth can only be established by their destruction" (Marcuse 1941: 27).[8] At the level of the Absolute Idea, which Marcuse holds to be a "totality," he concedes that the Absolute is also "dialectical thought and thus contains its negation, it is not a harmonious and stable form but a process of unification of opposites." However, what he ultimately stresses with regard to the Absolute is what he sees as its totalizing moment, wherein "all negativity is overcome" (Marcuse 1941: 165).

Dunayevskaya's emphasis on the liberatory dimension of Hegel's dialectic underlines her similarities as well as differences with other thinkers, such as Theodor Adorno, also of the Frankfurt School. Adorno affirmed the liberatory character of Hegel's overall philosophy, writing in his "Aspects of Hegel's Philosophy" (1957), "In Hegel reason finds itself constellated with freedom. Freedom and reason are nonsense without one another. The real can be considered rational only insofar as the idea of freedom, that is, human beings' genuine self-determination, shines through it" (Adorno 1994: 28). As against those who contend that Hegel's dialectic ignores the actual and leaves it as mere notion of freedom, Adorno argued that Hegel "accomplishes the opposite as well, an insight into the subject as a self-manifesting objectivity" (1994: 7). Yet Adorno parted company with Hegel when it came to the concept of absolute negativity. Adorno, who sought to expunge the affirmative character of Hegel's dialectic, went so far as to link absolute negativity to Nazi genocide! In the midst of a discussion of the horrors of Auschwitz and its implications for philosophy in *Negative Dialectics* (1966), Adorno writes: "Absolute negativity is in plain sight and ceased to surprise anyone" (Adorno 1973: 362). On the basis of her own reading of Hegel's *Science of Logic*, Dunayevskaya attacks this view, terming it a "vulgar reduction of absolute negativity" (Dunayevskaya in Hudis and Anderson 2002: 187).

Adorno contended in "Aspects of Hegel's Philosophy" that Hegel's Absolutes "dissolve anything not proper to consciousness" by reducing all existence to the self-movement of the absolute subject. By holding fast to idealism, he said, Hegel's Absolutes invoke a totalizing subject which swallows up the actual. This, Adorno argued, bears a striking resemblance to what Marx conceptualizes as alienated labor. Just as Reason in Hegel subsumes all otherness into the self-movement of the concept, so the labor process in capitalism subsumes all human and natural contingency into the movement of mechanized, abstract labor. According to Adorno, "In Hegel, abstract labor takes on magical form.... The self-forgetfulness of production, the insatiable and destructive expansive principle of the exchange society, is reflected in Hegelian metaphysics. It describes the way the world actually is" (1994: 44)—but not, as in Marx, the way it can be transformed. This notion that Hegel's Absolutes provide, at best, a philosophical gloss for the self-expansive power of the capitalist production process, rather than, as Dunayevskaya contends, the ground for a philosophy of human emancipation, is shared in different ways by a wide variety of contemporary thinkers, including Jürgen Habermas, Gilles Deleuze and Tony Negri, Moishe Postone and István Mészáros.[9]

Another challenge to the concept of absolute negativity has come from Jacques Derrida's deconstructionism. To be sure, Derrida has acknowledged Hegel's creation of an "immense revolution" in philosophy "in taking the negative seriously," and has even tried to ground his concept of *différance* in Hegel's affirmation of the inseparability of identity and difference in the *Science of Logic* (Derrida 1978: 259). Yet Derrida argues that the self-activating power of absolute negativity means that "the concept of a general heterogeneity is impossible" in Hegel. As Derrida sees it, Hegel's Absolutes "determine difference as contradiction, only in order to resolve it, to interiorize it, to lift it up ... into the self-presence of an onto-theological or onto-theological synthesis" (Derrida 1971: 44). He therefore calls for a total "break with the system of *Aufhebung* [transcendence] and with speculative dialectics." Even more problematically, he has argued that such an "absolute break" with Hegel also characterizes Marx: "Marx [in his 1844 critique of Hegel] then sets out the critical moment of Feuerbach and in its most operative stance: the questioning of the *Aufhebung* and of the negation of the negation. The absolute positive ... hence must not pass through the negation of the negation, the Hegelian *Aufhebung*...." (Derrida 1986: 200–201).

We need to underscore that Adorno's and Derrida's characterizations of Hegel's concept of negativity, especially absolute negativity, are in our view quite different from those of Marx. It is true that Marx took sharp exception to Hegel, in his 1844 "Critique of the Hegelian Dialectic" and elsewhere, for dehumanizing the Idea by treating it as stages of disembodied consciousness instead of that of live men and women. As a result, Marx argued, Hegel's philosophy ends in a series of absolutes which elevate the abstract at the expense of life itself. For this reason he called Hegel's *Logic* "the money of the Spirit" (Marx 1975: 330). Yet this did not mean that he followed Feuerbach in rejecting "the negation of the negation" and Hegel's Absolutes as a mere idealist delusion.

Nor, like Adorno, did he view Hegel's concept of dialectical self-movement as simply expressing the self-expansive power of capitalism.

To be sure, Marx critiqued the way capital takes on a life of its own and becomes self-determining. He did not, however, limit the concept of self-determination to that of capital. Quite the contrary. For Marx the subjective struggle of the workers is capable of attaining a liberatory, *human* self-determination, by experiencing the dialectic of absolute negativity. Marx broke this down concretely in his 1844 *Economic and Philosophical Manuscripts* by showing that the abolition of private property is merely the first negation. To reach the goal of a truly new society, he writes, it is necessary to negate this negation. In contrast to what he called "vulgar communism," which stops at the mere abolition of private property, he stressed that only through the "transcendence of this mediation" is it possible to reach "*positive* humanism, beginning from itself." This "thoroughgoing Naturalism or Humanism," Marx continues, is the result of the negation. This is why he writes, in commenting on the chapter on "Absolute Knowledge" in Hegel's *Phenomenology of Mind*: "The greatness of Hegel's *Phenomenology*, and of its final result—the dialectic of negativity as the moving and creative principle—lies in this, that Hegel comprehends the self-production of the human being as a process...." (Dunayevskaya 1958: 308).[10]

Two decades later, in the closing pages of *Capital*, Vol. I, Marx makes recourse once again to Hegel's concept of absolute negativity, here also discussing the negation of the negation. In his discussion of "the absolute general law of capitalist accumulation" Marx refers to the brutal expropriation of the peasants from their land during the sixteenth-century agricultural revolution in England as "the first negation of private property," in which the peasants lose their property. Over the next centuries, capitalism develops and eventually "begets its own negation," the working class which it has called into existence. Marx concludes,

> This is the negation of the negation. It does not reestablish private property, but it does indeed establish individual property on the basis of the achievements of the capitalist era: namely, cooperation and the possession in common of the land and the means of production produced by labor itself. (Marx 1976: 929–930)

Thus, Marx sees Hegel's concept of negativity and of the first and second negation neither as purely destructive nor as limiting us to an overly affirmative stance toward existing society. In addition, contrary to the claims of Louis Althusser and others, Marx's critical appropriation of Hegel's dialectic was continuous, even in his late writings, as seen in his reference to the negation of the negation in his Mathematical Manuscripts.[11]

In the twentieth century the emergence of new objective crises has again and again stirred interest in this dialectic of negativity, no matter how often Hegel was declared dead and buried. This has been reflected not only in the work of such Western Marxists as Lukács, Gramsci, and Adorno, but also in the dialectical humanism of the African revolutionary Frantz Fanon. Fanon's profound return to Hegel in light of such realities as the "additive of color" in the contemporary freedom struggles demonstrates the importance of dialectical philosophy in meeting the challenges posed by new forces of liberation. This is no less true when it comes to today. The collapse of statist communism in the former Soviet Union and Eastern Europe has given new meaning to Marx's critique of the tendency to stop at first negation, the mere abolition of private property, without moving on to the negation of the negation, and the creation of new humanist social relations. As the power of capital continues to expand and globalize, bringing with it ever-greater social dislocations and inequities, the search for new alternatives rooted in the dialectic of second negativity is sure to show itself.

This can already be seen on one level in the appearance of a number of studies over the past decade of Hegel, such as those by Daniel Berthold-Bond and John Hoffmeyer, which sharply contest the notion that Hegel's Absolutes are a "closed ontology" signifying "the end of history" (Berthold-Bond 1989: 136).[12] As Berthold-Bond put it in his discussion of the final pages of Hegel's *Phenomenology*,

> Absolute Knowledge is not the End of history, but the sort of knowledge which is possible only at the end of an epoch of history, and which is required to comprehend the development of the world-spirit within that epoch, so as to prepare the rebirth and transformation of the world into a new shape, a new existence.... Recollection [is] not only a sort of memorial of the past but an anticipation of the future, a redemption or resurrection of spirit into a new birth in historical time. (1989: 136)

As Dunayevskaya noted in *Philosophy and Revolution*, "Hegel's Absolutes have ever exerted a simultaneous force of attraction and repulsion" (1989: 4).

We believe that Dunayevskaya's specific interpretation of Hegel, in emphasizing the cogency of the dialectic of absolute negativity for today's freedom struggles, takes on new life at the present juncture. [...] She views Hegel's Absolutes *as new beginnings*. Central to this is her belief that the concept of absolute negativity expresses, at a philosophical level, the quest by masses of people not simply to negate existing economic and political structures, but to create *totally new human relations* as well. As Louis Dupré put it in his Preface to *Philosophy and Revolution*,

> A notable difference separates Raya Dunayevskaya's from the earlier positions of [Lukács and Karl Korsch]. Their interpretation had limited the revolutionary impact of Hegel's philosophy to the sociopolitical order. Dunayevskaya aims for a total liberation of the human person—not only from the ills of a capitalist society but also from the equally oppressive State capitalism of established communist governments. (1989: xv)

In situating the concept of absolute negativity in the struggles of workers, women, youth, Blacks, and other minorities, Dunayevskaya opened new doors to appropriating and projecting this concept *philosophically*. Once the dialectic of second negativity is seen as intrinsic to the human subject, it becomes possible to grasp and project the idea of second negativity as a veritable force of liberation. Dunayevskaya's writings on Hegel and dialectics provide a new basis for working out a vision of the future—of totally new human relations, of an end to the division between mental and manual labor and of alienated gender relations— which can animate and give direction to the emerging freedom struggles of our time.

Our time is burdened by the absence of a vision of a future which transcends the horizon of existing society. Everywhere, we are confronted with the near-unchallenged assertion that we must accept the limits of actually existing capitalism as our sole alternative. The profound crisis of the socialist movement over the past decades has made this crisis of the imagination all the more overwhelming. The failure to project an alternative to both existing capitalism and statist communism is a more important facet of today's social crises than is generally recognized. Unless we rethink the meaning of Marx's Marxism in light of *this* problem, *this* reality, *this* contradiction, it is hard to see how it is possible to break through the stranglehold of retrogression which has engulfed the world ever since the Reagan-Thatcher era of the 1980s. For this reason, we believe, Dunayevskaya's studies of Hegel's dialectic and his Absolutes, in which she saw the vision of a liberatory future that post-Marx Marxists had failed to articulate, is more timely than ever.

DUNAYEVSKAYA'S WRITINGS ON DIALECTICS

Although Dunayevskaya founded the philosophy of Marxist-Humanism in the mid-1950s, the work which preceded this is of considerable importance. Foremost here is her theory of state-capitalism. As mentioned earlier, Dunayevskaya served as Russian-language secretary to Leon Trotsky in Mexico, in 1937–1938. Her break from Trotsky at the time of the Hitler-Stalin Pact in 1939 over his insistence that Russia remained a "workers' state, though degenerate" led to her birth as a theoretician. She contended that Russia had transformed into a state-capitalist society, and set out to prove it through a series of articles and essays analyzing the Russian economy.

In 1941 she joined forces with C. L. R. James, the Caribbean Marxist and author of *The Black Jacobins*, who had independently come to a state-capitalist position. The two formed what became known as the Johnson-Forest Tendency or State-Capitalist Tendency within the American Trotskyist movement, from the early 1940s to the early 1950s (Johnson was James's pseudonym; Forest was Dunayevskaya's). A third key member was the Chinese-American Grace Lee (Boggs). Dunayevskaya authored most of the Tendency's analyses of state-capitalism in Stalinist Russia.

A number of theories of state-capitalism had arisen on the anti-Stalinist Left by the 1940s. Dunayevskaya's was distinctive among them in seeing state-capitalism not just as a Russian phenomenon, but as part of a new world stage of capitalism emerging from the Great Depression. Moreover, from the start her theory of state-capitalism was no mere social and economic theory, for it reached for something more, for new forces and a new vision with which to oppose the horrors of this new phenomenon of totalitarian state-capitalism as well as the bureaucratic state-capitalism of the welfare state. Central to this was the conceptualization of new revolutionary forces, such as rank-and-file workers, anti-colonial movements, independent struggles of the Black masses in the U.S., and new struggles of women and youth. No less central was the way she began to carve out a form of dialectical philosophy with which to critique and oppose the crude and scientistic materialism found not only in Stalinist ideology, but also in Trotsky's work, as well as that of other Marxist intellectuals of the period. Her engagement with the dialectic in the 1940s took varying forms, such as exposing Stalinist distortions of the law of value in *The American Economic Review*, attacking their deletion of chapter one of

Capital with its section on commodity fetishism from the teaching of *Capital*,[13] and critiquing Trotskyists for failing to "keep their fingers on the pulse of human relations" (Dunayevskaya 1992: 25). Most importantly, she wrote one of the first discussions in the U.S. of Marx's 1844 *Manuscripts*, her 1942 essay "Labor and Society" (Dunayevskaya 1992: 17–23). In this period she also studied Lenin's 1914–1915 *Philosophical Notebooks* on Hegel, which she translated into English in the late 1940s.

James, Dunayevskaya, and Lee debated Hegelian dialectics intensely in this period. In the face of the phenomenon of counterrevolution from *within* the revolution, which they viewed as the "absolute contradiction" of the age, they began to speak of the need to explore the dimension of Hegel which Marxists had tended to shy away from—the last book of Hegel's *Science of Logic*, "Subjective Logic, or the Doctrine of the Notion," and especially its final chapter "The Absolute Idea." At the same time, they began to speak of the need to relate dialectics to questions of organization within the revolutionary movement. By the late 1940s the Johnson-Forest Tendency was moving away from the Leninist concept of the vanguard party to lead and had begun to pose the need for a new relation of spontaneity to organization. Working out such a new relation, they held, required a direct encounter with dialectics. As James put it in his *Notes on Dialectics* (1948), "We have to get hold of the Notion, of the Absolute Idea before we can see this relation between organization and spontaneity in its concrete truth" (1980: 119).

By 1949, however, underlying differences between James and Lee on the one hand, and Dunayevskaya on the other, began to surface. Some of this can be seen in the extensive three-way correspondence between James, Dunayevskaya and Lee in 1949–1951, the period in which Dunayevskaya completed the first English translation of Lenin's "Abstract of Hegel's *Science of Logic*." As she suggested in a letter to James of March 12, 1949 [...] James did not actually fulfill his stated aim of delving into the Doctrine of the Notion, in which Hegel most fully poses the concept of the negation of the negation. In his *Notes on Dialectics*, she writes, James had much less to say about the Doctrine of the Notion than did Lenin in his 1914–1915 Hegel Notebooks. Instead of delving into the Absolute Idea, she writes of James, "the thing you chose to stop at and say, *hic Rhodus, hic salta* to, was the Law of Contradiction in [the Doctrine of] Essence" (Dunayevskaya in Hudis and Anderson 2002: 352).[14]

When James finally responded to her letter he equivocated on the issue of Hegelianism and idealism altogether, at one point defending even so crude and mechanistic a work as Lenin's early *Materialism and Empirio-Criticism* (1908) with its notion that theory should be a photocopy of reality. James declared that, "reading the book now I find no inadequacy" in it (*The Raya Dunayevskaya Collection*: 1612–1615).[15] Though important dialogue between them on the dialectic continued until the mid-1950s, James never explored in depth the contemporary significance of Hegel's Absolutes. Nor, in Dunayevskaya's view, did he ever deal seriously with the young Marx. As she later put it, he "stopped dead" before reaching either Hegel's Absolutes or Marx's Humanism, thereby failing to project a full *philosophical* break from Trotskyism. This led, in 1955, to a political and theoretical break between Dunayevskaya and James.

In the years preceding that break, far from deterring her from a journey into Hegel's Absolutes, these differences spurred Dunayevskaya to continue to work out their meaning. New impulses for liberation arising from ongoing social struggles also helped impel her journey. For example, at the time she was translating Lenin's 1914–1915 notes on Hegel, with their strong emphasis on subjectivity, she was also active with coal miners in West Virginia, who in 1949–1950 conducted a massive wildcat strike against the introduction of automation. The strike was motivated not primarily by issues of wages and benefits, but by the nature of the labor process and the degree of worker control of production. Dunayevskaya saw that in asking questions such as "what *kind* of labor should man perform?," the workers were seeking to go beyond the traditional framework of leftist and trade union politics.[16] New questions were being raised about *what it means to be human* in the very course of the struggle against dehumanizing working conditions. The abstract question of second negativity became newly concrete to her, as in her view workers were attempting to go beyond the mere negation of the immediate structures of oppression by posing what *kind* of human relations they are *for*. Dunayevskaya remained closely attuned to the emergence of such sentiments from workers, women, Blacks and youth throughout the late 1940s and early 1950s, as seen in her extensive writings on the independent character of the Black struggle in the U.S. and her singling out of women as a force of liberation, as early as a 1950 essay on "The Miners' Wives."[17] In the same period, as she later acknowledged, the new type of worker-peasant revolution in Bolivia in 1952 became especially important to her (Dunayevskaya in Hudis and Anderson 2002: 273–288).

The most critical moment in this search for new revolutionary forces came with the death of Stalin in March 1953. The long-awaited death of this tyrant, she felt, was bound to lift an incubus from the minds of the Russian and East European masses. She was seeking to anticipate the kind of revolts that might follow Stalin's death and the challenges they would pose to revolutionary theoreticians.

This helped motivate her direct exploration of Hegel's Absolutes, in two letters written to Grace Lee in May 1953. Both letters [...] explore the relation of spontaneity to organization in light of Hegelian categories. The first letter, of May 12, 1953, focuses on the final chapter of Hegel's *Science of Logic*, "The Absolute Idea." A number of dialectical categories are discussed here, from the limits of the concept of causality, to the concept of the subject as "personal and free," to Hegel's notion of the "free release" of the Idea of absolute negativity as constituting an "absolute liberation." In the second letter, written on May 20, 1953, Dunayevskaya moves from Hegel's *Logic* to his *Philosophy of Mind*, a work which had not been explored before by Marxists. She takes up such issues as Hegel's concept of freedom, the relation of "will" to the dialectics of freedom, and most important of all, the final three paragraphs of the *Philosophy of Mind*, which represent a summation of Hegel's philosophy as a whole. Here she develops her own distinctive version of the dialectic, seeing Hegel's Absolute Mind not as a mere logical abstraction but as the expression of a *dual* movement—a "movement from practice that is itself a form of theory and a movement from theory that is itself a form of philosophy and revolution" (*The Dunayevskaya Collection*: 10726).[18]

Hegel's statement, made near the end of his *Philosophy of Mind*, that "practice implicitly contains the Idea," becomes her jumping off point for developing the view that mass practice from below in the grassroots freedom movements *is itself a form of theory*.[19] In this way, she posed a new vantage point for a total opposition to existing society, one which does not stop at a first or bare negation, but which moves on to the second negation, to the positive within the negative, to express philosophically the yearning of women, children, and men to be whole human beings. Dunayevskaya developed these new interpretations of the dialectic on the eve of two major revolts against totalitarian communism, the East German uprising of June 17, 1953 and Hungarian Revolution of 1956, which in opposing both capitalism and existing communism placed the *humanism* of Marx, especially his 1844 *Manuscripts*, onto the historic stage. This was also the period of the historic Montgomery Bus Boycott of 1955–1956. To Dunayevskaya, these new freedom movements were inseparable from the new stage of dialectical cognition she was attempting to work out.

In anticipating these new movements from practice, Dunayevskaya in her breakthrough on Hegel's Absolutes also discerned a new *movement from theory reaching for philosophy*. Once the Idea of absolute negativity was seen as intrinsic to the subject, it no longer became necessary (as with an older generation of historical materialists) to "fear" the self-determination of the Idea as some mystical abstraction. The Idea itself could now be *philosophically* developed, in order to give revolutionary action its *direction*.

In the 1980s, when Dunayevskaya was reviewing the 50-year development of the philosophy that she had termed Marxist-Humanism by 1957, she discovered that the 1953 letters represented nothing less than its philosophical moment.[20] Each stage of her development of this body of ideas constituted a further fleshing out and concretization of the new points of departure contained in the 1953 letters. But all of their ramifications were not evident from the start, even to herself. It took repeated returns to them on her part, in response to objective world events and developments in Marxist-Humanism, for the full meaning of these letters to show themselves.

This can be seen in her changing assessment of Lenin. Lenin was a crucial figure for her, not only because of 1917, but also because he was the one major Marxist leader after Marx to turn directly to Hegel, in 1914–1915, as part of his theoretic preparation for revolution. Moreover, his "Abstract of Hegel's *Science of Logic*" delved deeper into the dialectic than many Marxists who followed him, in that he engaged in a materialist reading of the most idealistic part of Hegel's *Logic*, the "Doctrine of the Notion." However, the 1953 letters also represent a philosophical departure from Lenin. As she notes in her letter of May 12, 1953, Lenin stopped short of the "free release" of the Idea in his encounter with Hegel and never went into Hegel's *Philosophy of Mind*—the work in which he most fully developed the concept of absolute negativity. By holding fast to "materialism," "objective world connections," and "practice," Dunayevskaya argued, Lenin failed to develop his own insight, posed in his Hegel Notebooks, that "cognition not only reflects the objective world, but also creates it." Yet although a philosophical critique of Lenin is already central to Dunayevskaya's 1953 letters, its full ramifications were spelled out fully only near the end of her life. These writings from the 1980s make more explicit the distinctiveness of her overall approach to dialectics.[21]

*   *   *

Dunayevskaya's determination to work out a new relation between philosophy and revolution is expressed in the very nature of her writing. Neither an academic nor a mere political polemicist, she writes passionately without being dismissive of abstract thought. To cite Adrienne Rich's Foreword to *Rosa Luxemburg, Women's Liberation, and Marx's Philosophy of Revolution*: "Raya Dunayevskaya caught fire from Marx, met it with her own fire, brought to the events of her lifetime a revitalized, refocused Marxism. Her writings, with all their passion, energy, wit, and learning, may read awkwardly at times because she is really writing against the grain of how many readers have learned to think: to separate disciplines and genres, theory from practice. She's trying to think, and write, the revolution in the revolution" (Reprinted in this volume, pp. 91–102: Rich in Dunayevskaya 1991: xviii).

If Dunayevskaya is correct that the "Absolute" is no closed ontology, no pinnacle, no endpoint of development, then the task that awaits a new generation, we would argue, is to work out these points of departure as a new beginning. At a time when even Marxists are jettisoning the dialectic in favor of pragmatism and what they often term non-totalizing modes of thinking, Dunayevskaya's confidence in the dialectic of Hegel, Marx, and Marxist-Humanism is the type of perspective that can help us to navigate through such a retrogressive period as today. Yet developing that is never easy. For even at great revolutionary turning points, as in the 1960s when the pragmatic radicals of the New Left rejected philosophy, and even in 1914–1917 when Lenin tried so valiantly, especially in his Hegel studies, to fill the philosophical void after Marx's death, the overemphasis on practice has tended to overwhelm and muffle the dialectic even for revolutionary thinkers and activists.

The need to overcome this has never been greater than now, in light of the need to renew the Marxian project by working out the unresolved question of this century—what happens *after* the revolution. For this reason, the content of these texts by Dunayevskaya on the dialectic in Hegel, Marx, and today can be seen as a letter to the future.

In 1987 Dunayevskaya focused anew on Marx's *Critique of the Gotha Program* (1875), where he outlined a perspective on revolutionary organization, one which never became the basis for the large Marxist parties of this century, who instead opted for either Social-Democratic reformism or Leninist vanguardism. We close with a passage from that essay:

The burning question of the day remains: What happens the day after [the revolution]? How can we continue Marx's unchaining of the dialectic organizationally, with the principles he outlined in his *Critique of the Gotha Program*? The question of "what happens after" gains crucial importance because of what it signals in self-development and self-flowering—"revolution in permanence." No one knows what it is, or can touch it, before it appears. It is not the task that can be fulfilled in just one generation. That is why it remains so elusive, and why the abolition of the division between mental and manual labor sounds utopian. It has the future written all over it. The fact that we cannot give a blueprint does not absolve us from the task. It only makes it more difficult. (*The Dunayevskaya Collection*: 10690)

NOTES

1. The protests against the World Trade Organization in Seattle at the end of 1999, and the demonstrations in Washington, DC against the International Monetary Fund and World Bank in April 2000, have proved of special importance in having many turn with new eyes to Marx's critique of capital.
2. See especially Coole (2000), Butler (1999), and Nicolapoulos and Vassilacopoulos (1999).
3. We should add that Ollman (1993) has steadfastly defended the dialectical core of Marxism throughout the recent period, often in the face of sharp opposition to dialectical thought.
4. Many of these writings have been recently published in Dunayevskaya (1992).
5. Most of her other correspondence and writings have been gathered in *The Raya Dunayevskaya Collection: Marxist-Humanism—A Half Century of Its World Development*, on deposit at Walter Reuther Archives of Labor History and Urban Affairs in Detroit, Michigan.
6. For some discussions of Dunayevskaya's standpoint on Hegel, see Johnson (1989) and Jeannot (1999). See also the entry for Dunayevskaya in *Women Building Chicago, 1790–1990: A Bibliographical Dictionary* by Terry Moon (2001).
7. For background on Lukács's overall position, see especially Rockmore (1992).
8. The best overview of Marcuse's work remains Kellner (1984).
9. For a critique of Moishe Postone's *Time, Labor and Social Domination: A Reinterpretation of Marx's Critical Theory*, in which this position is articulated, see Hudis (1995, 1997).
10. We have used here Dunayevskaya's more lucid first English translation of Marx's "Critique of the Hegelian Dialectic," which appeared in her

Marxism and Freedom (1958). See also the more pedestrian rendering in Marx and Engels, *Collected Works* (1975).

11. See Ron Brokmeyer, Raya Dunayevskaya, et al. (1984).
12. See also Hoffmeyer (1996).
13. See Dunayevskaya (1944: 531–537). The essay has been reprinted in Dunayevskaya (1992: 83–87).
14. This is from a Letter of Dunayevskaya's to James of March 12, 1949, in Hudis and Anderson (2002): 351–354.
15. This statement is from a letter of James to Grace Lee on May 20, 1949. In the same letter James also says he has found nothing of significance in Hegel's *Philosophy of Mind*.
16. For an account, see Phillips and Dunayevskaya (1984), as well as Dunayevskaya (2000).
17. Dunayevskaya later reprinted this in her *Women's Liberation and the Dialectics of Revolution* (1985).
18. This is from a letter of Dunayevskaya written on January 13, 1987.
19. She was later to term this (in *Marxism and Freedom*) "the movement from practice to theory" (2000: 276).
20. See Dunayevskaya in Hudis and Anderson (2002: 3–13).
21. For a further discussion of her changing views about Lenin's philosophic ambivalence, see Anderson (1995).

References

Adorno, Theodor. 1973. *Negative Dialectics*, trans. by E. B. Ashton. New York: Seabury Press.

———. 1994. "Aspects of Hegel's Philosophy." In *Hegel: Three Studies*, trans. by Shierry Weber Nicholsen. Cambridge: MIT Press.

Anderson, Kevin. 1995. *Lenin, Hegel, and Western Marxism*. Champaign-Urbana: University of Illinois Press.

Berthold-Bond, Daniel. 1989. *Hegel's Grand Synthesis, a Study of Being, Thought and History*. Albany: SUNY Press.

Brokmeyer, Ron, Raya Dunayevskaya, et al. 1984. *The Fetish of High Tech and Marx's Unknown Mathematical Manuscripts*. Chicago: News and Letters.

Butler, Judith. 1999. Introduction to a new edition of *Subjects of Desire: Hegelian Reflections in 20th Century France*. New York: Columbia University Press.

Coole, Dianne. 2000. *Negativity and Politics*. London: Routledge.

Derrida, Jacques. 1971. *Positions*, trans. by Alan Bass. Chicago: University of Chicago Press.

———. 1978. "From Restricted to General Economy, a Hegelian Without Reserve." In *Writing and Difference*, trans. by Alan Bass. Chicago: University of Chicago Press.

————. 1986. *Glas*, trans. by J. P. Leavey and R. Rand. Lincoln: University of Nebraska Press.

————. 1993. *Specters of Marx*, trans. by Peggy Kamuf. New York: Routledge.

Dunayevskaya, Raya. 1944. "A New Revision of Marxian Economics." *American Economic Review* 34(3): 531–537.

————. 1982. *The Raya Dunayevskaya Collection: Marxist-Humanism—A Half Century of Its World Development*, on Deposit at Walter Reuther Archives of Labor History and Urban Affairs in Detroit, Michigan.

————. 1985. *Women's Liberation and the Dialectics of Revolution*. Detroit: Wayne State University Press.

————. 1989 [1973]. *Philosophy and Revolution, from Hegel to Sartre and from Marx to Mao*. New York: Columbia University Press.

————. 1991. *Rosa Luxemburg, Women's Liberation, and Marx's Philosophy of Revolution*. Champaign Urbana: University of Illinois Press.

————. 1992. *The Marxist-Humanist Theory of State-Capitalism: Selected Writings by Raya Dunayevskaya*. Chicago: News and Letters.

————. 1997. "May 1972 letter 'On C.L.R. James' Notes on Dialectics.'" Reprinted in *News & Letters*, October.

————. 2000 [1958]. *Marxism and Freedom, from 1776 Until Today*. Amherst, NY: Humanity Books.

Engels, Friedrich. 1990. *Ludwig Feuerbach and the End of Classical German Philosophy*, *Marx-Engels Collected Works*, Vol. 26. New York: International Publishers.

Habermas, Jürgen. 1987. *The Theory of Communicative Action*, Vol. 2, trans. by Thomas McCarthy. Boston: Beacon.

Hegel, G. W. F. 1969. *Science of Logic*, trans. by A. V. Miller. Atlantic Highlands, NJ: Humanities Press.

Hoffmeyer, John H. 1996. *The Presence of the Future in Hegel's Logic*. Rutherford: Associated University Presses.

Hudis, Peter. 1995. "Labor, High-Tech Capitalism, and the Crisis of the Subject: A Critique of Recent Developments in Critical Theory." *Humanity and Society* 19(4): 4–20.

————. 1997. "Conceptualizing an Emancipatory Alternative: István Mészáros' Beyond Capital." *Socialism and Democracy* 11(1): 37–54.

Hudis, Peter and Kevin B. Anderson, eds. 2002. *The Power of Negativity: Selected Writings on the Dialectic in Hegel and Marx*. New York: Lexington Books.

James, C. L. R. 1980. *Notes on Dialectics, Hegel, Marx, Lenin*. Westport, Connecticut: Lawrence Hill & Co.

Jameson, Fredric. 1997. "Interview with Fredric Jameson." In *Lukács After Communism, Interviews with Contemporary Intellectuals*, edited by Eva L. Corredor. Durham and London: Duke University Press.

Jeannot, Thomas M. 1999. "Raya Dunayevskaya's Conception of Ultimate Reality and Meaning." *Journal of Ultimate Reality and Meaning* 22(4): 276–293.

Johnson, Patricia Altenbernd. 1989. "Women's Liberation: Following Dunayevskaya in Practicing Dialectics." *Quarterly Journal of Ideology* 13(4): 65–74.

Kellner, Douglas. 1984. *Herbert Marcuse and the Crisis of Marxism*. Berkeley: University of California Press.

Lukács, Georg. 1975. *The Young Hegel*, trans. by Rodney Livingstone. Cambridge: MIT Press.

Marcuse, Herbert. 1941. *Reason and Revolution*. New York: Oxford.

Marx, Karl. 1958. "Critique of the Hegelian Dialectic." In *Marxism and Freedom* by Raya Dunayevskaya. New York: Bookman.

———. 1975. "Critique of the Hegelian Dialectic." In Marx and Engels, *Collected Works*, Vol. 3. New York: International Publishers.

———. 1976. *Capital*, Vol. I, trans. by Ben Fowkes. London: Pelican.

Moon, Terry. 2001. "Dunayevskaya." In *Women Building Chicago, 1790–1990: A Bibliographical Dictionary*, edited by Rima Luin Schultz and Adele Hast. Bloomington: Indiana University Press.

Nicolapoulos, Toula and George Vassilacopoulos. 1999. *Hegel and the Logical Structure of Love*. London: Ashgate.

Ollman, Bertell. 1993. *Dialectical Investigations*. New York: Routledge.

Phillips, Andy and Raya Dunayevskaya. 1984. *The Coal Miners' General Strike of 1949–50 and the Birth of Marxist-Humanism in the U.S.* Chicago: News and Letters.

Postone, Moishe. 1993. *Time, Labor, and Social Domination*. New York: Cambridge University Press.

Rockmore, Tom. 1992. *Irrationalism: Lukács and the Marxist View of Reason*. Berkeley: University of California Press.

CHAPTER 3

Unchaining the Dialectic on the Threshold of Revolution: Dunayevskaya's Discovery of Hegel in the Birth of Marxist-Humanism

Alessandra Spano

The decade of the 1950s was one of the richest and most turbulent phases in Raya Dunayevskaya's life. The definitive break with Trotskyism (1950), the end of the collaboration with C. L. R. James and Grace Lee, which lasted over a decade, and the founding of a new political group (1954–1955), News and Letters Committees, all took place on a political-organizational level. At the same time, the 1950s marked a real theoretical turning point, the moment of "philosophic break" (Hudis 1992: XVI), through which she developed from the theory of state capitalism to the founding of Marxist-Humanism, the position that constituted the framework within which her subsequent reflections developed and from which the paths of her subsequent theorizations unfolded. This "breakthrough", as Dunayevskaya was to describe it (1987b: 5–6), was centrally grounded in her encounter with Hegel, and, in particular, in her grappling with

A. Spano (✉)
Department of Political and Social Sciences, University of Catania, Catania, Italy

© The Author(s) 2021
K. B. Anderson et al. (eds.), *Raya Dunayevskaya's Intersectional Marxism*, Marx, Engels, and Marxisms,
https://doi.org/10.1007/978-3-030-53717-3_3

Hegel's notion of the "Absolute" as a "vision of the future" investigated from the point of view of the present. In this chapter I will focus on this pivotal engagement so as to investigate the philosophical and political grounds of her Hegelian turn and the constitutive role it can be said to have played in her later writing. In doing so, we will see how the theory of state capitalism elaborated in the 1940s is not only a historical but also a *logical* precursor to the philosophy of Marxist-Humanism.

"Why Hegel? Why Now?"

"Why Hegel? Why now?" is the title of the first part of *Philosophy and Revolution* (1973), the second work of Dunayevskaya's "trilogy of revolution"; but we can also use it as a point of departure from which to investigate how the very moment of her Hegelian turn is achieved. Her arrival at this Hegelian departure can be dated back to 1953, coinciding with the letters regarding Hegel's *Absolutes* that she sent to Grace Lee, with whom Dunayevskaya collaborated for a decade, together with James, first in the Johnson-Forest tendency (also known as the State Capitalist Tendency) within the American Workers Party and the Socialist Workers Party and then, after their break-up, which occurred in 1950, in the organization Correspondence Committees. Dunayevskaya's plunge into dialectical thought did not come out of the blue: her reflections on the Hegelian dialectic had already begun in the Johnson-Forest Tendency in the late 1940s, mediated by Lenin's *Philosophical Notebooks* of 1914–1915, and conditioned by the need to rethink the role of the party and organizational forms in general. What confronted them was the need to free the party from the myopia of the radical left which, from Stalinism to American Trotskyism, was largely unable to read the real movement of the present, manifested in the world-historical phase of state capitalism at the global level.

Indeed, during the 1940s, Dunayevskaya, James, and Lee carried out their critique of Stalin's Soviet Union, developing an original theory of state capitalism that contrasted with those who maintained a focus on the *form* of property relations. Integral to this theory was a challenge to the position that continued to see the USSR as a workers' state, albeit degenerate (Trotsky), or identified in it a third way between socialism and capitalism, i.e., a form of bureaucratic state socialism or bureaucratic collectivism (Burnham 1941; Carter 1941; Shachtman 1940,

1942). Instead, according to the Johnson-Forest tendency, it was neces-sary to look at both material relations *and* production relations in order to penetrate the reality of Stalinist society. Dunayevskaya was to follow up on this premise through a thorough and seminal economic analysis of Stalin's Five-Year Plans, a period of engagement that saw her atten-tion turn to the "secret laboratories of production" and the relationship between capital and labor in the production process. At the very center of her analysis of the state-managed centralization of capital we find "socialist accumulation" (Dunayevskaya 1942a: 46), realized through collectiviza-tion and the tax system, as well as the "socialist" governance of labor. This accumulation consisted of several policies—both at the legislative level and at the level of factory discipline—aimed at producing hier-archy and differentiation in the working class through the formation of a labor bureaucracy. The result was the effective replication of the capitalist command over labor, with its stunning effectiveness. On the other hand, accumulation, as well as the authoritarian organization of labor, had to deal with the subversive "fluidity" and the actual flight of labor, which is read by Dunayevskaya as a workers' tactic in the daily struggle to escape the factory regime through mobility:

> The workers became restless [...] In 1932 it was decreed that the worker could be fired for a single day's absence [...] While the factory director had control over the workers' food and lodging, the worker had no trade unions independent of the state to take up his grievances. But it was impos-sible to *decree* slavery. So long as the industry was expanding and workers were necessary to man the machines, the workers took advantage of that one fact and continued to shift job to job. (1942a: 60)

Such a focus on the autonomy and political relevance of workers' subjectivity is surely one of the most innovative aspects of Dunayevskaya's analysis of the USSR, especially considering she understood state capi-talism not simply as a totalitarian exception or as a manifestation of the "Russian question," but rather as a new phase of world capitalist devel-opment, directly linked to the political situation in the United States. In these terms, her theory differed also from the main Trotskyist critique of Trotsky, proposed by Tony Cliff in *The Nature of Stalinist Russia*, in which, whilst the centrality of capitalist productive relations in Russia is recognized, the main focus of the critique is nevertheless on state capi-talism as a Russian question, not as a new global stage of capitalism. In contrast, Dunayevskaya underlined the global level at which state capitalism was developed and the specific connection with the situation in the United States. If the 1930s and the Second World War mark a period of considerable increase in terms of state intervention in production relations at both an economic and political level, at the same time wildcat strikes and creative forms of workers' revolt against the factory regime and industrial discipline continually undermined the attempt to curb social conflict. In this "social war", Black workers were the protagonists: since the oppression of the Black worker was not limited to the increasingly ferocious exploitation in the factory, but also intensified by the political and social conditions of that exploitation—from racial segregation to the extremely inhumane conditions of life in the black ghettos,

> [it] will give his developing class consciousness a hostility to the existing society and a keener determination to destroy it. The proletarian vanguard must respond by recognizing not only the validity but the inevitability of Negro mass movements against this double oppression and strive to lead this movement and harness its revolutionary potentialities for the struggle against capitalist society. But only that revolutionary party can do this which understands the objectively revolutionary role that these independent mass movements can play in the reconstruction of society on communist beginnings. (Dunayevskaya 1948: 26)

Yet that party was not the Workers Party. The "Negro question" led Dunayevskaya and the other Johnsonites to criticize the Workers Party harshly for its incapacity to grasp the specificity of the Black dimension, which rather than being homogenized in the name of the abstract unity of the working class, needed to be recognized as a protagonist in the American radical movement and in the revolutionary process in and of itself. In other words, the very notion of *class*, understood as a subjective antagonistic positioning—self-movement, creative self-activity—within a given relationship of domination, needed to be seen in the way it was shaped by the emergence of racial and gender contradictions among the rank and file. From this position, it was clear that the urge to broaden the concept of the party was strongly influenced by the need to grasp its revolutionary potential: the function of the party is not politicization from the top of the grassroots movement—this movement is *already* political—but assisting the autonomous organization of the working class against capital. In the era of state capitalism, in which the centralization of capital and the bureaucratization of labor effectively transformed the Russian Communist Party and the Third International into executive agents of the plan, was it still possible to think of a party that "means independence of the proletariat as organization and uninterrupted revolution [...] powerful – overthrow of the bosses' state" (Negri 1973: 84)? The need to investigate this issue, as much theoretical as practical, forced Dunayevskaya to go beyond the boundaries of the category of state capitalism in a search for a theory capable of grasping and showing the real possibility of overcoming the present social relations.

Therefore, in order to enrich the discussion within the Johnson-Forest Tendency, Dunayevskaya decided to translate into English Lenin's *Hegel Notebooks*, previously published in 1929 in Russian. Dunayevskaya's choice of this specific text may have been motivated by a number of factors, but one clear influence was surely her first encounter with the Hegelian dialectic through Herbert Marcuse's *Reason and Revolution* (1941). This work had been widely diffused in the American context and was relevant in Marxist debates considering its polemical critique of positivist and pragmatist approaches (one of the greatest exponents of which in Marxist tradition being Sidney Hook, who had already been the target of Trotsky's attacks). At the same time, the Stalinist censorship of those aspects of Marxian thought considered to be too Hegelian—and therefore contrary to the orthodox formulation of scientific Marxism— certainly reinforced in Dunayevskaya the idea of the necessity to plunge into the dialectic. Just as Lenin had turned to the Hegelian dialectic to face the historical impasse of the Second International—soon after the vote by the German Social Democratic Party in favor of war credits— Dunayevskaya grasped in Lenin's elaboration the possibility of rethinking Marxism, starting from its dialectical content, in the very moment in which it seemed to be unable to respond to counterrevolutionary forces within the revolution, coming at that time from within the established Communist and Socialist Party.

The translation of the Notebooks was a part of a collective study that first resulted in James' *Notes on Dialectics* (1948). In his introduction, James explains that the need to deepen the study of Hegelian logic pertained to the grasping of its movement by testing it in relation to the history of the labor struggle (1948: 8). This need is found in the will to subtract the *absolute idea*, "the concept of the development of the proletariat in capitalist society viewed in the whole of its universality" (1948: 41), from the possible defeats of the organizational

forms that it gives itself in its development, interpreting them as temporary stages in the advancement of thought (1948: 96). James also used
Hegelian categories to portray Stalinism as a "transitional stage" of capitalism and *not* of the labor movement. In this analysis, the concept of
the *universal* stands for *socialism* in the present as well as denoting the
conflict between the level of consciousness (the party) and the object (the
proletariat). But, James adds, when the forms of organization no longer
correspond to the free creative and revolutionary activity of the workers,
they become nothing more than the internal opposition that must be
overcome. According to James, the time has come for the end of organization as such: "*there is nothing more to organize* [...] The task today
is to call for, to teach, to illustrate, to develop *spontaneity*." Just as the
Soviet in 1917 was the concrete universal that could invert socialism, for
James the universal for 1948 was the abolition of organization. However,
at the same time he claimed that "the vanguard can only organize itself on
the basis of the destruction of the stranglehold that the existing organizations have on the proletariat by means of which it is suffering such ghastly
defeats" (1948: 117). Thus, abolishing organization did not mean the
end of the vanguardism; rather, the question that now arose was: how to
think about the relationship between vanguard and masses without taking
into account the dialectic between spontaneity and organization? Therefore, it seems that James' study of Hegelian dialectics through Lenin's
Notebooks resulted in an essentially non-dialectical outcome.

Dunayevskaya did not hold back on criticism, sharing her desire to
explore the issue in a three-way correspondence with James and Lee at
the end of the 1940s during the period at which she was completing her
English translation of Lenin's Notebooks. In particular, she highlighted
the dialectical character of the relationship between essence and appearance: the latter cannot be reduced to the former simply because it has its
own *objectivity*. This explains why the problem of forms of organization
(appearance) cannot be dismissed as James did, because appearance itself
is "one of the determinations of the essence" (Dunayevskaya 1949: 348–
351). Moreover, she underlined the complications of the very concept of
causality, which Lenin no longer understood in an empirical and deterministic sense (as in his 1905 work, *Materialism and Empirio-criticism*),
but defined it as a dialectical relationship, wherein the cause can become
the effect and vice versa. Certainly, what emerges here is Dunayevskaya's
disagreement with James's reductionism, which places the contradiction
at the level of capital without grasping how the revolutionary movement

itself can pass through it. Therefore, through the dialectical method, Dunayevskaya starts to point out how it is not enough to get rid of anachronistic organizational forms to face the puzzle of the revolution and its subject. The need to connect theory and practice, subjectivity and objectivity will mark the next steps of her conceptual development.

The attempt to publish her English translation of Lenin's notebooks did not achieve the desired result, neither in her group nor outside of it (Anderson 1995: 202–203). In fact, as she says in the *Introduction* to Volume XII—*Retrospective and Perspective* (Dunayevskaya 1986) of the *Raya Dunayevskaya Collection*, the translation was only published after almost a decade, in 1958—together with the translations of parts of Marx's *Economic and Philosophical Manuscripts of 1844*—as an appendix of the first edition of *Marxism and Freedom*, a book that was defined by her as "the organization of thought which will determine our future organizational life" (1957: 12186). Even if reflections within the Johnson-Forest Tendency constituted the theoretical background of Dunayevskaya's dive into the Hegelian dialectic, the urgency of a philosophical leap beyond the theory of state capitalism (and toward the foundation of Marxist-Humanism) marked the need for the interruption of the collaboration with James and Lee.

One of the first reasons for their disagreement can be clearly found in the conclusion of *State Capitalism and World Revolution* (1950), which we can consider the expression of the position of both James and Lee, authors of this part of the text: "There is no longer any purely philosophical answer [...] Philosophical questions [...] can be solved only by the revolutionary action of the proletariat and the masses. [...] The proletarian revolution alone will put science in its place" (1950: 128–129). In addition, humanism is here identified with Christian and existentialist interpretations and considered to be a reactionary and individualistic theory because it would project within the subject the objective contradiction that belongs to the state-capitalist system. This answer obviously did not satisfy Dunayevskaya, who then entered what she came to define as her "transition period" (1984: 284). This period, which stretched from 1950 to 1953, was a period of the deepening of her study of Hegel following the example of Lenin, as mentioned above. What Dunayevskaya was concerned with here, above all, was to extrapolate upon the deepest meaning of Lenin's dialectical notion that "consciousness not only reflects the objective world but also creates it."

THE PHILOSOPHIC TURN

In May 1953, Dunayevskaya wrote two letters to Lee on Hegel's absolutes that marked her philosophical breakthrough and the theoretical foundation of the philosophy of Marxist-Humanism. The first letter (May 12, 1953) is focused on the final chapter of Hegel's *Science of Logic* on the *Absolute Idea*, while in the second (May 20, 1953) Dunayevskaya moves from Hegel's *Logic* to his *Philosophy of Mind*—and particularly to the final three paragraphs of the section on *Absolute Mind*. Both of these letters are essential to an understanding of how Dunayevskaya's passage from the theory of state capitalism to the philosophical formulation of Marxist-Humanism is articulated. In fact, this transition is to be understood in the dialectical movement that characterizes it: the theory of Marxist-Humanism is thus configured as an *Aufhebung* of the theory of state capitalism, that is, as an overcoming that reaffirms the validity of the previous theory on a broader level. This means that Dunayevskaya's Marxist-Humanism is a philosophy capable not only of indicating the negative character of Stalinism and economistic Marxism, but also of grasping the subjective novelty of the historical movement in which it is inscribed. Because of the centrality of these 1953 letters, we will put them in dialogue with some texts written before and after, in order to emphasize their continuity and discontinuity with her other writings.

Dunayevskaya wrote these letters to Lee at what was a particularly significant time, in the aftermath of a series of quarrels and misunderstandings that had arisen between members of the group in the previous months, especially after the death of Stalin, in March of that year. The death of Stalin, which for Dunayevskaya marked an epoch-making turning point in world history, did not interest Lee and James as much. What happened thereafter was that Dunayevskaya decided to isolate herself while reading of Hegel, looking for answers, or rather questions, that neither James nor Lee were willing to articulate.

> I have taken the plunge. But I will restrain myself from beginning with the conclusions and the differentiation of us from Lenin and even us from 1948 [James's *Notes on Dialectics*] but I will have you bear with me as I go through the whole last chapter of the *Logic*. However, before I do so, let me state what I am *not* doing: 1) I am not touching upon the mass party; the workers will do what they will do and until they do we can have only the faintest intimation of the great leap. 2) This is not 1948, but 1953; I am not concerned with spontaneity versus organization, nor with

Stalinism which the workers will overcome. I am concerned only with the dialectic of the vanguard party [or] of that *type* of grouping like ours, be it large or small, and *its* relationship to the mass. (Dunayevskaya 1953a: 16)

Dunayevskaya was approaching the dialectic of the absolute idea, looking for the dialectic of the party in a broad sense, going beyond the critique of the vanguard party. The Workers' Party and Stalin's death were behind her and, therefore, for a thinker such as Dunayevskaya, who always looked forward, the absolute idea was to be investigated from the point of view of the present. The time had come to pose the question of the form of the organization a revolutionary group should take. If "the absolute idea has shown itself to be the identity of the theoretical and the practical idea" that contains the highest opposition within itself (Hegel 1812: 735), for Dunayevskaya this meant that "the unity of leadership activity and grassroots activity," according to which the absolute idea (party/organization) is "the only object and content of philosophy," contains in itself all the determinations in a wealth of differences.

In this passage, we can identify an element that is crucial to Dunayevskaya's thought and especially to her humanistic reading of Marxism in particular. The need to overcome the division between theory and practice, grasping them in their unity as a totality, recalls in her philosophy of Marxist-Humanism the reflections on the division between manual and mental labor elaborated during the 1940s. Rank and file workers as masses in motion cannot be seen just as "force," but need also to be seen as the "reason" of revolution: political activity should not reproduce the hierarchy of the division of labor, between the bosses who rule and those who must listen and obey. As Dunayevskaya wrote in the 1940s in "Labor and Society" (1942b: 19), the division of labor under the capitalist mode of production means the alienation of the worker not only from the product and the means of production, but also from labor itself as a creative activity: labor as value, abstract labor, is opposed to that of the concrete, individual worker. The alienation of labor as human creative activity that transforms nature produces not only exploitation, but also labor's "enslavement" to capital. It is not by chance that we find the term *enslavement* used here, since in the same essay Dunayevskaya reiterates the fact that capitalism needs free labor—that is to say, labor free to sell itself on the market, to be transformed into a commodity— as an integral component of its own development. Thus, a comparison to outright slavery is made in order to highlight how the past persists in the present, namely in the bureaucratization and authoritarian organization of labor implemented as much by the state as by the party and the trade-union leadership in the era of state capitalism. The relationship between capital and labor is based both on economic exploitation and on a form of domination that commands the cooperation of individuals, as Dunayevskaya sees in the early 1940s through *The German Ideology*:

> The social power, i.e., the multiplied productive force, which arises through the co-operation of different individuals as it is determined by the division of labour, appears to these individuals [...] not as their own united power, but as an alien force existing outside them, of the origin and goal of which they are ignorant, which they thus cannot control, which on the contrary passes through a peculiar series of phases and stages independent of the will and the action of man. (Marx and Engels 1846: 54)

Uniting mental and manual labor means overcoming the relationship of domination that lies behind their separation, tackling the question of power directly in the productive process. It is here that "the undisputed authority of the capitalist," tracked by Dunayevskaya in *Marxism and Freedom* as the "despotic plan of capital that reveals itself in the specific form of the hierarchic structure of control over social labor," imposes its command over social cooperation (1958: 92). But, at the same time, this hierarchical power relationship lies within the organizational forms of the labor movement, at the service of the state-planned capitalism. In this sense, the focus on the problem of the party, in this phase of approaching and discovering the dialectic, comes from the specific concern to challenge Stalinism and state capitalism as a form of counterrevolution which emerged within the revolution: the party, on the one hand, is the historical negation of the revolution, on the other hand, it is the possible independence of proletariat as a revolutionary organization, of the worker's reappropriation of power to transform reality.

Willing thereby to confront the question of the party's ambivalent character—as counterrevolutionary and *potentially* revolutionary at the same time—Dunayevskaya took up the challenge of going further to grasp the essence of the concept of the second negation. This concept is defined by Hegel in the *Doctrine of Being* in the *Logic* as distinguished from "the *first* negation, negation as negation *in general*," because "the second negation, the negation of negation which is concrete, *absolute* negativity, just as the first is on the contrary only *abstract* negativity" (1812: 89). Significantly, the need to go beyond the concept of the "positive in the negative," that is, the overcoming of Stalinism in general, implies the need to discover how Hegel, in the last pages of the chapter on the absolute idea is able to state that the second negation is capable of transcending contradiction as the "deepest and most objective moment" of self-development of spirit, thanks to which a "subject is personal and free" (Dunayevskaya 1953a: 20). In this passage of Dunayevskaya's commentary on the *Science of Logic* her full enthusiasm emerges: the moment of the second negation, that is, of the revolution that will negate state capitalism's negation of the revolution, is constituted as a revolution that is also the means through which the revolutionary subject affirms its own personality and freedom. Here, Dunayevskaya finds the philosophical grounding of her theoretical and political path, which is aimed at making central to both revolutionary subjectivity and the struggle for freedom. Indeed, the emphasis given to the "personal and free" character of the subject means for Dunayevskaya the impossibility of identifying socialism with Stalinism or any form of scientistic and economistic Marxism, precisely because they subordinate individual and concrete workers, and their freedom on the altar of an abstract development and of production for production's sake. Moreover, second negation in Hegel is something richer than *die Furie des Verschwindens,* the "fury of the disappearance" of the old: it is also the moment that discloses the revolutionary subject as personal and free. Making socialism, the concrete universal, requires the full and thorough self-development of "human power" as "its own end." It is this that Dunayevskaya will reaffirm in the following years as the essence of her system.

Hegel's second negation provides the author with a philosophical basis for thinking the very possibility of revolution within the age of state capitalism, starting from the point of view of creative subjectivity and its struggle for freedom. But, if in Dunayevskaya this subjectivity emerges in the antagonistic relationship with the despotic plan of capital, in which the state is centrally implicated, the way toward the freedom of the political subject is developed in the Hegelian system as intimately linked to the concept of the state. Negative freedom is fulfilled in its positive and productive power as normativity, so that the real and historical dimension of freedom lies in the poietic activity of the law (Sciacca 1996: 75; 79): "reality in general, as the existence of the free will, is law [...] which as such includes all the determinations of freedom" (Hegel 1830: §486).

According to this, the subject realizes itself and its freedom in the state, so that the conceptualization of the transformation of the political order, namely revolution, is therefore not a radical negation of the contents and forms of that order, but rather its—even sudden—adaptation to the transformations of the historical reality (Ricciardi 2001: 128).

This contradiction unveils the political context of Dunayevskaya's immersion in Hegelian dialectic, which is concretized as a displacement of the Hegelian framework on the basis of the challenge of the present. Therefore, the point is not tracing and reestablishing the persistence of Hegel in Marx, but rather displacing the Hegelian dialectic on the basis of reestablishing Marxism as theory of revolution at the very time that state capitalism is engaging in counterrevolution. Recalling the first paragraph, the question of *Why Hegel?* cannot be figured out without thinking about *Why now?* The dialectic is redefined starting from the reversal determined by the age of state capitalism as the time of "absolute contradiction," i.e., of the antagonism between labor and capital.

The *second* negation as the moment in which the subject realizes itself as personal and free also implies, therefore, that contradiction is put at the very core of the dialectic, liquidating the Hegelian moment of the recon-ciliation of opposites. The process of "unchaining" the Hegelian dialectic begins with the central role of absolute negation as a split that cannot be reassembled, but instead shows in itself the possibility of something that is not yet, of a new beginning in history. This is the meaning of a passage in Dunayevskaya's letter to Lee, in which the whole movement of the absolute idea is seen as the path of liberation that constitutes freedom: nothing but the "absolute dialectic [...] that *frees* itself" (2002: 20).

To understand how the concept of the second negation can trans-form into a dialectic of revolutionary rupture, capable of interrupting the unfolding of the movement of becoming that continuously recom-poses and overcomes contradictions by reabsorbing them within itself, it is necessary to read this specific notion together with the last paragraph of the absolute idea chapter.

> The idea, namely, in positing itself as the absolute *unity* of the pure concept and its reality and thus collecting itself in the immediacy of *being*, is in this form as *totality* – *nature*. – This determination, however, is nothing that *has become*, is not a *transition* [...] The pure idea into which the deter-minateness or reality of the concept is itself raised into concept is rather

an absolute *liberation* for which there is no longer an immediate determination which is not equally *posited* and is not concept; in this freedom, therefore, there is no transition that takes place. (Hegel 1812: 752–753)

Here Hegel breaks with the concept of dialectical transition and instead uses the term liberation: the absolute idea freely releases itself and "no transition takes place." The idea's final action is neither a *Gewordensein*, continuity of becoming, nor an *Übergang* or passing over to a different but still *logical* sphere. It is rather an *absolute Befreiung*, or liberation as a new beginning originating from the very end of the absolute idea *as* internal to the Logic: the idea releases of itself (*sich selbst frei entlässt*) and finds the possibility of radical transformation of itself as such. Thus, this "absolute liberation" is the act whereby the idea, on the threshold between logic and nature, can retrospectively free itself from the past and prospectively free itself for a new beginning of history (Nuzzo 2018: 302–304). The absolute liberation in the final development of the absolute idea, as the unity of theory and practice represented by the dialectic of the party, opens a fault line on the edge of the Logic, that is the logic of capital as the dialectic of development of bourgeois society (Dunayevskaya 1953a: 23) that overlooks Nature, where the idea emerges from itself: namely, where revolutionary action takes place. The possibility of revolution, of a new beginning moving toward socialism as concrete universal lies in this fault line, in this discontinuity.

In this respect, revolution as the possibility of a new beginning paves the way for what in the essay "Private property and Communism," in the *Economic Philosophical Manuscripts*, Marx defines the "fully developed naturalism" that is humanism, "resolution of the strife between [...] freedom and necessity [...] the riddle of history solved" (1844: 296–297). In this way, recalling the historical nature of the concept of the "human" helps us to move a step forward in the understanding of the relevance of the final development of the absolute idea.

Firstly, the party grows in capitalist society: this means that if it constitutes itself as a subject in an antagonistic relationship to the "despotic plan of capital," it has at the same time been constituted as object. This contradiction impacts the party: for the new subject to come into being the old one must die. This means, in essence, the necessary end of the party, to the extent that it also carries within itself the shape given by the past. Yet only the subject itself can carry out this activity of transformation that is also self-transformation, where "not the means of production create the new type of man, but the new type of man will create the means of production" (Dunayevskaya 1942b: 20).

Secondly, the absolute liberation of the idea as end and the new beginning is neither a precise moment in a progressive and linear historical development, nor something metahistorical. It is the immanent *possibility* of revolution seen through the discontinuity of reality, that unveils the contingent nature of the relationship of capitalistic domination and that *appears* as if its reality were immutable and eternal. This appearance results in a form of legitimation of the hierarchical structure underpinning society: the despotic nature of capital's command unfolds itself in the "specific capacity of preventing individuals from accessing history," crushing the present under the weight of the past (Ricciardi 2019: 13; 91). Specifically, in Stalinist state-capitalist planning, the despotism of the state apparatus uses the past revolution against the worker in order to legitimate a new social hierarchy, this after the 1917 revolution had swept the former ones away. Therefore, the affirmation of the Soviet Union as a form of state capitalism, also shows the 1917 revolution as a historical process that was contingent and always exposed to the emergence of contradictions and even counterrevolution from within.

As a result, the absolute idea, interpreted as the dialectical movement of the party, that it is the unity of theory and practice, is related to the two fundamental aspects of revolution as well: the immanent possibility that unveils the contingency of capital, that is, theory as critique of reality, and revolution in its actuality, in the movement of the masses that makes history. These two aspects must be kept together because one depends upon the other: "the old must be overthrown, root and branch – its ideology (false consciousness) as well as its exploitation" (Dunayevskaya 1970: 26).

The relationship between these two aspects is dealt with directly in the second of the letters sent to Lee (May 20, 1953), focusing on the third part of Hegel's *Encyclopedia, Philosophy of Mind*, and on its final syllogisms in particular. If the absolute idea was identified with the dialectic of the party, then mind here is rather read as the "new society gestating in the old." This "new society" is not something that is yet to come, but evident everywhere (Dunayevskaya 1953b: 25), and shows in itself the very unity of the two aspects of revolution: its possibility is embedded in reality, and reality shows the concrete possibility of revolution, here and now. Thus the issue of revolution breaks the boundaries of the party to become a movement that pours into the new society. The last three syllogisms of the section on the absolute mind trace and define how here the unity between theory and practice is shaped.

In the first syllogism (Hegel 1830: § 575), the unity between Logic (theory) and Mind (the new society) has Nature (practice) as its middle term: in linking theory with the new society, practice sunders them by a movement from theory to practice and from practice to theory but also to the new society. Therefore, practice is implicitly theory and reaches out directly to the new society. This formulation will be fundamental for the foundation of Marxist-Humanism: revolutionary practice has a *direct* relationship to the constitution of the new society because it participates in it; however, it is also the middle term between theory and the new society. From this formulation it is possible to understand the affirmation, which is expressed in *Marxism and Freedom*, of the movement of the masses toward freedom not only as also force but as "reason" of revolution.

The second syllogism finds Mind, that is the new society, as the middle term between theory and practice. Presupposing practice, in the new society theory becomes a "subjective cognition, of which liberty is the aim, and which is itself the way to produce it" (Hegel 1830: § 576). This "subjective cognition" is a philosophy that vitalizes the idea, gives lifeblood to theory taking it from real human beings who struggle for freedom. It must be underlined that this syllogism is also quoted by Dunayevskaya in another form: in this second form, "which is itself the way to produce it" becomes the "self-bringing forth" (Dunayevskaya 1987b: 9), using Reinhart Klemens Maurer's translation in his *Hegel und das Ende der Geschichte* (1965) (Hudis and Anderson 2002: 13 n.22). In the original version *to produce* is in German *hervorbringen*: to create, produce, but also giving a kind of direction that is an expression, opening the act of production outward. So, the new society produces philosophy as its subjective cognition, theory enriched with living practice, not only aiming toward freedom and producing it in the process, but also the process of self-development that brings the struggle for freedom always beyond itself, grasping the direction of practice and giving it subjectivity.

In this way, the absolute universal is also transformed and enriched. The Idea of philosophy has its middle term in the absolute universal which, in the third syllogism (Hegel 1830: § 577), divides itself into Mind (the new society) and Nature (practice): in this way the former becomes the presupposition of theory, now subjective activity, and the latter a process in which the Idea implicitly exists.

Consequently, the movement that shapes the new society is nothing less than the absolute universal of socialism that has become real and subjective, unifying the two aspects: "it is the nature of the fact, the notion, which causes the movement and development, yet this same movement is equally the action of cognition" (Hegel 1830: § 577). Dunayevskaya refers to the Paris Commune and the Soviet as historical materializations of the new society: a new stage of development of freedom consisting in a "movement from practice that is itself a form of theory and a movement from theory that is itself a form of philosophy and revolution." She herself will define this double movement as "our unique characteristic from the original 1953 breakthrough on the absolute idea" (1987a: 10726).

Conclusion

Clearly, these theorizations by Dunayevskaya paved the way for the development of a new dialectic of philosophy and organization, namely the birth of Marxist-Humanism and the foundation of News and Letters Committees just few years after. After Stalin's death, the point for Dunayevskaya was not only to think of revolution as the upheaval that would have swept away what was already becoming history, but how to think of revolution itself as the moment of creation of a new world, a human one. This humanism has nothing to do with offering a solution to what is "human": it is, rather, to restore human beings as the protagonists of history. No development can be considered human if it is not a self-development, a subjective transformation that rests upon the human being as a whole of potentialities. Only in this way can society become the place where individuals enjoy their full dimension of social being, the realm of subjective freedom, instead of the realm of abstract necessity. Through absolute idea and absolute mind as the new society, the dialectic itself undergoes a twist. It is unchained by breaking the boundaries of a closed ontology to open up new beginnings of history and the emergence of new revolutionary subjects: the Black movement, the women's movement, and the anti-colonial movements, which were on the threshold of revolution.

In fact, these new beginnings would come soon enough: the East German uprising (June 17, 1953) and the 1956 Hungarian Revolution, and also the historic Montgomery Bus Boycott of 1955–1956 in the United States. In each of these struggles, and in those to come, there was a "movement from theory reaching for philosophy" (Hudis and Anderson 2002: xxix). Dunayevskaya found in Hegel's absolutes that the creative moment can only be put in place by revolutionary subjectivity liberating itself from the despotism of capitalist domination and from the remains of such despotism that continue to persist even inside its own fibers. On a theoretical level, Hegel's discovery allowed her to put Marxism on its feet: through dialectics it was possible to go beyond the scientific method, which analyzes, separates, reproduces the order of reality on the level of thought. The dialectic is what makes theory critical and self-critical, what has in itself that *surplus* that is given in matter as living energy, as a possibility for the transformation of reality itself: the ability to grasp how the movement from practice exceeds the conditions of its existence allows the dialectic to express both the subjectivity of that excess and its movement toward freedom.

In this respect, getting beyond state-capitalist theory alone meant restoring Marxism as a theory of human liberation that keeps theory and practice dialectically intertwined. The dialectic is capable of grasping the subjective movement in its struggle for freedom, and by doing so the very same dialectic releases itself as a new beginning. Where subjectivity is expressed, the theory is put to the test: this means the absolute method of philosophy, that comes from practice and returns to it to be tested and renewed. It does not develop in a linear progressive line but goes backward and forward as does the movement of reality itself: the dialectic of philosophy and organization shows how none of the previous forms of the new society as unity of theory and practice (such as the Commune, or the Soviet) has been left behind or lost, but become a source for a further development, becoming "incorporated" into the new dialectic of philosophy and organization (Dunayevskaya 1953a: 21).

James and Lee did not see that the urge to go beyond state-capitalist theory was for Dunayevskaya the need to move forward in order to understand how the world was changing, transformed by masses in motion toward liberation from oppression. She sought to grasp and absorb the lifeblood of this movement. This need resulted in the dialectic cracking the closed ontology of reality so as to become a subjective movement of liberation: a dialectic unchained that reveals the unity of theory and practice through the connection between the objective side of subjectivity, the new society that struggles to emerge, and the subjective side of objectivity, that is the self-movement within the objectivity of the subject searching for freedom. Unchaining the dialectic is a further step forward on the threshold of revolution, breaking with the present and opening it to an unwritten future. As she will write in *Marxism and Freedom*:

> the Absolute is the vision of the future. Whether one accepts it as the new society or thinks of it only as the ontological unity of the human and divine, the simple truth is that *this* unity of the human and divine is not up in heaven but here on the earth. (1958: 41)

Thus, the task was to make this vision of the future a reality by transforming the present. For Dunayevskaya, this meant catching the fire while it was still burning, "to think, and write, the revolution in the revolution" (Rich 1991: xviii).

REFERENCES

Anderson, Kevin. B. 1995. *Lenin, Hegel, and Western Marxism: A Critical Study.* Urbana and Chicago: University of Illinois Press.

Burnham, James. [1941] 1975. *The Managerial Revolution: What Is Happening in the World.* Westport, CT: Greenwood Press.

Carter, Joseph. 1941. "Bureaucratic Collectivism," in *New International*, Vol. VII No. 8 (Whole No. 57), September 1941, pp. 216–221.

Dunayevskaya, Raya. 1942a. "An Analysis of Russian Economy," in *The Marxist-Humanist Theory of State Capitalism.* 1992. Chicago: News and Letters, pp. 35–70.

———. 1942b. "Labor and Society," in *The Marxist-Humanist Theory of State-Capitalism*, pp. 17–24.

———. 1948. "The Industrialization of the Negro," in *Fourth International*, Vol. 9, No. 2, Jan–Feb 1948, pp. 24–29.

———. 1949. Letter to James. February 25, 1949, in Hudis and Anderson (eds.), *The Power of Negativity*, 2002, Boston Way, MD: Lexington Books, pp. 348–351.

———. 1953a. Letter on Hegel's *Science of Logic*. May 12, 1953, in *The Power of Negativity*, pp. 15–24.

———. 1953b. Letter on Hegel's *Philosophy of Mind*. May 20, 1953, in *The Power of Negativity*, pp. 24–32.

———. 1957. Letter to Saul Blackman of July 26, 1957, in volume XIV, *Supplement* to *The Raya Dunayevskaya Collection*, pp. 12185–12186. Wayne State University, Detroit, MI (The Collection is also digitalized and available on the web at the link: https://rayadunayevskaya.org/).

———. [1958] 2000. *Marxism and Freedom: From 1776 Until Today.* Amherst, NY: Humanity Books.

———. [1970] 1985. "The Women's Liberation Movement as Reason and as a Revolutionary Force," in *Women's Liberation and the Dialectics of Revolution*, pp. 19–28. Detroit: Wayne State University.

———. [1973] 2003. *Philosophy and Revolution: From Hegel to Sartre, and from Marx to Mao*. Lanham, MD: Lexington Books.

———. 1984. "Not by Practice Alone: The Movement from Theory," in *The Power of Negativity*, pp. 273–288.

———. 1986. "Introduction/Overview to Volume XII," in volume XII, *The Raya Dunayevskaya Collection*, pp. 8442–8470. Wayne State University, Detroit, MI.

———. 1987a. Letter to "Dear Friends," January 13, 1987. P. 10726. in "The Year of Only 8 Months," mimeographed bulletin published by News and Letters Committees January 12, 1987, in volume XIII, *Supplement* to *The Raya Dunayevskaya Collection*, pp. 10690–10726. Wayne State University, Detroit, MI.

———. 1987b. "Presentation on the Dialectics of Organization and Philosophy." June 1, 1987, in *The Power of Negativity*, pp. 3–13.

———. 1992. *The Marxist-Humanist Theory of State-Capitalism*. Chicago: News and Letters.

Hegel, G.W.F. [1812] 2010. *The Science of Logic*. New York: Cambridge University.

———. [1830] 2012. *Philosophy of Mind*. Oxford: Clarendon Press.

Hudis, Peter. 1992. "Introduction," in *The Marxist-Humanist Theory of State Capitalism*, pp. VII–XXVI.

Hudis, P., and Anderson, Kevin B. (eds). 2002. *The Power of Negativity: Selected Writings on the Dialectic in Hegel and in Marx*. Boston Way, MD: Lexington Books.

James, C. L. R. [1948] 1980. *Notes on Dialectics. Hegel, Marx, Lenin*. Westport, CT: Lawrence Hill & Co.

———. [1950] 1986. *State Capitalism and World Revolution*. With Raya Dunayevskaa and Grace Lee Boggs. Chicago: Charles H. Kerr Publishing Company,

Marx, Karl. 1975. "Private Property and Communism," in Marx, Karl and Friedrich Engels (eds.), *Collected Works*, pp. 293–306. New York: International Publisher, Vol. 3 (1843–1844).

Marx, Karl and Friedrich Engels. [1846] 1970. *The German Ideology*. New York: International Publishers.

Nuzzo, Angelica. 2018. *Approaching Hegel's Logic, Obliquely*. New York: SUNY Press.

Negri, Antonio. [1973] 2005. "Workers' Party Against Work," in *Books for Burning*, pp. 51–117. London and New York: Verso.

Ricciardi, Maurizio. 2001. *Rivoluzione*. Bologna: Il Mulino.

————. 2019. *Il potere temporaneo. Karl Marx e la politica come critica della società*. Milano: Meltemi.

Rich, Adrienne. 1991. "Foreword," in Raya Dunayevskaya *Rosa Luxemburg, Women's Liberation, and Marx's Philosophy* of *Revolution*. Champaign-Urbana: University of Illinois Press.

Shachtman, Max. 1940. "Is Russia a Workers' State?" in *New International*, Vol. VI No. 10 (Whole No. 49), December 1940, pp. 195–205.

————. 1942. "Russia's New Ruling Class. An Examination of New Materials," in *New International*, Vol. VIII No. 8, September 1942, pp. 237–242.

Sciacca, Fabrizio. 1996. *Imago libertatis. Diritto e Stato nella filosofia dello spirito di Hegel*. Torino: Giappichelli.

CHAPTER 4

The Indispensability of Philosophy in the Struggle to Develop an Alternative to Capitalism

Peter Hudis

PART I: WHITHER PHILOSOPHY? WHITHER MARXISM?

The role of philosophy in revolutionary politics has proven to be one of the most contentious and unsettled issues in the history of Marxism. Since Marx's death the vast majority of socialists have taken it as a given that philosophy "as such" comes to an end with Marx's critique of capitalism. Friedrich Engels provided the classic formulation of this position in *Ludwig Feuerbach and the End Classical German Philosophy* in arguing that Marx's "materialism" accomplished the transition from philosophy to positive science. Although Engels's judgment was by no means unanimously accepted even among the first generation of post-Marx Marxists,[1] the notion that Marx "exited" from philosophy as he turned to the critique of political economy remains the standard interpretation among many commentators on Marx to this day.[2] Given this, the notion that philosophy has a direct or pivotal role to play in revolutionary politics may

P. Hudis (✉)
Oakton Community College, Des Plaines, IL, USA

© The Author(s) 2021
K. B. Anderson et al. (eds.), *Raya Dunayevskaya's Intersectional Marxism*, Marx, Engels, and Marxisms,
https://doi.org/10.1007/978-3-030-53717-3_4

seem highly problematic, if not anachronistic. It is one thing to acknowledge that Marx was a product of a rich philosophical tradition, and quite another to view philosophy as a factor in advancing emancipatory politics today.

The claim that philosophy "as such" comes to an end with Marxism has of course been contested by numerous figures within the Marxist tradition, most notably Georg Lukács and Karl Korsch (in the 1920s), the Frankfurt School (beginning in the 1930s), and strands of independent Marxism since then.[3] However, even many of those who emphasized the philosophical substance of Marx's thought tended to argue that its development represents a move (to use Herbert Marcuse's phrase) from a philosophical critique to a critical *theory* of society. More recent iterations of this viewpoint (by Hans-Georg Backhaus, Moishe Postone, C. J. Arthur et al.) have taken this much further by arguing that Hegelian philosophy is important solely insofar as it expresses Marx's object of critique—*capital*. "Philosophy," according to this viewpoint, is nothing but a reflection of the alienated, abstract forms of domination that define value production—not an activity that can point the way out of it.[4] Ironically, many figures associated with Hegelian-Marxism in over the last three decades are no less willing to dismiss philosophy as an independent branch of inquiry than structuralists and post-structuralists who aim their sharpest theoretical barbs at "Hegelianism."

The claim that philosophy comes to an end with Marxism never made much sense, given the plethora of philosophical standpoints and positions that have been produced over the last century and a half. But while philosophical inquiry and creativity show no sign of disappearing (despite the effort to *make them disappear* by corporatizing education), matters are less straightforward when it comes to the relation between philosophy and revolutionary politics. Although one of the most promising developments in recent years is the emergence of a new generation of thinkers and activists seeking to reconstitute the idea of socialism, it remains to be seen whether this can be achieved without a *philosophical* reconstruction of the socialist project.

This makes Raya Dunayevskaya's work newly relevant, since it addresses *the indispensability of philosophy* for developing a viable alternative to capitalism. As she stated in *Marxism and Freedom* (originally published in 1958): "Our life and times impart an urgency to the task of working out a new relationship of philosophy to actuality. Thought and deed cannot forever stand far apart" (2000: 16). What *compels* philosophy today, she argued, is the rise of *counterrevolution from within revolution*, most starkly expressed by the transformation of the 1917 Russian Revolution into Stalin's totalitarian dictatorship: "Until the development of the totalitarian state, the philosophical foundation of Marxism was not fully understood. Only today is it possible to comprehend that Marx's rejection of the Communism of his day was not a nineteenth-century humanitarian adjunct to his scientific economic theories" (Dunayevskaya 2000: 22). Philosophy, she held, is needed not just to grasp the *roots* of Marx's thought but to *reconstitute* Marxism for realities that Marx himself never had to face.

Yet this raises a critical question: why did Dunayevskaya stress the need to philosophically reconstitute Marxism as humanism when many others from the Left who opposed Stalinism did not? Her background actually provides few signs that she would turn to philosophy at all. Born to an impoverished family in Western Ukraine in 1910, she and her family migrated to the U.S. during the Russian Civil War, and she grew up in a Chicago ghetto. She never had the opportunity to attend college, earning her "education" from the radical movement, which she joined as a teenager. Unlike Hegelian-Marxists who came from privileged backgrounds (such as Lukács, Marcuse, and Theodor Adorno), she never had the formal philosophical training that they had. Indeed, prior to the 1940s there was little indication that she was even headed to become a theoretician: she was known instead as an energetic rank-and-file activist in the labor, civil rights, and Marxist movement. So how did she manage to find her way to philosophy, and what does this tell us about whether or not philosophy remains an indispensable activity of humanity?

PART II: FROM STATE-CAPITALIST THEORY TO MARXIST-HUMANIST PHILOSOPHY

An original philosophy is a rare creation, born after much travail only when called forth by a new stage of world consciousness of freedom. It does mean that a viable philosophy must be capable of meeting the challenge of human experience, of the new revolts symbolic of the lack of specific freedoms. (Dunayevskaya 2000: 16)

Dunayevskaya's path to philosophy was paved by the theory of state-capitalism that she began developing in 1940, shortly after parting ways with Leon Trotsky (she served as his Russian language secretary in 1937–1938). What was *distinctive* about her theory of state-capitalism is that it was not a mere *political* designation (as with Karl Kautsky, Anton Pannekoek, and Friedrich Pollock). It instead consisted of an *economic* analysis of Stalinist Russia through the lens of Marx's *Capital*. Since *Capital* pinpoints capitalism's "law of motion," the nature of the USSR could best be comprehended, she held, by seeing whether or not it conforms to the law of value and surplus value delineated in *Capital*. In a series of exhaustive analyses that established her as an incisive economic theorist, she showed that Stalinist Russia represented a new form of capitalist class domination.

In 1941 she joined forces with C. L. R. James, who independently had come to a state-capitalist position,[5] to form a dissident faction within the Workers' Party, the Johnson-Forest Tendency (JFT). The JFT viewed state-capitalism as a new *world* stage of capitalism that arose out of the Great Depression and took such forms as Stalinist Russia, FDR's New Deal, and Hitler's Four-Year Plans. The JFT defined its task as developing a comprehensive redevelopment of Marxism for the age of state-capitalism as Lenin had earlier achieved for the era of monopoly capitalism. To achieve this, they formed a theoretical nucleus in which Dunayevskaya focused on economics, James on politics and culture, and Grace Lee (who had formal philosophical training) on Hegel.[6] Over the next decade they produced a formidable body of work dealing with state-capitalism, workers' revolts, the vanguard role of U.S. Black freedom struggles, forms of organization, and Hegel's dialectic. Their work represents a distinctively *American* version of Hegelian-Marxism that is far too often ignored or passed over in discussions of that tradition.

Although Dunayevskaya made no pretense of having expertise in Hegel or dialectical thought prior to the late 1940s, several dimensions of her theory of state-capitalism proved of critical importance in taking her on the path toward philosophy.

First, in contrast to the intellectual fashions of the time—which viewed Stalinist totalitarianism as rendering implausible any serious internal resistance and revolt[7]—Dunayevskaya argued that it was an inherently unstable and crisis-ridden formation. This flowed, she maintained, from the fact that economic relations in the USSR adhered to the capitalist law of value.[8] Most Marxists and socialists of the time held that capitalism is defined by "market anarchy" and socialism by a planned economy.

Dunayevskaya disagreed, arguing that capitalism had learned to plan while "socialist" Russia had failed to overcome chaos:

> Yes, planning is essential to capitalism and has always characterized the factory production and production relationship for it is the wherewithal of extraction of the greatest amount of surplus value. No, planning is not essential, chaos is, because while within production there resides the tendency to go outside the limits of production, class relations and existing values impose a limit on it, which expresses itself in the anarchy of the market. At the same time capitalism can never really plan because its law of motion is impelled by reproduction according to socially necessary labor time set by the world market, and thus even if all conditions are met as to planning in factory, external planning as to market, and labor paid at value, the incessant revolutions in production of necessity mean the "development of productive forces of labor at the expense of the already created productive forces." (1949: 9217)

While it appeared that economic planning from above—and hence *statist* control of society—was total in Stalin's Russia, this was actually not the case. The law of value signifies that it is not the *actual amount* of labor time expended in producing a commodity that establishes its value; instead, a commodity's value is determined by the *average* amount of time that is *socially necessary* to produce it on the world market. Since this average constantly shifts with technological innovations that alter the productivity of labor, no plan from above—not even a totalitarian one—can succeed in overcoming the constant imbalances and disequilibrium associated with value production. Totalitarian systems replace conflicts between competitive firms in the "free market" by shifting them to conflicts *within* the state bureaucracy (hence Stalin's constant purges and the endless feuds between the Gaue in Hitler's Germany).[9]

Moreover, since Stalinist Russia retained universalized commodity production and wage labor, it encountered the same problem as any "normal" capitalist society: an inability to efface the resistance of the human subject. In capitalism, as Marx never ceased to emphasize, labor is *not* a commodity—it is an *activity*. The commodity is *labor power*—the *capacity* of labor, which is paid in the form of wages. Human relations in capitalism take on the *form* of things, but they are not themselves things—if they were, capital accumulation would be impossible, since *living* labor is the only source of value. Dunayevskaya therefore insisted that revolts *within* the Soviet empire were inevitable.

Hence, even in her early economic writings, Dunayevskaya's analysis was grounded in the *dialectical* relation of subjective and objective—which prepared her for later encounters with Hegelian philosophy, in which this relation is central.

Second, in researching the USSR's economy (in 1942) Dunayevskaya came across the Russian publication of parts of Marx's *Economic and Philosophical Manuscripts* of 1844. At first, she knew only the essay "Alienated Labor"—which doesn't mention humanism (nor does she do so in her initial work of the early 1940s). Yet she was moving toward the concept of humanism, as seen in the 1942 essay "Labor and Society" (her first discussion of the 1844 Manuscripts): "The difference between the science of economics 'as such,' as a science of objective elements, wages, value, etc., and the Marxian science of economics is that for Marxism, all economic categories are social categories and thus in the science of economics it incorporates the subjective element, the receiver of wages, the source of value, in other words, the laborer" (1942: 21).

Third, in this period she also discovered Lenin's 1914–1915 "Abstract of Hegel's *Science of Logic*," in which he broke from his vulgar materialist past (a materialism most prominently expressed in his 1908 *Materialism and Empirio-Criticism*) in proclaiming that "cognition not only reflects the objective world but creates it."[10] Lenin's statement that no Marxist had understood Marx's *Capital* because they hadn't mastered the whole of Hegel's *Logic* was provocative enough. But even more so was his comment that "the whole chapter on the 'Absolute Idea' [in the *Science of Logic*]...contains almost nothing that is specifically *idealism*, but has as its main subject the *dialectical method*...in this *most idealist* of Hegel's works there is the least idealism and the *most materialism*" (Lenin 1961: 233).

Emboldened by Lenin's enthusiasm for Hegel's "Absolute Idea" and "Doctrine of the Notion"—which no Marxist prior to Lenin had paid the slightest attention to—the JFT took up the task of providing a "materialist interpretation" of Hegel's Absolute Idea for the era of state-capitalism. It led to intense studies of Hegel's work in relation to Marx's *Capital*, contemporary capitalism, and the problem of revolutionary organization. Its best-known expression is James's 1948 *Notes on Dialectics*.[11] In this work, James aimed to explore Hegelian categories in light of the search for an alternative to the traditional Marxist concept of the "vanguard party," from which the JFT was beginning to break. As he put it, "We have to get hold of the Notion, of the Absolute Idea, before we can see this relation between organization and spontaneity in its concrete truth" (James 1980: 119).

James's work in this period has many insights. He writes of Lenin's "Abstract," "The core of dialectic is self-movement through opposition. Good. But that is the core of dialectic—for him, in 1914. But for us, 1948, in our world, the core of dialectic is the materialist interpretation of Hegel's last chapters in the *Logic*, the complete interpenetration of subjective and objective, idealism and materialism." He adds, "We are poles apart from [Hegel] but very close to him in another respect. As materialists we root man in his environment, but now that the real history of humanity is about to begin, the Hegelian concept of speculative reason, comes to life with us, as never before, *and on our basis*" (1949a: 1614). And he contends, "The 'real history of humanity' is being worked out in Notion. When the masses, not a few philosophers, grasp the dialectic, the logic, the unity of theoretical, practical, methodological, we have reached the Absolute Idea of society, i.e., social man. There begins the development of human power for its own sake." James moves very quickly to apply such conceptions to politics, writing, "Notion = the growth of the proletariat, which is expressed in its subjective, i.e. political organizations. Today, 1949, we are faced with the dialectic of the party. We have to trace its [the party's] growth, development, how it perishes, must perish" (1949b: 1626).

Although far less known or acknowledged, no less important in this period was the work of Grace Lee.[12] She penned dozens of letters and draft essays on Hegel's *Phenomenology*, the *Science of Logic*, Leibniz and the European Enlightenment, Freud and modern psychoanalysis, etc.[13] She wrote to James in 1949, "Every great step forward in philosophic cognition was made only when a new category, a new way of making the plunge into freedom became possible" (1949a: 1662). She also stated,

> The importance of the dialectic as method of thought is the way in which it enables us to see this counterrevolution within the revolution itself. The moment the revolution begins, the counterrevolution seeks to legalize the institutions which have been created by the masses, i.e., particularize their tasks [and] transform them into fixed and isolated determinations. The method of thought of the counterrevolution is the particularization of the universal, carrying it to the Absolute like a shot out of the pistol. The permanent revolution is the overcoming of this particularization. (Lee 1949b: 1676)

Dunayevskaya likewise delved into Hegel in this period in a series of letters and essays on Hegel's *Logic* and Marx's *Capital*. She discussed the general contradiction of capitalism in light of Hegel's discussion of "limit" and "barrier;" Marx's delineation of the value-form in terms of Hegel's syllogism of Individual-Particular-Universal; and the way "The Doctrine of the Notion" informed Marx's theory of commodity fetishism and the absolute general law of capitalist accumulation. This is a *distinctive* achievement, since she was reaching for a recovery of the philosophical basis of Marxism *through* the critique of political economy. This was very different from the approach of other Hegelian-Marxists (like Lukács, Gramsci, and the Frankfurt School) who had little to say about political economy or limited the philosophical dimension to the young Marx.[14]

In 1949, Dunayevskaya moved to Pittsburgh and spent time in West Virginia. She was in Morgantown during the Miners' General Strike of 1949–1950, one of the first (and most massive) wildcat strikes against automation in U.S. history. It had an enormous impact on her. As she later put it, the strike "seemed to touch, at one and the same time, a concept Marx had designated as alienated labor *and* the absolute opposite to it, which Marx spelled out as the end of the division between mental and manual labor" (1984: 33). In striking not so much for higher wages and benefits as in opposition to the degraded conditions of labor produced by automation, the miners' raised the question "what *kind* of labor should people perform?" In her view, these were *theoretical* questions which brought to life Marx's notion that the central problem of modern society is not solely the alienation of the product from the producer but most critically the alienation in the very *activity* of laboring. In response, she returned to the 1844 Manuscripts, this time singling out Marx's affirmation of "a thoroughgoing naturalism or humanism [that] is distinct from both idealism and materialism, and constitutes at the same time the truth uniting them both" (Marx 1975: 336). The strike showed her that the time had come to reconstitute Marxism on the basis of Marx's conception of a new humanism.

However, it is precisely at this point that theoretical differences began to emerge *within* the JFT. Shortly after the strike the JFT issued *State-Capitalism and World Revolution*, a lengthy document that bid their final adieu to Trotskyism.[15] Its final section (written by Lee) was devoted to a discussion of philosophy—a first in the U.S. Marxist movement. But while it proclaimed, "the totality of these contradictions today compels philosophy, a total conception," it dismissed humanism as a Christian humanist and/or Existentialist departure from Marxism.[16] Thus, while Dunayevskaya was drawing closer to humanism, James and Lee were pulling away from it.[17]

What explains this internal differentiation, which was to lead (by 1955) to the breakup of the JFT? The answer is intimated in James's 1948 *Notes on Dialectics*. Its concluding section discusses Hegel's Absolute Idea in relation to the problem of organization. He rejects the notion of a "vanguard party" of professional revolutionaries on the grounds that, "The task today is to call for, to teach, to illustrate, to develop, *spontaneity*— the free creative activity of the proletariat (James 1980: 117). He calls for a party of a new type that does not "represent" the workers but *constitutes* them as a class—"a party which consists of all the workers...that is what the *soviets* represented" (1980: 141). With this new kind of mass party, broader in scope than even the most massive trade union, "the difference between being and knowing as separate functions would vanish." Such an organization, he asserts, would be the expression of Hegel's Absolute Idea, the apex of the dialectic. He writes, "Now if the party is the knowing of the proletariat, then the coming of age of the proletariat means the abolition of the party. That is our new Universal, stated in its boldest and most abstract form... That is *our* Universal—the question of the party" (1980: 175–176).

Yet this poses a problem: If the new form of organization, the mass party that is not *for* but *of* the workers, is the Absolute made manifest, what is the role of theory and theoreticians—let alone philosophy? It would seem that their role is to mirror or express the spontaneous forms of consciousness and organization forged by workers. And this is exactly what James argued for in the years following the JFT's break from Trotskyism and their establishment of an independent organization, Committees of Correspondence, from 1951. The role of the theoretician, James and Lee argued, is to be a "full fountain pen" taking down the thoughts of the masses, who constitute the Absolute in action. But in that case, theory or philosophy has no independent value of its own, since spontaneous forms of consciousness and organization exhaust philosophy's conceptual content.[18] The logical conclusion of James's unmediated identification of Hegel's Absolute Idea with "the dialectic of the party" is a denial of the *indispensability* of philosophy.[19]

Dunayevskaya, in contrast, did not rush to "answer" the problem of organization on the basis of the JFT's reading of Hegel. She moved in a decidedly different direction in a series of letters on Hegel's Absolutes written to Lee and James in May 1953. In a letter of May 12, she states she will explore Hegel's Absolute Idea in terms of "the differentiation of us from Lenin but even from 1948"—a clear reference to James's *Notes on Dialectics* (1953: 15–16). She writes,

> I am not touching upon the mass party; the workers will do what they will do and until they do we can have only the faintest intimation of the great leap. This is not 1948, but 1953; I am not concerned with spontaneity versus organization, nor with Stalinism that the workers will overcome. I am concerned only with the dialectic of the vanguard party [or] of that *type* of grouping like ours, be it large or small, and its relationship with the mass. (1953: 16)

After making a detailed commentary on the final chapter of Hegel's *Logic*, she states that Lenin failed to develop his insight that "cognition not only reflects the objective world but creates it" when he reached "The Absolute Idea." She writes, "We, however, can go further, and not only further than Lenin but further than we ourselves did in 1948" (1953: 20). The implication is that James's *Notes on Dialectics* likewise fails to develop the creativity of cognition. As noted earlier, his *Notes* directly map forms of mass self-organization onto Hegel's Absolute Idea. There is something to be said for this, since, as Dunayevskaya avers, the section on the "*absolute law of capitalist accumulation*" in Marx's *Capital* is based on Hegel's Absolute Idea insofar as the former consists of the *absolute contradiction* between the accumulation of capital at one pole and the revolt of the workers at the other. However, she now points out that the Hegelian "system" does not end with the Absolute *Idea*. The conclusion of Hegel's *Logic* intimates a "new sphere" that follows it—the realm of *Mind* or *Spirit*[20]—just as the end of Marx's *Capital* intimates a sphere beyond the accumulation of capital, *the new society*. James's identification of the Absolute with spontaneous forms of organization forecloses the need to philosophically articulate what is central to the *Philosophy of Mind*—the achievement of *freedom* through the transcendence of alienation.

Earlier, James wrote that he studied the *Philosophy of Mind* (the third part of Hegel's philosophical system) and found "nothing there for us" (1949d: 1612). Dunayevskaya now responds, "we couldn't get very far when we…equated Mind to party, but now that I believe…that Mind is the new society gestating in the old I feel sure we could get a lot of very valuable dialectical developments there" (1953: 24). She proceeds to explore Hegel's *Philosophy of Mind* in a letter of May 20, 1953, in which she emphasizes that the movement from Logic to Nature—which Lenin and James interpreted as the move from the abstract logical Idea to Practice—is *not* the culmination of Hegel's dialectic. What *follows* the movement from Logic to Nature is the movement from Nature to *Mind*, the realm of subjectivity or freedom.[21] By prematurely treating the movement from Logic to Nature as the culmination of Hegel's system, James reaches what was to Dunayevskaya is a premature conclusion about the relevance of Hegel's Absolutes for organization. He defines its role solely in terms of reflecting mass spontaneity, whereas Dunayevskaya comes to see the role "of that type of grouping as ours" in terms of embodying and projecting a humanist vision of a new society that transcends capitalist alienation. The difference in perspective was the philosophical point underlying the breakup of the JFT in 1955.

In the 1953 Letters Dunayevskaya discerned a *dual* movement in Hegel's Absolutes—a movement from practice that is itself a form of theory, and a movement from theory that is itself a form of philosophy. Spontaneous revolts raise and develop *theoretical* questions in struggling against oppression and adverse conditions under capitalism, but what is needed, as well, is a philosophically grounded alternative to capitalism that can give action to its direction. The latter calls for a philosophy of a *new* type, one that listens to and absorbs the liberatory aspirations of masses of people even as it takes responsibility for developing the creativity of cognition. Each movement by itself is one-sided. A philosophy of liberation is indispensable, since the movement from practice is *a* form of theory—not *the* form of theory. James's unmediated identity of theory and practice foreclosed recognition of the *necessity* for such a new relation of philosophy and action.[22]

Part III: The Self-determination of the Idea of Marxist-Humanism

The breakup of the JFT in 1955 led Dunayevskaya to form a new organization, News and Letters Committees, whose first publication was a pamphlet containing her translation of Lenin's Hegel Notebooks and her 1953 "Letters on Hegel's Absolutes"—this in an organization based in Detroit and largely composed of factory workers.[23] Its first convention assigned her to complete a book elaborating the philosophy that would guide the organization; it was published as *Marxism and*

Freedom in 1958, the first book-length statement of Marxist-Humanism. Dunayevskaya sought to develop a new relation of philosophy and political action by having theoretical essays and articles by "voices from below" in the same newspaper; insisting that workers, women and Blacks take leading positions in the group; and encouraging all of its members to directly explore philosophy. Her work on Hegelian dialectics further intensified after the publication of *Marxism and Freedom*, with lectures and seminars on Hegel's *Phenomenology*, the *Science of Logic*, Marx's 1844 Manuscripts, etc., given in academic as well as nonacademic settings with workers, activists, etc.

While a small but important number of activists in the 1960s were drawn to her tendency, especially since it provided a forum for oppressed people to speak for themselves and supported spontaneous, rank-and-file initiatives, the anti-theoretical bent of many in the U.S. New Left hardly won her a mass audience. Even members of her own organization often expressed discomfort at her decision to embark on an even more extensive engagement with the Hegelian-Marxian dialectic in her book *Philosophy and Revolution*. Published in 1973, its first part was entitled "Why Hegel? Why Now?" The failure of the movements of 1968 to lead to a single successful revolution, she argued, underlined the need to *directly* engage the dialectic of negativity.

> I must confess that the temptation to begin at the end, with the immediate concerns of our critical period, was hard to resist for one living in a land where empiricism is part of its very organism. But to have begun with the end would, in fact, have made it impossible to comprehend the "why *now*" of the "why Hegel"? The preoccupation with what Leon Trotsky called "the small coin of concrete questions" has ever been the road away, *not* from the mystical Absolutes of Hegel, but from the revolutionary principles of Marx. (Dunayevskaya 1989: xxvi)

Dunayevskaya held that moving beyond the theoretical void that held back the movements of the 1960s (and not in the U.S. alone) poses a serious challenge: "It requires the spelling out of [the] dialectic in its totality for each individual subject" of revolution (1985: 12). She devoted a considerable body of work to concretizing this for Black freedom struggles, a subject on which she had written extensively from the early 1940s. Its fullest development is found in *American Civilization on Trial: Black Masses as Vanguard* (first published in 1963 and reprinted with a new introduction in 1983). She held that it is no less important to spell out the dialectic for the new stage reached with the emergence of the modern women's liberation movement. It led her, by the late 1970s, to embark on a new study focusing on the greatest woman theoretician of revolutionary Marxism—Rosa Luxemburg.

Dunayevskaya originally intended the book to focus exclusively on Luxemburg—in large part because she was being ignored by most second wave feminist theoreticians, thereby making it all the harder to find a bridge to the humanism of Marx. And Dunayevskaya intended the high-point of the book to be 1910, when Luxemburg broke from the "Pope of Marxism," Karl Kautsky, over his refusal to take a firm stand against imperialism and for spontaneous forms of mass self-organization (like the mass strike) on the grounds that this would jeopardize the Social Democratic Party of Germany's (SPD) election prospects. It turned into a more extensive study, however, largely because of the dualities she discovered in Luxemburg's original contribution, her theory of class-consciousness.

Luxemburg never wavered from the view that *class-consciousness* is the critical determinant in creating a new society. This represented a break from the crude materialism and determinism that defined the Second International. She held that unlike the transition from feudalism to capitalism, socialism cannot and will not arise through historical forces that operate despite the wishes of conscious social agents. Instead, socialism is the first social system that arises from the *free, conscious,* and *democratic* deliberation of the masses. The greatest expression of this was her response to the 1905 Russian Revolution. Its central lesson, she held, is that mass strikes, like revolutions, are never "made" by intellectuals or leaders from above; they arise spontaneously from revolts that are nurtured by *class-consciousness.* This did not mean she counterposed spontaneity to organization. She believed in the need for revolutionary parties as much as any Marxist. But she held that their role is defined by *enlightening* the masses about the nature of capitalism and the goal of socialism. Since the class-consciousness generated by spontaneous revolts and revolutionary organizations is the key to social transformation, she held that *democracy*—the free and open exchange of *ideas*—is essential not just for "making" the revolution but to ensure that all vestiges of class domination are uprooted *after* the seizure of power. She wrote in 1905,

The present revolution is costing us terrible sacrifices. May these sacrifices buy not only formal political rights and freedoms, which are indispensable for waging the class struggle, but also that which is most valuable, the class-consciousness and class organization of the proletariat. May the bourgeoisie…find itself facing, not groups of workers who are dispersed, disoriented, and exhausted by the struggle, but the compact class power of the proletariat, steeled and hardened in the fire of the revolution, knowing, on the day after the revolution, how to turn the blade of the struggle against the bourgeoisie with the same strength they used, the day before, to smash the governments of despotism. (2018: 153)

And yet despite these insights, Luxemburg refused to break from the SPD in 1910 on the grounds that it was necessary to maintain the unity of the party. Nor did she fully break from the Second International even after the great betrayal of 1914. *Why* did her prescient critique of some of her fellow socialists (such as Kautsky) not lead to a total break from them and a return to *Marx's* Marxism? Dunayevskaya argues that the problem flows from Luxemburg's conception of class-consciousness. Luxemburg so emphasized class-consciousness that she reduced all forms of revolutionary cognition to it. That left little space for other forms of consciousness, such as national consciousness. Most of all, if revolutionary cognition is completely reduced to class-consciousness, wherein lies the *necessity* for a *philosophical* reconstruction of Marxism? Luxemburg clearly didn't see the need for this. She viewed Marx's work as the venue through which the proletariat gets to know itself, but she showed little interest in philosophy as such. The point at issue is that "the question of class-consciousness does not exhaust the question of cognition, of Marx's philosophy of revolution" (Dunayevskaya 1982: 60). However, if it is presumed that the class-consciousness that arises from the self-activity of the masses does *exhaust* cognition, it follows that a philosophy of revolution that can give spontaneous revolts a direction is completely superfluous. This denies the indispensability of philosophy.

Luxemburg's approach has been followed by much of the anti-Leninist and anti-vanguardist Left, which has resulted in an abdication of responsibility for providing spontaneous revolts with a vision of the future. In some respects, the most glaring example of this is James himself, who argued in *Facing Reality* (written only a few years after separating from Dunayevskaya) that socialism already exists in the self-activity of the masses.[24] It goes without saying that if James were right there would be no need to articulate an emancipatory alternative to capitalism. It can simply be left to spontaneity.

The experience of the past 100 years, however, plainly shows that emancipatory change *cannot* be left to spontaneity. Nor can it be left to forms of thought that fall short of philosophical cognition. At one time, the alternative to capitalism seemed straightforward to most people— replace market anarchy by planned production and private property by nationalized property. But it is now clear neither of these frees society from the stranglehold of the law of value. Nor does having democratically owned worker-cooperatives on a local or regional level. What, then, *can* free society from the law of value? It is a very difficult question to answer, because capitalist value production is so *mystifying*. Since the value of a commodity can only show itself through relations of exchange, it naturally (and indeed *necessarily*) appears that social planning that effects a "fair" redistribution of value is the solution—even though history shows that this simply replaces one version of capitalism for another. The question of how to *actually* abolish the law of value in light of capital's mysti-fied forms of appearance remains the least theorized issue in the history of Marxism. It can be answered only by marshaling the most powerful cognitive resources at our disposal. And a most critical one is the concep-tion of an alternative to capitalism that is implicit in Marx's critique of capital.[25]

The depth of today's crises demands that the implicit become *explicit*. For this reason, Dunayevskaya decided that her book "on Luxemburg" could not be about her alone. Nor could its highpoint be 1910. The limitations of even the greatest post-Marx Marxists, she held, shows that what has been missing from the purview of the radical movement are the ramifications for *our* day of Marx's transformation of Hegel's revolu-tion in philosophy into a philosophy of "revolution in permanence." She therefore devoted the last part of the book to one of her most extensive discussions of Marx's body of work. It ranges from his earliest writings, such as his doctoral dissertation, to his very last ones, in which he held that developing societies in the non-Western world could potentially reach socialism without undergoing capitalistic industrialization.

The red thread that runs through her work—from her 1953 "Let-ters on Hegel's Absolutes" to her three major books, as well as her last writings of the late 1980s—is this: "The question of cognition and actuality—like the gulf between thinking and doing—touches on the rela-tionship of philosophy and revolution" (1985: 4). If "philosophy" is detached from actuality—from the aspirations of masses in motion—it gets reduced to an intellectualistic exercise that is readily dispensable. And if "cognition" is held to be exhausted in spontaneous activity, philosophy becomes no less dispensable. But the immanent need for philosophy does not disappear because of such limitations. It lives on, because without philosophy the alternative to capitalism remains out of sight.

PART IV: DOES MARXISM HAVE A FUTURE?

Dunayevskaya directly addressed the problem of the alternative to capitalism shortly before her death in May 1987, as she was working on an unfinished book entitled "Dialectics of Philosophy and Organization: 'The Party' and Forms of Organization Born from Spontaneity." She wrote,

> The point is that of the years 1924-29, 1929 to today, World War II, and all those national revolutions, the rise of a Third World and the endless continuing struggle, and nowhere in sight, not even in telescopic sight, is there an answer to the questions, what happens after the conquest of power? Why so many aborted revolutions? What type of party or organization? What have the various forms of spontaneity—councils, soviets, committees, associations, communes—achieved? (1987a: 10955)

These words were penned in 1987—several years before the collapse of "actually existing socialism" in the USSR and Eastern Europe. In its aftermath, the void left by the failure of radical theoreticians to develop a conception of socialism that offered an alternative to both statist and private capitalism was filled by neoliberalism, which promoted the ideological claim that "there is no alternative" to "free market" capitalism. The veritable collapse of neoliberalism in the aftermath of the 2008 global recession has in turn left a void that is now being filled by resurgent xenophobic nationalism, racism, and misogyny. It seems hard to avoid the conclusion that these developments are a consequence of the fact that "and nowhere in sight, not even in telescopic sight, is there an answer to the question" of what constitutes a *viable* alternative to capitalism.

Needless to say, spontaneous revolts and movements continue to arise—from the Occupy Movement and the Arab Revolutions of 2011 to today's protests in Sudan, Algeria, Chile, Hong Kong, and elsewhere. Nor were they absent in the 1980s, prior to the collapse of the Stalinist regimes. One of the most crucial movements was the self-mobilization of the Polish proletariat in an organization ten million strong—*Solidarnosc*. Founded on September 17, 1980, it claimed *nine million members* a mere three months later. As one analyst puts it, *Solidarnosc* "amounted to a flat rejection of the Leninist precept that only the party could represent the working class and act on the basis of the masses' true interests" (McAdams 2017: 433). It might seem that by claiming the allegiance of almost the entire Polish working class it was the incarnation of the kind of mass party that C. L. R. James envisioned in his 1948 *Notes on Dialectics*— and this is indeed exactly what James himself proclaimed in the early 1980s.[26] However, while the *form* of organization was in accord with James's vision, it soon enough became clear that the political content of *Solidarnosc* would not lead to a new beginning. As early as 1981 many of the leftwing inspirers of *Solidarnosc* in "The Committee in Defense of the Workers" (KOR) had broken from Marxism and said they aspired for a "normal" capitalist society. Bereft of a concept of a viable, emancipatory alternative to capitalism, *Solidarnosc* became part of the political architecture of neoliberalism in the 1990s—until its being evicted from power by the utterly reactionary forces of rightwing Populism. The form of organization did not make up for the lack of an emancipatory project organized around an explicitly Marxian content.

A parallel development occurred in South Africa. There, after the collapse of the USSR, the apartheid regime entered into negotiations with the African National Congress (ANC) for a transfer of power. The two-stage theory of revolution[27] that had long been promoted by the ANC and its allies in the South African Communist Party dovetailed with the effort of the white minority to maintain its hold on economic power while allowing for the ANC's monopolization of political power. Neoliberalism thereby came to South Africa by disarming one of the most powerful and creative mass struggles in the global south. It was an expression of the "new moments" of Marx's last decade[28] *not* becoming a trail to the 1990s. Dunayevskaya's discussion of the late Marx's view of revolutions that could potentially bypass the stage of capitalistic industrialization in *Rosa Luxemburg, Women's Liberation, and Marx's Philosophy of Revolution* was not merely a historical discussion of the possibilities facing Russia in 1881. It was about the indispensability of *Marx's* philosophy of *permanent* revolution for meeting the challenges of *our* times.

In her 1986–1987 writings for a projected book on the "Dialectics of Organization and Philosophy," Dunayevskaya indicated that once the indispensability of philosophy is denied, the historic reason for the existence of an organization of Marxist theoreticians is left unclarified. Yet such groups clearly have a role—especially when it comes to articulating the ultimate goals that movements are reaching for. The question therefore remains, as she put it in her last presentation, just before her death in June 1987, "What happens to a small group 'like us' who know that nothing can be done without the masses, and [we] are with them, but such [groups] of theoreticians always seem to be around too. So, what is the objectivity that explains their presence? In a word, I was looking for the objectivity of subjectivity" (1987b: 7).

Two things can happen to "small groups" of revolutionaries that should be avoided. One is taking the results of philosophy as a pillow for intellectual sloth by failing to rethink the group's concepts in light of new realities. For example, some have misconstrued Dunayevskaya's notion that "the movement from practice is a form of theory" by uncritically heralding every movement, revolt, or strike, as if they are free of internal contradictions. This may be at least partly due to the fact that she was associated for many years with James—who, like her, sought to understand the new social movements of their time in light of Hegel's Absolutes. However, it bears noting that for Hegel the fullest expression of the Absolute is *absolute negativity*—the process of subjecting every phenomenon, no matter how appealing, to reflection and critique. Unmediated and unreflective celebrations of "everyday resistance" hardly do justice to what Hegel termed "the labor, patience, seriousness, and suffering of the negative" (2018: 13).

The second problem is transforming a philosophy into an ideology by popularizing it without conveying its wealth of content or by repeating its conclusions as an article of faith. Engels's transformation of Marx's philosophy of revolution into "positive science" that presumably is the master key for resolving all questions, whether theoretical or practical, is one of many examples of such ideologization. There is nothing that prevents any given body of thought, no matter how critical and revolutionary, from being turned into a frozen, closed ideology—Marxist-Humanism included. This became a burning issue in the organization founded by Dunayevskaya in the years after her death, which led to its demise and brought forth a new organizational effort to develop Marxist-Humanist principles anew.[29] Time will tell as to how successful the efforts will be.

In a reflection on her life and work, Dunayevskaya stated, "Our age has focused on the dialectics of revolution as the determinant. Nothing, including organization, the party, can find any escape from that determinant" (1985: 11). If every phenomenon, including organization, is subject to "absolute negativity," it follows that a very different understanding of organization is needed than has tended to prevail in much of the radical movement. Parties and organizations are neither ends in themselves nor the greatest good; they are no less ephemeral than spontaneous forms of organization. They have a reason to exist insofar as they meet the central challenge of the times; if they do not, they have little reason not to dissolve. And the central challenge facing us today is to articulate a conception of a noncapitalist future that is clear, concise, and profound enough to speak to those searching for a way to uproot the logic of capital before it makes life on this planet uninhabitable. Dunayevskaya herself spoke to this, I believe, when she wrote in 1987,

> It never fails that, at momentous world historic turning points, it is very difficult to tell the difference between two types of twilight—whether one is first plunging into utter darkness or whether one has reached the end of a long night and is just at the moment before the dawn of a new day. In either case, the challenge to find the meaning—what Hegel called "the undefined foreboding of something unknown"—becomes a compulsion to dig for new beginnings, for a philosophy that would try to answer the question, "where to begin"? (1987b: 321)

NOTES

1. The works of Antonio Labriola and Georgi Plekhanov come to mind, although their understandings of "philosophy" hardly escaped the conceptual horizons of the Second International.
2. For a re-affirmation of this position by a young scholar of Marx's work that has produced a very valuable account of Marx's ecological writings, see Saito (2017).
3. One of the most powerful critiques of the "end of philosophy" thesis was penned by Karel Kosik: "The eschatological formulation of abolishing philosophy through realizing it obscures the *real problem* of modern times: does humanity still need philosophy? Have the position and the mission of philosophy in society changed? What role does philosophy play? ... Does philosophy continue to be a special form of consciousness, *indispensable* for grasping the *truth* of the world?" (Kosík 1976: 103)

4. In at this this sense, their standpoint is not as far from the crude materialism of the Second International—aptly expressed in Karl Kautsky's notion that philosophy is "nothing but" the reflection of economic conditions—as it may appear.

5. James and Dunayevskaya, who did not know each other at the time, submitted separate theses to the 1940 Convention of the Workers' Party with the same title. Moreover, since she had earlier adopted the penname "Freddie James," it was not clear at first that they were separate documents. Upon meeting James, she changed her pseudonym to "Forest" while James adopted "Johnson."

6. See James (1942) for his initial foray into Hegel's work, written in connection with his debates with Max Shachtman and other bureaucratic collectivists.

7. This position typified such figures as Hannah Arendt, George Orwell, and Arthur Koestler, who neglected the deep internal fissures that characterize so-called "totalitarian" societies.

8. The Stalinist regime had admitted as much in 1943. See Dunayevskaya (1944) for her exposé of this.

9. The Gaue was series of administrative units or regions, led by Gauleiters. Since each Gauleiter had considerable power, they engaged in incessant competition and conflict with one another. Such tensions proved insurmountable within the Nazi system.

10. Dunayevskaya was the first to publish an English translation of Lenin's "Abstract" on Hegel in the 1958 edition of *Marxism and Freedom*. She provided James with an on-sight translation in 1942.

11. James' *Notes* was originally circulated within the JFT as a mimeographed bulletin. It was first published in book form in 1980.

12. See James (1949c: 1697) for his acknowledgment of this. Referring to Lee's writings, he states, "After much trouble and patient work, we have it at last…we shall build the whole thing on that."

13. None of these were ever published. The marked disregard of Lee's creative philosophical labors of the late 1940s and early 1950s is in part due to herself, since she completely dismissed her earlier philosophical work after she broke from Marxism in the early 1960s.

14. See Marcuse (1958) for his admission of this: "Dunayevskaya's book goes beyond the previous interpretations. It shows not only that Marxian politics and economics are throughout philosophy, but that the latter is from the beginning economics and politics" (xxi). Lukács was also weak on political economy; *History and Class Consciousness* tried to correct the defect by relying heavily on Luxemburg's *Accumulation of Capital*.

15. The JFT left the Workers' Party in 1947 to join the Socialist Workers Party. It split from it to form an independent organization, Committees of Correspondence, in 1951.

16. See James et al. (1950: 74–76). Since Dunayevskaya's and Lee's names were left out of some of the later editions of the work by James's followers, I am using the original edition, signed "Johnson-Forest."

17. James in fact never identified himself as a Marxist Humanist. To the end of his life he defined himself as a Marxist-Leninist.

18. See Hoffman (2019) for how this impacted the publication issued by James, Dunayevskaya, and Lee from 1953 to 1955: "*Correspondence* did not eliminate the division of workers and intellectuals in its version of workers' inquiry so much as aspire to invert it. The collective sought to invert this division through a radical diminution in the space in its publications accorded to theorizing by intellectuals" (63).

19. At issue is not, of course, whether or not one has a *personal interest* in philosophy. At issue is whether philosophy is indispensable for a critical political project or for human existence in general. James's and Lee's positions led them to deny the latter.

20. The final section of *The Philosophy of Mind* is "Absolute Mind," which contains three final syllogisms in which Hegel sums up the entire movement of the dialectic. "Geist" can be translated as either Mind or Spirit. Hence the differences in the translations of Hegel's *Phenomenology of Mind* vs. *Phenomenology of Spirit*, *Philosophy of Mind* vs. *Philosophy of Spirit*, etc.

21. Dunayevskaya's emphasis on the critical importance of Hegel's *Philosophy of Mind* (or *Spirit*) accords with the perspective of such important Hegel scholars as Otto Pöggeler: "In opposition to the usual interpretations of the Hegelian text, I should like to propose the following: that the actual Science of Spirit is not the Logic, but the philosophy of Spirit" (Pöggeler 1961: 282–283).

22. By no accident, James never returned to a serious study of Hegel or philosophy after the early 1950s. Lee took his view of the role of the intellectual as a "full fountain pen" to its logical conclusion by explicitly dismissing her own theoretical work of the 1940s and 1950s. After breaking from Marxism in 1962, she applied the notion of the intellectual as a "full fountain pen" to an uncritical affirmation of identity politics. James was less consistent on such issues, since he remained a Marxist and never doubted the need for theory—but he also never resolved the question of the role to be played by an *organization* of Marxist theorists. This explains his support for spontaneous forms of organization in some contexts and defense of traditional vanguard party formations in others (such as in the developing world) in his writings from the late 1950s onward.

23. Most of the intellectuals in the Committees of Correspondence went with James and Lee during the 1955 split, whereas most of the workers

(including Charles Denby, the Black autoworker who wrote *Indignant Heart: A Black Worker's Journal*) went with Dunayevskaya.

24. See James 1958: "It is agreed that the socialist society exists. Then we have to record the facts of its existence… Thus, these workers had struck a blow against common injustice, racial discrimination, and the disorder in production which management creates. That is the socialist society. It hasn't to be organized in the future. It exists" (106–107).

25. For a much fuller discussion of this issue, see Hudis (2013).

26. See James (1984: 271): "And now we have reached the final stage with Solidarity in Poland. Commune—Soviet—Solidarity. That is the movement. They haven't come by accident. They are part of the organic movement of the working class in capitalist society."

27. This was the notion, borrowed from European orthodox Marxism, that a technologically underdeveloped country needs to first experience a bourgeois-democratic revolution before it could be ready for a socialist revolution.

28. Dunayevskaya entitled her chapter on the late Marx (in Dunayevskaya 1982) "The Last Writings of Marx Point a Trail to the 1980s."

29. For a detailed discussion of this issue that led to the breakup of News and Letters Committees and the subsequent formation of a new group, the International Marxist-Humanist Organization, see Hudis (2009).

References

Dunayevskaya, Raya. [1942] 1992. "Labor and Society." In *The Marxist-Humanist Theory of State-Capitalism*. Ed. Peter Hudis. Chicago: News and Letters, 17–24.

———. 1944. "A New Revision of Marxian Economics." *The American Economic Review*. 34:3, September. 31–37.

———. 1949. Letter to Grace Lee [February 1]. In *The Raya Dunayevskaya Collection—Marxist-Humanism: A Half Century of its World Development*. Detroit: Wayne State University Archives of Labor and Urban Affairs.

———. 1953. "Letters on Hegel's Absolutes." In Dunayevskaya 2002, 15–34.

———. [1958] 2000. *Marxism and Freedom: From 1776 Until Today*. Amherst, NY: Humanity Books.

———. [1973] 1989. *Philosophy and Revolution: From Hegel to Sartre and from Marx to Mao*. New York: Columbia University Press.

———. 1982. *Rosa Luxemburg, Women's Liberation and Marx's Philosophy of Revolution*. Atlantic Highlands, NJ: Humanities Press.

———. 1985. "Dialectics of Revolution: American Roots and Marx's World Humanist Concepts." In Dunayevskaya 2000, 1–12.

———. 1987a. "Another 'Talking to Myself,' This Time on What Has Happened Since 'Not by Practice Alone,' 1984–87" [May 19]. In *Supplement to the Raya Dunayevskaya Collection.*

———. 1987b. "Presentation on the Dialectics of Organization and Philosophy." In Dunayevskaya 2002, 3–14.

———. 1987c. "Letter on Hegel's *Phenomenology of Mind*. In Dunayevskaya 2002, 319–323.

———. 2002. *The Power of Negativity: Selected Writings on the Dialectic in Hegel and Marx*, by Raya Dunayevskaya, Eds. Peter Hudis and Kevin B. Anderson. Lanham, MD: Lexington Books.

Hegel, G.W.F. 2018. *The Phenomenology of Spirit*. Trans. Terry Pinkard. Cambridge. Cambridge University Press.

Hudis, Peter. 2009. "Towards an Organizational History of the Philosophy of Marxist-Humanism in the U.S." In *The International Marxist-Humanist* [September 8] https://www.imhojournal.org/articles/towards-an-organizat ional-history-of-the-philosophy-of-marxist-humanism-in-the-u-s.

———. 2013. *Marx's Concept of the Alternative to Capitalism.* Chicago: Haymarket.

James, C. L. R. 1942. "Production for Production's Sake." In *The Raya Dunayevskaya Collection,* 225–240.

———. [1948] 1980. *Notes on Dialectics: Hegel-Marx-Lenin.* Westport, CT: Lawrence & Hill Co.

———. 1949a. Letter to Grace Lee [May 20]. In *The Raya Dunayevskaya Collection.*

———. 1949b. Letter to Raya Dunayevskaya [June 13]. In *The Raya Dunayevskaya Collection.*

———. 1949c. Letter to Friends [August 25]. In *The Raya Dunayevskaya Collection.*

———. 1949d. Letter to Grace Lee [May 29]. In *The Raya Dunayevskaya Collection.*

———. 1958. *Facing Reality*. Detroit: Correspondence.

———. 1984. "Poland," in *At the Rendezvous of Victory*. London. Allison & Busby.

James, C. L. R., Raya Dunayevskaya, and Grace Lee. 1950. *State-Capitalism and World Revolution*. New York: Socialist Workers Party.

Hoffman, Marcelo. 2019. *Militant Acts: The Role of Investigations in Radical Political Strategies*. Albany: SUNY Press.

Kosík, Karel. 1976. *Dialectics of the Concrete: A Study on the Problems of Man and World*. Dordrecht-Holland: D. Reidel.

Lee, Grace. 1949a. Letter to C. L. R. James [July 5]. In *The Raya Dunayevskaya Collection.*

———. 1949b. Letter to C.LR. James [July 9]. In *The Raya Dunayevskaya Collection*.

Lenin, V. I. [orig. 1914–1915] 1961. "Abstract of Hegel's *Science of Logic*." In *Lenin, Collected Works*, Vol. 38. Moscow: Progress Publishers.

Luxemburg, Rosa. 2018. "The Cards Are on the Table" [June 1905]. In *The Complete Works of Rosa Luxemburg*, Vol. 3. Eds. Peter Hudis, Axel Fair-Schultz, and William A. Pelz. London and New York: Verso Books, 149–153.

Marcuse, Herbert. 1958. "Preface." In Dunayevskaya [1958] 2000, xx–xxv.

Marx, Karl. [1844] 1975. *Economic and Philosophical Manuscripts of 1844*. In *Marx-Engels Collected Works*, Vol. 3. New York: International Publishers.

McAdams, A. James. 2017. *Vanguard of the Revolution: The Global Idea of the Communist Party*. Princeton: Princeton University Press.

Pöggeler, Otto. 1961. "Zur Deutung der *Phänomenologie des Geistes*." In *Hegel-Studien*, Band 1, 255–294.

Saito, Kohei. 2017. *Karl Marx's Ecosocialism: Capital, Nature, and the Unfinished Critique of Political Economy*. New York: Monthly Review Press.

PART II

Gender, Race, and Revolution

CHAPTER 5

Raya Dunayevskaya's Marx

Adrienne Rich

Raya Dunayevskaya was a major thinker in the history of Marxism and of women's liberation—one of the longest continuously active woman revolutionaries of the twentieth century.[1] In fierce intellectual and political independence, her life and work defied many mind-numbing labels that self-described conservatives, liberals, and radicals have applied to voices for political and social change. Born in 1910, between two revolutions, she said of her beginnings:

> I come from Russia 1917, and the ghettos of Chicago, where I first saw a Black person. The reason that I'm starting that way—it happens to be true—but the reason that I'm starting that way is that I was illiterate. You

Adrienne Rich: Deceased.
This chapter has been reprinted with permission from "Raya Dunayevskaya's Marx," in *Arts of the Possible: Essays and Conversations* by Adrienne Rich. Used by permission of W. W. Norton & Company. This selection may not be reproduced, stored in a retrieval system, or transmitted in any form or by any means without the prior written permission of the publisher.

A. Rich (✉)
Santa Cruz, CA, USA

© The Author(s) 2021
K. B. Anderson et al. (eds.), *Raya Dunayevskaya's Intersectional Marxism*, Marx, Engels, and Marxisms,
https://doi.org/10.1007/978-3-030-53717-3_5

know, you're born in a border town—there's a revolution, there's a counterrevolution, there's anti-Semitism—you *know* nothing, but experience a
lot. ... That is, you don't know that you're a revolutionary, but you're
opposed to everything.

Now, how does it happen that an illiterate person, who certainly didn't
know Lenin and Trotsky, who as a child had never seen a Black, had begun
to develop all the revolutionary ideas to be called Marxist-Humanism in
the 1950's? It isn't personal whatsoever! If you live when an idea is born,
and a great revolution in the world is born—it doesn't make any difference
where you are; *that becomes the next stage of development of humanity.*

Dunayevskaya was using her own early life to illustrate a core theme of
her writing: the inseparability of experience and revolutionary thinking,
the falseness of the opposition between "philosophy" and "actuality."
Her readings of past history and contemporary politics were drenched
in the conviction that while thinking and action are not the same, they
must continually readdress and renew each other. For the spontaneous
responses of a Russian Jewish girl, growing up in a climate of revolution, brought at the age of twelve to the Jewish ghetto in Chicago (in the
twenties she "moved herself" to the black ghetto), to become the ongoing
catalyst for a lifetime's commitment to human freedom, required a structuring of her experience that Marx's (not Marxist) theory was soon to
provide her. She was to become not just literate, but learned in philosophy and history—and here again labels fail us, since for Dunayevskaya
philosophy was the making of history: the envisioning of "the day after,"
"the creation of a new society." At the same time, her political activities—
first among black activists, then with the West Virginia miners' strike of
1949–1950, and so on into the Women's Liberation Movement of the
past two decades—set her on a lifelong path of both participating in and
reflecting on mass movements.

The separation—willed or unaware—of intellectuals from the people
they theorize about, the estrangement of self-styled vanguards and their
"correct lines" from actual people's needs and aspirations, is hardly news.
Dunayevskaya tried, in the very structure of her life and writings, to show
us a different method. What does it look like when, as part of a movement, we try to think *along with* the human forces newly pushing forth, in
ever-changing forms and with ever-different faces? How can we conceptualize a miners' strike, a poor people's march, a ghetto revolt, a women's
demonstration *both* as "spontaneous activity" *and* as the embodiment of

new ideas—not yet perhaps written down except in rain-blurred flyers—about power, resources, control of the products of one's labor, the ability to live humanly among other humans? How do we extract new kinds of "reason" or "idea" from the activities of "new passions and new forces" (Marx's phrase) without losing continuity with past struggles for freedom? How do we think clearly in times of great turmoil, revolution, or counterrevolution without resorting to a party line based only on past dogma or on internecine graspings for power? How do we create a philosophy of revolution that itself helps make revolution possible? The American Communist party was to lose its way among such questions.

Dunayevskaya's way of grounding herself was to turn to Marx. Not, I should emphasize, as a *turning backward* but as rescuing for the present a legacy she saw as still unclaimed, having been diminished, distorted, and betrayed by post-Marx Marxists and the emerging "Communist" states. But she didn't simply turn to Marx, or to Hegel (whose work she saw as a living, still uncomprehended, presence in Marx's own thought), as texts. Her work, including *Rosa Luxemburg*, is an explication of the fullness of Marx's thought *as she came to live it*, in living through the liberation movements of her own era. She translated Marx, interpreted Marx, fitted together fragments of Marx scattered in post-Marxist schisms, refused to leave Marx enshrined as dead text, ill read, or relegated to "the dustbin of history."

It was Marx's humanism above all that she felt had never been adequately understood—in particular his recognition of what she called the black and women's dimensions, but more largely as he sought not merely the "overthrow" of capitalism but a vision of "revolution in permanence," a dynamically unfolding society in which the human individual could freely develop and express her or his creativity; not a static Communist utopia but an evolving human community.

I come out of a strain of feminism that saw itself as a leap forward out of Marxism, leaving the male Left behind, and for which a term like *Marxist-Humanism* would, in the late sixties and early seventies, have sounded like a funeral knell. A major problem (a problem not just of language but of organizing) was to break from a paradigm of class struggle that erased women's labor except in the paid workplace (often even there), and also from a "humanist" false universal deriving from the European Renaissance glorification of the male. Radical feminists were of necessity concerned with keeping the political focus on women because in every other focus—race, class, nation—women had gotten lost, put down, marginalized. In addition, we were fighting a dogma of class as the primary oppression, capitalism as the single source of all oppressions. We insisted that women were, if not a class, a caste; if not a caste, an oppressed group *as women*—*within* oppressed groups *and* within the middle and ruling classes.

And, as Dunayevskaya is quick to point out, "the Women's Liberation Movement that burst onto the historic scene in the mid-1960s was like nothing seen before in all its many appearances throughout history. Its most unique feature was that, surprisingly, not only did it come out of the left but it was *directed, against it,* and not from the right, *but from within the left itself*". It's clear how eagerly she welcomed this new force as it sent shock waves through radical group after radical group, starting with the Student Nonviolent Coordinating Committee in 1965. But although her own thinking was obviously incited and nourished by the contemporary Women's Liberation Movement, she had, even in the forties, recognized "the woman dimension," and one of her earliest essays in *Women's Liberation and the Dialectics of Revolution* is an account of organizing by miners' wives in the 1949–1950 automation strikes in West Virginia. Dunayevskaya recognized women not just as revolutionary "Force" (contributing courage, support, strength) but also as "Reason"—as initiators, thinkers, strategists, creators of the new.

The first thing to strike a reader, ranging through Dunayevskaya's books, is the vitality, combativeness, relish, impatience of her voice. Hers is not the prose of a disembodied intellectual. She argues; she challenges; she urges on; she expostulates; her essays have the spontaneity of an extemporaneous speech (some of them are) or of a notebook—you can hear her thinking aloud. She has a prevailing sense of ideas as flesh and blood, of the individual thinker, limited by her or his individuality yet carrying on a conversation in the world. The thought of the philosopher is a product of what she or he has lived through.

Marxism and Freedom (1957) is a history of the process of Marx's thought, as it evolved out of eighteenth-century philosophy and Hegel's dialectic through the mass political movements of the nineteenth century, as it became adapted and modified by Engels, Trotsky, and Lenin and, finally, in Dunayevskaya's words, "totally perverted" by Stalin. She traced the shift from Marx's idea of a workers' state with no separation of manual and mental labor, to Lenin's failed attempt to create a "workers' state," to Stalin's creation of a corporate totalitarian state run by the Communist party—which she defines as counterrevolution. She saw, in the East

German workers' strike of 1953 and the Hungarian Revolution of 1956, evidence of a continuing revolutionary spirit in Eastern Europe (which was to capture world attention in the upheavals of 1989). She ends the first edition of *Marxism and Freedom* with the Montgomery bus boycott as a spontaneous movement kept within the hands of black people.

In *Marxism and Freedom*, Dunayevskaya grapples, in the face of the Stalinist legacy, with the question: *What happens after?* What happens when the old oppression has been successfully resisted and overthrown? What turns revolutionary leaders into tyrants? Why did the Russian revolution turn backward on itself? How do we make the "continuing revolution" "the revolution in permanence" in which this cannot happen? She is passionate about "the movement from theory to practice and from practice to theory" as a living process and about the necessity for new voices speaking for their own freedom to be heard and listened to, if a movement is to keep on moving. She had the capacity, rare in people learned in Western philosophy and theory—including Marxists—to respect and learn from other kinds of thinking and other modes of expression: those of the Third World, of ordinary militant women, of working people who are perfectly aware that theirs is "alienated labor" and know how to say that without political indoctrination. Maybe Dunayevskaya would claim she originally learned this from Marx.

Marxism and Freedom has as its focus the "movement from practice to theory." Dunayevskaya writes of the shaping impact of American slavery and the Civil War on Marx's thought when he was writing *Capital*; she acknowledges the unfinished legacy of Reconstruction and recognizes the acute significance of the Montgomery bus boycott—the "Black dimension." Women's liberation is not yet a focus, although already in the fifties, long before *Marxism and Freedom* was written, Dunayevskaya was keenly attuned to women's leadership and presence both within and outside radical groups. In "The Miners' Wives" (1950) she notes that while the press depicted the women as bravely going along with the strike, they were in fact activists, sometimes pushing the men. In a long-unpublished essay of 1953, she sharply criticizes the Socialist Workers party for failing to recognize that the women who had streamed by the millions into factories in the United States during World War II were "a concrete revolutionary force" searching for "a total reorganization of society." "By continuing her [sic] revolt daily at home, the women were giving a new dimension to politics" (*Women's Liberation and the Dialectics of Revolution*, p. 34). Perhaps it's not by mere oversight that this essay remained so long unpublished. In it Dunayevskaya makes clear that the equality of some women as leaders within the party did not extend to any real recognition of women as a major social force. Possibly her own consciousness of women, though keen, received only negative responses in the organization of which she was then a part. But her entire life was a demonstration of "Woman as Force and Reason," activist and thinker.

Philosophy and Revolution (1973) retraces some of the history of philosophy in *Marxism and Freedom*, moving on from there to discuss the Cuban revolution and the student and youth uprisings of the sixties, along with the emergence of the Women's Liberation Movement. This work feels—until the last chapter—less dynamic and more laborious, more like a political-philosophy textbook. But in both books, Dunayevskaya is on a very specific mission: to rescue Marx's Marxism from the theoretical and organizational systems attributed to him; to reclaim his ideas from what has been served up as Marxism in Eastern Europe, China, Cuba, and among Western intellectuals. She insists that you cannot sever Marx's economics from his humanism—humanism here meaning the self-emancipation of human beings necessarily from the capitalist mode of production, but not only from that. The failure of the Russian revolutions to continue as "revolution in permanence"—their disintegration into a system of forced labor camps and political prisons—was the shock that sent Dunayevskaya back to "the original form of the Humanism of Marx," translating his early humanist essays herself because "the official Moscow publication (1959) is marred by footnotes which flagrantly violate Marx's content and intent." "Marxism is a theory of liberation or it is nothing." But she refuses to "rebury" Marx as "humanist," shorn of his economics.

Rosa Luxemburg (1982) is much more than a philosophical biography. But that it certainly is: a sympathetic yet critical account of Luxemburg as woman, thinker, organizer, revolutionist. A central chapter is devoted to Marx and Luxemburg as theorists of capital, dissecting Luxemburg's critique of Marx in her *Accumulation of Capital*. Dunayevskaya dissents at many points from Luxemburg's effort to fulfill, as she saw it, Marx's unfinished work. But beyond the economic debate Dunayevskaya asserts that Luxemburg, despite her eloquent writings on imperialism, never saw the potential for revolution in the colonized people of color in what is now called the Third World; and, despite the centrality of women to her antimilitarist work, never saw beyond the purely economic class struggle. Where Marx had seen "new forces and new passions spring up in the bosom of society" as capitalism declined, Luxemburg saw only the "suffering masses" under imperialism.

Luxemburg was "a reluctant feminist" who was "galled in a most personal form" by the "Woman Question" but, "just as she had learned to live with an underlying anti-Semitism in the party, so she learned to live with ... male chauvinism." (Does this have a familiar ring?) In particular, she lived with it in the figure of August Bebel, a self-proclaimed feminist who wrote of her "wretched female's squirts of poison," and Viktor Adler, who called her "the poisonous bitch ... clever as a monkey." However, when she was arrested in 1915 it was on the eve of organizing an international women's antiwar conference with Clara Zetkin. Of their relationship Dunayevskaya says: "Far from Luxemburg having no interest in the so-called 'Woman Question,' and far from Zetkin having no interest outside of that question, ... both of them ... were determined to build a women's liberation movement that concentrated not only on organizing women workers but on having them develop as leaders, as decision-makers, and as independent Marxist revolutionaries." In fact, from 1902 on Luxemburg had been writing and speaking on the emancipation of women and on woman suffrage; in 1911 she wrote to her friend Louise Kautsky, "Are you coming for the women's conference? Just imagine, I have become a feminist!" She debated Bebel and Kautsky over the "Woman Question," and broke with Kautsky in 1911, yet, in her short and brutally ended life, feminism and proletarian revolution never became integrated. Dunayevskaya is critical of Luxemburg but also impatient with present-day feminists who want to write her off.

In Luxemburg, Dunayevskaya portrays a brilliant, brave, and independent woman, passionately internationalist and antiwar, a believer in the people's "spontaneity" in the cause of freedom; a woman who saw herself as Marx's philosophical heir, who refused the efforts of her lover and other men to discourage her from full participation in "making history" because she was a woman. But the biography does not stop here. The book opens into a structure generated, as Dunayevskaya tells us, by three events: the resurgence of the Women's Liberation Movement out of the Left; the publication for the first time of Marx's last writings, the *Ethnological Notebooks*; and the global national liberation movements of the seventies that demonstrated to her that Marxism continues to have meaning as a philosophy of revolution. Luxemburg's life and thought become a kind of jumping-off point into the present and future—what she saw and didn't see, her limitations as well as her understanding. We can learn from her mistakes, says Dunayevskaya, as she begins developing the themes she would pursue in *Women's Liberation and the Dialectics of Revolution*.

In this thirty-five-year collection of essays, interviews, letters, lectures you see Dunayevskaya going at her central ideas in many different ways. Agree or not with her analysis here, her interpretation there: these working papers are some of the most tingling, invigorating writing since the early days of Women's Liberation when writing and organizing most often went hand in hand. In her irresistible depiction of women in movement, across the world and through history, Dunayevskaya really does hold to an international perspective. She chides and criticizes Simone de Beauvoir, Sheila Rowbotham, Gerda Lerner; she praises *Wuthering Heights*, *A Room of One's Own*, the "Three Marias" of the *New Portuguese Letters*, the poetry of Gwendolyn Brooks and Audre Lorde; she says Natalia Trotsky went further than Trotsky; she chastises Engels for diluting and distorting Marx, and post-Marxists and feminists for accepting Engels's *Origins of the Family* as *Marx's* word on women and men. Her quarrel with the Western post-Marxists is that they've taken parts of Marx for the whole, and that what has been left out (especially the dimensions of women and the Third World) is crucial in our time. Her quarrel with the Women's Movement is that feminists have jettisoned Marx because he was a man, or have believed the post-Marxists without looking into Marx for themselves. She insists that Marx's philosophy, far from being a closed and autocratic system, is open-ended, so that "in each age, he becomes more alive than in the age before." That Marx was himself extraordinarily open to other voices than those of European males.

But why do we need Marx, anyway? Dunayevskaya believes he is the only philosopher of "total revolution"—the revolution that will touch and transform all human relationships, that is never-ending, revolution in permanence. Permanence not as a party-led state that has found all the answers, but as a society all of whose people participate in both government and production and in which the division between manual and mental labor will be ended. We need such a philosophy as grounding for organizing, since, as she says in *Rosa Luxemburg*, "without a philosophy of revolution activism spends itself in mere anti-imperialism and anti-capitalism, without ever revealing what it is *for*."

Dunayevskaya bases her claims for Marx on her reading of his entire work, but attaches special importance to the *Ethnological Notebooks* (only transcribed and published in 1972) as showing that at the very end of his life, as in his early writings, he was concerned with humanism—not simply class struggle but with the values and structures of precapitalist, non-European societies and the relationship of the sexes in those societies. In these manuscripts, jotted between 1881 and 1882, Marx reviewed the anthropological-ethnological writings of Lewis Henry Morgan (Engels based his *Origins* on Marx's notes on Morgan), John Budd Phear, Henry Maine, and John Lubbock. And indeed, as I read the *Notebooks*, Marx seems to be on a search for how gender has been structured in precapitalist, tribal societies.

Marx didn't go along with the ethnologists in their definitions of the "savage" as measured against the "civilized." Capitalism doesn't mean progress; the civilized are also the damaged. He saw "civilization" as a divided condition—human subjectivity divided against itself by the division of labor, but also divided *from* nature. He was critical of Morgan for ignoring white genocide and ethnocide against the American Indians, of Phear's condescension toward Bengali culture, and of the ethnocentricity of the ethnographers in general.

But neither did Marx idealize egalitarian communal society; he saw that "the elements of oppression in general, and of woman in particular, arose from *within* primitive communism, and not only related to change from 'matriarchy,' but began with the establishment of ranks—relationship of chief to mass—and the economic interests that accompanied it." He watched closely how the family evolved into an economic unit, within which were the seeds of slavery and serfdom, how tribal conflict and conquest also led toward slavery and the acquisition of property. But where Engels posited "the world historic defeat of the female sex," Dunayevskaya notes that Marx saw the resistance of the women in every revolution, not simply how they were disempowered by the development of patriarchy and by European invasion and colonization. The *Ethnological Notebooks* are crucial in Dunayevskaya's eyes because they show Marx at a point in his life where his idea of revolution was becoming even more comprehensive: the colonialism that evolved out of capitalism forced him to return to precolonial societies to study human relations and "to see the possibility of new human relations, not as they might come through a mere 'updating' of primitive communism's equality of the sexes ... but as Marx sensed they would burst forth from a new type of revolution."

Dunayevskaya vehemently opposes the notion that Marx's Marxism means that class struggle is primary or that racism and male supremacism will end when capitalism falls. "What happens after?" she says, is the question we have to be asking all along. And this, she sees in the Women's Liberation Movement, both women of color and white women have insisted on asking.

And, indeed, what is finally so beautiful and compelling about the Marx she shows us is his resistance to all static, stagnant ways of being, the deep apprehension of motion and transformation as principles of thought and of human process, the mind-weaving dialectical shuttle aflight in the loom of human activity.

Raya Dunayevskaya caught fire from Marx, met it with her own fire, brought to the events of her lifetime a revitalized, refocused Marxism. Her writings, with all their passion, energy, wit, and learning, may read awkwardly at times because she is really writing against the grain of how many readers have learned to think: to separate disciplines and genres, theory from practice. She's trying to think, and write, the revolution in the revolution. Anyone who has tried to do this, in any medium, knows that the effect is not smooth or seamless.

Rosa Luxemburg may not fit the expectations of many readers schooled in leftist, feminist, or academic thought. It is, first of all, not a conventional biography but rather the history and critique of a thinking woman's mind. It supplies no anecdotes of Luxemburg's childhood, no dramatic version of her assassination. It does, however, explore the question of how Luxemburg's sexual and political relationship with Leo Jogiches expressed itself both in intimate letters and in her theory. But Luxemburg's central relationships, in Dunayevskaya's eyes, were her intellectual relationship with the work of Marx as she understood it and the relationship of her whole self to the revolution. Most biographers of women still fail to recognize that a woman's central relationship can be to her work, even as lovers come and go. And Dunayevskaya doesn't end the book with Luxemburg's death, because she doesn't see that death as an ending. She goes on to throw out lines of thinking for the future, lines that pass through Luxemburg's fiery figure but don't finish with the woman who "joyfully [threw her] whole life 'on the scales of destiny.'"

"No one knows where the end of suffering will begin," writes Nadine Gordimer about the 1976 Soweto schoolchildren's uprising in her novel *Burger's Daughter*. In her 1982 essay "Living in the Interregnum," she muses about the sources of art and goes on, "It is from there, in the depths of being, that the most important intuition of revolutionary faith comes: the people know what to do, before the leaders."

Dunayevskaya concludes:

It isn't because we are any "smarter" that we can see so much more than other post-Marx Marxists. Rather, it is because of the maturity of our age. It is true that other post-Marx Marxists have rested on a truncated Marxism; it is equally true that no other generation could have seen the problematic of our age, much less solve our problems. *Only live human beings can recreate the revolutionary dialectic forever anew* [emphasis mine]. And these live human beings must do so in theory as well as in practice. It is not a question only of meeting the challenge from practice, but of being able to meet the challenge from the self-development of the Idea, and of deepening theory to the point where it reaches Marx's concept of the philosophy of "revolution in permanence."

And this work is indeed going on. Chicana lesbian-feminist poet, activist, and theorist Gloria Anzaldúa writes, in 1990:

What does being a thinking subject, an intellectual, mean for women-of-color from working-class origins? ... It means being concerned about the ways knowledges are invented. It means continually challenging institutionalized discourses. It means being suspicious of the dominant culture's interpretation of "our" experience, of the way they "read" us. ...
... Theory produces effects that change people and the way they perceive the world. Thus we need *teorías* that will enable us to interpret what happens in the world, that will explain how and why we relate to certain people in specific ways, that will reflect what goes on between inner, outer and peripheral "I"s within a person and between the personal "I"s and the collective "we" of our ethnic communities. *Necesitamos teorías* that will rewrite history using race, class, gender and ethnicity as categories of analysis, theories that cross borders, that blur boundaries. ... We need theories that point out ways to maneuver between our particular experiences and the necessity of forming our own categories and theoretical models for the patterns we uncover. ... And we need to find practical applications for those theories. ... We need to give up the notion that there is a "correct" way to write theory.

It's made so difficult, under the prevailing conditions of capital-shaped priorities, male supremacism, racism, militarism to envision that revolution without an end to which Dunayevskaya devoted her life. Most of us, even in our imaginations, settle for less. Living under these conditions, we can lose sight of the fact that *we* "live human beings" are where it all must begin—lose sight even to the point of denying the degree to which we are suffering. At certain moments, if we're lucky, we touch the experience, the flash, of *how it would feel to be free*. Raya Dunayevskaya clearly never let go of her experiences of the fullness of being human, of "how it would feel"—and she wanted that experience to be the normal experience of every human being everywhere.

NOTE

1. This chapter was previously published in: Rich, Adrienne. *Arts of the Possible: Essays and Conversations*. New York: W. W. Norton & Company, 2001. https://www.amazon.com/Arts-Possible-Conversations-Adrienne-Rich/dp/0393323129.

CHAPTER 6

Women as Force and Reason: Dunayevskaya, Marx, and Revolutionary Subjectivity

Heather A. Brown

We live in an era of counterrevolution. From ecological concerns, to neo-imperialist war, to increasing restrictions on women's rights and the rights of minorities; politically and socially, the clock has been rolled back throughout the world. In short, this is a world that seems foreign to the optimism of Marx's predictions of an end to capitalism and of full democratic control of political and economic life by the producing class. However, much of Raya Dunayevskaya's work, which reinterprets Marx's ideas for the crises of her time, points to precisely the relevance of Marx and his ideas of permanent revolution. More importantly, Dunayevskaya goes beyond Marx, creatively applying these insights to the twentieth-century world where counterrevolution seemed to be the order of the day, and yet where she discerned aspects of revolutionary consciousness.

Despite writing in an era that is long over with the end of statist communism in Russia and Eastern Europe (to say nothing of China, which has ended nearly any pretense to being "communist" with its

H. A. Brown (✉)
Department of Political Science, Westfield State University, Westfield, MA, USA
e-mail: hbrown@westfield.ma.edu

© The Author(s) 2021
K. B. Anderson et al. (eds.), *Raya Dunayevskaya's Intersectional Marxism*, Marx, Engels, and Marxisms,
https://doi.org/10.1007/978-3-030-53717-3_6

market reforms and severe exploitation of workers, among other things),[1] her efforts to rethink Marx for the Cold War period suggests to the contemporary reader how to carry out a similar project for today. Truly listening to and interpreting the voices from below calling for fundamental social change is just as significant today as it was at her death over thirty years ago. Moreover, having a vision for what comes after the revolution to overthrow capitalism is also essential to building a truly inclusive, non-racist, non-sexist society.

What is perhaps one of the most significant aspects of Dunayevskaya's work is her emphasis on the need to continually deepen the nature of revolutionary action. This can only be done when those on the margins of society are treated as true revolutionary subjects and theoreticians in their own right.[2] Following Marx and his theory of "permanent revolution," Dunayevskaya put forward a concept of women as revolutionary subjects who engaged both in revolutionary action and in theorizing for positive change. She illustrated how women behaved as both force and reason in the struggles surrounding the Abolitionist Movement and in various precapitalist societies. From these examples, and her lifelong project of remaining tuned into the radical movements of her time, she provides an important method for understanding and overcoming gender oppression as it manifests today.

Marx and "Permanent Revolution"

In 1850, following the defeat of the revolutions of 1848, Marx pointed to the fact that a new era was upon them. This would call for a new understanding of "the party." In an era of counterrevolution that was marked by significant political repression, the next revolution would not come easily. Instead, it would be necessary to rethink exactly what a democratic revolution might look like when bourgeois democracy was far from being up to the task of creating institutions that could bring true economic and political liberation.

> The relation of the revolutionary workers' party to the petty-bourgeois democrats is this: it marches together with them against the faction which it aims at overthrowing, it opposes them in everything whereby they seek to consolidate their position in their own interests. (Marx 2000a: 305)

Here, Marx suggests that the working class needs to be strategic concerning how it deals with the bourgeoisie. Certainly, in its battles with the feudal aristocracy, it was the more progressive group, but it still had its own interests to look out for, and these were often far from the interests of the working class. Thus, for purposes of liberation, the workers needed to align with those groups that shared their interests and oppose those that did not. This required that the workers not only knew what they were opposing but also that they envisioned what the new society itself must contain. Marx seems to be arguing that the workers themselves would have to be theoreticians, or at the very least that theoreticians would have to truly listen to the ideas and needs of the working class. This was far from the only time that Marx would use the concept of "revolution in permanence," even though the phrase itself was used in his work just on this occasion.

Dunayevskaya singles out a number of instances where Marx appropriates the activity (both practical and theoretical) of various oppressed groups in his own studies of capitalism and precapitalist societies. For Marx, "The nodal points of a serious revolutionary theory are rooted in self-activity of the masses who make the revolution, and the leadership's singling out of those live forces of revolution, not only as Force, but Reason" (Dunayevskaya 1991: 172). Whether in *Capital*, his writings on the political issues of the day, or his notebooks on precapitalist societies, Dunayevskaya notes how Marx singles out women as active subjects who influence society in general and initiate efforts to bring about social change: "He was forever 'transforming historic narrative into historic reason.' That is the dialectic of Marx's seeing, not merely the statistics he had amassed, but the live men and women reshaping history" (Dunayevskaya 1985: 196). Dunayevskaya borrowed this method from Marx, and creatively reread history and the current events of her day to point out how women were important theorists of revolution.

REVOLUTION IN PERMANENCE: FROM PRACTICE TO THEORY

Dunayevskaya often honed in on those instances where women and other oppressed minorities worked to further the revolutionary movement, by pointing to the inconsistencies in theory and practice engaged in by others in the movement, and demonstrating how it has often been oppressed groups that have been the true leaders of many political and social move-ments. Perhaps one of the most significant examples of this can be found in the Abolitionist Movement in the U.S. , where often Blacks and women led the way to expand the vision of a possible new society.

Dunayevskaya consistently focuses on how the revolt of one oppressed group enables others to see their own oppressed state. In the case of the institution of slavery in the U.S., Dunayevskaya points out that it was the leadership role of Black women that encouraged white women to push for greater rights in their own spheres. While "the Sojourner Truths and Harriet Tubmans were speakers, 'generals,' leaders" white women "[were] mainly the ones who arranged picnics, raised the money, and in every way were subordinate to the male abolitionist leaders" (Dunayevskaya 1985: 21). Although one could perhaps read this as discounting the traditional role of white middle-class women in progres-sive movements as doing only the seemingly less important work of providing food and serving the needs of male leaders, Dunayevskaya's point seems to be quite different on at least two fronts. She certainly does not go out of her way to value the traditionally female tasks discussed here, but instead points to the constraining nature of these activities from the perspective of the women involved.

First, she points to Black women as leaders, something that is rarely done when discussing the Abolitionist Movement, which has often tended to focus on the work of white men and women. She takes this point further by arguing that "When the white middle-class women saw the Black women being and acting as leaders of the Underground Railway, the white women decided to be more than handmaidens. The suffragist movement arose out of the Abolitionist Movement" (Dunayevskaya 1985: 21). It was the bravery and action of Black women like Sojourner Truth and Harriet Tubman that led many white women to question the patriarchal ideology which kept them out of politics and public life more generally. To Dunayevskaya, all of this illustrated the importance of the human drive for freedom and how the struggles of one group can reveal to others the binding nature of their own chains. Moreover, it illustrated how the struggle for freedom can take particularized forms, while the essence of freedom is universal: "There is no such thing as Black history that is not also white history. There is no such thing as woman's history that is not the actual history of humanity's struggle toward freedom" (Dunayevskaya 1985: 105).

Second, Dunayevskaya moves on to discuss the nature of a modern feminism that does not seek to challenge the alienation present in contemporary society, but only seeks to reinscribe it in new forms. For these "feminists," women are deemed to be free when they can choose to dress as they wish and buy whichever commodities they wish to buy. Rejecting this notion, Dunayevskaya critically opines: "today we must face those degrading TV commercials that try to sell us the idea that the hard-fought battle for equality has been met by our right to wear mini-skirts (at least until fashion dictators tell us otherwise) and having 'our own' brand of cigarettes!" (1985: 22). The only choice that we are offered is between commodified forms of femininity that fortify the power not of the individual but of the commodity itself.

In fact, Dunayevskaya elsewhere points to the way that Marx denounces the fetishized relations between commodities, where "human relations under capitalism are so perverse that it [the fetishism of commodities] is not appearance; that is indeed what they really are: Machine is master of man; not man of machine" (1964: 51). For Dunayevskaya, the problem is that clothing, cigarettes, or any other commodities are the things defining femininity and not real human beings.

Further, Dunayevskaya does not limit her critique to the position of women. Instead, she notes how the Women's Liberation Movement of the 1960s and 1970s shows that men are also in a far from an ideal position: "The young women feel that men, too, are alienated beings, and they want to be whole human beings... they have added to their own sense of world revolution that it be not only against the old exploitative system, but aim *for* a totally new society on truly human foundations" (Dunayevskaya 1985: 22—emphasis in the original). Again, the activity of others working for a better world shows the need for the universality of struggle against oppression and for something totally new.

This reading of late twentieth-century gender politics is based both on a close study of Marx as well as of the historical events since his death which called for an expanded and deepened understanding of the dialectics of history. One place where Dunayevskaya draws on Marx and his views on the new society relative to the gender divide is in a passage from the *1844 Manuscripts* where Marx argues that the position of women in society may offer some kind of measure as to how far humanity has developed (Marx 2004: 103). Under capitalism, this relationship necessarily has some element of commodification associated with it, but both

Marx and Dunayevskaya seek to go beyond this. As Dunayevskaya says of Marx: "In his early Humanist essays, he kept reiterating that so long as we talk only about different property forms, we will never get to new human relations, least of all the relationship of man to woman. Private property, Marx insisted, has made us so stupid that we only think about possessions. We are constantly substituting a 'to have' for a 'to be'" (1985: 23–24). Thus, it was the alienating nature of work under capitalism that leads to a separation between individuals who become commodified. We can only view other human beings on the basis of ownership or control, rather than seeing them for who they really are and valuing this.

Dunayevskaya uses this passage from the *1844 Manuscripts* as a jumping off point for illustrating how Marx sought to uproot *all* oppressive relations, including those involving gender and the family: "Marx called for a 'revolution in permanence' which would abolish and transcend all exploitative relations and see, in place of either the profit motive of capitalism or the state-form of property in vulgar communism, the self-development of man, woman, and child—with all of humanity in the process of 'the absolute movement of becoming'" (1985: 54). Marx would continuously point to a need to deepen the revolutionary movement and work to overthrow all forms of oppression. Dunayevskaya noted that Marx paid particular attention to the position of women, especially as he looked to those societies on the margins of capitalism.

Women as Subjects in Precapitalist Societies

Dunayevskaya is one of only a few scholars to take seriously Marx's notebooks on a number of contemporaneous studies on issues ranging from mathematics to ethnology and agricultural issues. Arguably the most fascinating and most overlooked of these notebooks are his *Ethnological Notebooks* from 1880 to 1882.[3] These notebooks contain Marx's research and comments on a number of important ethnological works of the time. Perhaps the most famous of these, in part due to the emphasis that Engels placed on them in his *Origin of the Family*, was Lewis Henry Morgan's *Ancient Society*. But Morgan is not the only scholar that Marx studied. In fact, Marx also took extensive notes on John Budd Phear, Henry Sumner Maine, John Lubbock, and Ludwig Lange. While Marx took up many issues beyond gender and the family, it is perhaps here that he made his most original and useful contributions to these topics.

Engels made his own attempt to take up the ideas of Morgan's *Ancient Society* in his *Origin of the Family*. Using Morgan's work, Engels argued that the introduction of private property brought about the end of matrilineal society and thus created the conditions in which gender oppression could arise. Since men became responsible for providing food for the clan, and because it was necessary to use heavy tools for this purpose, men gained power in terms of acquiring private property. Also, Engels stresses that with the development of the new form of the family—the pairing family—the paternity of children could be determined more easily. Finally, within these arrangements, the fathers of the children wanted to be sure to pass their property on to their own children. For Engels, these factors taken together led to the change from the matrilineal to the patrilineal determination of family (Engels 1986: 84–85), which led in turn to a significant change in social position of the women:

> The overthrow of mother right was the *world historical defeat of the female sex*. The man took command in the home also; the woman was degraded and reduced to servitude; she became the slave of his lust and a mere instrument for the production of children. This degraded position of woman, especially conspicuous among the Greeks of the heroic and still more of the classical age, has gradually been palliated and glossed over, and sometimes clothed in a milder form; in no sense has it been abolished. (1986: 87)

Women from this point forward would be subject to the oppression of men. Moreover, they had no subjectivity of their own, according to Engels, and would only be liberated with the end of private property and the introduction of communism.

For Marx, women were not passive victims, and were not condemned to be completely subject to the will of men after the fall of matrilineal society, waiting for society to advance far enough to liberate them. This said, Marx saw that women did not have complete control over their lives. In fact, Marx frequently noted that while women's position in precapitalist societies was at times preferable to that in the Europe of his era, one should aim higher than these limited rights (Dunayevskaya 1991: 184–186). Marx's analysis of women's position in these non-capitalist societies is something that has profound consequences both for understanding women's history and for efforts to overcome the current gender counterrevolution that threatens to force at least some women from many of those spaces that have been opened to them.

This difference in the accounts of Engels and Marx is extremely important to socialist politics, given the fact that it is Engels's voice that has been dominant within Marxism as it relates to the intersectional oppressions of class and gender. Many feminists have been rightly critical of the economic determinism of Engels's *The Origin of the Family*, which leaves women necessarily in a state of oppression until *after* the overthrow of capitalism. One of the most important of these responses includes the claim that Engels's framework is relatively determinist and that this severely weakens his argument in the context of the position of women today. On the one hand, Engels is fairly clear that bringing women into the public sphere through their introduction to wage labor and the abolition of the bourgeois family would not be sufficient to emancipate them: "it will be plain that the first condition for the liberation of the wife is that this in turn demands that the characteristic of the monogamous family as the economic unit of society be abolished" (1986: 105). On the other hand, there is no mechanism within his theory that can account for societal change other than in the abolition of the family following the destruction of capitalism. According to Engels, the abolition of the family will ultimately lead to the end of women's oppression, but he offers no specific theory of how this would come about. It seems as though he is arguing that because private property and patriarchy were born together, they would also fail together. However, as we have seen, both institutions are very adaptive and in fact, patriarchy can exist without capitalist relations.

According to Michèle Barrett (1986), this becomes especially important because the introduction of women into the workforce has not abolished the patriarchal family and its oppressive relations. Despite Engels's prediction that the family among proletarians would be abolished in its oppressive form, this has not been the case. Because Engels focused so heavily on the factory system, he was unable to see that the oppression of women would not end, nor would their conditions even necessarily improve, with the further involvement of women in the workforce:

> Engels did not attend sufficiently to the amount of domestic work women have to do even when they go out to work full time, and he certainly did not see how heavy the familial and household burden was and is on working-class women. Hence he ignored the factors that have continued

to depress women's wages and keep them in part-time and insecure work, and he failed to appreciate the far-reaching effects of ideologies of what was appropriate as men's work and women's work. (Barrett 1986: 25)

Thus, for Barrett, it was Engels's narrow focus on the oppressive nature of the monogamous family that was a serious problem with his work (1986: 29).

Lise Vogel (1983) brings up a related point. Vogel argues that Engels does not go far enough in his discussion of the means of reproduction of workers (1983: 91) Engels is right to make the distinction between the mode of production and the mode of reproduction but "he simply takes a very primitive distinction between natural and social phenomena to its logical conclusion" (1983: 91). Therefore, the somewhat crude materialism that characterizes Engels's writings results in his leaving out important aspects of socialization. This constitutes a major flaw in his work. Marx, on the other hand, takes a more nuanced approach that allows for more discussion of these kinds of issues.[4] Vogel tends to conflate the views of Marx and Engels, frequently pointing to similarities between statements made in *The Origin of the Family* and statements made in Marx's works without examining their differences (1983: 84, 85, 86, 90–91).

This was not the case in Dunayevskaya (1991), where she made a sharp distinction between Marx and Engels in terms of their respective positions on women's oppression. Most significant for Dunayevskaya in this respect is Marx's multilinear theory of women's oppression in contrast to Engels's unilinear, monocausal formulation in *The Origin of the Family*. For Marx, the origins of women's oppression were much more complicated and began much earlier than "the world historic defeat" that Engels posited with the beginning of private property (Dunayevskaya 1991: 180–181). Dunayevskaya writes, "Marx drew no such unbridgeable gulf between primitive and civilized as Engels had... The pivotal point was that everything 'depends on the historical environment in which it occurs'" (1991: 185). In contrast to Engels's relatively uncritical account of early societies and their treatment of women, Marx saw the need to go beyond this still limited sense of freedom (Dunayevskaya 1991: 184).

A central part of Dunayevskaya's focus is on the degree to which Marx charts a dialectical course for the development of the family, one that includes significant evidence of women's subjectivity, even in the most limited of circumstances. Marx regularly commented in his notes on the position of women before and after the colonial experience:

> What was crucial to Marx in seeing the great freedom of the Iroquois women was to show how great was the freedom the women had before American civilization destroyed the Indians. Indeed, first, it was true throughout the world that "civilized" nations took away the freedom of the women, as was true when British imperialism deprived the Irish women of many of their freedoms when they conquered Ireland. Marx's hatred of capitalism as he studied precapitalist societies grew more intense... (Dunayevskaya 1985: 201)

Thus, it was not an issue of the "progressive" West showing the rest of the world its future. Instead, the West was taking away rights and freedoms of women in these supposedly primitive societies. Women's position in society varied on the basis of real conditions on the ground, not due to any abstract formulation of mode of production and familial superstructures, although these could certainly influence the options available. As Marx sardonically noted when discussing how the leaders of early societies dealt with the change from mother to father right: "Innate casuistry! To change things by changing their names! And to find loopholes for violating tradition while maintaining tradition, when direct interest supplied sufficient impulse" (quoted in Dunayevskaya 1991: 181–182). Tradition had to be made to service a new practice that was in the interest of a few at the expense of the others.

As Dunayevskaya notes, Marx was not content with noting the sometimes-elevated position of women in these precapitalist societies, however. While their position may have been better than that of the Victorian women of his day, it was far from ideal for both men and women in these societies:

> Marx demonstrated that, long before the dissolution of the primitive commune, there emerged the question of ranks *within* the egalitarian commune. It was the beginning of a transformation into opposite—gens into caste. That is to say, within the egalitarian communal form arose elements of its opposite—caste, aristocracy, and different material interests. Moreover, these were not successive stages, but *co-extensive* within the communal form. (Dunayevskaya 1991: 181)

In contrast to Engels, Marx showed that the position of women at the dawn of class society was not due to any essentialist biological need of women for protection or based on a preference for monogamy (Engels 1986: 83), but instead was based on a real social struggle that extended beyond the man/woman question. As Marx and Engels had argued in *The German Ideology*, slavery was "latent in the family" (1998: 38). Already as the family moved to reduce the partners available for marriage, men began buying and capturing women from other clans. These women were outsiders who did not have to be fully incorporated into the clan with similar rights. This paved the way for others to be brought into the clan on less equal terms and eventually led to rank being ossified in what was a once egalitarian group.[5] Thus, the position of women was intertwined with the structure of rank in the clans and eventually with the state as it began to gain power over clans and subsume much of the authority held by clan elders. However, their position varied based on the rank that they held and the social forces available to them at the time.

As Dunayevskaya reads Marx in these notebooks, he continuously points to the continuing conflict within the family rather than to a long-term defeat of women:

> The point at all times is to stress a differentiation in the family, both when it is part of the gens and as it evolves out of the gens into another social form, at which point Marx again differentiates between the family in a society that already has a state and the family before the state emerged. The point at all times is to have a critical attitude to both biologism and uncritical evolutionism. (Dunayevskaya 1991: 184)

This difference with Engels is significant not merely for understanding the history of precapitalist societies, but also points to the idea that women have always been actual and potential subjects who are often erased by those who write history. If women have always had a role to play in history, then there is no reason to wait until after the revolution to demand equality with men.

In fact, as Marx is discussing the role of women in Greek society, he "held that the Greek goddesses on Olympus were not just statues, but expressed myths of past glories that may, in fact, have reflected a previous stage, and/or expressed a desire for a very different future..." (Dunayevskaya 1985: 201). Dunayevskaya again focuses on how Marx, even where women faced some of the harshest oppression, saw a yearning for a better future, if only in fictional representation. More importantly for today, these studies helped Marx to produce a positive view of what the future could look like based on critical analysis of the past: "Marx envisioned a totally new man, a totally new woman, a totally new life form (and by no means only for marriage)—in a word, a totally new society" (Dunayevskaya 1991: 186).

WOMEN AS FORCE AND REASON TODAY

Raya Dunayevskaya's reading of Marx provides a number of openings for theorizing alternatives to the oppressive gender relations that we see throughout the world. Dunayevskaya reminds us to keep our eyes on the movements from below as they fight against oppression in their own lives. Despite (or perhaps in some cases because of) our differences, these struggles against what is, can prompt us to examine our objectives. Dunayevskaya learned from the LGBT movement of her time that:

> You can't make your right to your own kind of love-making as if that is the answer for everyone. People want to have a conclusion on the question of love—what is love, whether it's physical, whether it's emotional, whether it's total, and all that sort of thing. But I don't think it's correct for us to try and solve it for others. I think what we have to do is to create the conditions for everyone to be able to experiment with choices, in love, in the family—and I don't think we'll really have those choices until we get rid of capitalism. (1985: 180)

This interview from 1984 leaps from the pages it was transcribed onto as if it were written to speak to the issues of today. From same-sex marriage, to reproductive rights, to the right to live without being sexually harassed or assaulted, radical movements are fighting worldwide against the counter-revolutionary actions of conservatives that seek to turn the clock back. As women and LGBT individuals are again showing themselves as activists in their own particular causes, there is also a need to return to philosophy, and to unite the movement from practice with the movement from theory. Today's gender and sexual rights movements can move toward the role of acting as "new passions and new forces" for revolution only when theory and practice are combined into a dialectical whole. There is much work to do in terms of theorizing a positive alternative to capitalism. Women and non-traditional gender conforming individuals throughout the world provide new avenues for inquiry as they say "no" to many of the most oppressive aspects of patriarchal capitalism. Dunayevskaya reminds us of the need to stand with these individuals in their opposition to the status quo and to assist in making concrete how a new society would organize gender relations. Theory can only be successful when it responds to real human needs:

> Only live human beings can recreate the revolutionary dialectic forever anew. And these live human beings must do so in theory as well as in practice. It is not a question only of meeting the challenge from practice, but of being able to meet the challenge from the self-development of the Idea, and of deepening theory to the point where it reaches Marx's concept of the philosophy of "revolution in permanence." (Dunayevskaya 1991: 195)

It has become clear that state regulation of civil rights is not nearly enough to secure full emancipation for women and non-traditional gender conforming individuals, as is indicated by a multinational debate over reproductive rights for women and transgender civil rights. As Marx points out, simple political equality is not tantamount to human emancipation. In fact, the abolition of a distinction must presuppose that the distinction actually exists.[6] This distinction is then alienated from the individual's species being, the conception (and requisite activity) of belonging to a common humanity, as they have individual qualities that do not conform to the abstract individual of the classical liberal state. Therefore, the state ignores the difference of the individual in order to bring them into the community, since abstract equality demands abstractly equal individuals who will not be subject to any special treatment, whether it affects the individual positively or negatively, as it would necessarily lead to unequal treatment of such individuals by the state.[7] The individual is fractured into multiple parts where only the most abstract aspects of humanity are acknowledged by the state and by other human beings. One remains a citizen, but qualifiers must always be added which can ultimately lead to a sort of second-class citizenship. For example, women are politically equal to men in the U.S. but face discrimination on the job market, in the political sphere, and in terms of the right to control their own bodies, in part because they contain an identity that is not part of the abstract citizen that is recognized by the state. They have the capacity to produce new human life—something that is difficult, labor intensive, and that can take away from the standard of what abstract civic duty or the employer-employee contract represents. In the liberal state, difference is acknowledged and alienated from the individual's species being, leading to a separated public and private individual that must constantly fight to retain the full rights seemingly granted with citizenship. Hence, the constant back and forth on civil rights for all the oppressed minority groups.

It is necessary at this point to return to the issue of identity, this time from the perspective of what a new society might look like. Perhaps there is something that we can learn from reading Marx and Dunayevskaya in their discussions of gender from today's perspective, even if Marx's interest was likely far from supporting what would become the LGBT community or fundamental change in gender roles. In the same passage of the *1844 Manuscripts* that Dunayevskaya singles out as representing an important element of Marx's understanding of gender, he takes up in an extremely brief and abstract way, the progression of gender relations and how it illustrates progress toward the fully developed human being:

> The immediate, natural and necessary relation of human being to human being is also the *relation* of *man* [Mann] to *woman* [Weib]. In this *natural* species relationship the human being's [Mensch] relation to nature is directly his relation to the human being [Mensch], and his relation to the human being [Mensch] is directly his relation to nature, to his own *natural* function. Thus, in this relation is *sensuously revealed*, reduced to an observable *fact*, the extent to which human nature has become nature for him. From this relationship humanity's [Mensch] whole level of development can be assessed. It follows from the character of this relationship how far *the human being* [Mensch] has become, and has understood himself as, a *species-being*, a *human being*. The relation of man [Mann] to woman [Weib] is the *most natural* relation of human being to human being. It indicates, therefore, how far the human being's [Mensch] *natural* behavior has become *human*, and how far his *human* essence has become a *natural* essence for him, how far his *human nature* has become *nature for him*. It also shows how far the human being's [Mensch] *needs* have become *human* needs, and consequently how far the other person [Mensch], as a person, has become one of his needs, and to what extent he is in his individual existence at the same time a social being. (adapted from Marx 2004: 103)

Of particular note here is how Marx moves from the abstract universal— the unmediated, "natural" human understanding of species being where survival and thus reproduction is the primary link between individuals—to the concrete universal where every human being regardless of gender (and today we could add sexuality) are both beings for themselves and for others—i.e., individuals are valued both in terms of who they are and what they can become as well as being a representative of the species being for others. In order for human beings to develop in this way, it is necessary that we become true individuals, detached from those primordial bonds with the community. As Marx notes later in the *Grundrisse* and elsewhere, this is part of the progressive element of capitalism.

Today, however, this individualism has become an impediment to further progress toward gender equality. This is where the *politics of difference* comes in. Certainly, the ability to express one's gender identity without harsh social, political, and economic repercussions is important; but one can begin to wonder where the possibility for common ground between these identities comes in. However, even between the seemingly most different individuals, there is always some element of commonality. Marx, for example, points to many such commonalities in the *1844 Manuscripts* where he notes that as human beings, we are all "suffering beings," i.e., there is something outside of ourselves that is necessary to our survival such as, the material necessities of life (2004: 140); love and companionship (2004: 168); recognition from others of our humanity (2004: 105); and physical and intellectual enrichment (2004: 82). While the way that we carry out these activities will necessarily vary, they all require a human community to be fulfilled. Moreover, it is this commonality of needs that provides the ground for difference to even be discussed.

It is this commitment to difference qua difference on many sides of the debate that needs to be questioned. For example, in the U.S. , it is now clear that same-sex marriage does not contain the full solution: discrimination can and does come in various forms, whether a refusal to provide business services because of religious belief, bathroom policing, or even outright physical violence. Simply asserting identity and difference is not enough—some commonality must be found. This is not a call for some abstract and unmediated unity, but instead for dialogue about these intersections among those committed to full human emancipation for all. While Marx was far from flawless on these issues, Dunayevskaya reminds us that his work seems to point in the direction of showing how changes in gender relations come about, and more importantly, how to work toward such changes, citing him on the extremely difficult yet extremely important goal of "creat[ing] a new economic [and social] foundation for a higher form of the family and of relations between the sexes" (Marx 1976: 620) (and one could add gender) today.

The battles over gender and sexual rights, equality, and emancipation for all that we have witnessed in previous centuries, and up until today, are of great significance. Capital has opened up a great deal of space for the expression of difference on many fronts, but however important the expression of individuality is, it is nothing without the recognition of humanity within each individual. The struggle to come to terms with these multiple identities for all human beings throughout the world, regardless of their sex, gender, and sexuality, is one of the foremost challenges of our time. On these issues, Raya Dunayevskaya's work offers us a vantage point from which to interpret and overcome the challenges of our age.

NOTES

1. In fact, Dunayevskaya made clear in many of her writings that she never saw the People's Republic of China as Communist, but instead as a state capitalist dictatorship. The same was true for the Soviet Union and its satellite states. See for example Dunayevskaya (2000).
2. This is, of course, something that is rarely done in academic circles and in seemingly progressive social movements. One only need to look at the recent history of socialist parties regarding gender and sexism both in the U.S. and in Britain to get a flavor of how voices from oppressed groups can get silenced even by those claiming to be for all of the working class.
3. This is likely due to the fact that these are research notebooks and not a draft of a text that Marx was working on. Thus, much of it is quotations from the texts that he was studying as well as paraphrases and occasional comments. It is not clear exactly why Marx was researching this material and what he would have eventually use it for. For speculation on this, see Anderson (2002, 2010), who argues that Marx was looking at the possible resistance that capital would face as it expanded, and Smith (2002), who argues that Marx was doing this research to expand the scope of *Capital*.
4. For a detailed discussion of this see Brown (2013).
5. For a more detailed discussion of this issue see Brown (2013).
6. "Far from abolishing these factual differences, its existence rests on them as a presupposition, it only feels itself to be a political state and asserts its universality by opposition to these elements" (Marx 2000b: 53).
7. It is important to note that the classical liberal state in this context only concerns itself with equality of opportunity which assumes away difference so that everyone seems to start at an equal position, and therefore, pays

no attention to the actual outcome of events. A just policy is one where everyone starts at the same starting line for the race. Any obstacles that are encountered by the participants are ignored in the classical liberal state. It is this sort of logic that makes it seem as though affirmative action policies are "reverse discrimination," since they try to take into account that not every individual starting the race has the same chance of finishing first (or at all).

BIBLIOGRAPHY

Anderson, Kevin B. 2002. "Marx's Late Writings on Non-Western and Precapitalist Societies and Gender." *Rethinking Marxism*. Vol. 14, Issue 4, pp. 84–96.

———. 2010. *Marx at the Margins: On Nationalism, Ethnicity, and Non-Western Societies*. University of Chicago Press.

Barrett, Michèle. 1986. "Introduction," in Friedrich Engels, ed. *The Origin of the Family, Private Property and the State*. New York: Penguin Books.

Brown, Heather. 2013. *Marx on Gender and the Family: A Critical Study*. Chicago: Haymarket Books.

Dunayevskaya, Raya. 1985. *Women's Liberation and the Dialectics of Revolution: Reaching for the Future*. Atlantic Highlands, NJ: Humanities Press.

———. [1982] 1991. *Rosa Luxemburg, Women's Liberation, and Marx's Philosophy of Revolution*. Chicago: University of Illinois Press.

———. [1958] 2000. *Marxism & Freedom: From 1776 Until Today*. New York: Humanity Books.

———. 1964. "The Theory of Alienation: Marx's Debt to Hegel," in Mario Savio, Eugene Walker, Raya Dunayevskaya, eds. *The Free Speech Movement and the Negro Revolution. News & Letters* Pamphlet.

Engels, Friedrich. [1884] 1986. *Origin of the Family, Private Property and the State*. New York: Penguin Books.

Krader, Lawrence. 1972. Introduction to *The Ethnological Notebooks of Karl Marx*. Assen: Van Gorcum.

Marx, Karl. 1972. "Ethnological Notebooks," in Lawrence Krader, ed. *The Ethnological Notebooks of Karl Marx*. Assen: Van Gorcum.

———. 1976. *Capital*, Vol. I. Trans Ben Fowkes. London: Pelican Books.

———. [1850] 2000a. "Address to the Communist League," in David McLellan, ed. *Karl Marx: Selected Writings*. Second Edition. New York: Oxford University Press, pp. 303–312.

———. [1843] 2000b. "On the Jewish Question," in McLellan, David, ed. *Karl Marx: Selected Writings*. Second Edition. New York: Oxford University Press, pp. 46–70.

———. [1844] 2004. *The Economic and Philosophic Manuscripts of 1844*, in Erich Fromm, ed. *Marx's Concept of Man*. New York: Continuum.

Marx, Karl and Friedrich Engels. [1846] 1998. *The German Ideology*. Amherst, NY: Prometheus Books.

Smith, David Norman. 2002. "Accumulation and the Clash of Cultures: Marx's Ethnology in Context." *Rethinking Marxism*. Vol. 14, Issue 4, Winter, pp. 73–83.

Vogel, Lise. 1983. *Marxism and the Oppression of Women: Toward a Unitary Theory*. New Brunswick, NJ: Rutgers University Press.

CHAPTER 7

Raya Dunayevskaya on Race, Resistance, and Revolutionary Humanism

Ndindi Kitonga

The renewed interest in socialism in the United States today is propelled not only by a need for a new economic theory that can pull the masses out of capitalism's cruel hands but also the quest for developing a new society, one that is free from violence, alienation, and distorted human relations. In our present historical moment, this struggle reveals itself in the widespread resistances of people of color, who at every turn in history have defied dehumanization. How can we, in our current moment, move beyond the orthodox Marxist notion of creating economic programs to align with the dogmatic ideologies that have produced failed "socialisms" across the globe and inflicted suffering on so many? How should racialized and gendered forms of oppression be addressed in this work? The historical record shows that people of color are not willing to address economic questions outside of those related to their recognition and participation as full humans in society.

The founder of the Marxist-Humanist tradition in the U.S., Raya Dunayevskaya, understood the significance of Black liberation movements

N. Kitonga (✉)
Los Angeles, CA, USA

© The Author(s) 2021
K. B. Anderson et al. (eds.), *Raya Dunayevskaya's Intersectional Marxism*, Marx, Engels, and Marxisms,
https://doi.org/10.1007/978-3-030-53717-3_7

and those of other oppressed minorities and made a case for returning to the totality of Marx's philosophy of liberation. She noted, "[t]he unmasking of Western civilization's racism by its Black dimension in revolutionary moments of mass upsurge makes imperative a most serious return, on this centenary of Marx's death, to his critical, revolutionary unmasking of Western civilization's capitalist foundations," also writing that "[t]he Black dimension is crucial to the total uprooting of the existing, exploitative, racist, sexist society and the creation of new, truly human foundations" ([1963] 2003: 14). In her development of Marxist-Humanism, Dunayevskaya reclaims the concept of the *politicization of philosophy*:

> Because politicalization has, in the hands of the Old Left, meant vanguardism and program-hatching, we have kept away from the very word. It is high time *not* to let the "vanguard party to lead" appropriate the word, politicalization. The return is to its original meaning in Marx's new continent of thought as the uprooting of the capitalist state, its withering away, so that new humanist forms like the Paris Commune, 1871, emerge. (1986)

In *Marxism and Freedom: from 1776 until Today*, Dunayevskaya applies the concept of the politicization of philosophy to reveal the revolutionary humanism of Marx through an analysis of his *Economic and Philosophical Manuscripts of 1844*. In these early manuscripts, Marx extends Hegel's dialectic to address material questions. He also demonstrates how the capitalist mode of production obscures human relations, reducing these relations to nothing more than relations between things. At the center of this mode of production is alienation: the alienation of humans to their work, to nature, to each other, and to themselves. For persons of color, this alienation occurs doubly: as both workers and as racialized beings (Hudis 2019). Without this understanding of the dual nature of alienation, we are left with a class reductionism that suggests that overthrowing capitalism without addressing other systems of domination will of itself lead to a classless, democratic, and free society. In *Marxism and Freedom*, and in successive works, Dunayevskaya does something else that the dogmatic Marxist left fails to do: namely, search out and identify the revolutionary subjects of the time, be they persons of color, women, or youth. As she tells us, Marxist-Humanism, checks before and after each movement from practice also the movement from theory, *and* measures how we anticipated some of the events as well as created the fabric – the single dialectic in both subjectivity and objectivity. (1984b)

This chapter will, in this spirit, focus on the specific struggles of people of color, with a particular emphasis on the activities of Black peoples. It will seek to show Dunayevskaya, through an exploration of her extensive writings, not only as an astute Marxist but also as a revolutionary humanist, with an enduring relevance for our times.

IDENTITY AND THE MOVEMENTS OF BLACK AND BROWN MASSES

And I wish I knew how, it would feel to be free, I wish I could break,
All the chains holdin' me
I wish you could know, what it means to be me, then you'd see and agree,
That every man should be free.
Sung by Nina Simone, written by Billy Taylor and Dick Dallas (1967)

Over the past 10 years, we have seen the rise of authoritarianism, state repression, and white supremacy all across the globe. As always, people of color tend to bear the brunt of these dehumanizing structures. Some of the structural issues Black and Brown populations are currently experiencing in the United States include over-policing, police brutality, gentrification of already under-resourced communities, depressed wages, lowered health outcomes, and mass incarceration, to name a few. Movements like Black Lives Matter have been at the forefront not only of fighting police violence, and the incarceration of Black and Brown people, but have also taken on issues such as mental health concerns, LGBTQ rights, and reproductive justice for people of color. The brutal 2014 murders of Eric Garner and Michael Brown at the hands of police mobilized the Black masses around the cry "I can't breathe!"—a reference to Garner's last words as police manhandled him, cutting off his circulation—and "We have nothing to lose but our chains!"—a phrase found in the *Communist Manifesto* but popularized by Assata Shakur in the 1970s. Throughout this decade, the United States public has been forcefully confronted with what many communities of color have long understood: namely, that their bodies are considered disposable in this society. A 2015 study by the Harvard Public Health Review confirms this, revealing that

Black men are three times more likely to have a fatal encounter with the police as compared with White men. The same study also shows that there has been a sharp rise in such fatal incidents since the 1980s.

Similar movements have developed among Indigenous women in North America. Native American women suffer greatly from gendered violence and continue to be "disappeared" and murdered at very high rates. According to the Urban Indian Health Institute, murder is the third leading cause of death among Native American women (Lucchesi and Echo-Hawk 2018). Currently, grassroots movements are mobilizing to address the issues of Missing and Murdered Indigenous Women & Girls (MMIWG) through community watch groups, raising awareness, demanding visibility, and juridical recognition. Awareness-raising might not seem like a revolutionary act, but it is of great importance in this case, especially since it is unclear how many women are missing, or whether they are even alive. Local governments have been reluctant to keep records or investigate these atrocities, prompting Indigenous women to mobilize and demand to be heard.

With this systematized, ongoing, and cruel dehumanization of Black, Brown, and Red people, it is no wonder that we see the rise of identity-first or race-based revolutionary movements. These struggles often take the form of marginalized racial groups fighting for judicial protections and systemic changes to their material lives. These politics are also used to inspire pride, self-expression, and self-creativity for marginalized identities and draw upon similar aesthetics and attitudes that were prevalent in the consciousness-raising movements of the past. In this way, phrases like "I/we am/are unapologetically Black!" are the "Say it loud, I'm Black and I'm proud!" of today.

Identity politics, or the politics of recognition, are sometimes viewed with suspicion by some on the Marxist left who remain interested in class-first solutions to the problems we experience under capitalism. The critics claim that these forms of identity politics undermine class solidarity in favor of neoliberal reforms and other individualist bourgeois freedoms. Understanding that the politics of recognition do not develop in a vacuum, Dunayevskaya (1982) did not reject these politics wholesale. In fact, and in a clear evocation of Hegelian concepts, she saw that,

> it is clear that for the Black masses, Black consciousness, awareness of themselves as African-Americans with their dual history and special pride, is a drive toward wholeness. Far from being a separation from the objective,

it means an end to the separation between objective and subjective. Not even the most elitist Black has quite the same arrogant attitude as the White intellectual toward the worker, not to mention the prisoner. (1982: 281)

Dunayevskaya recognizes something that scholars like Keeanga-Yamahtta Taylor (2016) point to: that even the Black elites in U.S. society cannot escape racialization. This is an important observation that the class reductionists are usually not able to make. Their fear of being derailed from struggling against a global class war prevents them from understanding how comparatively little power Black and Brown elites hold in a racist society. They also fail to realize that even the bourgeois Black and Brown classes are willing to fight against racialized oppression and have historically done so. Indeed, almost all U.S. mainstream politicians of color at our present time are willing to proclaim, "Black Lives Matter!"

Concerning the issue of identity-first or race-based movements, Dunayevskaya (1982) rejects the idea that the Black self-development of subjectivity is bourgeois. Over the span of her career, Dunayevskaya remained committed to understanding structural racism and its relationship to capital. She also followed the activities and self-development of people of color, particularly that of the Black dimension in the United States. Determined always to get to the root of racial domination, she was consistently willing to take the class reductionist left, as well as the Black bourgeois leadership, to task.

It is important to state that Dunayevskaya does more than champion the rights of racialized minorities or simply explain how their oppression is connected to a larger class war. Through her dialectical exploration of history, she is able to demonstrate that not only are the United States Black populations always at the forefront of liberation movements but that no system of domination can eradicate the human desire to be free. In *American Civilization on Trial: Black Masses as Vanguard*, she wrote, "[the Black dimension] at each turning point in history, anticipates the next stage of development of labor in its relationship with capital. Because of his dual oppression, it could not be otherwise" (1963: 81). To make this claim, Dunayevskaya analyzed the creativity of Abolitionists in relation to the slave revolts, Black anti-imperial resistances during the turn of the twentieth century, Black labor battles of the Reconstruction era, the courageous actions of the Little Rock Nine in their quest to desegregate schools, and the Black wildcat strikes in Detroit. Crucially, she saw that many of the struggles she highlighted appeared to have no obvious or immediate class character. Dunayevskaya takes a special interest in the 1955–1956 Montgomery bus boycott, asserting that this struggle was as relevant and radical as the Hungarian revolution that occurred the same year. She writes extensively not only on the relatedness of these movements but also on the underlying humanism that propels them. Dunayevskaya warned the left not to undermine the activities of the Black masses and to learn from vibrant and radical movements and their potential to usher in a new humanist society. She wrote,

> Above all, we hold fast to the one-worldedness and the new Humanist thinking of all oppressed from the East German worker to the West Virginia miner; from the Hungarian revolutionary to the Montgomery Bus Boycotter; as well as from the North Carolina Sit-Inner to the African Freedom Fighter. The elements of the new society, submerged the world over by the might of capital, are emerging in all sorts of unexpected and unrelated places. What is missing is the unity of these movements from practice with the movement from theory into an overall philosophy that can form the foundation of a totally new social order. ([1963] 2003: 98)

Hudis (2019) makes a case for creating what he describes as an "intersectional historical materialism," i.e. a framework that works through the analysis of political economy but also reckons with issues of identity and the politics of recognition as they relate to current day movements. An often relied upon concept for understanding how the politics of recognition operates can be found in Hegel's master/slave dialectic and his thoughts on the social contract found in his work *Phenomenology of Spirit*. For Hegel ([1807] 1977), one is admitted to a political community based on a form of social contract (a social contract being the way in which personhood is legitimized as the individual's internal conceptions of self are acknowledged or externalized in relation to others.) To be included into the social contract is to be considered human. Fanon moves Hegel's dialectic beyond a "struggle to the death," noting that the racialized subject cannot acquire recognition and inhabits, "the zone of non-being" (1952: 7). Being outside of the social contract, people of color are never considered fully human.

Fanon's work is growing in popularity in the United States as the variegated masses try to make sense of their particular struggles as racialized beings. Some of the articulations we see are based on an incomplete inter-pretation of Fanon's work, focusing on his theories of recognition and the effects of racism on the psyches of the oppressed (see Wilderson 2014 on Afro-Pessimism), but never arrive at his radical humanism, where he posits that it is possible to "reach out for the universal," the "creation of a human world ... of reciprocal recognitions" (1952: 217). Also lacking in this analysis is the revolutionary subjectivity of people of color over the centuries. More than anything, those who espouse these ideologies are able to carefully describe dehumanization of the racialized body but do not offer any liberatory way out of this plight. These kinds of politics sometimes overshadow the project of dismantling capitalism and over-coming other systems of domination. They can also live quite comfortably and, in fact, thrive within the neoliberal order, particularly if the groups seeking recognition limit their demands to matters of culture, inclusion, representation, or aesthetics. Dunayevskaya's work becomes very impor-tant here, not only because she recognized the revolutionary humanism of Fanon's anti-racist, anti-colonial philosophy, but also because she takes the activities of workers seriously. For her, theory and practice must be united: "the actions of the proletariat create the possibility for the intel-lectual to work out theory" (1958: 91). Her lifelong commitment to the struggles of both workers and marginalized peoples reveals that ordinary people always strive for emancipation regardless of what theoreticians say.

While some articulations of Fanon's work by theorists ends in social death for racialized beings, Dunayevskaya asserts that human strug-gles against dehumanization always point to "nothing short of a new humanism" (1958: 287). Her position is very close to that of Fanon, who always points us to the creation of a new humanism in which humans will have achieved genuine mutual recognition. If we are to embrace the poli-tics of recognition, they should not follow a dead-end into various forms of social death or nihilism. As Fanon affirms, "Man is a yes that vibrates to cosmic harmonies" ([1952] 2008: xii).

BLACK ANTI-IMPERIAL RESISTANCES

Njeri is an African woman. Her home is in Kenya, a country in East Africa which has been in the grip of civil war for almost three years. The civil war was started by the British authorities when they declared an Emergency in October 1952 because the people of Kenya were trying to help themselves.

They want their rights as human beings which the minority of white settlers had taken from them.

Njeri is a woman of about 53... Like Harriet Tubman during our own Civil War, she cannot read or write legibly. She is in a prison camp with about 9,000 other African women. She has been very badly treated and everybody thought she was going to die. This remarkable woman founded the first independent women's movement in East Africa. She started her work in 1940 when, independently of any man, she organized African women to establish, at the Kenya Teachers College, facilities for girls to equal those enjoyed by the boys. But there is more behind the African women's movement... It is not simply for equality with African men. It is for equality of Africans in relation to anyone else in the world.

Njeri's story, and the story of the people of Kenya, is told by Mbiyu Koinange in THE PEOPLE OF KENYA SPEAK FOR THEMSELVES, which is dedicated to her.

From the first issue of News & Letters, June 1955

The African independence movements of the late 1950s and 1960s raised important questions about the kinds of human societies we would create after the revolution. While these revolutions mainly lay unfinished, they have many implications for our current struggles against neo-colonialism. Dunayevskaya was quick to notice that these movements were "[opening] a new page, in the dialectic of thought as well as in world history" ([1973] 2003: 213). Dunayevskaya also observed the class character of many of the freedom struggles, being careful to note that these struggles did not originate in the 1960s, but were, in fact, part of an ongoing resistance to European imperialism on the African continent. She particularly points to the 1905 Maji Maji rebellion of Tanganyika (current day Tanzania), and to the 1945 general strike in Nigeria (1973). Lakemfa (2009) chronicles the events of this historic strike, noting that, "the workers' communiqué said that '...the situation can no longer be sustained.' It gave a one-month ultimatum emphasizing that 'not later than Thursday, June 21, 1945, the workers of Nigeria shall proceed to seek their own remedy with due regard to law and order on the one hand and starvation on the other unless their demands are met.'" There are many other examples that demonstrate that Africans were agentic and could organize against oppression without Western intervention. Dunayevskaya's work here is of great significance, particularly because she was writing at a time when the responses from the left concerning issues of colonialism in Africa tended to be somewhat anemic.

At a time when both White liberals and the Marxist left were leery of Black consciousness-oriented liberation movements, Dunayevskaya supported the Pan-African and Black consciousness struggles, understanding their revolutionary potential to emancipate not only Black people but also to undermine the entire system of colonialism for the purpose of producing new, creative, and free humans. For Dunayevskaya, Africa and Africans were not lacking in self-creativity or the ability to theorize. In *Africa Today* (1962), when Dunayevskaya is asked to comment on humanism in relation to Gambia anti-colonial struggles, she writes: "They [the Gambian people seeking independence] thought that they had an advantage in being the last in West Africa due to get freedom, for they hoped to unite thought and action instead of using 'Pan Africanism' as a mere umbrella to cover contending tendencies" (Dunayevskaya [1973] 2003: 331). So committed is Dunayevskaya to potential new humanisms emerging from the anti-colonial movements that she featured something about them in almost every issue of the Marxist-Humanist publication she founded, *News & Letters*.

As aforementioned, Dunayevskaya considers Fanon to be an important revolutionary humanist who articulated a total philosophy—one that addresses the psycho-affective dimensions of domination, as well as material conditions, and is concerned with the total overthrowing of colonial subjugation in order to realize the creation of a new humanity. Dunayevskaya and her coauthor and longtime colleague, the Black autoworker and *News & Letters* editor Charles Denby, consider Fanon's work to be not only a "Manifesto of the Third World, but a Manifesto with global dimensions he called 'a new humanism'" (Denby and Dunayevskaya [1978] 1986: 12). She shares Fanon's confidence in the theoretical and practical work of Africans struggling for independence over predetermined programs from the West, agreeing with his contention that "[we must] combine our muscles and our brains in a new direction. Let us try to create the whole man, whom Europe has been incapable of bringing to triumphant birth" ([1961] 2004: 235).

So important is Fanon to Dunayevskaya that she and other members of News and Letters Committees go on to publish an important piece on his anti-colonialism and new humanism, *Frantz Fanon, Soweto and American Black Thought*, in 1978, co-authored by Lou Turner and John Alan. In the introduction of this work, Denby and Dunayevskaya detail and comment on both the subjective and objective situation in South Africa, relating it to the Black workers' struggles in the United States.

They take particular interest in the work of anti-apartheid activist and leader of the Black consciousness movement, Steve Biko. Denby would go on to write in his autobiography, "What both Fanon and Biko are saying is that the struggle for freedom has no national boundaries, and everywhere that you have a battle for human liberty helps the worldwide movement for freedom" (1979: 293).

The interrelatedness of the Black struggle everywhere is an important theme that Dunayevskaya continued to revisit in her scholarship, here in an essay co-authored with Lou Turner and John Alan:

> What is crystal clear in the high intensity of the Black dimension's struggle – whether we are talking of Labor, Women, or Youth – is that the post-World War II world manifests the presence of an unquenchable thirst for freedom. What the emergence of the Third World as a whole world has revealed is just how continuous are those freedom struggles. It is this movement *from* practice that is itself a form of theory which has been challenging revolutionary intellectual-theoreticians to develop a new unity, a new relation, of theory to practice. (Dunayevskaya, Turner, and Alan [1978] 1986: 6)

In the 1986 edition of this book, written at a time that is hardly considered revolutionary, Dunayevskaya and her co-authors also look to the unwavering revolutionary activities of the U.S. Black masses. They maintain the concept of "Black masses as vanguard" when describing the "*little shorties*," very young youth who took to the streets during three Black uprisings in Miami (1980, 1981, 1982) that erupted after the acquittal of four police officers who fatally assaulted a Black man named Arthur McDuffie. These events were barely acknowledged by the white Marxist left, given as their ostensible lack of relation to standard questions of class politics. We notice similar attitudes on the left today when it comes to issues of race. In this essay, Dunayevskaya and her co-authors also note the anti-capitalist and anti-imperialist rejection of Reaganism by U.S. Blacks, thereby dismantling the narrative on the left that an increase in Black elites was dulling consciousness among Black populations. The fact was that, while some Blacks experienced upward social mobility, many did not, and in fact continued to struggle materially. In their introduction to the first edition of this pamphlet in 1978, Denby and Dunayevskaya maintained that the Black masses in the U.S. remained in fact revolutionary over time:

"contrary to the reports in the white press, Black America's actual rejection of white capitalistic-imperialistic exploitation, with or without Black lackeys, is, at one and the same time, a time-bomb that is sure to explode, and a time for thinking and readying for action" ([1978] 1986: 11). Later on, Dunayevskaya also points to the creativity and revolutionary spirit of the Black dimension noting, "[t]o grasp the Black Dimension is to learn a new language, the language of thought, Black thought. For many, this new language will be difficult because they are hard of hearing. Hard of hearing because they are not used to this type of thought, a language which is both a struggle for freedom and the thought of freedom" (1985: 49).

While the reactionary neo-conservative politics of the Reagan years raged on, the Black dimension held steadfast in their demands for total emancipation. Throughout the 1980s, Dunayevskaya continues to write about new Pan-Africanisms connecting Black struggle everywhere. During this time, Dunayevskaya writes often about a renewed Black American identification with Biko's Black Consciousness Movement in South Africa and Fanon's anti-colonial thought. She also points to the participation of the Black masses in anti-apartheid demonstrations in the U.S. and the complete rejection of U.S. imperialist investments in South Africa. While the anti-apartheid struggle was widely supported, the Western left mostly allied with the African National Congress and the South African Communist Party rather than the Black Consciousness Movement or other more radical tendencies; their analysis did not extend as far as that of Dunayevskaya, who understood that the Black Consciousness Movement was not an expression of narrow nationalism, but a wider humanist struggle that could offer an anti-colonial liberatory framework.

Across the 1960s, 70s, and 80s Dunayevskaya continued to connect the liberation struggles in Africa to all other struggles of the time, always being careful to include the activities of youth, women, and workers. Her dedication to youth, in particular, is of great importance. Dunayevskaya relates the 1976 youth Soweto uprising to the 1968 revolts of young people in Paris, dispelling the bourgeois liberal logic of the time that suggested that Black youth could not theorize about their own conditions. Turning this argument on its head, Denby and Dunayevskaya praise the Soweto youth's desire for freedom, urging the U.S. left to pay attention and learn from their creativity and from, "the triangular development of ideas and actual achievement of liberation, not for history's sake, but as a preparation for the American revolution to be" ([1978] 1986: 14).

While always committed to anti-colonial movements in Africa and the Caribbean, Dunayevskaya was not uncritical of the unfinished revolutions of this era. There are many contradictions and questions to work out concerning the new independent African states of the 1950s–70s that have yet to be explored. It is worth noting that not all of the revolutionary left supported the various African quests for independence on nationalistic terms, and instead asked for the colonial subject to abandon the aspiration for national identity for the sake international solidarity and a commitment to the workers of the world. The question of eschewing one's national or local struggle for a collective international solidarity continues to plague the left. Dunayevskaya did not suffer from this affliction, sharing, as she did, Fanon's perspectives on transcending narrow nationalisms for a broader form of national consciousness (a particularly prescient aspect of Fanon's analysis given the many African nations that have failed to this day to fully complete their revolutions).

> But if nationalism is not made explicit, if it is not enriched and deepened by a very rapid transformation into a consciousness of social and political needs, in other words into humanism, it leads up a blind alley. The bourgeois leaders of underdeveloped countries imprison national consciousness in sterile formalism. It is only when men and women are included on a vast scale in enlightened and fruitful work that form and body are given to that consciousness. Then the flag and the palace where sits the government cease to be the symbols of the nation. The nation deserts these brightly lit, empty shells and takes shelter in the country, where it is given life and dynamic power. The living expression of the nation is the moving consciousness of the whole of the people; it is the coherent, enlightened action of men and women. The collective building up of a destiny is the assumption of responsibility on the historical scale. (Fanon [1961] 2004: 98)

Dunayevskaya also predicted a transformation into opposite when newly independent African states were faced with the task of self-governance and social and economic development after decades of being dispossessed and exploited by colonial powers. She also understood the pitfalls newly independent African nations needed to avoid, wondering, in 1959, if the new socialisms proposed by freedom fighters now turned heads of state could "hide the old smell of exploitative capitalism" (1959: 5). She acknowledged the challenges of new nation-building, noting that "Of course, industrialization of Africa is a necessity. Of course, this cannot be done outside of a relationship to technologically advanced industrial powers. But must the method be capitalistic?" (1959: 5). When the national independence struggles lead to incomplete freedom from colonial structures, new forms of nationalism that only served capital and its sergeants emerge. In many senses, the full project of anti-colonialism in Africa remains unfinished.

Over some four decades of scholarship, Dunayevskaya continued to dialectically relate matters of neo-colonialism, authoritarianism, class politics, and racism to struggles of Black people internationally. She remains an important revolutionary humanist to engage within light of our current anti-colonial struggles.

WOMEN OF COLOR, REVOLUTION, AND ABOLITION FEMINISMS

Each generation of revolutionaries must theorize and act based on current conditions. One of the most pressing issues of the day in the United States is that of mass incarceration. The number of U.S. state and federal prisoners actually dropped in the tumultuous 1960s but began to rise steadily in the 1980s after disastrous policies such as the war on drugs, three-strike rules for repeat offenders, and the passing of "tough on crime" legislation by conservative—and also liberal—local and state governments. To date, the United States houses 21% of the worlds' prisoners but only 4.3% of its population (Sawyer and Wagner 2019). While Black and Latinx adults make up 12 and 16% of the U.S. adult population respectively, they account for 33 and 23% of the people in prison (The Bureau of Justice Statistics of the U.S. Department of Justice 2017). The overrepresentation of incarcerated Black and Brown persons in our prisons is such that if these groups were incarcerated at the same rates as Whites, the prison population would decrease by 40% (Sawyer and Wagner 2019).

The growth of the "for-profit" prison industry since the 1980s adds an interesting layer to issues of mass incarceration. Most of the products needed in prisons are produced by workers in the global south, who are paid even less than the slavery wages prisoners receive here in the U.S. So, while mass incarceration is a United States concern, it has far-reaching global implications. Theorists and activists who challenge mass incarceration have rightfully termed this system the Prison Industrial Slavery Complex (PISC). One framework socialist feminists of color are rallying around presently is that of "abolition feminism" (Lober 2018). Abolition feminism is an anti-capitalist framework with Marxist roots which seeks to not only dismantle the carceral state but also to project a new world. According to Maureen Mansfield (2018), this framework, "invites us to consider the world we want, and how to organize to build it. Seeking a world beyond prisons, Abolitionist Feminism focuses our attention on developing stronger communities and bringing about gender, race and economic justice. It encourages us to consider our approach systematically and collectively rather than individually…Abolitionist Feminism asks us to consider the violence and harm caused by the state, as well as inter-personally, and seek alternative strategies for addressing these harms."

While most of the U.S. prison population is male, the number of women, particularly women of color, in prisons has increased tremendously over the past 30 years. About three out of five incarcerated women have children and four out of five are victims of abuse. This abuse persists in prisons, with trans women in particular finding themselves the most vulnerable (Sawyer and Wagner 2019). Abolition feminism is perhaps the new revolutionary phase of the women's liberation movement, as it seeks to identify, understand, and uproot the PISC. It does so not only because of the gender violence and exploitation the PISC pushes onto women and their communities but also because prison is a most egregious manifestation of gender-based oppression. To be fair, there have been abolitionists as long as there has been any kind of enslavement of human beings in the United States. The women, mostly of color, engaged in this work regard it as more than simply the unfinished work of the women's liberation movement; it is tantamount to any anti-capitalist, anti-imperialist, or anti-racist praxis. It is a matter of solidarity with all prisoners of the world.

Dunayevskaya always carefully studied the activities of women's movements. She noticed the increasingly bourgeois character of some of the women's movements of the 1980s, which she accused of falling into the position of the "existential other" that considered "man to be the enemy" (Dunayevskaya 1982: 102). She admonished those who would "simply turn the other side of the coin" for a woman-centered analysis that was no longer revolutionary or inclusive of the unique contributions of women of color. Having been not only a philosopher but also an activist in her own right, Dunayevskaya recognized the early work of Black women like Harriet Tubman, who carried on despite the "short sighted" Black male leaders who refused to fight for women's suffrage after the U.S. Civil War. Among them were prominent abolitionists like Frederick Douglass, who championed the fight for what he called the "Negro hour" of Black male suffrage (1982: 103). Dunayevskaya was also present to witness and analyze the dynamics of the work of women of color, showing great admiration for the creativity and radical movements of women who struggled both against misogyny from within their organizations and from the racism of White women's movements. Over the course of her scholarship, Dunayevskaya examines the intersections of class, race, and gender as she writes about the activities of U.S. activists Fannie Lou Hammer and Gloria Richardson, Rosa Muki Bonaparte of East Timor, and women's groups in Nigeria and South Africa.

Over time, some in feminist movements have become wary of Marxism, claiming that Marx himself had little to say about issues of gender. Always committed to the entirety of Marx's philosophy of revolution, Dunayevskaya points us to the humanist man/woman concept in the *Economic and Philosophical Manuscripts of 1844* (1959) where he "extended the concept of alienation to the Man/Woman relationship and to all life under capitalism" (1982: 10). Throughout her scholarship Dunayevskaya returned to Marx's manuscripts (and related works on gender) to theorize alienation, capitalism, and gender oppression. In *Women's Liberation and the Dialectics of Revolution: Reaching for the Future* (1985) she noted "that until we end the division between mental and manual labor—and every single society has been characterized by that, and it was even in primitive communism—we will not really have a new man, a new woman, a new child, a new society" (Dunayevskaya 1985: 10). From this, it follows that our feminist movements should not only be anti-capitalist but should also theorize ways to overcome gendered domination.

Addressing issues of class, race, and sexuality presents an interesting task for women's movements. The slogan, "my feminism will be intersectional, or it will be bullshit!" was born out of current day feminist struggles. While intersectionality frameworks are not always revolutionary, they require that the oppressions that women and sexual minorities face to be understood as interlocking. White liberal feminist organizations of the day have set their sights on increasing representation for women in politics, dealing with harassment in places of work and contesting prescribed gender roles. Needless to say, addressing these concerns does not in itself lead to the upsetting of capitalist social relations. The abolitionist feminist movement is currently taking the bourgeois feminists to task over their reliance on the carceral system. This approach certainly goes beyond liberal intersectional feminisms, as it is a framework interested in theoretically and practically taking hold of systems produced by patriarchy and capitalism and irreversibly changing them from the bottom up (Lorber 2018).

Currently, liberals and radicals alike are organizing around exposing sexual assault, creating harassment free spaces for women, and bringing abusive men to account as part of what is known as the #MeToo movement. For Abolitionist feminists, the #MeToo moment is about addressing public and private forms of violence against women while simultaneously working to uproot the carceral state. This means addressing interpersonal and community violence through alternative means, taking on issues of social reproductive labor, examining the violence purveyed on humans by exploitation, poverty, disease, and by theorizing a world without prisons as we know them. Because carceral violence mostly harms women of color and sexual minorities, transcending the bourgeois family structure which locks many into coercive and violent relationships is of great importance to the abolition feminist movement. To get a sense of Dunayevskaya's thinking on non-heterosexual unions and non-nuclear families, I harken back to her response on the question of Marxism and new family forms posed to her on International Women's Day in 1984:

> People want to have a conclusion on the question of love—what is love, whether it's physical, whether it's emotional, whether it's total, and all that sort of thing. But I don't think it's correct for us to try and solve it for others. I think what we have to do is to create the conditions for everyone to be able to experiment with choices, in love, in the family—and I don't think we'll really have those choices until we get rid of capitalism. (Dunayevskaya 1985: 180)

The abolitionist feminist movement is currently theorizing and working out what human societies could look like without the capitalist carceral state. This framework refuses to explore the "woman question" or the "prison abolition question" after the revolution but demands that it be theoretically worked on in the here and now. Time will tell if these and related movements can potentially uproot the capitalist mode of production and overcome the mental and manual division of labor that creates alienated human relations.

CONCLUSION

Without a philosophy of revolution, activism spends itself in mere anti-imperialism and anti-capitalism, without ever revealing what it is for. (Dunayevskaya 1982: 194)

The Marxist left has continued to struggle when it comes to issues of race and gender. Identity-based intersectional theories remain relevant as people try to make sense of their experiences. Our task as revolutionaries is to try to project better alternatives that take the everyday material conditions of folks' lives seriously and to "recognize that there is a movement from practice—from the actual struggles of the day—to theory; and, second, to work out the method whereby the movement *from theory* can meet it" ([1965] 2012: 73). Dunayevskaya, who always had a long and dialectical view of history, invariably and systematically related capital's latest crisis to mass movements and issues concerning people of color. She did so by developing Marxist-Humanism, a philosophy that reanimates the totality of Marx's Marxism and that posits alienation at the heart of the dehumanization we suffer under capital. She remained situated in the struggles of the day, paying special attention to the activities of the Black dimension, which she identified as an historically important force for liberation. Always working from Marx's concept of revolution in permanence, she also posed the question "what comes next," taking care to articulate the potential to produce new humanisms during each revolutionary struggle. For these reasons, Dunayevskaya's revolutionary Marxist-Humanism offers a relevant framework that can point us to the irreversible uprooting of dehumanizing systems of domination.

Instead of becoming frustrated with the consciousness-raising and empowerment projects some identity-based movements have turned to, we should position ourselves to do the theoretical and practical labor required to be in critical solidarity with Black and Brown movements. I propose that this project be taken on by theorizing around the psychic components of racialized and gendered oppression while seeking out ways to move incomplete articulations of intersectionality and emerging movements to a place of radical criticality. In a quest to identify and be in solidarity with the revolutionary subjects of our day, scholars like Monzó (2019: 80) ask us to transpose. Dunayevskaya's concept of the Black masses as vanguard to what she calls "women of color as vanguard." This is a significant proposal, as much of the revolutionary work we see today is being led by Black, Brown, and Indigenous women and transgendered folks in the United States. Others like Hudis (2019) propose developing an intersectional historical materialist framework that can theorize around women's oppression and capitalism. Such a framework will surely reveal the limitations of either a class reductionist or an identity-based bourgeois framework. One thing remains clear, however: we must continue to strive for "a unity of the struggles for freedom with a philosophy of liberation. Only then [can] the element of revolt release new sensibilities, new passions, and new forces-a whole new human dimension" (Dunayevskaya 1973: 292).

REFERENCES

Alan, John. 2003. *Dialectics of Black Freedom Struggles: Race, Philosophy and the Needed American Revolution*. Chicago: News and Letters Publications.

Anderson, Kevin B. 2016. *Marx at the Margins: On Ethnicity, Nationalism, and Non-Western Societies*. Expanded ed. Chicago: University of Chicago Press.

Anderson, Kevin B. and Russell Rockwell, eds. 2012. *The Dunayevskaya-Marcuse Fromm Correspondence, 1954–1978: Dialogues on Hegel, Marx and Critical Theory*. Lanham, MD: Lexington.

Biko, Steve. 1977. "Black Consciousness: Steve Biko Speaks for Himself." *News & Letters* 22: 9 (November).

Brown, Heather A. 2013. *Marx on Gender and the Family: A Critical Study*. Chicago: Haymarket.

Denby, Charles. 1979. *Indignant Heart: A Black Worker's Journal*. Quebec: Black Rose Books.

Denby, Charles and Raya Dunayevskaya. [1978] 1986. "Introduction," pp. 111–114 in Turner and Alan [1978] 1986.

Dunayevskaya, Raya. [1958] 2000. *Marxism and Freedom: From 1776 Until Today*. Amherst, NY: Humanity Books.

———. 1959. "The African Revolution I." *News & Letters* (January). http://newsandletters.org/PDF-ARCHIVE/1959/1959-01.pdf.

———. [1963] 2003. *American Civilization on Trial: Black Masses as Vanguard*. Chicago: News and Letters Publications.

———. [1973] 2003. *Philosophy and Revolution*. Lanham: Lexington Books. https://www.marxists.org/history/etol/newspape/news-and-letters/1970s/1977-11.pdf.

———. [1982] 1991. *Rosa Luxemburg, Women's Liberation, and Marx's Philosophy of Revolution*. 2nd ed. Foreword by Adrienne Rich. Urbana: University of Illinois Press.

———. 1983. "A 1980s View of Two-Way Road Between the U.S. and Africa," pp. 5–14 in Dunayevskaya [1963] 2003.

———. 1984a. "On Listening to Marx Think as Challengers to All Post-Marx Marxists." *Raya Dunayevskaya Collection* [RDC], 8183.

———. 1984b. "Marxist Humanist Perspectives, 1984–1985." *News & Letters* (July). https://rayadunayevskaya.org/ArchivePDFs/8193.pdf.

———. 1985. *Women's Liberation and the Dialectics of Revolution.* Atlantic Highlands, NJ: Humanities Press.

———. 1986. "A Post-World War II View of Marx's Humanism, 1843–83; Marxist-Humanism, 1950s–1980s." News and Letters. https://rayadunayevs kaya.org/ArchivePDFs/11588.pdf.

Dunayevskaya, Raya, Lou Turner, and John Alan. 1986. "New Introduction/Overview," pp. 1–10 in Turner and Alan 1986.

Fanon, Franz. [1952] 2008. *Black Skin, White Masks,* trans. by Richard Philcox. New York: Grove Press.

———. [1961] 2004. *Wretched of the Earth,* trans. by Richard Philcox. New York: Grove Press.

Hegel, Georg and Wilhelm Friedrich. [1807] 1977. *Phenomenology of Spirit,* trans. by Arnold V. Miller. Oxford: Oxford University Press.

Hudis, Peter. 2015. *Frantz Fanon: Philosopher of the Barricades.* London: Pluto Press.

———. 2019. "How Is an Intersectional Historical Materialism Possible? The Dialectic of Race and Class Reconsidered." Paper presented at. Toronto, April, 2019.

Krieger, Nancy, et al. 2015. "Trends in US Deaths Due to Legal Intervention Among Black and White Men, Age 15–34 Years, by County Income Level: 1960–2010." *Harvard Public Health Review,* Vol. 3 (January).

Lakemfa, Owei. 2009. "One Hundred Years of Trade Unionism in Nigeria." *The Nigerian Vanguard* (November 18).

Lober, Brooke. 2018. "(Re)Thinking Sex Positivity, Abolition Feminism, and the #MeToo Movement: Opportunity for a New Synthesis." *Abolition: A Journal of Insurgent Politics* (January).

Lucchesi, Annita and Abigail Echo-Hawk. 2018. *Missing and Murdered Indigenous Women & Girls.* Urban Indian Health Institute.

Mansfield, Maureen. 2018. "What Is Abolitionist Feminism, and Why Does It Matter?" *The Progressive Policy Think Tank.* https://www.ippr.org/juncture-item/what-is-abolitionist-feminism-and-why-does-it-matter.

Marx, Karl. 1959. *Economic and Philosophical Manuscripts of 1844.* Moscow: Progress Publishers.

———. 1976. *Capital,* Vol. I, trans. by Ben Fowkes. New York: Penguin Books.

Monzó, Lilia D. 2015. "Women and the Revolution: Marx and the Dialectic." Paper presented at the 1st International Conference on Critical pedagogy. Changchun, China, October 8.

———. 2019. *A Revolutionary Subject: Pedagogy of Women of Color and Indigeneity*. New York: Peter Lang.

The Bureau of Justice Statistics of the U.S. Department of Justice. 2017. *Prisoners in 2017*. By Jennifer Bronson and E. Ann Carson. https://www.bjs.gov/content/pub/pdf/p17.pdf. Accessed July 6, 2019.

Sawyer, Wendy and Wagner, Peter. 2019. "Mass Incarceration: The Whole Pie 2019." *Prison Policy Initiative Journal*.

Taylor, Keeanga-Yamahtta. 2016. *From #BlackLivesMatter to Black Liberation*. Chicago: Haymarket.

———. 2017. *How We Get Free: Black Feminism and the Combahee River Collective*. Chicago: Haymarket.

Turner, Lou and Alan, John. [1978] 1986. *Frantz Fanon, Soweto & American Black Thought*. Second Edition. Chicago: News and Letters.

Whalley, Elizabeth and Hackett, Colleen. 2017. "Carceral Feminisms: The Abolitionist Project and Undoing Dominant Feminisms." *Contemporary Justice Review*, 20: 4, 456–473.

Wilderson, Frank B., III. 2014. "We're Trying to Destroy the World: Anti-Blackness & Police Violence after Ferguson." *Ill Will Editions*. https://illwilleditions.noblogs.org/files/2015/09/Wilderson-We-Are-Trying-to-Destroy-the-World-READ.pdf.

Woods, Donald. 1987. *Biko*. New York: Henry Holt & Company.

CHAPTER 8

The Dialectic in *Marxism and Freedom* for Today: The Unity of Theory and Practice and the Movement of Today's Concrete Struggles

Lilia D. Monzó

Along with the increasingly fascist, conservative tide that is sweeping our world today—including White nationalist agendas and xenophobic reactionary attitudes and policies—a new generation of courageous activists is taking to the streets, even in the belly of the beast here in the United States, where such vociferous protests have not been heard since the Civil Rights movements of the 1960s. For those of us who dream of bringing down capital and developing a new Marxist-Humanism, we find tremendous hope in these movements, but we also recognize the need to take heed of the lessons that have been gleaned from revolutionary histories, including those to be learned from the work of Raya Dunayevskaya, whose humanist interpretation of Karl Marx's philosophy of revolution

L. D. Monzó (✉)
Chapman University, Orange, CA, USA
e-mail: monzo@chapman.edu

© The Author(s) 2021   141
K. B. Anderson et al. (eds.), *Raya Dunayevskaya's Intersectional
Marxism*, Marx, Engels, and Marxisms,
https://doi.org/10.1007/978-3-030-53717-3_8

was developed in light of the concrete struggles she witnessed during her own lifetime.

Today's movements, and the activists that shepherd them, are full of energy and impelled by indignation against the multiple forms of violence directed against both humanity and the Earth, the latter of which is being threatened with oblivion (Jobin-Leeds and AgitArte 2016). However, many of these movements are fragmented, perhaps unable to recognize the relationship between the myriad forms of oppression that exist, as well as lacking a philosophy that can guide their movement against capital and toward building a socialist alternative (Larkin 2017). Such a philosophy cannot be merely extrapolated from the pool of intellectual activity of an historical and intellectual elite. The experiences and insights of the people whose lives are most affected by these oppressions are key to movement building. People do not just act without thinking. While their actions may be constrained and highly influenced by the need for employment, they are conscious beings who think and reflect on their conditions and strategize for the best ways to ameliorate conditions of oppression. The spontaneous activity within which the revolutionary Subject arises is as much theory as it is practice, and is a clear testament to our human potential to recognize, understand, and act with agency against injustice.

Beginning with her earliest major work, *Marxism and Freedom*, Dunayevskaya (2000) engages with this dialectical relation between theory and practice and between organization and spontaneity that will prove crucial to bringing down capital, as well as to our ability to take advantage of the moments wherein history opens up possibilities for the creation of what she referred to as a "new humanism." Without a clear understanding of this dialectical relationship we risk losing opportunities for change or, worse, creating something that only *reorganizes* the existing dehumanizing social relations that exist under capitalism. In this chapter, I draw on Dunayevskaya's profound insights into these dialectical relations to consider how our current social movements can become better prepared to take on the massive task of challenging capital and its many antagonisms and of building a Marxist humanism grounded in freedom, love, and dignity for all life forms.

Philosophy of Revolution

In *Marxism and Freedom*, Raya Dunayevskaya examines the relationship between Marx's body of work and the Hegelian dialectic. She posits that Marx's work was not mere economic theory, but rather, an entire system of thought and method of movement toward liberation—i.e., a philosophy of revolution. Dunayevskaya begins her discussion with Hegel, articulating his philosophy, wherein history is viewed as a series of stages of development toward freedom. For Hegel, and later for Marx, freedom was the ultimate reason for struggle and the ultimate human achievement. To be free, and to fight for our freedom, is our human vocation and the ultimate precondition to becoming fully human. Both Hegel and Marx recognized that objective forces existed that could prevent us from attaining our true human potential (Dunayevskaya 2000).

The Hegelian dialectic is a form of reasoning and a method of resolving contradictions that is concerned with enabling our further movement toward freedom (Hegel 1812, 1977). Hegel posited that within each concept there exists an underlying contradiction of presumed opposites— one positive and one negative—that must be resolved, the resolution of which furthers the positive move toward liberation. Dunayevskaya (2000) points out that although Hegel's focus was on freedom as developed through human consciousness or Absolute Knowledge, his overall philosophy was *not* one of mere ideas, but was rooted in history and was thus a philosophy of the world rather than purely of the mind (although it was in the Idea wherein he focused his resolution of contradictions). Dunayevskaya points out that Hegel was highly influenced by the French Revolution, through which he came to recognize alienated labor as a dehumanizing experience but also a context from which "true" consciousness could develop. Indeed, Hegel's Absolutes are not abstracted from reality but, rather, are laden with history, making freedom in consciousness the achievement of science and history: that is, social and scientific development has been a process by which humanity has sought to free its thoughts from the constraints imposed upon them by religious doctrines and ideologies that serve the interests of the ruling classes.

Central to the process of realizing freedom in history, for Hegel, is the notion of "negation." Negation is the process by which something is nullified. The first negation is a challenge to oppressive forces wherein the positive emerges as triumphant. However, this first negation retains the underlying contradiction; a second negation is necessary in order to disavow the existence of the contradiction, allowing for a new unifying concept to emerge. Hegel posited:

To hold fast to the positive in *its* negative, to the content of the presupposition in the result, is the most important factor in rational cognition.
(2010: 744)

For Marx, this kind of statement signaled that the working classes were
capable of the self-activity necessary to transcend the capitalist order and
in doing so affirm their human nature in the struggle for freedom. Taking
Hegel as his point of departure, Marx took a step forward in the development of the dialectic, adding the crucial material-ideal component that
enabled him to comprehend, intellectually and practically, the movement
toward freedom. Marx's dialectical materialism must not be misconstrued
simplistically as the correction of Hegel's stress on consciousness through
a stress on materialism but rather as a further development of Hegel's
dialectic, wherein consciousness (Idea) and reality (material) are recognized as presumed opposites that must be unified (Marx and Engels
1998). The ideal and the material are each an aspect of the other, and
their unity creates not only a new understanding of what it means to
be human, but a new human being, one that rejects capitalist social
relations, including the hierarchical division of labor, which ultimately
continues to thwart our efforts to bring the monster of capital to its knees.
Dunayevskaya captures this complex process of negation and unification.

Hegel's LOGIC moves. Each of the previously inseparable divisions
between opposites – between thought and reality – is in constant process
of change, disappearance and reappearance, coming into head on collision
with its opposite and developing thereby. It is thus, and thus alone, that
finally achieves true freedom, not as a possession, but as a dimension of
his being... (2000: 36)

Unlike the often-made assumption that Marx merely stood Hegel
upright, and planted him on the ground, transplanting Hegel's idealism
with materialism, Dunayevskaya points out:

Marx did not reject idealism. "Thoroughgoing naturalism or humanism"
as the young Marx designated his own philosophic outlook, "distinguishes
itself from both idealism and materialism and is at the same time the truth
uniting both." (2000: 42)

This dialectical view of history, as contradictions that are overcome to create and overcome new contradictions—an evolution toward freedom—demands a Subject. This was Hegel's significant accomplishment—to recognize the human capacity to free itself—bringing the will and agency of the people to life. It was Marx who, from the vantage point of this new discovery, examined the reality of the movement around him and fully identified the working class as the revolutionary Subject of his time.

A Revolutionary Subject

Dunayevskaya established a new interpretation of Marx's work that centers on the humanism he established in his *Economic and Philosophical Manuscripts of 1844* and developed throughout his entire body of work, including *Capital*. Part of her new interpretation of Marx was the notion that central to Marx's philosophy of revolution and the historical movement to liberation that he articulates is the development of the revolutionary Subject—persons whose lived social conditions provide the understanding and impetus to challenge existing dehumanizing conditions.

Dunayevskaya points out that Marx was the first to recognize the working class as a human Subject, continuously in motion, moving through contradiction toward freedom. For Hegel, human freedom was the ultimate goal, the ultimate contradiction to be solved. However, for Hegel, human freedom was gained through consciousness—the Idea of freedom acting as the site of the necessary struggle of humanity. To be free was to gain freedom in consciousness, to see the world as it was, with clarity gained through education or philosophy.

Marx introduced the human being as an agentic Subject who acts (in addition to thinking) and is grounded in material reality. Without this elementary human component, consciousness is nothing more than a mystical movement handed down by God or some other spirit. When grounded in material reality, consciousness and freedom of consciousness becomes something that we as human beings can create through the struggle against injustice—the injustice that inhibits actual freedom *and* our freedom of consciousness. Marx focused on the injustices of capitalist social relations, recognizing class as a historical human development, such that the social relations human beings create, our lived realities, shape and are shaped by consciousness. Once this material component of humanity was recognized, the revolutionary Subject became someone who not only sought freedom in consciousness but also through the struggle against capitalist social relations.

For Marx, this revolutionary Subject was to be found among the working classes. Capitalism would be brought down only when workers recognized their oppression, challenged the processes of production, and affirmed their humanity in the process. The working class has the greatest potential to transform itself into a revolutionary Subject because its deplorable living conditions support both a consciousness of injustice and the impetus to act against the structures that impinge upon its very humanity. This is not merely a theoretical statement, but is evidenced in the many revolutionary struggles and uprisings that have taken place from the onset of industrialization to today, including the struggle for the eight-hour workday, the development of trade unions, and the constant strikes across industries to demand higher wages and better working conditions. Dunayevskaya points out that although Hegel recognized alienated labor, he was unable to see—and could not have seen, because their revolutionary activity was not yet revealed in his life-time—the positive that emerged from alienated labor. It is during Marx's time that alienated labor reveals its human nature—its agentic activity toward liberation by developing consciousness, organizing, striking, and actively resisting. Furthermore, it is the working class whose productive labor is capable of arresting the processes of production, thereby bringing capital to its knees. By dialectically grounding the Subject in its material reality, in history, Marx was able to recognize the class struggle as the fundamental objective of human agency in our quest for liberation.

One of the most common mistreatments of Marx's work is the imputation of a narrow conception of the "working class," which has been used as "proof" that his philosophy is no longer pertinent to today's revolutionary efforts. Of course, the chapter of *Capital* on "The Working Day" depicts factory scenes that have been legislated against in the majority of the industrialized world (although not so in the so-called developing world). Indeed, labor has become more diverse. Although manufacturing jobs continue to exist, many companies in the industrialized world now outsource these jobs to the "developing world," where they find cheaper and more exploitable labor. In the west, especially, the service sector of the economy has expanded tremendously, as has the educated professional workforce that produces intellectual labor. These jobs are often perceived as less dehumanizing and associated with social mobility—even though this labor can also be subject to the same capitalist principles of forced labor and surplus value. Indeed, the capitalist tendency to squeeze the greatest possible amount of labor out of the worker within "the limits of the working day" takes on new proportions as workers are given salaried jobs and manager titles, which can lift legal restrictions to the eight-hour day, with inconsequential pay increases or change in job responsibilities. Nonetheless, these shifts in types of work and the perceived social mobility that comes with them, support narratives of meritocracy and opportunity that are often equated with freedom to pursue one's interests (under capitalism, this is equated with freedom of the market). This diversification of the working class proves only that capitalism is flexible and capable of delivering concessions to the working class in order to sustain itself. At the same time, such concessions show that the working class is capable of bringing capital to its knees; that is, when the system diversifies to make itself appear more humanistic and democratic, it indicates a built-in recognition of the power of collective labor. Indeed, Dunayevskaya articulates the many ways in which the people, through spontaneous uprisings, have garnered concessions, such as the shortening of the working day, and also brought down capitalist regimes. That these have, without exception, been eventually defeated or reversed into a new statist capitalism does not change the fact that the possibility of getting it right exists.

For Marx, the working class referred to the people who are forced to sell their labor power for a wage. As such, the term "working class" or "proletariat" has a far broader applicability than is often assumed. In today's labor market, the proletariat includes teachers, doctors, and other professionals, those who produce intellectual labor, and those who work for nonprofit agencies or the social service sector. Some may argue that this excludes those who do not work within the formal capitalist system, such as the unemployed or those who work in the informal sector, which involves some of the most oppressed and impoverished communities, most of whom are Black, Indigenous, and other People of Color (BIPOC). While these sectors of the population, in and of themselves, do not have the capacity to bring down the processes of production, they certainly embody the fact that pauperization exists. It is also clear that their role in capitalism—as the reserve army of workers capable and willing to take over jobs—helps to keep existing labor from making more demands than the system can handle. The consciousness of the "lumpen proletariat," and their capacity to resist the capitalist ploy of pitting them against existing labor remains crucial to bringing down capitalism.

The working class is reproduced in each successive generation—most working-class people grow up in working-class homes and communities, with few opportunities for social or economic mobility. Yet, the ideological apparatus that creates narratives of meritocracy—especially in the west—is so well ingrained in society that people believe its related antirevolutionary dogma that blames the working class for its lot. Others become complacent, believing that class relations can never be changed or that the alternative may be even more horrific and destructive. The stratification of the working class—with significant differences in economic and social conditions and opportunity structures as well as race and gender relations—become an additional way in which the working class is subdued from joining forces to bring down capital.

Thus, the revolutionary Subject is not born, but *made* in the process of struggle. It is through struggle, the act of confronting injustice and taking risks, that we become courageous warriors for freedom. It is in collective action that we come to recognize our shared oppression and the ways in which this benefits the capitalist class. It is through struggle and its initial gains that we recognize our human capacity to change the world and, thereby, develop the hope that is necessary in order to rise up against injustice and to develop new social relationships. Revolutionary attitudes, values, and beliefs are learned and developed as individuals take collective action in processes that draw upon their human capacities. This "revolutionary practice" involves simultaneously making change within and outside the self. Lebowitz argues that such struggles are also a process of production—but one that challenges the logic of capital. In Lebowitz's words:

> Struggles are a process of production: they produce a different kind of worker, a worker who produces herself or himself as someone whose capacity has grown, whose confidence develops, whose ability to organize and unite expands ... The working class makes itself fit to create the new world. (2012)

It is important to note that the revolutionary Subject can initially be formed in any type of freedom struggle. Any struggle against oppression reveals the revolutionary Subjects' potential consciousness and, with it, their capacity to act. Indeed, Marx himself championed national and ethnic/racial liberation struggles that may, on the surface, have seemed unrelated to the fight against capital. He recognized that these struggles for sovereignty and human rights were, however, not only necessary to the broader struggle against capital but also important struggles to champion in and of themselves.

This is especially important today, at a time in which racism has functioned as one of the greatest dividers of the working class. Donald Trump and his administration, from as early as his campaign for the presidency, revealed to the world just how significant an ideological tool racism is. With outright disdain leveled against all but White men, and fear-inducing tactics to boot, Trump was able to galvanize a conservative base to elect him president. Thus far he has been able to retain this support, even as he imposed hateful and inhuman policies against children and families seeking refuge. Of course, this was surprising only at a time in which many people had been lulled into believing we were close to becoming a racism-free society, given that outright racial attacks, discrimination, and segregation had been made illegal and politically incorrect since the Civil Rights movement of the 1960s. Yet, the reality is that racism, although less visible, has remained a foundational element of U.S. society, evident across every institution.

Marx, in his day, recognized how race, ethnicity, and other markers of difference were effective tools for dividing the working class, breaking up the potential for revolutionary action in class unity. In a letter to his friends Sigfrid Meyer and August Vogt written in 1870, Marx explains this division between the working class of England and Ireland:

> Every industrial and commercial center in England now possesses a working class divided into two camps, English proletarians and Irish proletarians. The English worker hates the Irish worker as a competitor who lowers his standard of life ... He regards himself as a member of the ruling nation, and consequently, he becomes a tool of the English aristocrats and capitalists against Ireland, thus strengthening their domination *over himself*. He cherishes religious, social, and national prejudices against the Irish worker. His attitude towards him is much the same as that of the "poor whites" to the Negroes in the former slave states of the U.S.A. (1870)

Marx continues:

> This antagonism is artificially kept alive and intensified by the press, the pulpit, the comic papers, in short by all the means at the disposal of the ruling classes. This antagonism is the secret of the impotence of the

English working class, despite its organization. It is the secret by which the capitalist class maintains its power. And the latter is quite aware of this. (1870)

At the same time, racism in the United States has become a central and unifying experience among BIPOC communities. Dunayevskaya's analysis of the history of revolutionary struggles across the world led her to note the revolutionary potential of the Black masses, because their experiences of racism and oppression bound them together and created a force to be reckoned with, a collective force of action. This is why Dunayevskaya elaborated the theoretical concept of the Black masses as vanguard.

Paulo Freire also discussed the role of the oppressed in transforming social relations, but was not specific about any particular axis of oppression. For Freire, the oppressed faced a set of interlocking forms of oppression—class, race, gender, and others. When we conceive of the goal of freedom as the "historical vocation" of becoming more fully human, then we see that *every* axis of oppression and exploitation must be challenged. In this process, it really matters not around which axis the revolutionary struggle is built, since they must dialectically incorporate the struggle against all forms of oppression. However, like Marx, Freire too recognized that it would be the oppressed who would pave the path to freedom. He believed that the oppressors were not likely to have either the capacity to see clearly the structures of oppression or the impetus to change social conditions. Freire aptly stated:

> The great humanistic and historical task of the oppressed [is] to liberate themselves and their oppressors as well. (1970: 44)

Freire's work also brings to light that the revolutionary Subject cannot develop in contexts where their humanity is not affirmed. Only when the oppressed recognizes her own humanity—her "force and Reason"—does she become a revolutionary Subject willing and capable of taking action. From this perspective, the revolutionary Subject can be neither the intellectual nor the capitalist who denounces their position—both have historically been complicit in the dehumanization of the working class, whose work has historically been effectively reduced to simpler and simpler forms of manual labor with little opportunity for the utilization of their human mental functions. Only through the simultaneous recognition and application of their full human capacities, do the oppressed become a revolutionary Subject. The intellectual who seeks to "liberate" the working class invokes a "false generosity" that reestablishes dehumanization through a failure to trust in the human capacity of the oppressed.

As Marx noted, it is the very conditions of oppression that create the spaces for contradictions to develop and for struggle to ensue, just as it is in the very heart of capitalist relations that we find non-alienating relations of solidarity among the oppressed that provide the vision for and possibility of the alternative to capitalism. As Dunayevskaya points out, the most important revolutionary movements have been spurred on by those whose conditions of oppression place them in close contact with others facing the same conditions, coming together in spaces where people begin to talk, question, and act against their conditions. These are the spaces where revolutionaries are formed.

THEORY AND PRACTICE

One of the most important contributions that Dunayevskaya made was her formulation of a theory of state capitalism. The theory of state capitalism, which was simultaneously concerned with the inability to develop a dialectical movement from theory to practice and from practice to theory, is based on the articulation of the so-called communism(s) established by Stalin in the Soviet Union and Mao in China—a devastating perversion of Marx's humanism toward totalitarian regimes (Dunayevskaya 2000). This is the potential consequence that Dunayevskaya warns will result from movements designed by intellectuals who perceive themselves superior to the workers. What happens in these situations, as Dunayevskaya shows us, is that the revolutionary activity and philosophy of the proletariat is negated, and the relations of domination that structure capitalist social relations are reproduced. Unlike the democratic processes articulated by Marx as necessary to establish the human Subject through collective control of the means of production by the producers themselves, statist communism(s) became bureaucratic nightmares controlled by the state. Such systems were products of the exacerbation of the monopoly rule of capital and possessed an inevitable tendency toward dictatorship at the hands of those who controlled the state.

Dunayevskaya argued for a dialectical approach to the question of philosophy and practice. Adrienne Rich said that Dunayevskaya's work was "drenched in the conviction that while thinking and action are not the same, they must continually readdress and renew each other" (1991: xi). This "conviction" speaks to Marx's critique of the hierarchical division of labor, the separation of mental and manual tasks, such that workers become mere instruments of production, alienated from the essence of what it means to be human—namely, the use of their intellectual capacities. The worker is reduced to an appendage of a machine, performing compartmentalized tasks in rote that require minimal thought for an eight-hour day. This division of labor sits at the heart of capitalist relations of production, the alienation it creates naturalizing class relations through the ideology that class is a function of people's varying capacities, with workers incapable of the mental labor necessary to reap more fully the presumed benefits of the capitalist system.

Dunayevskaya's concern, which remains central to building an alternative to capitalism, is with the question of organization and the role of intellectuals in revolutionary action. The same question haunted revolutionary organizations as far back as Hegel and Marx. The question boils down to the issue of who possesses the impetus and insights necessary for planning and executing the revolutionary activity that will challenge oppressive forces and also develop a new alternative. Such revolutionary activity must engage in a democratic process that negates the relations of domination and the division of labor that are at the heart of class societies and that are reflected not merely in the ownership of the means of production but also in the social relations that define gender relations, race relations, and ultimately, all human relations.

In Marx's time, Pierre-Joseph Proudhon and Ferdinand Lassalle, both important members of the first international could not conceive that the workers would be able to set the agenda for revolutionary action. As Dunayevskaya (2000) notes, these intellectuals could not recognize that revolutionary philosophy does not come out of a mental abstraction but rather is rooted in the actual lived experiences of those who suffer capitalism's greatest impact. It is the workers, whose impetus for change necessarily sets the stage for revolution. But these arrogant men could not see that they could learn from the workers who they believed to be beneath them; for Proudhon, Lassalle and their followers, theory and philosophy was not a capacity of all human beings but rather only of a select few.

Thus, Proudhon opposed mass movements because they did not align with his own intellectual Ricardian thinking, which had little basis in what was actually happening in the factory. Instead, he proposed developing "people's banks" which would give free credit and unite labor and property. His school of radical socialists believed that if attitudes and values for justice and equality were cultivated, property would become available to all. Similarly, Lassalle "could not rid himself of the concept of the 'backwardness' of labor" (Dunayevskaya 2000: 74). He believed science was "classless" and that he could represent both science (or the intellectual) and the worker. Lassalle, as Dunayevskaya pointedly put it, foreshadowed "the state socialist administrator of our day" (2000: 77). Dunayevskaya attributed the failure of statist communism(s) to establish a true alternative to capitalism to the elitism of the intellectuals who failed to recognize, learn from, and work with the actual workers—those whose alienation provided the experiential element which often eludes those who are removed from the daily reality of working life and from the positive impetus to move toward revolutionary activity and philosophy.

Dunayevskaya points out that without the worker, intellectuals can only grasp the revolutionary movement as an abstraction. They cannot know, in actuality, what is possible. Only the lived reality of the workers creates real movement. Only the workers know when they are materially and psychologically ready for revolution; when their hopes and spirits are such that large numbers of them will be willing to stop production; what the psychological and material consequences of such stoppage will be; and how they will find support and build morale to continue the struggle even in the face of hunger, or worse. Indeed, a certain level of material security is sometimes necessary for people to embark upon striking or other activities that may have a negative material impact.

Perhaps more importantly, the workers' experience with production allows them the capacity to theorize the process of production: what aspects of existing production are consistent with supporting a humanist alternative to capitalism; how to create relations that are non-alienating, and thus prevent an alternative that merely replicates the horrifying oppressions that capitalism creates and/or exacerbates. As Dunayevskaya wrote in 1958:

> ... the workers have been acting out Hegel's Absolute Idea and have thus concretized and deepened the movement from practice to theory. On the other hand, the movement from theory is nearly at a standstill because it blinds itself to the movement from practice. (2000: 37)

Dunayevskaya accurately depicts the typical role of the intellectual in revolution:

> The crying inequality of distribution, arising from this method of production, could not but arouse the sympathy of the intellectual for the proletariat. Being outside of production the intellectual could not see that the working class had power to overthrow the contradictory conditions of production. For the intellectual the proletariat existed only as a suffering class. (2000: 48–49)

Indeed, intellectuals, sometimes called "armchair philosophers" by activists, often presume that they can find answers to the world's problems by combing through theoretical and historical accounts of particular phenomena. While this approach can certainly be helpful, it cannot anticipate the actual movement of workers in production; that is, the real and ideological challenges, resistance, beliefs, relationships, and organizing efforts of the only group that can actually stop and overthrow capitalist relations of production. Intellectuals often create organizations that fail to include actual workers or fail to create the spaces where the experiences, knowledge, insights, and theories of workers are shared and recognized as critical components to revolutionary practice, which includes having some insights into the possibilities for transformation and what alternatives workers desire and are perceived as possible or worth moving toward.

Dunayevskaya (2000: 73) points out, quoting Marx, that intellectuals are often separated from the working class "as widely as heaven from earth" and that "they are consequently driven theoretically to the same tasks and solutions to which material interests and social position practically drive [the petty bourgeoisie]." Furthermore, their lack of faith in the working classes often results in "radical intellectuals [who are] forever planning to do something *for* the worker, substituting their activity or at least planning for the self-activity of the working class" (2000: 73). In this sense, the intellectual, even when well-meaning, offers a "false generosity" that at the very least signals the same alienating relations that characterize capitalist social relations and at worst, when unchecked and perhaps unknowingly, may thwart activity that actually has the potential to negatively impact capitalism.

It is thus the dialectic that makes Marx's work a humanist philosophy. The dialectic insists on the unity of theory and practice (or praxis), and on the recognition of the worker as human Subject. Without the recognition of their humanity—their concrete activity for change (which involves movement both in consciousness and reality)—the intellectual's theorizing remains disconnected from the actual concrete conditions and desires of those who are actually moving. A dialectical treatment recognizes that workers are both actively engaged in struggle and that they *theorize* about their activity, and that the so-called intellectual must be grounded in struggle through active participation. Dunayevskaya writes of Marx:

> It was no accident that his Communist Manifesto was published on the eve of the 1848 revolutions. He could do this because of his idea of theory as the generalization of the instinctive striving of the proletariat for a new social order, a truly human society, a striving that arises out of the dialectic of the economic process which at each stage produces what Marx called the new passions and forces for the next social order. Although no one can see the concrete form of the new society until it actually appears, Marx's vision did anticipate the future society. He was not left behind, not because of his individual genius, but because of his dialectical method of uniting theory and practice. He thereby gave the intellectuals who aligned themselves with the proletariat as a political tendency that new human dimension to enable each to become as tall as the proletariat straightened up to its full height in the creation of the new society. (2000: 65)

As Dunayevskaya points out, Marx not only kept his eyes glued to the workers' movements but also participated in them. Marx was fully attentive to the struggles of his day and he was especially engaged with the Civil War in the United States and the struggle for the abolition of slavery, which he perceived "a world upheaval" (Marx, quoted in Dunayevskaya 2000: 82). Marx recognized American slavery as particularly atrocious and did not lump it together, as other Marxists of the time, with "all slavery, wage and chattel," instead recognizing the racial dimension as inexcusable under any form of class struggle (Dunayevskaya 2000: 84). Marx writes:

> In the United States of America every independent movement of workers was paralyzed so long as slavery disfigured a part of the republic. Labor cannot emancipate itself in the white skin where in the black it is branded. But out of the death of slavery a new life arose. The first fruit of the civil war was the eight hours agitation, that ran with the seven leagued boots

of the locomotive from the Atlantic to the pacific, from New England to California. (1972: 275)

Thus, Marx recognized the significance that the Civil War had on labor more generally and its foundational role in the struggle to shorten the working day. Marx derived theory from the "masses in motion." It was by following the revolts of his day—the Civil War in the United States, the Paris Commune, the movement of the Fenians in Ireland—and later in his life examining the history of movement among non-western peoples in his *Ethnological Notebooks*, that he developed a philosophy of revolution.

THE "WOMAN QUESTION" AND THE "BLACK DIMENSION"

Following Marx's example, Dunayevskaya examined the social upheavals of her time. In particular, she was attentive to women's roles in revolutionary movements, noting that as opposed to what is typically assumed, women had a strong presence in revolutionary movements that was not only perceptible in terms of force but also in terms of Reason. Dunayevskaya capitalized the term Reason to emphasize her challenge to common assumptions of women as passive supporters of revolution and, instead, to articulate their very active *and* theoretical contributions. She also declared the *Black masses as Vanguard*.

> Far from Black being a detour, we know that it has been the keystone of all of American history. The first Woman's Rights Movement arose on the shoulders of the Blacks; that is to say, in working with Blacks against slavery, middle-class American women learned the value of organizations and established the first Woman's Rights Movement. (Dunayevskaya 1991: 102–103)

We see this argument especially in *Rosa Luxemburg, Women's Liberation, and Marx's Philosophy of Revolution*, wherein Dunayevskaya points out the revolutionary activity of Black women, in Africa and in the United States, honoring their strength of character in standing up to both Black men and White women and in doing so demonstrating unequivocally their "revolutionary force and Reason."

In *Rosa Luxemburg, Women's Liberation, and Marx's Philosophy of Revolution*, Dunayevskaya also articulates the force and Reason of Rosa Luxemburg, not only in terms of her contributions to Marx's theory, but especially as the first Marxist to take on the task of vociferously critiquing the horrors of colonialism and imperialism and also in recognizing that the spontaneous activity of the masses, especially the general strike, was crucial to revolution. While Dunayevskaya is critical of Luxemburg on a number of theoretical issues, she takes up Luxemburg's contributions and gives life to the people for whom Luxemburg advocated. Dunayevskaya points out that the people's spontaneous eruptions are not just the machinations of a disorganized "mob" but, rather, that they are spurred on by their ideas—ideas that emerge from their location as workers struggling for better conditions. While Luxemburg repudiated the treatment of Indigenous peoples under colonialism, she failed to support anti-colonial liberation. While perhaps not always dialectical in relation to philosophy and activity, Luxemburg correctly perceived the important role that women could play in revolution. Dunayevskaya points out that although Luxemburg did not call out the chauvinism within her own party and perhaps did not recognize fully the ways in which she (and women generally) was ridiculed by her male counterparts, she worked closely with Clara Zetkin to develop a socialist feminism and to bring women into Marxist politics (Dunayevskaya 1991).

At the same time that Dunayevskaya recognized women as Subjects— she remained true to her belief that philosophy needed to be closely connected to and, in fact, to follow the actual revolutionary movements of the people. Her historical analysis of women's contributions to revolution also led her to recognize the important role that Black women had played in the United States and in Africa. Dunayevskaya traces not only the force of Black women, noting that it was a Black woman seeking abolition, Maria Stewart, who was the first American-born woman ever to speak in public, but also that the ideas of these early Black women revolutionaries held insights and significance that reflected their lived experiences. In particular, she points out that Sojourner Truth had not only negated her object position as the master's property by changing her name (once freed) but that she had also chosen a name that reflected the future she sought. Her new chosen name reflected *the future*—the freedom that comes from negation (1991).

Dunayevskaya engaged in a systematic analysis of revolutionary movements around the world, and from this she articulated the theory that the Black masses had been the vanguard of revolution that had changed the face of American civilization (2003). Especially significant to Dunayevskaya's articulation of the role of the Black masses as vanguard was the struggle for abolition, which evidenced people from multiple paths moving in unity. As she writes of the Abolitionists:

> They were inter-racial and in a slave society preached and practiced Negro equality. They were distinguished as well for inspiring, aligning with, and fighting for equality of women in an age when the women had neither the right to the ballot nor to property nor to divorce. They were inter-nationalist, covering Europe with their message, and bringing back to this country the message of the Irish Freedom Fighters. (Dunayevskaya 2003: 34)

As noted above, the Civil War had also led to the struggle for the eight-hour day, a struggle that was fought on numerous fronts and brought together workers across the world. Certainly, continuous and subsequent struggles for Black Civil Rights have led the way for numerous gains for other groups who have followed in the wake of the Black commu-nity. The Civil Rights Movement of the 1950s–1960s, initiated by Black activists and their allies, as seen in the Montgomery Bus Boycott and the Freedom Riders, brought down Jim Crow laws and legal segregation but also initiated the anti-war movement and led to a string of other move-ments and demands, including the next wave of the feminist movement, the Black Panther Party, the Chicano movement, bilingual education, and affirmative action.

Dunayevskaya's articulation of Black masses as vanguard was not based solely on the impetus and Reason of Black Americans in the United States, however, but also had an international focus, recognizing that the movement from theory was equally important and rejected any notion that communism could develop in one country in isolation from others. Dunayevskaya's Marxist theoretical development allowed her to see that in a global capitalist economy, a socialist revolution would eventually need to become an international effort. Thus, Dunayevskaya examined the Black masses and their revolutionary activity and potential in Africa and other contexts, noting their significant resistance to western imperialism. She specifically discusses "The Women's War" that took place in 1929 in Nigeria, wherein 10,000 Igbo women organized themselves across tribal lines to challenge the British tax on women but also the male chiefs that had sided with the British, in what they called "making war" or "sit-ting on a man." While 50 women were killed and 50 others wounded, the women won this battle and taxes were not imposed on them. For

Dunayevskaya, the Black dimension referred to the specific character to the alienation of Black workers, one that added creative passions and Reason (Dunayevskaya 2003).

SPONTANEITY AND ORGANIZATION IN TODAY'S MOVEMENTS: WOMEN OF COLOR AS VANGUARD

Regarding our further development to freedom, we must turn once again to the Hegelian dialectic and to Marx's dialectical materialism. The question of how to prevent our revolutions from turning into their opposites, requires understanding the dialectic, not just in terms of what we chose to challenge but of *how* we seek to engage with the various tensions between philosophy and practice.

Related to the tension between theory and practice is the tension between organization and spontaneity. The perception of spontaneous movements as dramatic eruptions among the people that lack theoretical rigor, direction, or organization is again an articulation made with little attention to the concrete development of movements—i.e., to what actually is happening among the people as they rise up against the horrors they experience. A careful examination of historical movements demonstrates that the majority of so-called spontaneous eruptions were in fact philosophically grounded. That is, there had been a significant activity that had raised the consciousness among the people as to the causes of their oppression and of the potential impact and potential outcomes of deciding to rise up. Important examples of such philosophical development have been well documented among the women who spearheaded the Paris Commune and the Russian Revolution of 1917. In both cases, attempts to describe these movements as simply activist social forces without Reason, have been clearly challenged by important historical accounts that document significant prior political activity among the people (Monzó 2019).

The recent Occupy Movement in the United States, for example, has been accused of failing because of their lack of organization and/or leadership. However, there is significant political organizing in the United States on the left that can be said to have powerfully influenced the people that joined this movement. To suggest that there was no philosophy in such spontaneous revolution is to dismiss the theoretical rigor of the people most affected by oppressive forces—who live out the daily injustices of our capitalist system. Jobin-Leeds and AgitArt (2016) have pointed out that it was not the lack of theoretical analysis that brought down Occupy but the inability to recognize the racial and the gender divide among the protestors. They further discuss that although claiming itself leaderless, some Occupy members have suggested that there was indeed a de facto leadership of White men who supported a class-only analysis, ignoring the significant differences among the 99 percent.

However, whether the philosophical grounding of such movements will lead to immediately improved conditions, greater mass movements, the end to major historical forms of oppression, and/or a socialist alternative depends on the particular type of organization that is influencing and/or is connected to the movement. The philosophical orientation that the movement espouses, the vision for short and long-term changes, whether democratic processes are employed, how diversity of gender, race, sexual orientation, religion, and other identities will be incorporated, not only in terms of the people involved but of the ideas and concrete activity that informs these ideas, what checks to power are created, are just a few of the issues that must be worked out for any long-term social change. Thus, organization and philosophy are critical components of revolutionary social movements. The grounding of these organizations in the realities of the people—following their lead, recognizing how and when their passions are ignited, understanding who can lead the way and what the limits may be—is critical. This dialectical relationship between spontaneity and organization is a significant factor in the development and achievement of any revolution.

The dialectic shows us that these binaries between mental and manual labor, philosophy and practice, and organization and spontaneity are more appearance than reality; that, in fact, all mental labor involves some form of practice to be "rational" and all practice engages some mental activity. Of course, these binaries have been created to support capitalist relations of production and replicated in many ways across the various institutions of civil society that support the ruling class. The dialectic teaches us that the negation of these binaries and the creation of a unity of presumed opposites is what can lead us toward a humanizing pedagogy that will help us move toward freedom.

The movement from theory to practice and from practice to theory requires, following Dunayevskaya and Marx before her, that we examine today's movements closely, noting the liberatory proclivities across movements and countries, applying our philosophical articulations to both understand these movements, and collaborate with them so as to co-construct theory in light of the actual forces and thinking at play.

In light of this process, there are some key themes of today's movements that stand out. One of these is the increasing evidence of women as active makers of these revolutions and women's liberation as central to or connected to their other goals. Black, Indigenous, and other Women of Color, especially, are exhibiting great revolutionary thinking and activity, understanding that women tend to engage the world differently than men, and also the racialized and other dimensions of their positions in the world. Movements such as Black Lives Matter, the Zapatistas, Idle No More, Rojava, and the numerous Im(migrant) rights groups in the United States have all either originated with Women of Color coming together or have been significantly impacted by their participation and decision-making and have been instrumental in shaping the movement's goals and activities. There is no denying that women are at the heart of these movements, and that their voices are clearly present in terms of both force and Reason (Monzó 2019).

Black Lives Matter, first organized in response to the police killings of unarmed Black men, has evolved to develop articulations about how Black women, Indigenous and other Women of Color (including Transgender) are also disproportionately mistreated, and calling for both analysis of and interventions into the ways in which the police perceive and interact with racialized women (Taylor 2016). Current uprisings have further radicalized BLM to demand for defunding the police. The Zapatista movement, a two-decades-old revolution with autonomous territory in Chiapas, Mexico, was initiated by both men and women. However, women have played a significant role from the outset, transforming their lives within their own communities and on their own terms, without the need to adhere to outside (or western) definitions of feminism (Klein 2015). Idle No More was started by three Indigenous women and one non-Indigenous woman in response to the issue of land and water rights of First Nation communities in Canada but has since evolved into one of the strongest Indigenous rights organizations, reaching across borders to the United States, New Zealand, and Ukraine. According to Caven (2013), what has made this movement so powerful is that people have shared their stories of pain and colonialism online, allowing others to make an emotional and spiritual connection. Although Idle No More includes many male members, it too is predominantly a women's movement that remains closely tied to the grassroots. Caven (2013) explains:

"The nature of the fluid, nonviolent, and unifying movement is one that both reflects and engages women's agency."

The Rojava Revolution, in Syrian Kurdistan, is a revolution that began with women's involvement from its inception, and that has since become a beacon of feminist activity, bringing both equal women's participation within the People's Defense Units (YPG), which includes women and men, and the Women's Defense Units, which give exclusive voice to women on issues that pertain predominantly to women or in which they have key interests (Gupta and Taylor 2017).

Another important element that seems to characterize the movements of today is public identification as inclusive organizations that seek goals for equality and justice across differences. They are also characterized by the notion of "intersectional identities," something that has contributed to attracting people from a wide spectrum of identities. For Black Lives Matter, intersectionality has been a key founding element, given that the founders represent multiple identities—Black, LGBTQ, working class, and Latinx, with important connections to the interests of immigrant communities. The Rojava Revolution is also strongly grounded in the idea of inclusiveness of ethnic, language, cultural, and religious diversity. This is important for a revolution that seeks justice and peace in a zone that has been riddled with war and tensions for decades, and whose goals are to meet the basic needs and equality of all (Iltis and Munckton 2015). Likewise, Im(migrant) rights organization are situated across racial, ethnic, Indigenous, refugee, documented and undocumented, gender, and sexual identities. Although some tensions exist between these groups, they are building coalitions that widen their base of support. The fact that the Trump administration has targeted families by separating asylum seekers from their children and detaining them as criminals, has drawn indignant criticism from mother's groups and family advocates that cut across most other identities. These connections across diverse identities make it clear that the class-reductionist Marxist critique of "identity politics" must be rethought in light of what it actually means to the people who are making revolution. Rather than argue against identity politics because it can divide us, an examination of these movements suggests that the opposite is true—that the intersections of our identities can garner support from multiple communities. Furthermore, it shows that BIPOC communities understand "colorblindness" to be racist and instead prefer to be "seen" through their racial positionings and that this "recognition" can bring people together by creating empathy for their diverse oppressions (Monzó 2019).

A third element of contemporary social movements is the recognition that the "leadership," as has traditionally taken shape in previous revolutionary efforts, has been generally male and White and has kept Black, Indigenous, and other Women of Color outside of the realm of decision-making. In the socialist revolutions of the past, the leadership has often mistakenly argued that women's liberation would follow automatically, as a natural result of bringing down capitalism or colonialism. Other times, it has been discussed as an "issue" that would be addressed after the system was brought down in order to avoid dividing the people by gender. In this way, women's liberation has often taken a "back seat," relative to what the male leadership has determined to be "important." In fact, often upon the triumph of these revolutions, women have been relegated to less than equal status, or their interests have continued to be seen as secondary to other national interests. Beyond gender, other forms of oppression (including racism, and LGBTQIA concerns) have generally been absent from discussion. Thus, contemporary movements, founded and/or held up by Women of Color, are increasingly defining themselves as "leaderless," or practicing "horizontalism"—a process of decision-making through a system of decentralized direct democracy (Monzó 2019). Marxist-Humanism can be quite useful in developing such praxis, since one of its central principles is the dialectical relationship between class and all forms of oppression. Marxist-Humanists argue that class reductionism is undialectical and also fails to recognize the movement from practice to theory.

CONCLUSION

Raya Dunayevskaya, with her insistence on the unity of philosophy and activity, and spontaneity and organization, has left a legacy for us to carry forth into the next generation with the keen awareness of the need to not only observe and listen to the workers, whose daily action reflects their oppression, but also to believe in and trust their Reason such that our philosophy can be grounded in the reality of the exploited classes whose interests and experiences have yet to be fully grasped. We who have studied Hegel, Marx, and Dunayevskaya, and non-western philosophers and theorists, such as Frantz Fanon, Paolo Freire, and Gloria E. Anzaldúa have an important place too, especially in helping these movements to

develop creatively and overcome the contradictions facing them. So long
as these theories are understood in light of the workers' thinking and
activity, we can perhaps see how their activity connects with the past and
with the future.

In order to grasp what is happening in today's most important movements, we must take heed of the revolutionary force and Reason of Black,
Indigenous and other Women of Color. They are too few in our organizations, and too often silenced in ways that have yet to be grasped. An
important challenge for us as Marxist-Humanists is to create the social
spaces that can draw in and draw on racialized women's unique epistemological diversity. Only then can our philosophical renderings capture
today's revolutionary activity so that together with them we can move in
the direction of freedom, where we can experience dignity and justice and
love for ourselves, each other, and the Earth that sustains us—where we
can be fully human.

REFERENCES

Cavens, Febna. 2013. "Being Idle No More: The Women Behind the Movement." *Cultural Survival*, March. https://www.culturalsurvival.org/public
ations/cultural-survival-quarterly/being-idle-no-more-women-behind-mov
ement.
Dunayevskaya, Raya. 1991. *Rosa Luxemburg, Women's Liberation, and Marx's
Philosophy of Revolution*. Urbana: University of Illinois Press.
———. 2000. *Marxism and Freedom: From 1776 Until Today*. Amherst, NY:
Humanity Books.
———. 2003. *American Civilization on Trial: Black Masses as Vanguard*.
Chicago, IL: News and Letters.
Freire, Paulo. [1970] 2000. *Pedagogy of the Oppressed, 30th Anniversary Edition*.
New York: Bloomsbury.
Gupta, Rahila and Kimmie Taylor. 2017. "Women on the Front at Raqqa: An
Interview with Kimmie Taylor." *50.50: Gender, Sexuality and Social Justice*,
February 14. https://www.open-democracy.net/en/5050/women-on-front-
at-raqqa/.
Hegel, Georg Wilhelm Friedrich. 1977. *Hegel's Phenomenology of Spirit*. Trans-
lated by A. V. Miller. London: Oxford University Press.
———. [1812] 2010. *The Science of Logic*. Edited and translated by George di
Giovanni. New York: Cambridge University Press.
Iltis, Tony and Stuart Munckton. 2015. "Rojava's Democratic Feminist Revolution a Source of Hope Among Horror." *Truthout*, November 22. http://
www.truth-out.org/opinion/item/33752-rojava-s-democratic-feminist-rev
olution-a-source-of-hope-among-horror.

Jobin-Leeds, Greg and AgitArte. 2016. *When We Fight We Win! Twenty-First-Century Social Movements and the Activists That Are Transforming Our World.* New York: The New Press.

Klein, Hilary. 2015. *Compañeras: Zapatista Women's Stories.* New York: Seven Stories Press.

Larkin, Mark. 2017. "What Is a 'Universalizing Politics' and Why Does the Left Need It?" *Truthout*, August 27. https://truthout.org/articles/what-is-a-universalizing-politics-and-why-does-the-left-need-it/.

Lebowitz, Michael A. 2012. "What Makes the Working Class a Revolutionary Subject?" *Monthly Review* 64, no. 7. https://monthlyreview.org/2012/12/01/what-makes-the-working-class-a-revolutionary-subject/.

Marx, Karl. 1870. "Letter to Sigfrid Meyer and August Vogt, April 9, 1870." In *Marxists Internet Archive.* https://www.marxists.org/archive/marx/works/1870/letters/70_04_09.htm.

———. 1972. *Karl Marx: On America and the Civil War.* New York: McGraw-Hill.

Marx, Karl and Friedrich Engels. 1998. *The German Ideology.* New York: Prometheus Books.

Monzó, Lilia D. 2019. *A Revolutionary Subject: Pedagogy of Women of Color and Indigeneity.* New York: Peter Lang.

Rich, Adrienne. 1991. Forward to *Rosa Luxemburg, Women's Liberation, and Marx's Philosophy of Revolution, 2nd Edition.* By Raya Dunayevskaya. Chicago: University of Illinois Press.

Taylor, Keeanga-Yamahtta. 2016. *From #BlackLivesMatter to Black Liberation.* Chicago, IL: Haymarket Books.

PART III

Connections and Debates

CHAPTER 9

Marxism and Freedom: Apropos of Raya Dunayevskaya's Book

Rodolfo Mondolfo

By introducing Raya Dunayevskaya's book to readers in Italy,[1] Gaetano Arfé nostalgically evokes the polemics among Italian socialists at the turn of the century, which were animated by a sincere and unprejudiced concern for truth, that united Marxists from different tendencies, even with all their reciprocal differences.[2] Moreover, maybe what linked us to each other was nothing less than the fact that all of us understood Marxism as Humanism; that is, we were already conscious of the central importance of the problem of man in Marx, even at a time that the Marx-Engels writings of 1844–1845—as yet unpublished —had not appeared to document this more decisively, and were even believed to have been irredeemably lost.

Given this Humanist interpretation, I remember that even as early as 1912—in a study entitled *Rousseau nella formazione della coscienza*

Rodolfo Mondolfo: Deceased.

R. Mondolfo (✉)
Buenos Aires, Argentina

© The Author(s) 2021
K. B. Anderson et al. (eds.), *Raya Dunayevskaya's Intersectional Marxism*, Marx, Engels, and Marxisms,
https://doi.org/10.1007/978-3-030-53717-3_9

moderna[3]—I had recalled the essential bond that binds Marx to the Genevan thinker with regard to the idea of the *alienation* of man. Rousseau did not use such a term, which Marx drew directly from Hegel (*Phenomenology of Spirit*); but the connection between that idea and the division of labor—which reduces the worker to a fraction of a man, wresting from him the possibility of being free—was derived undoubtedly from Rousseau, with the resulting demand and revindication for the integral unity of man: *make man whole!* Furthermore, it is from Rousseau himself that the idea of the alienation of labor, resulting from its mechanization, must have reached Hegel—an idea that the latter expressed in his youthful writings (1801), still unpublished at that time, and consequently unknown to Marx. It is only recently that these writings have been studied by Georg Lukács (*The Young Hegel*, 1948) and by Herbert Marcuse (*Reason and Revolution*, 1954).[4] Raya Dunayevskaya aptly cited from the latter the following passages: "The more mechanized labor becomes, the less value it has and the more the individual must toil... The value of labor decreases in the same proportion as the productivity of labor increases... The faculties of the individual are infinitely restricted, and the consciousness of the factory worker is degraded to the lowest level of dullness" (2000: 33).[5]

Marx did not know these Hegelian writings, but he very well knew, as I have pointed out elsewhere, the echo that the ideas of Rousseau had found in Vidal, Proudhon, Carlyle, etc.—all of whom were preoccupied with the reduction of the workers to *hands*. That relationship to Rousseau deserves to be pointed out especially today, when, with the publication of the *Economic and Philosophical Manuscripts of 1844* and *The German Ideology*, there has been a return to the Humanist interpretation of Marx, recognizing the relevance that human freedom—destroyed by the alienation of labor—has for man.

A sign of that recognition is the recent simultaneous appearance of several studies on the subject. After examining these studies by writers with different orientations, such as Raya Dunayevskaya, Erich Fromm, A. Sabetti, etc., I agree with them. But while (similarly to me) Sabetti has focused particularly on the genesis of Marx's Humanism through the relation with the Hegelian Left (though without thereby neglecting the influence of Hegel or that of the historical process, nor that of the proletarian movements—even while differing from me in his evaluation of Feuerbach's Humanism), Fromm has studied Marx's Humanism in and of itself; and Dunayevskaya, who also initially posits the problem of its genesis, has—in connection with the latter—been exclusively preoccupied with the theoretical influence of Hegelian philosophy and dialectic, and with the practical influence of the proletarian class movements. The various studies thus complement one another.

For Dunayevskaya, the modern age is the daughter of the three eighteenth-century revolutions (the Industrial, the American, and the French), revolutions that also gave birth to Hegelian philosophy with its dialectic and its process of negation, through which Marx understood all revolutionary dynamism.

Hegel had seen history as a chain of moments in the development of Spirit's freedom: the stages of development of humanity were for him stages of the struggle for freedom; Marx transferred that vision to the real world, to the world of labor and laborers. Following in the footsteps of Locke (who is always forgotten in this respect), classical political economy had placed the source of all value in labor—but which, as Marx writes, theorized "production for production's sake" (2000: 45)—and yet was disoriented by the emergence of crises and class struggles. At the same time, Utopian Socialism (especially with Proudhon) wanted to derive—from the principle that labor is the source of value—the conclusion that the fruits of labor rightly belong to the worker, believing that "a just idea" sufficed, and not seeing (according to Marx's reproach of Proudhon) that only struggle by the masses can resolve the conflict between the forces and the relations of production. This was Marx's own intuition, which was suggested to him by the new proletarian impulses that exploded in the Silesian weavers' insurrection in 1844, the same year that Marx was writing the *Economic and Philosophical Manuscripts*.

Classical political economy had brought to light the value of labor, but it was imperative to take the laborer—the man whose living labor had been *alienated* by its subjugation to dead labor (machines and capital), and who has thereby lost all light—directly into account. Therefore, the Hegelian dialectic had to be transferred from the sphere of the Idea to the world of real men: man must not be alienated and dismembered because of the division between mental and manual labor, but must instead reconquer his integrity in their reunification—"the free individuality of the laborer himself" (2000: 61).

The demand for a full and free human personality is affirmed in the *Manuscripts* of 1844: "We must above all avoid setting up 'the society' as an abstraction opposed to the individual. The individual *is* the social entity" (2000: 65). But in referring to the individual, Marx understands the personality, whose respect and development he reclaims: not against other men or against society, but in harmony and solidarity with them. Thus the designation of *individualism*, which not only Dunayevskaya, but also Fromm, apply to Marx's theory is evidently unwarranted: it is a *Humanism* that aspires to a society in which "the free development of each is the condition for the free development of all" (2000: 65), and for that reason makes evident (as Dunayevskaya summarizes) that "the abolition of private property inaugurates an essentially new social system only if free individuals, and not 'the society,' become masters of the socialized means of production."[6] It is because of this requirement, Dunayevskaya points out, that Marxian Humanism is clearly antithetical to the deformation of Bolshevism in practice.

Dunayevskaya does not dwell on proofs of Marxian Humanism from the works from 1843 to 1846 that accompany the *Manuscripts* of 1844 (*Critique of Hegel's Philosophy of Right*, *The Holy Family*, *The German Ideology*), but instead she sets out to demonstrate the continuity of that orientation in the subsequent works, beginning with the *Communist Manifesto*, which reveals the full understanding Marx had of the proletarian revolution of 1848—an understanding that was lacking in the utopians Blanqui, Blanc, and Proudhon. In the 1848 revolution, the proletariat acquired a consciousness of itself as a class, which the intellectuals could not understand. Marx understood it, but not Lassalle, whom Marx made the object of bitter and sometimes unjust criticisms, which Dunayevskaya wrongly repeats without any reservation.[7]

From Marx's perceptiveness concerning the real struggles of workers flows (and this is one of the most interesting parts in Dunayevskaya's analysis) some essential developments of his theory, the impulse for which he draws not "from the sheer development of his own thoughts" but instead "from living workers changing living reality by their actions" (2000: 81). The American Civil War, the foundation of the First International, and the workers' struggles for the shortening of the working day all have crucial importance for the development of Marx's thought and writings. It is in this influence from the historical action of real men, that the humanist character of Marx's doctrine is confirmed.

Undoubtedly, Marx's most important investigation develops—as it appears in the title of the incomplete *Critique of Political Economy*—with the theories of Smith and Ricardo as its point of departure. When he interrupts the *Critique* to dedicate himself instead to the writing of *Capital*, however, he transforms the history of theory into the history of class struggle, and he develops the chapter on the working day. The workers' struggle for the shortening of the working day illuminates the problem from a new angle: it is not only a question of reclaiming surplus value but also of the liberation of the worker.

"In place of the pompous catalogue of the 'inalienable rights of man'," writes Marx, "comes the modest Magna Carta of a legally limited working day which shall make clear when the time which the worker sells is ended, and when his own begins" (2000: 89). The worker, reduced to an instrument (*hand*) during work hours, reclaims a return in daily life to his quality as a *man*—as a free person with possibilities for development.

Humanism is reaffirmed, drawing inspiration and stimulus from the concrete action of the workers in defense of their own humanity. And no less decisive for Marx is the historical experience of the Paris Commune, whose action confronted the problem of workers' self-government in production. "The political rule of the producer," writes Marx, "cannot coexist with the perpetuation of his social slavery" (2000: 97). For that reason, the workers of the Commune took on the task of running the factories through "the cooperative association of the workers employed in them," in order to transform the means of production into means of "freely associated labor," which put an end to hierarchical distinctions. If it was not to be a fraud and a snare, Marx concluded, cooperative production must remain under the control of the workers (*The Civil War in France*). In this manner, the historical experience of the Commune revealed to Marx the way to achieve an association in which the free development of each becomes the condition of the free development of all.

This ideal of "a society in which the full and free development of each individual is the ruling principle" (2000: 125) is reaffirmed in *Capital*, and constitutes the humanistic inspiration that, according to Dunayevskaya, gives the work "its profundity and its force and direction" (2000: 125).

Beginning with the principle that all of human history can be reconstructed through the development of labor—because man is essentially *homo faber*—Marx demonstrates how labor is transformed—from the exteriorization of human creativity to its negation—when the worker must sell his labor-power; i.e., transform himself into a commodity. In this transformation, the power of labor—faced with constant capital (plant, machines, raw material)—becomes variable capital, the producer of surplus value: thus, accumulated labor dominates living labor, which is compelled to produce more and more, as it is intensified in order to compensate for the shortening of the working day.

In the chapter on the general law of capitalist accumulation, Marx writes: "All means for the development of production transform themselves into means of domination over, and exploitation of, the producers; they mutilate the laborer into a fragment of a man, degrade him to the level of an appendage of a machine, destroy every remnant of charm in his work and turn it into a hated toil (…). It follows, therefore, that in proportion as capital is accumulated, the lot of the laborer, *be his payment high or low*, must grow worse" (2000: 124–125). From there comes the resistance of the workers which—Marx says in the same chapter—tends to replace that fragment of a human being "by the fully developed individual, fit for a variety of labors, ready to face any change in production, and to whom the different social functions he performs, are but so many modes of giving free scope to his own natural and acquired powers" (2000: 119).

This essential inspiration in Marx—on account of which Dunayevskaya states, "Human freedom is the principle toward which he worked, and for that reason and his philosophy can most fittingly be called a new Humanism" (2000: 148)—is confirmed with an interesting analysis of the process of the composition of *Capital*, of its logic and its end, and of the drafting of the second and third volumes. Moreover, it has already been revealed that the name Humanism corresponds to Marxism not only on account of the end that it proposes itself (human freedom), but also on account of the derivation of its doctrines from the examples of concrete, historical human actions; i.e., of the real struggles of the proletarian masses. However, this interpretation of Marxist doctrine should not be translated into a dogmatic rule, according to which any revolutionary impulse or mass movement—even when arising where a proletariat does not yet exist—must always be transformed into a directing and constitutive element of socialist doctrine and action.

When Dunayevskaya reproaches the Second International and the German Social Democracy for not having incorporated into their own program and activity the new impulses of the year 1905 (that is, not only the first spontaneous creation of the soviet—which, as she recognizes, was not considered important by either Rosa Luxemburg, or even Lenin himself—but also the movements of backward Africa and the Zulu rebellion) she seems to replace the duty of sympathy and solidarity that every socialist party must feel toward any oppositional movement of the oppressed that demands its own freedom, with the possibility or duty of seeing in those independence movements a realization of socialism and an orienting element for the socialist program. She thus forgets that Marxist Humanism—which is realistic—is tied to a critical-practical conception of history that ties every historical program and action to the maturity of the objective and subjective conditions, and can therefore see the opening of a socialist horizon only where a developed and conscious proletariat enters the scene.

The abandoning of this requirement was precisely the historical error of Bolshevism, which believed it could establish Socialism by seizing state power in what was still a semi-feudal country—finding itself thereby constrained to assume a dictatorial and totalitarian character, something which Dunayevskaya deplores and rejects.

For this very reason, the historical reconstruction that Raya Dunayevskaya realizes in the fourth part of her book—treating the development of Lenin's thought, from the collapse of the Second International until his Will—is not only interesting but also filled with fruitful lessons. We limit ourselves to highlighting only a few points that reveal the contradiction—internal to Lenin's consciousness—between the democratic requirement (which Dunayevskaya brings to light) and the Bolshevik program (which she leaves in the shadows).

Following the repression of the 1905 revolution, Lenin had already championed the idea—somewhat contradictory—of a workers' and peasants' *revolutionary democratic dictatorship*, declaring that the proletariat's task in a bourgeois—not a socialist—revolution in an overwhelmingly peasant country was still being discussed: "Whoever wants to approach socialism by any other path than that of political democracy will inevitably arrive at absurd and reactionary conclusions, both economic and political" (2000: 185).

After the collapse of the Second International (1914), Lenin discovers Marx and Engels's critique of the bourgeoisification of the trade unions, and proclaims the necessity of going "deeper and lower" into the working class (2000: 187). But he still does not grasp the type of organization that the spontaneous revolt of the workers can provide for itself; until in 1917, the Russian workers—on their own initiative— took up again the fleeting example of 1905 (which Lenin considered unimportant at the time), and created Soviets all over the country: workers', soldiers', and peasants' Soviets. And in this spontaneous creation on the part of the masses, Lenin considers any danger of the formation of *elites* to have been superseded, and proclaims: "All power to the Soviets!" (2000: 190).

This means substituting *workers' direct control* at every level of government and for every technical and bureaucratic directive: "The workers must demand *immediate* establishment of control *in fact* to be exercised by the *workers themselves* (...). I 'calculate' *solely* and *exclusively* on the workers, soldiers and peasants able to tackle better than the officials, better than the police, the *practical* and difficult problems of increasing the production of foodstuffs and their better distribution, the better provision of soldiers, etc., etc." (2000: 191).

The only way to have a genuine proletarian democracy, declares Lenin in *State and Revolution*, is to suppress the bureaucracy and to give all power to the workers, with the "immediate introduction of control and superintendence by *all* (...) *Every* worker, *every* peasant, *every* toiler, *every one* who is exploited, the whole population to a man" (2000: 192). Only in this manner would the classless society that Marx wished be realized, and "the re-integration of man's manual and mental abilities in the producer himself ... first open[s] the real history of humanity" (2000: 194).

In the face of these declarations of ultra-radical democracy, with which Dunayevskaya sketches Lenin as a political figure, it is inevitable that we ask ourselves: How could such an orientation transform itself into the bureaucratic management of production and the dictatorship of the Communist Party, which was, moreover, a tiny minority? And how is it that Lenin found himself on the side of merciless repression when the revolt of the sailors and of the people of Kronstadt arose to demand the rights and freedom of the Soviets? The answer is not to be found in the situation of external war, in which Bolshevik Russia was surrounded by hostile forces on every front; but it is to be found most of all in the internal conflict of the party in power with the very masses of peasants and workers, with their demands and aspirations.

Lenin himself had observed that "the overthrow of the exploiter class is the easiest part of the social revolution. Now comes the prosaic, daily, hard, and more important work" (2000: 194): to actualize the creation of a socialist society, as had been proclaimed. It was not only about distributing food, but also about creating a whole productive and industrial organization throughout the immense country; it was not only about abolishing "the distinction between manual workers and brain workers" (2000: 194), but also about creating and organizing the necessary means of production for a Socialist society. This arduous preparation for the future required sacrifices in the present that the masses did not accept spontaneously: it required renunciation of their aspirations (like the hunger for land on the part of the peasants) that only an iron discipline could impose upon them.

Thus, while Lenin proclaimed the abolition of hierarchies—of *elites*, of technocracy—, he saw immediately in the party that attained power "a passion for bossing" (195); he saw the progressive affirmation of the bureaucracy; he saw the Soviets,[8] which he had greeted as free "schools of communism" (2000: 196) and self-discipline, subjugated instead to the "orders from above" (2000: 200) that he had condemned; he saw (and must have discussed with Trotsky and others) the conflict between the trade unions and the State. He saw that the "workers' state" was set to transform itself "into a State Capitalist society" (2000: 208).

But was that the result of bad will, arbitrariness, or usurpation from unscrupulous leaders whom Lenin could have opposed himself in order to prevent their advance? Certainly not. It was a necessarily intrinsic condition that Lenin and his party had imposed on the Russian Revolution.

As I have said in another occasion, in reality, Bolshevism—with its claim of skipping over in Russia the stages of historical evolution that the Western world had undergone with much difficulty, in order to pass from feudal society directly to the socialist one without going through the phase of capitalist development—did nothing other than to replace the bourgeoisie with the State in the task of creating and developing, with the forced sacrifice of the laboring masses, a formidable State Capitalism: more cruel and inexorable than private capitalism because it can directly employ the organization of political power and all the power of its apparatus to dominate individuals and the masses with an iron fist. Lenin himself did not reject the invocation of strong measures put in place against the opposition and the resistance of the "enemies of the revolution." The proclaimed requirement of democracy transformed itself into the exercise of dictatorial power, not only as a consequence of the state of external war imposed by the White Russians and by the hostility of capitalist states, but also (and even more so) by the internal conflict between the demands of the Bolshevik program and the spontaneous demands of the masses.

All of this must not be forgotten if one desires to understand historically the impressive picture that Dunayevskaya traces of the *Russian world* paralleled to the *American world* in the fifth part of her book, which studies "the problem of our age" as a conflict of "State-Capitalism vs. Freedom" (2000: 211).

For the Russian world, the roots of the subsequent developments clarified by the author must be searched for in the contradictions that she did not consider; contradictions in which Lenin's program and action were befouled from the very beginning, as I had the occasion to document at that time in my studies of 1920–1923 on the *Significato e insegnamenti della rivoluzione russa* [*Meaning and Teachings of the Russian Revolution*].[9] All of the subsequent conflicts with the masses—which Dunayevskaya entitles "State-Capitalism vs. Workers' Revolt"[10]—derive from those primary causes; and they cannot be considered only as deviations from Leninism, caused by the emergence of a mania for planning on the part of Trotsky, but principally on the part of Stalin.

The planners had of necessity to put themselves against the workers' aspirations in order to achieve the capital accumulation indispensable for industrial development. For that reason, Dunayevskaya is able to compare Stalin's work with the historic mission of accumulation and production that, as Marx pointed out, classical political economy attributes to the bourgeoisie. Classical political economy, Marx added, did not fool itself at any moment about the pain that accompanies the birth of wealth. "Stalin did not deceive himself either (...)" Dunayevskaya continues, "His iron will was the manifestation of the objective drive of the industrial development" (2000: 217–219).

The lengthening of the working day, the introduction of the piecework system and of Stakhanovism, the forced-labor camps, the tendency to pay to the worker the minimum and to extract from him the maximum surplus value, the draconian labor legislation, the perversion of the relation between man and machine (in which dead labor dominates living labor), are all aspects and moments—documented by Dunayevskaya—of this process of development of the totalitarian State whose motto was: reach and surpass the capitalist countries.

This was Stalin's obsession, which inspired his merciless liquidation of all resistance. The fact that his planning with a vengeance was an intrinsic demand of the self-same party and Bolshevik State is revealed from the fact that—as Dunayevskaya points out—Stalin's disappearance "does not mean that his battling heirs fundamentally changed a single part of the state capitalist structure they inherited, either before or after 'De-Stalinization'" (2000: 248).

At the same time, however, subsequent events demonstrate how the requirements of the party in power are in conflict with the laboring masses. Dunayevskaya traces briefly the history of the workers' insurrection in East Germany on June 17, 1953, which exploded with the cry, "We will not be slaves," as well as the Russian political prisoners' revolt in the forced-labor camps of Vorkuta in July 1953, the workers' insurrection in Budapest and in Hungary as a whole in October 1956; all of them subdued with the blood and iron of the Russian military forces, but not before demonstrating their momentous strength. And she asks herself: "Whoever before June 17th had heard of a mass revolt against a totalitarian dictatorship? Whoever had, before July, heard of slave laborers forcing concessions from a police State? Two pages in history that have shown the way to freedom" (2000: 254). And she comments on the Hungarian insurrection, observing that, because of the repression, the revolutionary forces "have been forced underground, but they have not disappeared. Nor was the impact exhausted within the national boundaries of Hungary. Thousands of Communist Party members all over Western Europe...now see Russian Communism as but another name for state capitalism" (2000: 256–257).

The diffusion of this consciousness in the proletariat—Dunayevskaya concludes—"is a beginning only, but it is a beginning" (2000: 257). The human demand for freedom can be suffocated temporarily, but it can never be extinguished. Totalitarianism cannot be assured of a definitive victory, which would suppose an irreconcilable adaptation (not only of resignation, but also of satisfaction) on the part of the workers to their *alienation* from themselves and from their labor.

The impossibility of such an adaptation is manifested above all in the American world, where the demand for freedom on the part of the workers arises against that supreme expression of industrial capitalism and its battle for productivity that is *automation*: an extreme form of subjugation of the worker to the machine, of the negation of his creativity and freedom, of his reduction to an automaton. Marx had foreseen these developments when he wrote: "An organized system of machines to which motion is communicated by the transmitting mechanism from a central automaton, is the most developed form of production by machinery... The lightening of the labor, even, becomes a sort of torture since the machine does not free the laborer from work, but deprives the work of all interest..." (cited by Dunayevskaya 2000: 272–273).

Man is transformed into machine and the machine into mind: "If you are the one who operates it, you feel its impact in every bone of your body: you are more sweaty, more tired, more tense, and you feel about as useless as a fifth wheel. You are never on top of the machine; the machine is always on top of you and keeps you isolated from your fellow-workers. In addition, you feel more isolated as more and more of your shopmates are displaced by the monster machine" (2000: 264). For the worker, it is no longer a question of wages, but of the quality of labor. This is not only because the latter becomes dangerous, accidents increase, and security diminishes, but even more because of the tensions to which the worker is subjected (which render him neurotic and push him to use *sedatives*, with their disastrous effects), and the reduction of his thinking humanity into a kind of appendage of the machine.

The demands of industrial workers, which Dunayevskaya expresses with phrases from the Marxist tradition—"work that would be completely tied up with life"; "doing that would not be separated from thinking"; "a new unity of theory and practice, unified in the worker himself" (2000: 276)—respond to a concept of labor as human activity that develops all human aptitudes, innate or acquired. How can we transform this concept into action? It is not enough to say, with Dunayevskaya, that the new impulse can come only from the workers, and to thereby proclaim that the control of production belongs to them. This responds to the problem of liberation from any totalitarian system and from any system of forced labor, but not to the problem of the relation between man and machine and automation.

If it is true that the solution to this second problem presupposes a new society (and that "the working people will build it, or it will not be built" [2000: 286]), the decisive question remains: In what direction will this society of workers be able to find the solution to the problem of alienated labor and to the construction of a new Humanism in the era of automated and mechanized production? Is an integral and complete solution possible in this, our modern epoch, which cannot return to the artisanal stage?

In *The German Ideology*, Marx, like Rousseau, attributed the reduction of man to a mere fragment of man to the division of labor. He demanded, on that account, that man be freed from his sentence of remaining limited to an exclusive form of activity for his entire life (hunter, fisherman, shepherd, or any other trade). Man, he claimed, must be free to hunt at certain hours, fish at others, pasture cattle at yet others; that is, to dedicate himself to the most varied activities in order to fully develop his human

faculties and to fulfill his propensities. But this somewhat utopian requirement (almost like the return to nature proclaimed by Rousseau) did not
make evident any real solution to the problem of *alienation* due to the
subordination of man to the machine.

In *Capital*, Marx tends toward more concrete demands, due to the
impetus from the workers' struggles for the shortening of the working
day, a demand that was made possible by the increased production that
the very use of machinery allows. The reduction of the working day means
the availability of free time for the worker; that is, the daily possibility,
if only for a few hours, of regaining his autonomy as a human being—
his capacity to carry out various activities in accordance with his tastes
and needs (material and intellectual); in short, the possibility to freely
develop his human personality. In this manner, the unity of manual and
mental labor—lost by the artisan as he was transformed into an industrial
worker—can reconstitute itself in a certain way: no longer as a simultaneous unity of the two moments, but at least as a succession of diverse
phases in a person's activity, which manages to restore from compulsory
work a part of his time and energy, in order to dedicate the latter to the
autonomous satisfaction of his human propensities and demands.

At any rate, this represents a partial compensation for the mortifica-
tion and drudgery of alienated labor, but it is still not a solution to the
problem of enlightening labor itself—constantly associating the intellectual and the manual, the comprehension and the mechanical, and thus
giving the worker the consciousness of being a functioning human being
and not a mere appendage of the machine, subjugated to its iron domination. The exigency of the new Humanism is to shed light on labor. But
is this possible in modern mechanized and automated production?

The steadily increasing requirement of modern industry for skilled
labor rather than undifferentiated brute force can show us the way to
the solution of the problem. Skill means education: development of the
intelligence required for the execution of one's task, as well as comprehension of specialized labor, of its means and methods, and the possibility
of cooperating in perfecting these; in short, the re-conquest of human
creativity. But the measure that suffices for industry, and for its leaders
and managers, is still not sufficient for the worker. The education that
is enough to make him into a skilled industrial worker is not enough to
bestow a fully developed consciousness upon him. He needs to deepen his
knowledge of the machine that he operates, and also of other machines
(whether connected to his or not), in order to feel that he consciously

controls the machine's functioning, rather than being blindly dominated by it.

The degree of education needed by the worker for this is very high, deeper than that needed to make him a skilled industrial worker. In order to overcome the humiliation of *alienation*, the worker must feel that he is almost like the engineer, who is the master of the secrets that he puts in action. Now, to bring the education of the workers to such a level could not be a necessity felt either by capitalism (private or State) or by the managerial hierarchies of industry: it can only be felt by those who want to withdraw themselves from the situation of dehumanized automatons and appendages of the machine, and want to reaffirm their own humanity in labor, enlightening it completely.

Here then comes into play the necessity, affirmed by Dunayevskaya, of workers' control over the construction of the new society and the new humanism: the limitation of the working day and as good a knowledge as possible of the means of production are two conditions for the solution of the important problem of alienated labor. And only to the degree to which this problem is solved will the end that Marx proposed to the workers be reached: an association in which the free development of each is a condition for the free development of all.

Beunos Aires, July 1963.

NOTES

1. First published in *Il Ponte* (Florence), Vol. XIX, Number 10 (October 1963), and soon after in Spanish in Mondolfo's *El Humanismo de Marx* (Buenos Aires, 1964). C. J. Pereira Di Salvo translated it from the Spanish and the Italian. Unless specified, notes are by the translator and Kevin B. Anderson.
2. A reference Gaetano Arfé's preface to the Italian edition of *Marxism and Freedom*. Excerpts of this preface appeared in English in *News & Letters* 8:1 (January 1963).
3. *Rousseau and the Formation of Modern Consciousness*, not translated into English.
4. This refers to the second edition of Marcuse's study, which first appeared in 1941, earlier than that of Lukács.
5. Here and below, parenthetical page numbers refer to the 2000 Humanity Books edition of *Marxism and Freedom*. In many cases, Mondolfo is citing passages from Marx or Lenin quoted by Dunayevskaya.
6. This seems to be a quote from Marcuse, *Reason and Revolution* (Boston: Beacon Press, 1960), p. 283.

7. Mondolfo note: For a more impartial judgment I refer the reader to my study, *La Filosofia della storia di F. Lassalle* [*The Philosophy of History of F. Lassalle*], in which I also do not withhold any relevant criticism (Cf. *Sulle orme di Marx* [*In Marx's Footsteps*]).

8. Actually, Dunayevskaya was referring not to the soviets, but to the trade unions, specifically to Lenin's characterization of them as "schools of communism."

9. Mondolfo note: *Sulle orme di Marx* [In Marx's Footsteps], 3rd ed., Vol. 1, 1923.

10. A reference to the title of Chapter 13 of *Marxism and Freedom*, "Russian State Capitalism vs. Workers' Revolt."

CHAPTER 10

Why Twenty-First Century Marxism Has to Be Humanist

Paul Mason

INTRODUCTION

In the aftermath of the Second World War an overt humanist turn took place both within Marxism and, in the case of some prominent Marxists, against it. Raya Dunayevskaya, who had been Trotsky's secretary, introduced the key ideas of the early Marx to the American left – producing arguably the quintessential statement of postwar Marxist humanism. (Dunayevskaya 1958)

Erich Fromm began his career as a social psychologist in the late 1920s allied to the Frankfurt School. However by 1941, his Marxism evolved in an explicitly humanist direction, leading him towards a theory of ethics and re-centering his work on the psychology of the individual. (Fromm 1994)

Manabendra Nath Roy, one of the founders of the Comintern, broke with Marxism completely by 1948, arguing that its under-estimation of the

P. Mason (✉)
London, UK

© The Author(s) 2021
K. B. Anderson et al. (eds.), *Raya Dunayevskaya's Intersectional Marxism*, Marx, Engels, and Marxisms,
https://doi.org/10.1007/978-3-030-53717-3_10

independent role of thought and individuality in its liberation narrative had made Marxism susceptible to the totalitarian system imposed under Stalinism. (Roy 1947)

Herbert Marcuse stands both as a forerunner and a counterweight to these postwar thinkers. His 1932 essay, which introduced Marx's early writings, addressed most of the key ideas embraced by the post-1945 converts. Marcuse called definitively for a Marxism focused on the human essence: "It is precisely the unceasing focus on the human essence that becomes the inexorable impulse for founding the radical revolution". (Marcuse 1972)

However, Marcuse's rediscovery of the humanist core of Marx proved to be just one stage in a journey towards philosophical despair in the early 1960s: both about the "one-dimensionality" of workers under the technological domination of capital, and in the very possibility of the working class becoming the gravedigger of capitalism. (Marcuse 1991)

In any case the humanist turn within Marxism in the 1950s was quickly overwhelmed by a counter-tendency, originating from within Existentialism, which stigmatised Enlightenment humanism and all its offshoots itself as the ultimate source of fascism, imperialism and genocide. (Geroulanos 2010)

By the mid-1960s, a fully theorised anti-humanism was embedded in both the official Marxism taught in Soviet and in the structuralist Marxism emergent in Western academia, as codified by Althusser, who depicts Marx and Engels' *The German Ideology* (hereafter *TGI*) (Marx and Engels 1968) as an absolute break with humanism. (Althusser 1964)

In this chapter I will argue that, for much of the twentieth century, the humanist roots of Marxism were unknown and misunderstood, even by its most subtle practitioners, even after the appearance of Marx's early writings in German in 1932. Official Marxism laid the basis for theoretical anti-humanism in the 1880s and 1990s because its authoritative thinkers adopted a hyper-determinist approach to both nature and society and clung to Marx's flawed theory of proletarian teleology long after it had begun to fall apart.

The key thinkers of the Second International did not break overtly from the humanist precepts embedded in Marx's then-unknown philosophical writings—but they did diverge in epistemological method. They adopted an essentially Kantian theory of knowledge—but with material reality seen as active, with thought as it's passive reflection. And they systematically minimized both thought, self-activity and the subjective intent of the working class. On this basis they began to make claims about the superiority of dialectics over the complexity theories emerging in the physical sciences, to disparage the Hegelian roots of early Marxism and to side-line the subjectivity of the working class (and indeed all human beings).

For the generation of leftists born before the First World War, this was the orthodox Marxism they learned. Their textbooks were classic summaries of historical materialism by Engels, Plekhanov, and Labriola. In each of these works, assertions about the process of economic determination of social phenomena were paired with claims about the nature of matter whose purpose was to present Marxism as a universal science of reality (Engels 1940; Plekhanov 1947; Labriola 1908).

However, this was also a generation whose practical experience of working-class struggle, of revolutionary dynamics, and of cultural modernism taught them the practical power of subjectivity. If we study the *lives and actions* of the generation who led the 1916–1923 revolutionary upsurge, they exist in permanent tension with the objectivist theories they had been taught in the pre-1914 social peace.

To renew Marxism in the twenty-first century, we need to return to its humanist origins. The proletariat, though it exists and has doubled in size since 1989 (Freeman 2007), can be demonstrated not to possess the *telos* identified by Marx. Instead, under neoliberal globalization, the plebeian masses are exploited through multiple value streams—at work, through rents, financially, behaviorally and through data collection—in a way that undermines the key teleological claim of nineteenth century Marxism: that the proletariat was destined to overthrow capitalism because of its absence of property.

Rather than the classic proletariat, it is the wider plebeian mass of exploited humanity that has both the reason and the motivation to transcend capitalism. And its high access to information and education, captured by the sociological label "networked individual," solves permanently the controversy within Marxism about whether the agent of history can act effectively while blinded by ideology. Henceforward it will act, and can only act, consciously.

In an ironic confirmation of Marx's dictum that "mankind always sets itself only such tasks as it can solve" (Marx 1977), capitalism has created the networked individual at the very moment its own future existence is called into question by the threat of climate change and the transformative potential information technology.

The rise of information networks creates the possibility of a prolonged transition beyond capitalism on the basis of abundance, not the scarcity-based project of twentieth century socialism (Mason 2015). Meanwhile the onset of artificial intelligence will pose point blank the question of human control over autonomous systems (Mason 2019). The ultimate form of alienation, in the sense Marx uses the word in 1844, will be the permanent alienation of our ability to control the technologies we have created, and the loss of our claim to human rights against the supposed rights of corporate- and state-owned machines.

In order to equip humanity for its struggle against machine control, and for a human-centric transition program beyond the market, historical materialism needs to leave behind permanently the objectivism of the Engels-Plekhanov generation, and to resolve crucial problems of agency introduced by Marx himself, in his flawed theory of the proletariat.

How Humanist Was Marx?

Marxism was, at its inception, the answer to a philosophical question posed throughout the Enlightenment: in a monist world, where there is only matter and no disembodied "spirit," what causes change? Marx's answer was: human labor. In the *Economic and Philosophical Manuscripts* (EPM) he espoused both a radical humanism and a basic ecology (naturalism). Human labor, for Marx, alters both the nature of human beings and the shape of the natural world (Marx 1959).

The purpose of human beings, says Marx, is to set themselves free. They are enslaved not just by capitalism, nor merely by any specific form of class society, but by their social nature, which obliges them to work in groups and to collaborate via language and consciousness, not simply instinct. When humans make things, or discover a new idea, we tend to embody our concept of "self" in the new object or the new idea— a process Marx calls self-estrangement or "alienation." We then allow our products, mental and physical, to exercise power over us, whether in the form of religions, superstitions, or by fetishizing consumer goods, or mindlessly obeying routines and disciplines that we have created for ourselves.

Communism, said Marx, is not simply the abolition of private property but the "appropriation of the human essence by and for man...the complete return of man to himself as a social (i.e., human) being" (Marx 1959).

A modern restatement of this might say: humans are, in their DNA, linguists, imaginers, team-workers, and technologists. Through their interactions with the natural world, they reshape both nature and themselves. Human nature is not, as the thinkers of the Enlightenment imagined, immutable, and thus the source of immutable ethical principles (and legal rights). It is historically constructed. Out of this arises the unique possibility that we, as a species, can liberate ourselves from both economic necessity and psychological self-oppression. This involves us recognizing and resisting both the physical and ideological power of the autonomous systems we have created.

Should we admit this view to be essentialist? Yes, as long as you are prepared to allow that the human "essence" is malleable through human activity. It is impossible logically to maintain the concept of alienation without possessing a concept of human essence, as Marx does in *EPM*.

Should we admit this view to be teleological? Again yes, as long as you understand the *telos* of humanity in its Aristotelian sense: that our "purpose" in the world, created randomly through our evolution toward consciousness and language, is to free ourselves. In fact, the discovery of the human potential for self-liberation through self-activity is the fundamental teleology of Marxism, from which the theory of the proletariat was a secondary conclusion, albeit reached simultaneously.

Marx had no need to spell out the continuity between his views in the 1840s and those of the late eighteenth century humanist thinkers of the German and Scottish Enlightenment, because the modern form of anti-humanism was not present in the intellectual discourse around him. It was, however, brilliantly foreshadowed in the work of Max Stirner. In *The Ego and Its Own* (Stirner 1907) Stirner argues that all forms of humanism originating from the Enlightenment are mere secular replacements for religion. Though he divides human history into a Hegelian, three-phase process of maturation, Stirner conceives freedom—the final phase—as the freedom of individuals from any universal claims and from all teleological views of the species.

It was Stirner's attack on left-Hegelian humanism which, as Alexander Green (1992) points out, provoked Marx and Engels to write *TGI*. The anti-humanist left has always framed *TGI* as Marx's "break" with both humanism and essentialism. However, as Green—a critic of Marx—demonstrates, the book is in fact an attempt to defend key concepts that Marx shared with the left-Hegelian humanists, and which Stirner had attacked.

Though Stirner's attack forced Marx to reappraise and reject Feuerbach's humanism, for its dependence on an a-historical conception of the human essence, Green shows that *TGI* was "the result of an attempt to preserve the Left Hegelian humanist heritage in spite of Stirner's challenge" (Green 1992).

And as Chris Byron (2013) notes, it is possible to trace the same dialectical-essentialist view of human nature through numerous reiterations, which permeate the *Grundrisse*, *Theories of Surplus Value*, and *Capital* itself. For example, in Vol. 3 of *Capital* Marx states:

> Freedom in this field can only consist in socialized man, the associated producers, rationally regulating their interchange with Nature... under conditions most favorable to, and worthy of, their *human nature*. (Marx 1991, emphasis added)

After 1845, then, Marx's humanism became reframed as a set of categories within political economy: alienation and fetishism, which are described speculatively in 1844, reappear as "alienated labor" and "commodity fetishism" in *Capital*. And the teleological implication of this humanism is also reframed, focusing less on general statements about humanity's propensity to self-liberate, toward a specific teleology focused on the working class within capitalism, and its necessity to abolish private property.

Throughout his later writings Marx remained, as Byron suggests, "a rigid essentialist who sees a fluctuating essence to man." And as Norman Geras (1983) has shown, it is a myth that the 1845 *Theses on Feuerbach* contradicts the claim that Marx had a theory of human nature.

The humanist core of Marxism was, however, obscured in the process of reframing the doctrine as a theory of history and political economy. The non-availability of the early writings aided but did not cause this. The real "epistemological break" comes not in Marx but in post-Marx materialist thinking.

WHAT GOT LOST IN THE 1890S?

From the work of Engels, Plekhanov, and Labriola it is possible to distill the core propositions of the "orthodox" Marxism taught to the generation of Lenin, Luxemburg, and Gramsci:

- That Marxism is a theory of the laws of motion of matter in general, and of human society as a subset of that matter.
- That a crude confirmation of the Hegelian dialectic can be found in the dynamics of matter—from the history of the earth's crust, to the evolution of species, to the life-cycle of plants and animals.
- That the dialectic is not only superior to the methods of formal logic but unsurpassable as a tool for comprehending the laws of motion thus described.
- That Marx, in 1845, "broke" with philosophy, refounding his theory of history on the basis of economic concepts rather than the human-teleological ones inherited from left-Hegelianism, with the implication that there were no further philosophical problems worth discussing.
- That Marx "inverted" Hegel's system, standing it "on its feet," thus converting the superior theory of change embedded in objective idealism into a newly dynamic form of materialism.
- That Marxism was thus both the perfection of the monist materialisms of the eighteenth century and the economic counterpart of late nineteenth century monism in physical science.
- That there was no place in the Marxist system for ethics or moral thought. Morals, like laws, are the superstructure of a given set of social relations.
- That all the teleological characteristics attributed to humanity in general by the left-Hegelian and Utopian socialist traditions were in fact embodied only in the proletariat: the proletariat was the "bearer" of the new social relations of communism and destined to achieve class consciousness (a class for itself) primarily though the experience of exploitation and class struggle.

However, as quickly as it was expounded, this doctrine began to fall apart on contact with three new developments.

First, with the birth of modern physics, we see the emergence of post-dialectical ways of thinking about complexity, randomness, and indeterminacy. This raised the possibility of a scientific method superior both to the dialectic and to formal logic, which was to enrage Lenin when embraced by Bogdanov and others (Lenin 1972).

Second, the modernization of academic philosophy. The Nietzschean challenge to rationalism, humanism, and teleological thought called forth a response both from the left and the liberal center which drove "official" philosophy back toward Kant, and secularized moral philosophy as a profession. Meanwhile, in the first decade of the twentieth century the philosophical turn in mathematics also raised the possibility of studying contradiction with more complex tools than the dialectic.

Thirdly, with the emergence of highly organized, state-led capitalism, a "labor aristocracy," plus a working class stratified by Taylorist management techniques, and early welfare states, the key teleological premise of orthodox Marxism was challenged.

Eduard Bernstein's revisionist intervention represents one logically consistent response to these changes: to abandon the teleological claims of Marxism altogether and to return to a moral socialism centered on timeless Kantian principles, while leaving science to the scientists (Bernstein 1912).

For Bernstein's opponents, the generation of revolutionary Marxists who emerged in the first two decades of the twentieth century, the practical solution was to swing toward subjectivity. Lenin's *What Is To Be Done?* for example, contains a view of the working class which is implicitly similar to Bernstein's: that the proletariat could not in itself develop revolutionary consciousness. From this Lenin drew the opposite conclusion to Bernstein: the proletariat would have to be injected with the will to overthrow capitalism by an external force (the intelligentsia and advanced workers, formed into a Jacobin-style party) (Lenin 1961).

Gramsci, Trotsky, and Luxemburg, among others, each contributed to the post-1900 subjectivist turn in Marxism, finding in the lived experience of national, democratic, and workplace struggles a source of belief in the possibility or revolution "against" the timetable laid down by economic development alone. Gramsci was to describe the 1917 Bolshevik revolution as a "revolution against *Capital*"—i.e., against Marx's masterwork—precisely because it was perceived as a voluntaristic escape from the rigid economic determinism of the 1890s (Gramsci 1917).

Yet the revolutionary Marxist generation which rose to prominence after 1914 left their break with the determinism of the 1890s only half-theorized. As a result, both in their minds and in the textbooks their followers produced, the fundamental tenets of hyper-determinist Marxism remained intact. You could be a Leninist and still subscribe to Engels's "dialectics of nature," to Plekhanov's rigid monism, and to the dogma that the working class was destined to introduce socialism because of its absence of property rather than its desire for an unalienated life.

For example, Marx's humanism was based on the assertion that humans alone, unlike the rest of nature, had the power to change themselves through action. By 1921, Nikolai Bukharin's *Historical Materialism* could assure the nascent Soviet bureaucracy of the exact opposite:

> Everything in nature, therefore, from the movements of the planets down to the little grain or mushroom, is subject to a certain uniformity or, as it is generally put, to a certain natural law. We observe the same condition in social life also, i.e., in the life of human society. (Bukharin 1925)

Luxemburg added to the classical Marxist theory of the proletariat an important variation specific to the twentieth century: that the working class is destined to overthrow capitalism not primarily because it will self-educate, or because it will be immiserated, or because it owns no property—but because (even if none of these criteria apply) the crisis-ridden nature of the imperialist epoch confronts the proletariat with existential threats in the form of extreme crisis, war, colonial barbarity, and fascism. However, even Luxemburgism remained a variant of the proposition, "the working class is destined to overthrow capitalism because..." only with an extra reason.

Today, as I argue in *Postcapitalism*, the Marxist theory of the proletariat has to be abandoned (Mason 2015). For certain, it moves spontaneously from forming "a class against capital" to a class "for itself" as Marx suggested (Marx 1955). But at no time in its history did the majority of the working class spontaneously develop a consistently pro-communist consciousness; and with the rise of a mass consumer society in the twentieth century, its stake—both in private property and the capitalist state—increased. As Luxemburg suggested, it was repeatedly prepared to take power in conditions of war and fascism, but it later proved historically incapable of holding power in the Soviet Union, Cuba, or China when faced with the rise of bureaucratism.

Instead, throughout its entire history, the working class wanted more than reform, but less than revolution. It wanted control—and when it got control it was often prepared to defend the islands of humanity and justice it could create in alliance with petit-bourgeois forces and, as in the USSR and beyond, bureaucracies. Simon Pirani's account of the Moscow working class's acceptance of early Stalinist bureaucratism after 1921, offers a convincing case study of this (Pirani 2008). The real experience of the Paris Commune, as opposed to the events filtered by classic Marxist accounts of it (e.g., Lissagaray 1976) tells the same story. The real experience—from Proudhonism in the 1860s to syndicalism in 1911 and Durruti's columns in 1936—suggests that for the factory proletariat it was control above all that embodied the condition of becoming a "class for itself."

In short, over its 250-year history, the urban/industrial proletariat was always able to achieve more than what Lenin condemned as "mere trade union consciousness" but always less that what Marx expected.

This refutation of Marx is more radical than the one outlined by Marcuse in *One-Dimensional Man* (Marcuse 1964). For Marcuse, it is the postwar emergence of state capitalism and its capacity for technological domination that led to a degeneration of the proletariat. For me, Marx's attempt to cast the proletariat as the objective embodiment of the "negation" in the form of propertyless social relations was wrong, and never factually based, even in the 1840s. It was certainly a revolutionary class—for the social republic, and in defense of itself against fascism and dictatorship but the theory of the "bearer" (*Träger*) does not stand up against the actual anthropology of working-class existence. The working class was, and still is, the historically lawful bearer of altruism and solidarity, but not of communism.

However, until the 1880s, the Marxist theory at least coincided with some of the facts. After that, the entire history of revolutionary Marxism since 1902 has to be read as series of theoretical convolutions designed to avoid confronting Marx's error.

Engels began the process with his theory of the labor aristocracy, originally applied only to Great Britain. He claimed in 1892 that the labor aristocracy was now a generalized *temporary* phenomenon, tying an upper section of the working class throughout the developed world to capital through the proceeds of colonial exploitation (Engels 1898).

Lenin, by 1916, had developed this into a general theory, describing the skilled reformist workers as a *permanent* stratum within the working class (again to be found across the imperialist countries) whose material interests require them to support capitalism. For Lenin, the bearer of the future social relations had now to be found "lower and deeper" among the masses (Lenin 1964). Marcuse, and indeed most of the Frankfurt School, came to believe that the working class had lost its historical capacity to overthrow capitalism, while from the 1960s onwards the New Left began to search for "replacement" agencies to overthrow the system—in the form of students, racial minorities, women an anti-imperialist national revolts.

What does this imply for the teleological claims of Marxism? Let us follow Marx's initial logic. In 1844, he elaborates a concept of the human essence based on self-activity (i.e., human labor). He discovers that the working class of Paris are spontaneously embracing communist ideas and extrapolates from that the theory that their material conditions (penury, propertylessness) will oblige them to destroy capitalism.

There are two, parallel claims here:

i. that humanity can self-liberate through technological progress and self-education; the working class, being the latest and last embodiment of the alienated human being, will be obliged to create the conditions for ending alienation;
ii. that the working class, because it can hold no property, will be the agent of capitalism's overthrow and the bearer (*Träger*) of the new social relations—whatever the specific ideas it holds in its head.

If you believe this second thesis is historically refuted, then you have two choices. You can begin the search for an alternative agent of history—the Leninist Party, or the bourgeois-nationalist guerrilla movement, the student nucleus, or sections of the masses "lower and deeper" than the semi-skilled proletariat. Or you can revert to the first thesis, which is the most consistent teleological statement in Marxism. Humankind in general, through its self-activity, is the agent of self-liberation—and the form that agency takes is not limited to the one in which Marx first encountered it—the solidarity of industrial workers. Human history is the history of class struggles, but the class struggle within capitalism turns out to be—as it was in all previous societies—over the forms and limits of alienation, not simply the distribution of the economic surplus.

If so, the most important question at a given stage of class society, including our own, is not "why has the working class failed, who is to blame, and/or who can replace it?" It is: "what is the current form of the alienated human being and what would creating the conditions to end its alienation involve?"

WHAT DID MARXIST HUMANISM ADD?

The contribution of the postwar Marxist humanists was to rediscover and reinsert the humanism of 1844–1845 into a coherent restatement of historical materialism. As compared to the orthodox Marxism of the 1890s (see above), by the time of the Hungarian Revolution in 1956 that restatement might be summarized as follows:

- That Marxism is primarily a theory of the dynamics of human society, indeed an anthropology.
- That the Hegelian dialectic is far from the crude idealist triad understood by Plekhanov's generation: it is in fact a subtle quasi-materialism that does not need much "standing on its head" at all. Though Marcuse had pioneered Western Marxism's reassessment of Hegel, it was Dunayevskaya who most significantly elaborated it, through her prolonged engagement with two key categories in Hegel's logical system—"the power of negativity" and the "absolute idea."
- That the dialectic was a contribution to scientific thought but does not replace it.
- That Marx's break with idealist philosophy does not give Marxists permission to disengage from philosophy but obliges them to engage and respond to developments in ontological, epistemological, logical, and moral thought.
- That Marxism has more in common with the dynamic idealism of Hegel than it does with the determinist monism of the eighteenth century materialists.
- That Marx's *Capital* is not merely a work of political economy, but an attempt to show how humanity's "social consciousness" is produced by its "social being"—i.e., also a work of anthropology. For Dunayevskaya, once *Capital* was thus interpreted, it became a guide for the working class to take control of machinery, factories, and entire industrial processes, not merely with the intent to end

exploitation, but as a way of immediately combating alienation and lack of control.

- That it is possible to conceive of a Marxist ethical system on the basis of the essential but changing human nature, and on a universalist premise drawn from that view of human nature.

- That the proletariat's fight against capitalism would have to take place on the basis of a conscious effort to overcome its own alienation, and therefore could not be a dumb, ant-like process described in the hyper-determinist era.

- That, though the proletariat's struggles arise out of historically specific conditions, they are a subset of humanity's long struggle against alienation and part of a wider arc: certain forms of alienation—e.g., women's oppression, racism, colonial subservience—may run deeper than class oppression.

- That the "negation" of modern capitalism, using Hegel's terminology, therefore consists of more than simply the factory proletariat, and thus the dynamics of feminism, the Black civil rights movement and the struggle against colonialism are essentially negative to capitalism. For Dunayevskaya, the importance of these non-economic struggles and oppressed groups lay not as "replacements" for a proletariat which had failed to live up to its teleological purpose: they were elements of an expanded revolutionary subject. This rethink of "who is the subject?" was only possible because of Dunayevskaya's determination to restore negativity to its primary role in the Hegelian thought-system.

Above all, both chronologically and logically, humanism is the core of Marxism. As Dunayevskaya put it:

Humanist philosophy is the very foundation of the integral unity of Marxian theory, which cannot be fragmented into "economics," "politics," "sociology," much less identified with the Stalinist monolithic creation. (Dunayevskaya 1965)

Given that Marxist humanism was so aligned with the spontaneous dynamics of social struggle in the 1960s, it is worth asking: why didn't it take off?

First, because many of its adherents remained loyal to the model of the Leninist party, long after they were prepared to denounce Stalinism as a twin phenomenon with fascism.

Second, and most obviously, because of the brief but spectacular return of proletarian agency in the years 1968–1975, when the factory workforce of the developed world adopted spontaneous practices of resistance like the factory committee, the occupation, the proto-soviet, and the mass strike. On first contact with the student-based fragments of the humanist and anti-Leninist left, the workers demanded something different.

My observations of the British left in the aftermath of the mid-1970s strike wave were that the most militant workers themselves demanded a turn to a practical form of Leninism—albeit of a highly economic-focused variety. Ian Birchall's biography of the far-left leader Tony Cliff demonstrates how it was under the influence of the 1968 radicalization of rank-and-file workers that the IS/SWP tradition abandoned its vestigial Luxemburgism and began to reframe its entire politics around Lenin's *What Is To Be Done* (Birchall 2011).

The social conditions for the take off of anti-humanist, structuralist Marxism influenced by Althusser were accelerated by the acute economic crisis after 1973 combined with the defeats of the late 1970s. From 1968 onwards, the Baby Boomers were radicalized in a world that looked and sounded like the one in the Leninist textbooks: Marcuse's lament that the working class had surrendered to one-dimensionality were derided; the later predictions of a Marxist humanist like Andre Gorz, of the proletariat's demise, were scorned (Gorz 1994).

A further impediment to the spread of Dunayevskaya's humanism was its determination to remain engaged with Soviet and Chinese Marxism as if with rival interpretations within a single doctrine. Only amid the hubristic return of Leninism in the 1970s, backed by Althusser's renewed hyper-determinist theory, did it became necessary for Marxist humanists to state what had only been implicit in the works of Korsch, Gramsci, and Marcuse: that there are, as Edward Thompson put it "two Marxisms"—incompatible with each other. A gulf has opened, he wrote:

> between idealist and materialist modes of thought, between Marxism as closure and a tradition, derivative from Marx, of open investigation and critique. The first is a tradition of theology. The second is a tradition of active reason. (Thompson 1978)

As long as they clung to the theory of proletarian agency, the Leninist party and the idea of Marxism as a unified canon of ideas, Marxist humanists such as Dunayevskaya were always going to be metaphorically "playing away," in the ideological sports stadium of their enemies.

During the long period of defeat for the working class which began in the late 1970s, and the rise of neoliberalism, it is possible to say with hindsight that Marxism was literally atomized. In academia, subtle and lucid Marxist analyses of capitalist social relations, or pre-capitalist anthropology, flourished precisely because they could exist in an anti-universalist world. Your Marxist masterpiece can sit on the shelf alongside my Foucauldian deconstruction of it, because the premise of the library's existence is that all knowledge is relative. In political activity, meanwhile, Leninist groups became re-enactment societies, losing power and influence to anarchism and environmentalism after missing the boat during the anti-globalization movement of 1999–2003. Stalinism, meanwhile, hibernated. It produced no account of its own downfall, only a nostalgia industry for the Spanish Civil War and 1917, and at its worst an international support network for Vladimir Putin and Bashar Al Assad.

Marxist political economy has made fruitful and at times devastating interventions into the battle between orthodox and heterodox economics. Alongside this, a revived philosophy function has emerged in Marxism, so that every school of bourgeois philosophy—from analytical to realist to metaphysical—now has a "Marxist" expression.

But Marxism as a holistic theory has been shattered and will remain shattered until it confronts the central philosophical questions raised by the falsification of Marx's "bearer" theory. Namely: who is alienated within this particular form of capitalist society? What gives them the material interest to overthrow it? And what qualities do they "bear" which enable them to create a society without exploitation, property, or oppression?

The Centrality of Marxist Humanism Today

Marx, famously, refused to describe communism except in very general terms. Though he outlined in the 1859 Preface (Marx 1977) the possibility of a clash between the industrialized forces of production and the social relations of capitalism, he never fully detailed what this would look like. Only once did he hazard a guess at the form the techno-economic revolution might take. In the 1858 *Fragment on Machines*, in what is known today as the *Grundrisse*, he imagined a time when machines do most of the work, where the workforce stands completely "to the side" of the process as an observer, and in which knowledge becomes "social," embodied in what he called a "general intellect." Since capitalism is based on profits generated by workers, it could not survive a level technological advance that eradicated the need for work. The clash between private property and shared social knowledge, he said, would blow the foundations of capitalism "sky high" (Marx 1973). This prophecy, so obviously relevant to our time of robots and networked knowledge, lay in the archives unread until the 1960s.

Today, the immanent contradictions of capitalism look very different from the way they've been presented in previous periods of crisis. During the pre-1914 period the Marxist orthodoxy, shared by revolutionaries and revisionists, was that the forces of production had further to mature, and that the form of a socialized economy was taking shape via the consolidation, monopolization, and state intervention already happening under finance capitalism.

During the Great Depression, a plausible underconsumptionist account of capitalism's endpoint was added to Hilferding and Lenin's thesis about monopoly and finance capitalism (Hilferding 1981). The collapse of growth, financial profits, and financial wealth would force the state to organize the economy; meanwhile the deep poverty and insecurity generated by mass unemployment would create an army of discontented workers and lower-middle-class people to make the revolution. They would seize the centralized state economy and use it to abolish the law of value.

During the post-1973 period, the source of crisis seemed the opposite: the wage bargaining power of the workers combined with the indebtedness of states, making it necessary for capital to attack trade unions and welfare systems.

Since neoliberalism peaked, and entered its downswing in 2000/2001, a very different narrative has emerged about how capitalism ends. Rifkin (2014), Drucker (1993), Bastani (2019) and I have each separately described how the rise of information technology disrupts the normal process of price formation in a market system. The postcapitalism thesis states that:

- There is too little exchange value in information goods to allow price formation through the marginal costs, and while mark-ups and monopoly pricing can delay this "zero marginal cost effect," they cannot do so forever.

- Infotech disrupts the ordinary defense mechanism of capitalism, whereby jobs and tasks automated out of existence are replaced by new, high-skilled, high paying jobs which sustain consumer demand and raise the level of subsistence required by the whole workforce.
- Thus capitalism faces a strategic crisis of the realization of surplus value. Productivity will go on showing up in the "use value" side of the Marxist accounting schedule but not on the "exchange value" side.
- As a result, an information-dominant capitalism is heavily reliant on monopolistic and rent-seeking business models, and on central bank money creation.
- In order to sustain demand, the system itself is becoming more and more reliant on fiat money, generating high private, corporate and government debt, none of which can be paid back without high inflation, which is unlikely given the long-term impact of infotech described above.
- These effects are exacerbated by contingent factors: the slowdown of population growth, the slowdown of innovation, the diminishing returns from catch-up growth, and the constrained nature of government finances in an era when global debt is 150% of global GDP and rising.

With or without climate change, these conditions would create the possibility of a transition beyond market-dominated production in the twenty-first century. But the climate crisis accelerates the clash between forces and relations of production, demanding swifter action by the state and civil society to produce a new model of capitalism from which we can build postcapitalism.

The question is: who has the material interest in making this happen? Two insights from within heterodox Marxism throw light on the answer.

As class identification has weakened, and information technology has begun to allow people to create multiple identities, and to move freely across distributed social networks, sociologists Wellman and Castells originated the concept of the "networked individual" (Wellman 2001; Castells 2001). At first used to describe a set of behaviors, this term has morphed into a description of the decisive change in lifestyle, attitude, behavior, and personality among people exposed to the combined effects of social networks and mobile digital communications.

As a term it has been appropriated in disciplines as far apart as psychiatry and marketing, but for Marxists there is an obvious and narrower meaning. Being a networked individual does not alter the fact that you are a proletarian, or a petit-bourgeois, or a member of the super-rich elite. But it does overlay your position within the exploitation process at work with more general features common to the most basic alienation process Marx described in 1844.

The human being as a slave of the thing it has created was easy to conceive for factory workers in the 1840s; how much clearer is our enslavement to the smart mobile digital comms devices, and the thought-control machines that stand behind them, which three billion people on the planet now possess, and which barely existed on the day Lehman Brothers went bust?

The second insight arises from the work of Mario Tronti, the Italian autonomist thinker who first theorized the "social factory." In classic Marxism, the process of exploitation takes place primarily in the factory. For Tronti, by the 1960s, capitalism had developed to the point where every living act of human beings had become a source of valorization for capital:

> At the highest level of capitalist development social relations become moments of the relations of production, and the whole society becomes an articulation of production. In short, all of society lives as a function of the factory and the factory extends its exclusive domination over all of society. (Tronti 2019)

Nearly sixty years on, after decades of atomization, privatization, and financialization of consumption we might re-state the argument as the *twenty-first century social factory thesis*:

> Under neoliberalism, after the destructive phase of the 1980s, the process of valorizing capital came to pervade the non-work social life in the developed world. A worker is still producing a steady stream of surplus value in the workplace—reflected in the average 10–12% pre-tax operating profits of corporations. But they are also producing a stream of interest from credit cards, student loans, healthcare loans, and mortgages at a substantially higher rate of return. In addition,

the consumer's actions are co-creating intellectual property for free. Meanwhile entire vistas of previously non-commercial interactions during leisure time are now commodified. And for giant data corporations like Facebook and Google, the mere behavioral existence of the human subject can be monetized: our location data, our heart rates, our speed of reading an e-book—all of these generate commercializable data. As a result, the networked individual—in successive iterations as Generations Y and Z—experiences exploitation at work as merely a device for servicing all the other value streams emanating from their consumption, borrowing, sex life, exercise, and cultural activities. Even in prison or while asleep we can be exploited by capital—and in multiple, subtle ways.

If this is so, Marxism must now stand as a kind of liberation theory for these multiply exploited, alienated, and oppressed individuals. Their material interest calls for ending the surveillance, intrusion, asymmetric power, and suppressed incomes from which they suffer. And they have the means to do so—through the activity Tronti described as "refusal": they can create conditions in which refusal to participate in commoditized friendship, or high-interest borrowing becomes possible through mass struggle—albeit of a variety in which swarms and temporary networks are more important than hierarchies and parties.

MARXISM'S SEARCH FOR THE SELF

With hindsight, the whole tradition of critical Marxism in the twentieth century can be interpreted as an unfulfilled search for a theory of the self. For the Frankfurt School, Marcuse included, it was only the failure of the working class, and the rise of all-powerful consumerist ideology, that freed Marxism from having to be a theory of struggle and gave permission for it to become a theory of self-reflection.

For Fromm and Dunayevskaya, the return to the early Marx was what allowed them to reintegrate the notion of individual human freedom as the ultimate objective in a communist project.

Roy, by contrast—in an unacknowledged return to the essence of Stirner's thesis—concluded that human thought, and therefore ideas of freedom, are not conditioned, even in a mediated form, by the social relations of production. They are primarily conditioned by previous ideas,

and by rationality, which sits at the center of *Homo sapiens* consciousness. Unlike Stirner, who rejected any attempt to derive a teleology or
morality from the autonomy of the idea, Roy advocated the replacement
of Marxism with a universal doctrine of self-liberation very close to that
of Feuerbach:

> Man is the maker of his world – man as a thinking being. And he can
> only be so as an individual. The brain is the means of production and
> produces the most revolutionary commodity... Spiritually free individuals
> at the helm of affairs will smash the chains of slavery and usher in freedom
> for all. (Roy 1947: 47)

Thompson wrote in the 1970s that, if humanist Marxism was proven
to be incoherent, then his line of retreat would be to Christianity or
bourgeois liberalism. It is clear from this that Roy had already travelled
that path by the late 1940s. Like Thompson, once you understand the
profound humanism at the core of Marxism, I do not think there is any
need to take it.

So, what is left of Marxism in our era of techno-euphoria and environmental doom? Since the rediscovery of the 1844 manuscripts the dilemma
for Marxism has been clear: either it is a theory of the liberation of individual human beings or it is a theory of impersonal forces and structures,
which can be studied but very rarely escaped. Either there is a "human
essence," which we can reappropriate by abolishing property and class, or
we are a sack of bones conditioned by our surroundings and our DNA,
and human essence is a myth. Either people make history, as Marx said,
or history makes history.

During the past 50 years, much of left-wing academic thought has
followed the path Althusser laid out: there is a clear genealogy from his
anti-humanist Marxism, to postmodernism, the attack on science and the
recent emergence "post-humanism" and vitalist "New Materialisms," in
which inert matter is alleged to have as much agency as human beings.

But the project of human liberation and communism can survive the
atomization and dispersal of the class that was supposed to bring it about,
and the emergence of multiple forms of exploitation. As the revolts
of 2011 showed, large masses of people now possess the capacity for
autonomous action, self-education, and collaboration that Marx admired
in the Parisian working class of the 1840s (Mason 2012). This multiple,

awakened, and connected self is the revolutionary subject—but not the amoral and nihilistic self, suggested by Stirner and Nietzsche.

As Dunayevskaya understood, the impulse toward freedom is created by more than just exploitation: it is triggered by alienation, the suppression of desire, and the humiliation experienced by people on the receiving end of systemic racism, sexism, and homophobia. Everywhere, capitalism follows anti-human priorities it stirs revolt—and anti-human priorities today form the entire basis of the society of networked behavioral control, surveillance, and financialization.

Dunayevskaya, who conceived the revolution as the ultimate negating act, always focused on the question "what comes after." Though impossible to predict, she wrote, the tasks of the post-revolutionary moment should preoccupy even those unlikely to experience it. This marks Dunayevskaya as one of the earliest adopters of prefigurative thinking in the Marxist tradition.

Today, however, the exploited masses face an even more urgent necessity: to adopt what most Marxists would see as post-revolutionary tasks as urgent ones for the present. Information technology plus the networked individual, basically makes Utopian socialism practical. The urgent deadline mandated by climate science means we no longer have the luxury of time.

In the coming century, just as Marx predicted in the *Fragment on Machines*, it is possible that automation plus the socialization of knowledge will present us with the opportunity to liberate ourselves from work. That, as he said, will blow capitalism "sky high." The economic system that replaces it will have to be shaped around the goal he outlined in 1844: ending alienation and liberating the individual.

To reunite the atomized strands of historical materialism into a coherent doctrine of human liberation may take years of work, but the outlines of a Marxist Humanist project are clear.

We need an *aretaic moral philosophy* based on the question: what does a society without class, exploitation, and alienation look like and what are the virtues needed by a human being living within it? This, in fact, was always the implicit content of what Marxists called "class consciousness": the practice of workers building solidarity in the workplace, the community, and the party itself.

We need to rebuild a Marxist *theory of knowledge* that can withstand contact with complexity and indeterminacy, most notably via quantum mechanics.

We need an account of the coming *transition beyond capitalism* based on the political economy of the information network.

We need a *theory of the earth's ecosystem* that accepts the fact there may be no technological fix to the depletion of the earth's atmosphere, and which revises the Marxist assumptions about human survivability accordingly.

We need a *complex and provisional anthropology of the species*, based on the ever-improving data about pre-capitalist social formations and socio-psychological studies of the self. And we need a *political economy of the "social factory"* which situates class, gender, racial, and psychological oppression in a more complex relationship to the exploitation process, both in history and today.

Above all we need a new practice based on the spontaneous struggles of the networked individual in the social factory. As Brecht put it in the final scene of his movie *Kuhle Wampe*: "Who will change the world? Those who are not satisfied with it!" (Brecht 1932).

References

Althusser, Louis. 1964. "Marxism and Humanism." *Cahiers de l'I.S.E.A*, June.
Bastani, Aaron. 2019. *Fully Automated Luxury Communism*. Verso.
Bernstein, Eduard. 1912. *Evolutionary Socialism*. B.W. Heubsch.
Birchall, Ian. 2011. *Tony Cliff: A Marxist for His Time*. Bookmarks Publications.
Brecht, Bertholt. 1932. *Kuhle Wampe: Or Who Owns The World*. Berlin.
Bukharin, Nikolai. 1925. *Historical Materialism: A System of Sociology*. International Publishers.
Byron, Chris. 2013. "Marx's Human Nature: Distinguishing Essence from Essentialism," *With Sober Senses*, March.
Castells, Manuel. 2001. *The Internet Galaxy: Reflections on the Internet, Business and Society*. Oxford University Press.
Drucker, Peter F. 1993. *Postcapitalist Society*. Butterworth-Heinemann.
Dunayevskaya, Raya. 1958. *Marxism and Freedom: From 1776 Until Today*. Bookman Associates.
———. 1965. "Marx's Humanism Today." *Socialist Humanism*. Edited by Erich Fromm. Doubleday.
Engels, Frederick. 1898. *The Condition of the Working-Class in England*. Swann, Sonnenschien & Co.
———. 1940. *Dialectics of Nature*. International Publishers.

Freeman, Richard. 2007. "The Great Doubling: The Challenge of the New Global Labor Market." *Ending Poverty In America: How to Restore the American Dream*. The New Press.

Fromm, Erich. 1994. *Escape from Freedom*. Henry Holt & Co.

Geras, Norman. 1983. *Marx and Human Nature: Refutation of a Legend*. Verso.

Geroulanos, Stefanos. 2010. *An Atheism That Is Not Humanist Emerges in French Thought*. Stanford University Press.

Gramsci, Antonio. 1917. "La Rivoluzione contro il Capitale." *Avanti!*, 24 December.

Green, Alexander. 1992. "Stirner and Marx." *Non Serviam*, 23.

Gorz, André. 1994. *Farewell to the Working Class*. Pluto Press.

Hilferding, Rudolf. 1981. *Finance Capital: A Study of the Latest Phase of Capitalist Development*. Routledge.

Labriola, Antonio. 1908. *Essays on the Materialistic Conception of History*. Charles H. Kerr.

Lenin, Vladimir Ilyich. 1961. What Is To Be Done? *Lenin's Collected Works*, Vol. 5. Foreign Languages Publishing House Moscow.

———. 1964. "Imperialism and the Split in Socialism." *Lenin Collected Works*, Vol. 23. Progress Publishers.

———. 1972. "Materialism and Emprio-Criticism." *Lenin Collected Works*, Vol. 14. Progress Publishers.

Lissagaray, Prosper Olivier. 1976. *History of the Paris Commune of 1871*. New Park.

Marcuse, Herbert. 1964. *One-Dimensional Man: Studies in the Ideology of Advanced Sndustrial Society*. Beacon Press.

———. 1972. *Studies in Critical Philosophy*. Beacon Press.

———. 1991. *One-Dimensional Man*. Beacon Press.

Marx, Karl. 1955. *The Poverty of Philosophy*. Progress Publishers.

———. 1959. *Economic and Political Manuscripts of 1844*. Progress Publishers.

———. 1973. *Grundrisse*. Penguin.

———. 1977. *A Contribution to the Critique of Political Economy*. Progress Publishers.

———. 1991. *Capital: Volume III*. Penguin.

Marx, Karl, and Friedrich Engels. 1968. *The German Ideology*. Progress Publishers.

Mason, Paul. 2012. *Why It's Kicking Off Everywhere: The New Global Revolutions*. Verso.

———. 2015. *Postcapitalism: A guide to Our Future*. Allen Lane.

———. 2019. *Clear Bright Future: A Radical Defence of the Human Being*. Allen Lane.

Pirani, Simon. 2008. *The Russian Revolution in Retreat, 1920–24: Soviet Workers and the New Communist Elite*. Routledge.

Plekhanov, Georgi. 1947. "The Development of the Monist View of History." *Selected Philosophical Works*, Vol. 1. Lawrence & Wishart.

Rifkin, Jeremy. 2014. *The Zero Marginal Cost Society: The Internet of Things, the Collaborative Commons, and the Eclipse of Capitalism*. Palgrave Macmillan.

Roy, M. N. 1947. *New Humanism: A Manifesto*. Renaissance Publishers.

Stirner, Max. 1907. *The Ego and His Own*. Benjamin R. Tucker.

Thompson, E. P. 1978. *The Poverty of Theory and Other Essays*. Monthly Review Press.

Tronti, Mario. 2019. *Workers and Capital*. Verso.

Wellman, Barry. 2001. "Physical Place and Cyber Place: The Rise of Networked Individualism." *International Journal of Urban and Regional Research*, 25 (2).

CHAPTER 11

On Capital Accumulation, the Tendential Fall in the Rate of Profit, and Crisis Theory

Karel Ludenhoff

In his *The Long Depression* (2016), Michael Roberts discusses the economic downturn experienced by global capitalism since 2007.[1] He writes that he "tries to provide an explanation of what has happened, an analysis of the causes, and some hypotheses (even predictions) of what will happen next." He critiques other explanations of economic depressions from a Marxist standpoint, which he conceives in this way: "the underlying cause of depressions in capitalist economies... can be found in Marx's law of the tendency of the rate of profit to fall" (Roberts 2016: 12). But he makes clear that he will examine other explanations of economic depressions "mainly based on using empirical evidence" (Roberts 2016: 6). Although he was already doing a lot of empirical work in *The Long Depression*, the publication of *World in Crisis* (2018), a series of empirical studies on the law of the tendency of the rate of profit to fall, edited by Roberts and Guglielmo Carchedi, serves to enhance this empirical work. To be sure, the empirical research in *The Long Depression* and

K. Ludenhoff (✉)
Amsterdam, The Netherlands
e-mail: k.w.ludenhoff@tele2.nl

© The Author(s) 2021
K. B. Anderson et al. (eds.), *Raya Dunayevskaya's Intersectional Marxism, Marx, Engels, and Marxisms*,
https://doi.org/10.1007/978-3-030-53717-3_11

World in Crisis affirms Marx's law of the tendency of the rate of profit to decline. Moreover, this empirical work has tremendous importance for evaluating Marx's theory of crisis under capitalism. It also gives a strong empirical support to the labor movement's struggle against capital.

As for the underlying theoretical concept of crisis in Marx and Marxism, Roberts declares that he will leave "the theoretical debates and in particular a theoretical defense of Marx's crisis theory to other authors and another day" (2016: 6). However, a *theoretical* defense of Marx's crisis theory based on his law of the tendency of the rate of profit can be found in Raya Dunayevskaya's notion of "economics" under capitalism, a notion embedded in a revolutionary philosophical foundation. In what follows we will look more closely at this revolutionary philosophical foundation. Specifically, we will take up how the creation of this revolutionary philosophy was "laying ground" for a "philosophic-economic" notion concerning the law of motion of capitalist society and its relationship to Marx's law of the tendency of the rate of profit.

In her "philosophic-economic" theorization, Dunayevskaya evaluated critically Nikolai Bukharin's perspective, but was more approving toward that of V. I. Lenin. These considerations are relevant to an understanding of both the law of motion of capitalist society and how it can be broken with or transcended. Briefly, she writes that although Bukharin "believes in social revolution" that "does not, however, seem to stop him from dealing with labor, *not as subject, but as object*" (Dunayevskaya 1967: 11). She adds that there was no "disagreement with Lenin about the major achievement of the Russian revolution—the destruction of bourgeois production relations. But the minute Bukharin tried to make an abstraction of that, tried to subsume production relations under 'technical relations' it became obvious to Lenin that Bukharin simply failed to understand the dialectic" (Dunayevskaya 1967: 13). The fact that Bukharin "simply failed to understand the dialectic" also meant for Lenin, as Dunayevskaya notes, "the failure to see self-activity of the masses." (Dunayevskaya 1967: 16). And in taking up Lenin's notion of practice— "Practice to Lenin was *workers practicing*"—she stresses that "*To the Marxist theoretician, this is where all theory must begin*" (Dunayevskaya 1967: 14).

Next, we will address more extensively the theories of Rosa Luxemburg, because it is in her critique of Luxemburg on "economics" and philosophy that Dunayevskaya reveals more clearly her own insights concerning the law of motion of capitalism, Marx's crisis theory, and the law of the tendential decline in the rate of profit.

DUNAYEVSKAYA ON THE ECONOMICS OF CAPITALIST SOCIETY: MARX'S HUMANISM AS GROUND FOR OUR ERA

An examination of her conceptualization of the overall law of motion of capitalist society is the best way to trace Dunayevskaya's interpretation of Marx's law of the tendential decline in the rate of profit. For Dunayevskaya, conceptualizing and extending this law for her era, and really our era as well, consists in establishing Marxist-Humanist ground for a consideration of the nature of economics under capitalism.

As to the law of motion of capitalism, Marx writes in the Preface to the first edition of *Capital* that "it is the ultimate aim of this work, to lay bare the economic law of motion of modern society" (Marx 1990: 17).

As Marx sees it, modern society is a capitalist one in which the contradiction between capital and labor is central. Also emphasizing the determinant role of production under capitalism, Marx writes concerning the *nature* of goods produced for the market: "This division of a product into a useful thing and a value becomes practically important, only when exchange has acquired such an extension that useful articles are produced for the purpose of being exchanged, and their character as values has therefore to be taken into account, beforehand, during production" (Marx 1990: 63–64). Marx formulated this in Chapter One of *Capital*, in a passage that a lot of Marxists overlook when they maintain that value comes into being in the sphere of commodity exchange. They forget that although value does realize itself socially during exchange, it does so when it, as Marx holds, was there *beforehand*, created in the sphere of production.

In capitalism it is the labor element, the working class, which is producing value and surplus value. The creation of surplus value makes possible the accumulation of capital. The capitalists who appropriate surplus value transform it either in nature or through money (surplus value realized as profit in money terms) into new and bigger means of production, thus expanding their production in order to try to obtain more profit in order to continue the process on an ever-greater scale. Inherent in the process of capital accumulation is the growth of constant capital (means of production and raw materials) in relation to variable capital (living labor power). Because value can be created only through the actions of living labor power in the process of production, the relation of constant to variable capital is actually at the root of the law of the tendency of the rate of profit to fall. This is because, when constant capital grows vis à vis variable capital there will be less labor power to produce value and surplus value in relation to investments in constant capital, all of which results in a lower rate of profit. Of course, we speak here of the overall relation between the capitalist class and the working class, not about individual capitalists and their workers.

When Dunayevskaya addresses Marx's analysis of capitalism, and in particular his notion of the law of motion of capitalist society, she writes "Marx wished, above all, to analyze the *law of development* of capitalism. For no matter what its beginnings were, the contradictions arise not from its origin but from its *inherent nature*, 'which begets with the inexorability of a law of nature, its own negation'" (Dunayevskaya 1988: 124). That is why, she notes, Marx put the analysis of its beginnings, the so-called primitive accumulation of capital at the end of *Capital*" (see Dunayevskaya 1988:124).

In discussing the *substance* of this law of motion, Dunayevskaya stresses that Marx is bringing to the fore the fact that

> The "general contradiction of capitalism" consists in the fact that capitalism has a tendency toward limitless production "regardless of the value and surplus value incorporated in it and regardless of the conditions of production under which it is produced." That is why, in "Unravelling the Inner Contradiction," Marx places in the center of his analysis, not the market, but the "Conflict between Expansion of Production and the Creation of Values." (Dunayevskaya 1991: 42)

Because the law of motion of capital exists as a contradiction, "the general contradiction of capitalism," Dunayevskaya concludes that for Marx, "*The law of motion of capitalistic society is therefore the law of its collapse*" (Dunayevskaya 1988: 124).

It is not by accident that we find this statement about the collapse of capitalism in Chapter VII of *Marxism and Freedom*, which deals with Marx's notions of *humanism* and *dialectic* in *Capital*, Volume 1. In this chapter, Dunayevskaya highlights that in *Capital*, Volume 1, Marx demonstrates that "the development of capitalism itself creates the basis of a new Humanism— the 'new forces and new passions' which will reconstruct society on new, truly human beginnings, 'a society in which the full and free development of every individual is the ruling principle.'"[2] She adds "It is because Marx based himself on this Humanism, more popularly called 'the inevitability of socialism,' that he could discern the law of motion of capitalist society, the inevitability of its collapse" (Dunayevskaya 1988: 125).

In these formulations we can see that for Dunayevskaya, Marx in *Capital* is continuing and *developing* the notions of humanism that he had already taken up in the *Economic and Philosophical Manuscripts* of 1844. Here, in a most original interpretation, she holds that Marx's law of the collapse of capitalism, itself grounded in a tendency toward limitless production based on the production of value and surplus value, is *connected* with Marx's 1844 humanism and his overall notion of dialectics. All this indicates that she is considering this law as more than only economics, more than only part of the critique of political economy. The close connection she draws between Marx's humanism and the collapse of capitalism is establishing ground for another type of linkage, that between the critique of political economy and its laws and, on the one hand, Marx's revolutionary thought, and on the other hand, what that means for later generations.

In approaching these issues, it is advisable to turn to the polemic between Dunayevskaya and Herbert Marcuse in the 1950s (in Anderson and Rockwell 2012: 40–44) about the question of the so-called American roots of Marxism. On this question, Marcuse, who was writing the preface to *Marxism and Freedom*, opines in a letter to Dunayevskaya of October 9, 1957: "To tell you the truth, I am getting a little uneasy about the publicity with the 'American roots of Marxism' and the statement that Marx 'completely recreated the structure' of *Capital* under the impact of the American civil war" (Marcuse 1957: 40). She answers in a letter of October 11, 1957: "My Chapter V, The Impact of the Civil War on the Structure of Capital shows that the decade of the 1860's was decisive for the structure of *Capital*. It was the period of the Civil War in the United States, the great mobilization of English workers on the side of the North, the Polish insurrection, the unrest in France, and the creation of the First International" (Dunayevskaya 1957: 41). Here, she is referring to Chapter V of *Marxism and Freedom* (which was to be published in 1958), "The Impact of the Civil War in the United States on the Structure of *Capital*."

We can use this letter of October 11, 1957 to Marcuse as a vantage point from which to see how Dunayevskaya's engagement with Marx's critique of political economy was developing and above all in which theoretical framework this engagement was taking place. For besides the above-mentioned passage—to which we will have to return because it alludes to how, when, and why Marx is structuring *Capital*—other points in this letter illustrate how she had begun to conceive of Marx's critique of political economy within the totality of his revolutionary thought. And by looking closer at the development of her conception of the critique of political economy we will also be able to get a handle on *how* she conceives of the tendential decline in the rate of profit in capitalist society, which Marx takes as ground for the law of motion of this society. We also incorporate, in this process of establishing ground, elements from works Dunayevskaya published after both this letter and the publication of *Marxism and Freedom*. These elements show more clearly what Dunayevskaya already had in mind qua the substance of "economics" during the period she was finishing *Marxism and Freedom*.

As we look closer at this letter to Marcuse, let us consider the *moment* of its writing. For the moment of writing, October 1957, has a specific relevance, for two reasons.

First, this letter was written shortly after the beginning of Marxist-Humanism *as organization*: the beginning of the functioning of News and Letters Committees, March 1955, immediately after the split between C. L. R. James and Dunayevskaya who cooperated before in the Johnson (James)-Forest (Dunayevskaya) Tendency or State-Capitalist Tendency. News and Letters Committees would go beyond the State-Capitalist Tendency by taking up *Marx's Humanism* so much that this step was a *recreating* of Marx's Humanism for their own age. Connected to this, they also were publishing a biweekly newspaper in Detroit, in which they tried to break down the divide between intellectual and worker, as seen in the appointment of a Black production worker, Charles Denby, as editor.

These considerations bring us to the second reason why we need to look at that month, October 1957: Marxist-Humanism as *Idea* at this point in Dunayevskaya's philosophical development. As to the origin of this "Idea," she writes in *25 Years of Marxist-Humanism in the U.S.*: "The major document of the [Johnson-Forest] Tendency, *State-Capitalism and World Revolution*, dismissed Humanism because, in the late 1940's it had appeared in the forms of Existentialism and of Christian Humanism. It was only after the final break with Johnson; it was only when new forms of workers' revolts sprang up— that the Humanism of Marx was brought onto the historic stage of our own age" (Dunayevskaya 1980: 5). As for the earliest beginning of her own notion of Marx's Humanism she goes back almost two decades: "It is true that the *germ* of Marx's humanism was present from the very beginning of my break with Trotsky at the outset of World War II and my subsequent study of the class nature of Russia as a state-capitalist society" (Dunayevskaya 1980: 5). Dunayevskaya wrote her first essay on the theory of state-capitalism, on the class nature of Stalin's Russia as a state-capitalist society, in "The Union of Soviet Socialist Republics is a Capitalist Society" (1941).

In talking, in 1958, about the re-emergence of Marx's Humanism, a theoretical development that was integral to fully conceptualizing capitalism in her age, she writes:

> Marx posed dialectically the fundamental problem— what *kind* of labor— which is today being battled out the world over. Automation has made this question urgent in the United States. In 1844 [in the *Economic-Philosophic Manuscripts*] Marx made this self-same question pivotal, *the* new theoretical response to the workers' revolt against the tyranny of factory labor. (Dunayevskaya 1988: 54–55)[3]

In the context of the fundamental problem, the *new and changed nature* of labor under capitalism in her age, she stresses:

> *It is important* that we look at the new stage of production, Automation, and the form of the workers' revolt against it—the 1949-50 Miners' General Strike— in the same way as, in 1953, we looked at the first revolt against state-capitalism and its work-norms in East Berlin. The point is that both stages of production and both forms of revolt were every bit as crucial for the re-emergence of Marx's Humanism in our age, as has been the outbreak of World War II for the birth of the State-Capitalist Tendency. (Dunayevskaya 1980: 1)

And Dunayevskaya notes that the questions brought to the fore by the miners in their strike, which she saw as summed up in the question from a coal miner, "what *kind* of labor should man do?," "were posed *not* as 'philosophical' questions, but as concrete and urgent matters affecting the workers' daily lives, they should have, *but didn't*, signify to theoreticians that philosophy, in Marx's sense of human activity, had become actual. Yet, if we are not to run a losing race with reality, all theory must begin here, *just here*" (Dunayevskaya 1967: 20–21).

Thus, she is observing that in the new stage of production, that of automation *and* revolts of the workers against it, philosophical questions arise that had to be worked out, and at the same time be developed as a contribution to, a philosophy of revolution geared to the transcendence of capitalism. These were not philosophical questions for the ivory tower, but questions of life and death: "The miners were concerned not just with the old grievances and hazards. This Automation was recognized as a 'man-killer' in a *total* way" (Dunayevskaya 1988: 267).[4] For Dunayevskaya, this observation and its critical elaboration result in the following question in which she situates the critique of political economy in the capitalist society of her era: "What excuse can there be now for any independent Marxist theoretician to persist in keeping economics, politics and philosophy in three separate compartments *just when* the 1950's disclosed a movement *from practice itself* toward theory?" (Dunayevskaya 1967: 23).

A few years later, in *Philosophy and Revolution*, she would write, again concerning Marx's critique of political economy, that the "dismal science" [as Marx called economics], "in its Marxian reconstructed form, it helped in discerning the law of motion of the capitalistic social formation" (Dunayevskaya 1989: 74). She proceeds to discuss Marx's reconstruction of economic science, offering this interpretation of the underlying framework of Marx's critique of political economy: "The reconstructed science meant not only that his original discoveries made all the difference, but also that these original economic categories were so philosophically rooted that a new unity was created out of economics, philosophy, revolution" (Dunayevskaya 1989: 74). She is careful, however, not to forget the specific theoretical and empirical element of this by also denying that such a recourse to philosophy "means that all economic problems have thereby been 'dissolved' into philosophic ones. That would be ludicrous" (Dunayevskaya 1967: 23).

Here we come to the heart of the matter of "economics" under capitalism as Dunayevskaya conceives it: "Economics is a matter not only of the economic laws of the breakdown of capitalism, but of the strife between the worker and the machine against dead labor's domination over living labor, beginning with *hearing* the worker's voice, which had been stifled 'in the storm and stress of the process of production'" (Dunayevskaya 1991: 140).

Having considered how Dunayevskaya developed a notion of "economics" in capitalist society, we can now return to Dunayevskaya's 1957 letter to Marcuse about "the American roots of Marxism." The reason that this letter is so useful for our purpose of tracing her thought about the decline in the rate of profit is that we can record that Dunayevskaya broaches in this letter to Marcuse different aspects of Marx's critique of political economy and refers to interpretations by Marxist tendencies of his economic science that are closely connected to Marx's notion of the tendency of the rate of profit to fall. The following passage from this letter is particularly relevant for our purposes:

> Heretofore I have concentrated on the warp and woof of the book [*Marxism and Freedom*]— the philosophy, dialectics, Humanism of Marxism. As publication date approaches, it is time to indicate the complementary thesis. I use the structure of *Capital* to illustrate this. The changes in the structure of this work meant nothing to the Second International, reformist and revolutionary wings alike. Until Rosa Luxemburg, in 1913, began to question what Engels "had made out" of the material left him by Marx, all Marxists treated the changes in the structure as a "literary question." The Communists continued this tradition (...). The battle of quotations with which Rosa Luxemburg was attacked, both by the Second and Third Internationals, never went into the structure of *Capital* until Henryk Grossman, in 1929. His was the first serious analysis of the changes in the structure. However, his interest was primarily economic; it was directed against Luxemburg's underconsumptionism and the reestablishment of the decline in the rate of profit as central to the theory of accumulation in its Marxist form. (Dunayevskaya 1957: 40–41)

Let us consider the above.

A first topic in this passage is the critique of political economy as "the complementary thesis" of "philosophy, dialectics and Humanism of Marxism." We already have seen above how Dunayevskaya situated "economics," the critique of political economy, in a framework that was a new unity of economics, philosophy, revolution. We see that Dunayevskaya refers in this letter to "the warp and woof of the book [Marxism and Freedom]" in which she conceives of "the philosophy, dialectics, Humanism of Marxism" as a unity. And she writes that it is now the "time to indicate the complementary thesis." By pointing to both sides—the one of philosophy, dialectics and Humanism of Marxism and the other the critique of political economy—as complementary sides means that she already had *substantially* in mind at the moment of writing this letter the "new unity of economics, philosophy, revolution."

The structure of *Capital* is the second topic to which Dunayevskaya refers. As we will see she will point to important changes by Marx in his original plan of *Capital* and why he makes these changes.

A third topic is that all the tendencies within the Second International were renouncing the importance of the structure of *Capital*. In the Second International, it is only Rosa Luxemburg who is questioning what Engels "had made out" of Marx's heritage, especially in his editing of the Volumes 2 and 3 of *Capital*.

The fourth and last topic we find in this passage is the reference to Henryk Grossman as the first Marxist theoretician after Marx who analyzed the law of the tendential fall in the rate of profit. He did so in the context of the 1929 crisis.

In these topics we are confronted firstly with the *how, why,* and *when* of the changes by Marx in the structure of *Capital*. Second, the connection between the three Volumes of *Capital* and the status of the *Theories of Surplus Value* (actually the biggest part of the *Capital Manuscript* of 1861–1863) arises. Third, the theoretical notions of Rosa Luxemburg—concerning the accumulation of capital, imperialism, and the tendency of the rate of profit to fall—will come up and be connected with this. Fourthly, we will see that both Dunayevskaya and Grossman criticize strongly the Luxemburg's notions about Marx's crisis theory.

Let us begin with what Dunayevskaya brings to the fore concerning "the American roots" of Marxism, an influence in the 1860s on the structure of *Capital*, as she bases her argument on what Marx actually writes. First, she refers to Marx's letter of January 11, 1860 to Engels where he writes that "the biggest things that are happening in the world today are on the one hand the movement of the slaves in America started by the death of John Brown and, on the other, the movement of the serfs in Russia."

Second, she refers to July 30, 1862, when Marx recounts to Engels his arguments with Ferdinand Lassalle, who doubted the revolutionary importance of the U.S. Civil War, about the contribution of the "Yankees." She also cites Marx's letter of August 15, 1863, "where he directly involves the structure of *Capital*: 'when I look at this compilation and see how I have had to turn everything around and how I had to make even the *historical* part out of material of which some was quite unknown, then he (Lassalle) does seem funny with "his" economy already in his pocket'" (Dunayevskaya 1957: 41).

Third, Marx reports to Engels in a letter of February 10, 1866: "Historically I developed a part about the *working day* which did not enter in my first plan [of *Capital*]." And later on, he writes "how happy he is that the American workers 'by correct instinct' came to the same formulation on the eight hour day that he had worked out for the Geneva Congress of the First International" (Dunayevskaya 1957: 42). Also, in the context of the instinct of the American workers, she writes that Marx notes in *Capital* that "Labor cannot emancipate itself in the white skin where in the black it is branded. But out of the death of slavery a new life at once arose. The first fruit of the Civil War was the eight hour agitation" (Dunayevskaya 1957: 42). She is demonstrating here that she is keeping an eye open for Marx's "new forces and new passions" in the development of capitalism. For the fact that Marx says that the workers "in the white skin" cannot emancipate themselves where racism is present means that he considers the struggle for human liberation as indeed *determined* by the struggle of labor, the class struggle, but *not as exhausted* in it. This opens the way to analyze and fight all forms of oppression in capitalist society in a Marxian sense. It will be clear that this is connected with Marx's notion of dialectics.[5]

Fourth, Dunayevskaya adds, "Finally the American roots are not only in the finished (by himself) Volume I but in the unfinished Volumes II and III" (Dunayevskaya 1957: 42). To buttress this interpretation, she refers to a letter by Marx to Nikolai Danielson in which he "asks him not to wait for Volume II before translating Volume I because of the mass of material he received from Russia and the United States" (Dunayevskaya 1957: 42). Dunayevskaya states that "it is clear that Russia and America were to play roles in volumes II and III that England played in Volume I, that Lenin filled out Volume II for Russia and that I believe American worker[s] are concretizing it for America in their attitude to Automation" (Dunayevskaya 1957: 43).

Fifth, as we read in chapter V of *Marxism and Freedom*, Marx, in finishing Volume I of *Capital*, "takes out the voluminous material on the 'History of Theory,' and relegates it to the very end of all three volumes, as book IV. *He is breaking with the whole concept of theory as something intellectual, a dispute between theoreticians*" (Dunayevskaya 1988: 91). (The history of theory drafts were later published as *Theories of Surplus Value*.)

These are five items illustrating how Marx, as Dunayevskaya writes to Marcuse, is "turning everything around." They show that the structure of *The Critique of Political Economy* (1859) is less dialectically developed than that of *Capital* (see Dunayevskaya 1957: 42).

We pointed earlier to Dunayevskaya's notion that the beginning of economics (in the Marxian sense) is with "*hearing* the worker's voice."

But, as she also writes, in the period of the 1850s the workers were quies-
cent and that meant to the theoretician Marx "that he must watch the
laws of economic development of the old social order without being able
to see the *specific* form of revolt with which the workers mean to meet
the new stage of production." The consequence was that *The Critique of
Political Economy* (1859) was "a theoretical answer to an actual problem...an *application* of dialectics to political economy, instead of the
creation of the dialectic that would arise out of the workers' struggles
themselves" (Dunayevskaya 1988: 87).

In *Rosa Luxemburg, Women's Liberation, and Marx's Philosophy of
Revolution* she will accentuate this notion:

> *Capital* is a very, very different book than either *Grundrisse* or *Critique of
> Political Economy*, and it is a very different book from the first chapter to
> the last. *It* is the Great Divide from Hegel, and not just because the subject
> is economics rather than philosophy. The other two also were economics,
> and the "first draft" (if that is what one wishes to call the *Grundrisse*) had
> a great deal more obviously philosophic language than *Capital*. No, it is
> that Great Divide because, just because, the Subject— not subject matter,
> but Subject— was neither economics nor philosophy but the human being,
> the masses. (Dunayevskaya 1991: 143)

And it is here, according to Dunayevskaya, that Marx is *creating* a new
dialectic that arises out of the workers' struggles themselves and that
"*Capital* is the work in which— as Marx works out the economic laws of
capitalism, not apart from the actual history of class struggles— historic
narrative becomes historic reason" (Dunayevskaya 1991: 143). In creating
this new dialectic she is not denying that Hegel was "the source of
all dialectic" (Marx 1990: 517), Dunayevskaya is stating that "precisely
because he began with that source that he could make the leap to the
live Subject who is the one who transforms reality" (Dunayevskaya 1991:
143).

Actually, she is emphasizing here the revolutionary potential Marx saw
in Hegel's thought. And as for Marx elaboration of "hearing the voice of
the workers" in relation to his transcending of the philosophy of Hegel
she phrases it for her age as follows: "Thus, the workers, the American
workers, made concrete and thereby extended Marx's most abstract theories of alienated labor and the quest for universality. Marx was right when

he said the workers were the true inheritors of Hegelian philosophy" (Dunayevskaya 1988: 76).

CAPITAL, VOLUME I, AS THE WHOLE OF MARX, BUT WHOSE DIALECTICAL STRUCTURE IS "ANATHEMA" TO ROSA LUXEMBURG

Unlike in Marx's writings, we do not find a critical transcendence of Hegel in Luxemburg. She had no great admiration for Hegel's thought. This becomes clear when we see her form of reasoning in a letter to Hans Diefenbach[6] of March 8, 1917 (Luxemburg 1984: 187–189). Here, she writes that Diefenbach will be the second reader after Franz Mehring of her manuscript for *The Accumulation of Capital—An Anti-Critique*, an answer to the critics of her *Accumulation of Capital* (1913). She reports that Mehring has read the manuscript a few times and "at first reading he called it 'simply brilliant,' since the death of Marx a book second to none" (Luxemburg 1984: 187). Later, however, she adds, he was more moderate in his opinion. She seems to view the *Anti-Critique* as a more mature work than *Accumulation of Capital*, "without any side issue, without any coquetry and delusion." And she adds that she "now in scientific labor as in art only estimates something that is simple, quiet and an open-minded way of thinking, because of which to me for example the strongly praised volume 1 of Marx's 'Capital' with its overloading of rococo-ornaments in Hegel's style is now an anathema" (Luxemburg 1984: 187).

We need to take Mehring's first reading of the manuscript of the *Anti-Critique* as "simply brilliant" with a grain of salt, for he was hardly proficient in Marx's critique of political economy. On the one hand, we find in Luxemburg a disdain for the "rococo-ornaments in Hegel's style" and on the other hand, neither Mehring nor Luxemburg had much knowledge of the significance that the dialectical, revolutionary framework of Hegel's thought had for Marx. Such ignorance was generally prevalent in the Second International. What concerns us here, however, is not the academic question of being knowledgeable about Hegel or not. As will be discussed shortly, in dealing with Luxemburg's theory of imperialism we will see that what is really at stake is Marx's notion of the revolutionary Subject.

The most shocking element in Luxemburg's letter is that she, with her method of "simple, quiet and open-minded way of thinking," considers *Capital*, Volume 1 to be an "anathema." Therefore, she is taking up Volume 2 of *Capital*, as *she conceives of it*, as the basis for her theory of accumulation of capital and imperialism. Luxemburg was living in the period of rising imperialism and when she is talking about an "explanation of the economic roots of imperialism" she holds that it "must be deduced from the laws of capital accumulation, since, according to common empirical knowledge, imperialism as a whole is nothing but a specific method of accumulation" (Luxemburg 1972: 61). For that explanation she turns to *Capital* Volume 2 and questions Marx's assumptions, "which are constructed for a society in which capitalist production is the only form, where the entire population consists solely of capitalists and wage laborers?" (Luxemburg 1972: 61). Marx also made this assumption in Volume 1.

She formulates her critique of Marx's assumption of a closed capitalist society with only two classes, workers and capitalists, in this manner in the *Anti-Critique*: "For you can twist and turn it as you wish, but so long as we retain the assumption that there are no other classes but capitalists and workers, then there is no way that the capitalists as a class can rid of the surplus goods in order to change the surplus value into money, and thus accumulate capital" (Luxemburg 1972: 58). In her notion of the accumulation of capital, she assumes that "there must develop right from the start an exchange relationship between capitalist production and the non-capitalist milieu, where capital not only finds the possibility of realizing surplus value in hard cash for further capitalization, but also receives various commodities to extend production, and finally wins new proletarianized labor forces by disintegrating the non-capitalist forms of production" (Luxemburg 1972: 59).

This means that she is looking for other forces, *outside* the capitalist milieu, to explain the process of accumulation of capital within capitalist society. To Luxemburg, it concerns those forces that are able to realize surplus value, i.e., to transform surplus value into money. She is starting with the *market* in capitalism, the process of selling in order to realize created surplus value, instead of the sphere of production, as Marx does. She assumes that a closed capitalist society with only workers and capitalists, the one that Marx assumes, cannot explain the transformation of all surplus value into money and thus cannot explain the process of accumulation.

We wrote above that the growth of constant capital (means of production and raw materials) in relation to variable capital (living labor power) is inherent to the process of capital accumulation. Luxemburg denies this. In *The Accumulation of Capital* (pp. 271–326), Luxemburg is considering the discussion in Russia—from the beginnings of the 1880s to the middle of the 1890s— about the relation c/v [constant capital/variable capital].

On this matter, Dunayevskaya writes that Luxemburg's notion was that "the Russian Marxists were deeply mistaken when they thought that the preponderance of constant capital over variable capital... 'alone' revealed the specific characteristic law of capitalist production, 'for which production is an aim in itself and individual consumption merely a subsidiary condition'" (Dunayevskaya 1991: 38). Luxemburg's focus on the market and individual consumption, instead of production "transforms the inner core of capitalism into a mere outer covering" (Dunayevskaya 1991: 38). Because for Luxemburg the relation of constant capital to variable capital "is merely 'the capitalist language' of the general productivity of labor," she "is depriving the carefully isolated c/v relationship of its class character" (Dunayevskaya 1991: 38). Again, according to Dunayevskaya, this means that Luxemburg identifies "what Marxism had considered to be the specific characteristic law of capitalist production—c/v— with 'all pre-capitalist forms of production' *as well as* with 'the future, socialist organization'" (Dunayevskaya 1991: 38).

In contrast to Luxemburg, when Marx deals with the accumulation of capital in *Capital*, Volume 2, he divides social production into two departments: means of production and means of consumption. He assumes a closed capitalist society with only the class of workers and the class of capitalists. His two departments reflect this class relation. Grossman writes concerning this key assumption by Marx:

> If Marx combines capitalist production not into one, but in two branches— and not into any arbitrary branches, but in such a way that means of production must *necessarily* be produced in one, and the means of consumption in the other— then this occurs because, in his schema, Marx wanted to illustrate all the necessary conditions for the existence of a capitalism that is conceived of as isolated. (Grossman 2013: 158)

Luxemburg, however, explicitly rejects Marx's assumption of two departments:

Here, however, we deviate from Marx. He included the production of gold (we have reduced the total production of money to the production of gold for the sake of simplicity) in the first department of social production. "The production of gold, like that of metals generally, belongs to department 1, which occupies itself with means of production." This is correct only in so far as the production of gold is the production of metal for industrial purposes (jewelry, dental toppings, etc.). But gold in its capacity as money is not a metal but rather an embodiment of social labour in abstracto. Thus it is no more a means of production than it is a consumer good. (Luxemburg 1951: 99–100)

She considers Marx's two departments as only a technical question and thinks that she can improve the division into two departments by intro-ducing a third one, the production of gold. Grossman remarks ironically as to this deviation from Marx: "Would Marx really have confused so elementary categories as means of exchange and means of production?" (Grossman 1971: 82).

We already saw above that Luxemburg is looking for a way whereby the capitalists as a class can rid themselves of surplus goods in order to change surplus value into money, and thus accumulate capital. Dunayevskaya's notion of the issue at hand is that "the whole complex question of the conditions of expanded reproduction can be reduced to the following: can the surplus *product* in which the surplus value is incorporated go directly (without first being sold) into further production? Marx's answer is: 'It is not needed that the latter (means of production) be sold; they can *in nature* again enter into new production'" (Dunayevskaya 1991: 35–36).

Concerning the structure of *Capital*, we referred above to Dunayevskaya's 1957 letter to Marcuse and to her *Marxism and Freedom*. We have to add another point Dunayevskaya introduces, in *Rosa Luxem-burg, Women's Liberation, and Marx's Philosophy of Revolution*, on the structure of *Capital*, Volume 1. There, she writes concerning the changes Marx introduced after 1867: "The most fundamental and greatest changes were introduced into [the chapter on] "The Accumulation of Capital" (Dunayevskaya 1991: 147) and that "'The Accumulation of Capital' was a substitute" for what Marx had in mind originally as the ending, to wit, "Results of the Immediate Process of Production" (Dunayevskaya 1991: 147). She writes further that it "is the centerpoint of volume 2, though it is entitled 'The Process of Circulation.' (It must not be forgotten that what we know now as volume 2 was considered by Marx to be book 2 of volume 1.)" (Dunayevskaya 1991: 147).

Part VI of *Capital*, Volume 1, "The Process of Accumulation of Capital," writes Dunayevskaya, "begins with 'Simple Reproduction'." She adds:

> So much of the section on "Erroneous Conception by Political Economy of Reproduction on a Progressively Increased Scale" answers Rosa Luxemburg, that it is almost impossible to understand how she could have failed to see that the problems in volume 2 are answered in volume 1, including even the reference to the fact that "the general change of places in the circulation of wealth of society... dazes the sight and propounds very complicated problems for a solution." (Dunayevskaya 1991: 147)

As to expanded reproduction in capitalist society Dunayevskaya writes, "there is hardly a fundamental point in this critique of classical political economy about expanded reproduction that isn't already anticipated here [in Volume 1]" (Dunayevskaya 1991: 147).

Grossman has the same opinion about Luxemburg's approach:

> Luxemburg refers to the incomplete character of the second volume of *Capital*, but she forgets that, while the *schematic* representation of the production process was only carried out in the second volume, the essential aspects of Marx's theory of reproduction and accumulation are developed in the first volume, which we have in a finished form. (Grossman 2013: 156)

Both Dunayevskaya and Grossman are pointing to the "wholeness" of *Capital* Volume 1 which structures the setting of Volumes 2 and 3. Where Dunayevskaya is above all emphasizing the Humanism of Marx in that Volume, his philosophy of revolution, Grossman is stressing more the inner logic of the economic ideas.[7]

We can speculate about why it was not possible for Luxemburg to follow Marx's development of the structure of *Capital*, Volume 1, but it is a fact that she did not do it. During her lifetime the *Grundrisse* (first time published in 1939 and 1941) was still unknown, except for the Introduction, which was published by Karl Kautsky in 1903. In her era, the *Critique of Political Economy*, the three Volumes of *Capital* and the *Theories of Surplus Value* had been published, although the latter was heavily edited by Kautsky. The French edition of *Capital* was also available. Dunayevskaya refers to Marx's Afterword to the French edition of *Capital* in 1875 in which he writes that the French edition "possesses a scientific value independent of the original and should be consulted even by readers familiar with German" (cited in Dunayevskaya 1991: 146). A question arises: What was Luxemburg doing with all this material?

We saw that she was rejecting the assumptions that Marx made concerning the theorization of the accumulation of capital. Instead of taking up these assumptions, writes Dunayevskaya, "Luxemburg falsely counterposed reality to theory." For she "argued that a precise demonstration from history would show that expanded reproduction has never taken place in a closed society, but rather through distribution to, and expropriation of, 'non-capitalist strata and non-capitalist societies'" (Dunayevskaya 1991: 36). Instead of analyzing how accumulation of capital results from the activity of labor or variable capital in the process of production she was describing the process by which capital invades non-capitalist lands (Dunayevskaya 1991: 36–37). Marx, however, was "not only" engaged with "a phenomenological analysis of his age" (Dunayevskaya 1991: 37). To be sure, we can see his attentiveness to the "phenomenological reality" in the very structure of *Capital*, especially in how he takes up the voices of alienated, exploited, and oppressed people, in his concern with their revolts. But he was in the first place interested in what was the "driving force" of this phenomenological reality. As we know, he conceived of the law of motion of capitalism as a contradiction, "the general contradiction of capitalism," which was the contradiction between labor and capital. Because the law of motion of capitalistic society is at the same time the law of its collapse, Marx had to study thoroughly the process of accumulation of capital in which the growth of constant capital in relation to variable capital is actually taking place. Dunayevskaya writes: "Marx's theory was so profound a dialectic of accumulation that, at one and the same time, it disclosed the different forms of revolt and how they revealed the logical development to the point where no alteration in exchange or distribution could fundamentally change anything" (Dunayevskaya 1991: 37).

The big difference we observe here between Marx and Luxemburg is that Marx holds fast in his analysis to *production* and Luxemburg's focus is the *market*. Actually, the status of *Capital*, Volume 1, is at stake here as well. In this context Dunayevskaya concludes "that Volume I, published by Marx is not only, as he put it, a whole in itself. *It is the whole*" (Dunayevskaya 1988: 146).

DUNAYEVSKAYA AND MARX: THE DIALECTIC IN PRODUCTION AND THE HUMAN SUBJECT

According to Dunayevskaya's synopsis, Marx concludes after an engagement with the *production process* in *Capital*, Volume 3: "(1) decline in the rate of profit, (2) deeper and deeper crises, and (3) a greater and greater unemployed army" (Dunayevskaya 1991: 43). She adds that because Marx grounds his analysis of the accumulation of capital on the production process in which the contradiction between capital and labor is fundamental, he sees that "the decay in capitalist production [had its foundation] in the tendency in the *rate* of profit to decline despite the growth in its *mass*" (Dunayevskaya 1991: 44). In contrast, according to Dunayevskaya, Luxemburg goes so far as to state that the mass of profit is such a strong counter-tendency that it counterbalances the tendency of the rate of profit to fall (Dunayevskaya 1991: 44).

When we consider the tendency of the rate of profit to fall, we have to realize that this fall is long-term and is not linear, for there are counter-tendencies. But the underlying tendential fall remains the determinant, even though the tendency has its ups and downs. That is why Roberts holds "that there is no permanent slump in capitalism that cannot be eventually overcome by capital itself. Capitalism has an economic way out if the mass of working people do not gain political power to replace the system....Capital will resurface for a new period of growth and development, but only after the bankruptcy of many companies, a huge rise in unemployment, and even the physical destruction of things and people in their millions" (Roberts 2016: 6).

Luxemburg, exactly as bourgeois economists, thinks the cause of capitalist crisis lies in a deficiency of effective demand. She focuses on the market. She does not realize that overproduction or underconsumption emerge "*because of the fundamental antecedent decline in the rate of profit, which has nothing whatever to do with the inability to sell*" (Dunayevskaya 1991: 43).

Actually, the theory of the tendency of the rate of profit to fall is a death blow for all theories that start from effective demand in order to explain the fundamental crisis in capitalism and that try to change the system by means of altering effective demand. The detailed scientific contributions of Marx concerning "economics" and the theoretical and empirical work of Grossman and many contemporary Marxist economists show that the law of motion of capitalism does exist in the sphere of production and that the law of the tendency of the rate of profit is its driving force and thus also the ground for crisis.

Also, theories of effective demand can at best point to the need for reforms *within* capitalism, but not why it is *necessary* to end value and surplus value production in order to break down and transcend an *inhuman* and *contradictory* system.

That is the significance of Dunayevskaya's notion that Marx's dialectic of accumulation disclosed the different forms of revolt and also revealed the logical development of the system to the point where no alteration in exchange or distribution could fundamentally change anything. It is here, just here, that Dunayevskaya's notion of economics connected at a fundamental level the economic laws of the breakdown of capitalism *with* the strife between the worker and the machine, against dead labor of the machine's domination over living labor. This notion, which began with *hearing* the worker's voice, was topical for her age just as it is for ours!

We saw earlier that in deviating from Marx's notion of expanded repro-duction in capitalism, i.e., his notion of capital accumulation, Luxemburg developed an historical description of how capital invaded non-capitalist societies. Moreover, she conceived the imperialist exploitation of these societies as *necessary* for the accumulation of capital. As a result, Luxem-burg theorizes that an outside force, rather than labor, will bring down capitalist society. But nowhere in Luxemburg's theory, as Dunayevskaya notes, do the colonial masses emerge as a revolutionary force. Thus, they remain only as victims of imperialism, not allies of the prole-tariat (Dunayevskaya 1991: 45). Dunayevskaya concludes concerning this notion of Luxemburg: "Put otherwise, the dialectic, both as movement of liberation and as methodology, is entirely missing. All these opposites coexist without ever getting jammed up against each other to produce a movement" (Dunayevskaya 1991: 45). Thus, in Dunayevskaya's critique of Luxemburg, it is by missing the dialectic as movement and method-ology that she is missing the human Subject in the anti-colonial struggles: "All her magnificent descriptions of imperialist oppression have no live Subject arise to oppose it [colonialism]; they remain just suffering masses, not gravediggers of imperialism" (Dunayevskaya 1991: 47).

The significance of Dunayevskaya's theorization of capital accumula-tion, of the law of the tendency of the rate of profit to fall, of Marx's crisis theory, and alongside that, her critique of Luxemburg's notions of capital accumulation and imperialism lies in the relation of all of this to a "philos-ophy of revolution": "Just as the relationship of dialectics to economics did not exhaust the significance of the dialectics of revolution, neither did the 'self-determination of the Idea' exhaust itself by being parallel with the struggle of self-determination of nations. Absolute negativity manifests its pivotal role in the Idea precisely because it is both totality (summation) and new beginning, which each generation must first work out for itself" (Dunayevskaya 1991: 194).

In short, Dunayevskaya's lifelong work has as a major theme the unity of dialectics and economics, and ultimately, of philosophy and revolution.

NOTES

1. "A depression is defined here as when economies are growing at well below their previous rate of output (in total and per capita) and below their long-term average. It also means that levels of employment and investment are well below those peaks and below long-term-averages. Above all, it means that the profitability of the capitalist sectors in economies remain, by and large, lower than levels before the start of the depression" (Roberts 2016: 4, 5).
2. We encounter again this formulation in *Capital*, Volume 1, about a society where the full and free development of every individual is the ruling principle, in Marx's *Critique of the Gotha Program* where he writes that the future communist society will be based upon the principle, "From each according to his abilities, to each according to his needs!" (Marx 1985: 15).
3. Because Louis Althusser denied Marx's notion of humanism and its development in all of Marx's works, he completely missed what Dunayevskaya in this context of the miners' strike called "*the* new theoretical response to the workers' revolt against the tyranny of factory labor" as Marx and Lenin conceived it (Dunayevskaya 1988: 55).
4. The notion "man-killer" is nowadays perhaps even more topical in the context of Artificial Intelligence and Robots which are threatening in their *capitalistic form* to become destroyers of humanity.
5. When Marx is writing about "new forces and passions" we have to consider this in relationship to what he writes in *Capital*, Volume 3 about *dialectics*: "It is always the direct relationship of the owners of the conditions of production to the direct producers — a relation always naturally corresponding to a definite stage in the development of the methods of labor and thereby its social productivity — which reveals the innermost secret, the hidden basis of the entire social structure and with it the political form of the relation of sovereignty and dependence, in short, the corresponding specific form of the state. This does not prevent the same economic basis — the same from the standpoint of its main conditions — due to innumerable different empirical circumstances, natural environment, racial relations, external historical influences, etc. from showing infinite variations

and gradations in appearance, which can be ascertained only by analysis of the empirically given circumstances" (Marx 1992: 732). For reasons of space we cannot work out this notion of dialectic, but it will be clear that it is highly important for a non-class reductionist analysis of social movements as to "race", gender, indigenous people, LBGTQ issues, and ecology.

6. Hans Diefenbach was at that time Luxemburg's lover.
7. During Dunayevskaya's lifetime most of the works of Grossman had not been translated from the German. Since she did not read German, it is possible that she gained indirect knowledge of Grossman's main work, *Das Akkumulations- und Zusammenbruchsgesetz des kapitalistischen Systems* (1929) through Paul Mattick's 1934 article in English on Grossman.

REFERENCES

Anderson, Kevin B. and Russell Rockwell, eds. 2012. *The Dunayevskaya-Marcuse-Fromm Correspondence, 1954–1978: Dialogues on Hegel, Marx, and Critical Theory*. Lanham, MD: Lexington Books.

Dunayevskaya, Raya. 1957. Letter to Marcuse October 11. In: Anderson and Rockwell 2012: 40–44.

———. 1967. *State-Capitalism and Marx's Humanism or Philosophy and Revolution*. Detroit: News & Letters.

———. 1980. *25 Years of Marxist-Humanism in the U.S.* Detroit: News & Letters.

———. [1958] 1988. *Marxism and Freedom: From 1776 Until Today*. New York: Columbia University Press.

———. [1973] 1989. *Philosophy and Revolution: From Hegel to Sartre and From Marx to Mao*. With a preface by Louis Dupré. New York: Columbia University Press.

———. [1982] 1991. *Rosa Luxemburg, Women's Liberation, and Marx's Philosophy of Revolution*. With a foreword by Adrienne Rich. Urbana and Chicago: University of Illinois Press.

Grossman, Henryk. 1971. "Die Goldproduktion im Reproduktionsschema von Marx und Rosa Luxemburg." In: *Aufsätze zur Krisentheorie*: 77–113. Frankfurt: Verlag Neue Kritik.

———. 2013. "The Change in the Original Plan for Marx's Capital and its Causes." *Historical Materialism* 21 (3): 138–164.

Luxemburg, Rosa. [1913] 1951. *The Accumulation of Capital*. With an introduction by Joan Robinson. London: Routledge & Kegan Paul.

———. [1917] 1972. *The Accumulation of Capital—An Anti-Critique*. In: Tarbuck, Kenneth J., ed., *Imperialism and the Accumulation of Capital*: 47–150. London: Penguin Press.

————. 1984. Letter to Hans Diefenbach of March 8, 1917. In: Laschitza, Annelies und Radczun, Günter, ed. 1984, *Rosa Luxemburg. Gesammelte Briefe-Band* 5: 187–189. Berlin: Dietz Verlag.

Marcuse, Herbert. 1957. Letter to Raya Dunayevskaya of October 9, 1957. In: Anderson and Rockwell 2012: 40.

Marx, Karl. [1875]. 1985. *Kritik des Gothauer Programms.* In MEGA I/25. Berlin: Dietz Verlag: 3–25.

————. [1887]. 1990. *Capital. A Critical Analysis of Capitalist Production.* In MEGA II/9. Berlin: Dietz Verlag.

————. 1992. *Ökonomische Manuskripte 1863–1867.* In MEGA II/4.2. Berlin: Dietz Verlag.

Mattick, Paul. 1934. "The Permanent Crisis- Henryk's Grossman's Interpretation of Marx's Theory of Capitalist Accumulation." *International Council Correspondence* 1 (2) (November): 1–20.

Roberts, Michael. 2016. *The Long Depression: How It Happened, Why It Happened, and What Happens Next.* Chicago: Haymarket Books.

CHAPTER 12

The Revolutionary Travels of *Marxism and Freedom*

David Black

RECEPTION OF DUNAYEVSKAYA'S MARXISM AND FREEDOM

Marxism and Freedom: From 1776 Until Today by Raya Dunayevskaya (1910–1987) was published in 1958 in hardback by Bookman, New York, with a preface by Herbert Marcuse. The first part of what follows briefly surveys the book's reception among European intellectuals. The second part charts Dunayevskaya's travels in Europe following the book's publication, in which she sought to find publishers for new editions, give university lectures, and meet other Leftists in person to seek out organizational cooperation. The third part addresses the "unfinished business" left by the book: (1) Lenin's "ambivalence" on philosophical questions and his shortcomings regarding the role of the "vanguard party"; (2) Dunayevskaya's interpretation of Hegel's philosophical "absolutes" as a call to unify theory and practice; and (3) her interpretation of "absolute negativity" as the "revolution in permanence" needed to uproot the capitalist value-form and liberate the human foundations for socialism.

D. Black (✉)
London, UK

© The Author(s) 2021   233
K. B. Anderson et al. (eds.), *Raya Dunayevskaya's Intersectional Marxism*, Marx, Engels, and Marxisms,
https://doi.org/10.1007/978-3-030-53717-3_12

In Britain, Dunayevskaya's book was distributed by Vision Press. Reviewing it in the *Universities and Left Review*, Autumn 1958, Alasdair MacIntyre lauds one of the book's most original and controversial themes—Dunayevskaya's explication of Marx's indebtedness to Hegel:

> Certainly Marx had to transform Hegel. But the ferment of the concepts of freedom, reason and consciousness in Marx's philosophy is the Marxist debt to Hegel. Hegel without Marx is unrealistic, and in the end obscurantist. Marx without Hegel would have been rigid, mechanical, inhuman... ([1958] 2008: 42)

The book, writes MacIntyre, has "three great merits":

> The first is that she has tried to write a history of Marxist theory in which development of the theory is linked at every point to the corresponding developments both in society and in the political experience of socialists. The second is that she has utilised some of the source material of Marxism more fully than any previous commentator [specifically Marx's Economic and Philosophical Manuscripts of 1844, Lenin's Hegel Notebooks of 1914-15, and the records of the Russian Trade Union Debate of 1920-21 - D.B.]... The third merit of this book, and it arises out of the other two, is that it provides a framework for a re-evaluation of Lenin in which a change can be noted from an emphasis on the party as the revolutionary manipulator of a passive working class to emphasis on the potential revolutionary spontaneity of the working class. And this change goes along with what we may call Lenin's Hegelian conversion.... ([1958] 2008: 42–43)

In his subsequent political development MacIntyre vacillated between Thomism—the Catholic doctrine based on Thomas Aquinas's appropriation of Aristotle's metaphysics—and anti-Stalinist Marxism. Surprisingly, he sees Dunayevskaya's analysis of the USSR as too "negative":

> For Miss Dunayevskaya this is the age of state capitalism, a form of economy common to both USA and USSR. This leads her into a fantastic under-valuation of socialist achievement in the Soviet Union... And the result is that this portion of her book is negative and sterile... Her only hope is the world-wide working class. And the suspicion grows as one reads that she has an entirely idealised view of that class. ([1958] 2008: 44)

Paul Mattick, a German emigrant, and anti-Bolshevik Left Communist, reviewed the book in March 1958 for the Boston-based *Western Socialist*, under the title, "A Marxian Oddity." For Mattick, like Dunayevskaya, the Soviet Union was never socialist, but he would seem to agree with MacIntyre's suspicions about an "idealized view" of the world working class. For Mattick, the idealism stems from Dunayevskaya's Hegelian Marxism: "an embarrassing, scatterbrained hodge-podge of philosophical, economic and political ideas that defy description and serious criticism," and "leads back into the murk of Hegelianism where it gets lost in incomprehensible philosophical gibberish." Mattick, who assumes that his rationalist, materialist-minded readers will share his dismissal of Hegel's philosophy as "mysticism," argues from a position of what Dunayevskaya would call "economism" and class-reductionism:

> ...she celebrates the proletarian aspects of the East German and Hungarian risings but she neglects to pay attention to their nationalist implications. She applauds the bus boycotts by Negroes in America's South. She sees in them expressions of working-class self-determination yet overlooks the striving for racial equality within the existing social system. She supports — as is proper — sporadic wild-cat and sit-down strikes but fails to notice their relative insignificance within the total American situation and with a working class fully in the sway of capitalist ideology. (1958)

Contra Dunayevskaya, Mattick sees no real value in Marx's *1844 Manuscripts* ("fragmentary early writings of Marx... which represent a stage of Marx's intellectual development which he himself was glad to get behind him").

Moreover, Mattick sees Dunayevskaya's analysis of Lenin's break with Second International Marxism as "astonishing":

> [Lenin] came to the conclusion, as he himself stated, that "it is impossible completely to grasp Marx's *Capital* ... if you have not studied through and understood the *whole* of Hegel's *Logic*." Consequently, Lenin added, "none of the Marxists for the past half century have understood Marx." It was a good thing that Lenin opened Hegel's *Logic*. If he had not, there would not have been a true Marxist for a whole century — until the day, that is, when Dunayevskaya herself opened the *Logic*. (1958)

George Lichtheim, another German emigrant (and like Mattick, an anti-Bolshevik Marxist), reviewed the second American edition of

Marxism and Freedom in the *New York Review of Books*, December 17, 1964. Lichtheim recognizes that Dunayevskaya "has a firm grasp of the essentials so far as the descent from Lenin to Stalin is concerned." However,

> Her own utopianism comes out in the chapter devoted to 1921, the NEP [New Economic Policy], and the failure of the "Workers' Opposition." It is true that Lenin in 1921 tried to salvage what was left of party democracy, where Stalin later ruthlessly destroyed it... "The tragedy of the Russian Revolution," in her view, was that "the masses" were not really drawn into public life, in the way Lenin had envisaged when he wrote State and Revolution. But in the absence of democracy, how could they have been so drawn in? Mrs. Dunayevskaya might have learned the reasons of the failure from Rosa Luxemburg, whose general outlook is somewhat akin to hers. (1964)

Dunayevskaya would later write a book taking up Rosa Luxemburg, which would indeed discuss Lenin's and Luxemburg's divergences on democracy and socialism. Lichtheim was one of those intellectuals she liked to refer to as a "friendly enemy."

The August 21, 1959 edition of the London *Times Literary Supplement* ran an unsigned review of the book, entitled "Marx's Heirs and Antecedents," which later turned out to have been written by the historian, E. H. Carr. According to Carr:

> Mrs. Dunayevskaya's assumption that the present regime in the Soviet Union, whatever it may be called, cannot and will not raise the living standard of the masses of workers seems particularly rash, and tends to discredit the case she builds on it... Automation is, one gathers, the ultimate and complete subjection of man to the machine – of the "alienation' of labour." It can only provoke the spontaneous revolt of the workers, which must be the beginning of any true process of liberation. The conclusion is lost in these floating clouds. But the book contains enough stimulating argument and enough glimpse of insight to prove attractive and valuable to those whose thinking can accommodate itself to the Marxist categories. (1959: 479)

DUNAYEVSKAYA'S TRIP TO EUROPE, 1959

Philosophical Letters to a Worker: Frank Williams

On September 9, 1959, Raya Dunayevskaya boarded the S.S. August, bound for Genoa. Relaxing under "floating clouds" on the deck, she studied Hegel's *Phenomenology of Mind*. Dunayevskaya, having brought out *Marxism and Freedom*, was already thinking about a follow-up which would fully engage with philosophy proper. In a letter to Herbert Marcuse (July 15, 1958), she had written:

> You once told me that what I wrote in the first letters in 1953 on the Absolute Idea and what appeared in Marxism and Freedom were miles apart and, in a sense it is. No public work, popular or unpopular, can contain the intricacies of thought as they develop in the abstract form before they become filled with more concrete content... But I do mean to follow up the book with further development, and I certainly would love to have your help, no matter how sharply critical, in breaking through those murky categories. (2002: 98)

Her most important contact in Britain was Frank Williams, a worker in East London, to whom she writes on September 11, 1959:

> You are obviously the "greatest find" of all and therefore it would be important that I see as much of you as possible, which means that if at all possible, you should try to take some time from work. I know what money means especially as you are a prospective father, but think seriously and we'll see what can be worked out. (1959d)

Her letters to Williams reveal how much philosophy was on her mind, and how its insights could speak to a worker-intellectual like Williams who was interested in theory and the history of class struggle:

> ...written from the boat, which means at one with a world free of details and an ocean stimulating to thought. This is not to say that details cannot be so. On the contrary. A great deal of this letter concerns the simple detail never noticed before, because England was never as actual to my thoughts and that is that the translation and translator's preface of Hegel's Phenomenology of Mind – one JB Baillie – comes from the University of Leeds... this is one of the few "interpretations" that has something to say. (1959d)

In her view, Baillie's preface captured,

> the very essence of the Hegelian concept that there are no "accidents"
> in history – that the sum total of accidents tells you the true course
> of history... In Hegel's view this is not accidental, but the principle
> underlying human experience. The individual is potentially capable of
> accomplishing all that humanity has explicitly realized. The wealth of
> human resources is his rightful inheritance and endowment, the achieve-
> ment of humanity is his own fulfillment, its range and its height, the
> measure of his stature and his worth. The proof that philosophy is concrete
> to [Baillie] is the fact that he refused to capitulate to anyone who thinks
> thought is abstract. He not only in his comments before each section
> relates each stage of consciousness to the historic period, from Greek civi-
> lization through the French Revolution to which it pertains. But he relates
> the whole movement from abstract to concrete in Hegel to the move-
> ment from potentiality to actuality. In a couple of places he reminds me of
> Marx... How could possibly a man like that [have] failed to be interested
> in some of Marx *if* he had ever heard of it outside its perversions, direct
> and indirect. (1959d)

Baillie's University in Leeds was, as it happened, one of the places where
Dunayevskaya was scheduled to give a lecture on Hegel and Marx. She
asks Williams to try and find out if Baillie is still alive and, if so, to track
him down so she could meet him (she did not know that Sir James Black
Baillie, born in Scotland in 1872, had died in 1940).

For Marxist-Humanism, the movement from abstract to concrete was
a relation of philosophy to revolution, and of ideas to class struggle:

> I take it for granted that the proletarian developments will be the basis
> always and that a country that is as rich and advanced in its prole-
> tarian history as England with its Levellers, Diggers, Chartists will produce
> many "firsts" to the preface of such an English edition [of Marxism and
> Freedom]. (1959d)

The importance of finding the British roots of class struggle was also to
"find the philosophic root which is at the same time method and result":

> In this case to combine root, method *and* result is neither dilettantish
> nor too all-encompassing. It means only that in *today's proletariat, English
> proletariat* you will find the continuators of the Hegelian tradition. And if
> that is not obvious it is because no intellectual has been looking seriously...

Marxism and Freedom gives us a platform. Now, I am *not* creating a theory out of the "accident." But here is the history of Hegelianism in England to show you why my confidence has a solid basis. (1959d)

Talk of a "Hegelian tradition" in the history of the British proletariat was by no means as "off-beam" as it might have appeared to historians of the 1950s, who had failed to take account of the profound Hegelian writings in the Chartist press of Helen Macfarlane, who is described by Marx in 1851 as a "rara avis" with "original ideas" compared to most empirically-minded Chartist leaders (Marx and Engels [1851] 1982: 291; Macfarlane, 2014). But neither Williams nor Dunayevskaya were aware of this at the time.

Looking forward to the Paris end of her trip she shares her thoughts with Williams on the writings of the Marxologist, Maximilien Rubel, whom she also wanted to meet:

Now Maximilien Rubel of Paris has decided that all Marx used was "Method" and that both "dialectical" and "historical" materialism are Engels's vulgarizations. Now there is no doubt Engels was just a follower and that the humanism of Marxism and the *simplicity* of the dialectic escaped him, so that his 1886 version of "Feuerbach" is vastly inferior to the young Marx's of 1844 which he was "bringing up to date." But to accuse Engels of not understanding that for Marx both reality and thought are one continuous process is to misread the young Marx's criticism of Hegel's idealism for a criticism of actual thought. In the end, Rubel had to say Lenin made the same mistake. So here is one who does understand "humanism" but because he doesn't see it *concretely* as [the] end of division of mental and manual he suddenly calls it all "ontology," i.e., a closed system, beginning and ending with thought's development and nothing else, and of course if it (Absolute Idea) were only "ontology" we would reject it... Now I say all this to you because if you have no Rubel's and Marcuse's bearing such names we will be meeting them bearing other names once we try to penetrate the intellectual closed circle – and we must have some first-class intellectuals in the proletarian movement. We will have to teach them to give up the million ways they have of avoiding the proletarian reality and *then* they'll be good – I'll even call them indispensable if they accept the proletarian discipline. Let's use my trip to go searching for some. (1959d)

The Italian Left

In July 1958, Dunayevskaya's sister, Bess, and her husband, Louis Gogol, attended a "regroupment" conference in Milan of revolutionaries who shared the view that Russia and the other Stalinist states were forms of bureaucratic or state capitalism. Those attending included Socialisme ou Barbarie (SoB) and Pouvoir Ouvrier from France; a number of Spanish exiles (including Alberto Vega); and the Italian groups, Battaglia Comunista, and Azione Comunista. The conference set up a tentative "Center of International Correspondence" to translate documents produced by the participating organisations (1958b).

Dunayevskaya accepted an invitation for a follow-up European International Conference to be held in Milan in September 1959. In preparation for her trip Dunayevskaya corresponded with the Polish-born novelist, Jean Malaquais, then based in Paris (1958a); the French philosopher Maximilien Rubel (1959b); the Spanish revolutionary exile, Grandizo Munis (1959c); and Onorato Damen (1893–1979), leader of the Italian group, Battaglia Communista. Dunayevskaya wrote to Damen:

> I believe that a conference of the groups who participated last summer [1958] and those who, like the Spanish and Greek, wish to do so now, should not only hear reports of the activities in the various countries, but to face soberly their theoretic responsibilities historically as Marxists. Time is not forever. The Berlin crisis, the moves toward to right in Italy, the African Revolution [and] the American-Russian war-like gestures may well make this *the* turning point in history. (1959a)

On September 23, 1959 Dunayevskaya disembarked in Genoa and was met by the philosopher Luciano Raimondi. A communist Partisan leader in World War Two, Raimondi (1916–1965) later broke with the Italian Communist Party to join the leftist *Azione Comunista* group. Dunayevskaya also met Luciano Bianciardi (1922–1971), novelist and translator, who was working with Raimondi on the prospective Italian edition of *Marxism and Freedom*; and Damen, who was arranging publication of the book in Italy by La Nuovo Italia press. As a close ally of Amadeo Bordiga (1889–1970), Damen had been one of the founders of the Italian Communist Party in 1921 and suffered imprisonment several times under Mussolini's fascist regime. In 1945 Bordiga founded the Internationalist Communist Party (ICP), with which Damen aligned himself. The "official," Moscow-line Communist Party general secretary

Palmiro Togliatti (1893–1964), in his capacity as the Italian Minister of Justice decreed a general amnesty of fascist leaders and party members at the very time his party was denouncing Damen and the leaders of the ICP as "saboteurs." The culmination of this defamatory campaign was the assassination by Stalinists of two ICP founders, Fausto Atti and Mario Acquaviva. Bordiga's advocacy of a return to the Left Communist positions of the 1920s was rejected by Damen as being somewhat mechanical and ahistorical. Also, whereas Damen regarded Russia as state capitalist, Bordiga regarded the Russian bureaucracy as a cabal of gangsters that did not amount to a capitalist class (Goldner 1997). In the early 1950s Damen's group took the name International Communist Party and published the paper, *Battaglia Comunista* and the journal *Prometeo*.

The Italian Left were critically engaged with the positions of the French group, Socialisme or Barbarie (founded and led by Cornelius Castoriadis, alias Pierre Chaulieu, alias Paul Cardan) regarding workers' councils. Castoriadis, who saw the Hungarian workers' councils of 1956 as exemplary forms for establishing a post-capitalist society, drew up a veritable blueprint for a new "system" of elected workers' councils, a central assembly and a national "planning factory."

But the collapse of the Fourth Republic in 1958 did not provide an opening for the radical Left; instead it led to de Gaulle's Fifth Republic and a new era of corporatism and neo-colonialism. Dunayevskaya comments:

> Damen says rightly… that workers councils arise on the crest of revolution – as in Russian Revolution, so in the Hungarian; where they do not, such a slogan could be entirely reformist, as it means functioning *within* capitalist framework. (1959d)

On the other hand, she disagreed with Damen's conclusion that the absence of a vanguard party had been the one and *only* cause of the defeat of the Hungarian workers councils. The Italian groups Battaglia Comunista and Azione Comunista were "re-evaluating their own failures to act as polarizing force and insisting that the intellectual responsibility must move toward working for a unity of theory and practice" (1959d).

But in Dunayevskaya's view, the weakness of Damen's position was "above all" his rejection of trade union and parliamentary interventions. On September 27, 1959, following the conference in Milan, Dunayevskaya reports concerning his introduction to the meeting:

Damen, in his introduction, stressed that we have much in common in the general Marxist theory and in the feel for the spontaneity of the proletariat.

There were however,

> different views on the role of the vanguard party, the role of philosophy in which he considers me an idealist, and on humanism... which in Italy, says he, is the excuse for all those who have left the movement and search communion with reformism, etc. He also stressed that the book *will* be published and is a very important contribution, especially in its economic parts, both of Marxist theory and on state-capitalism which from fundamental points unite the American movement with the Italian. (1959d)

Also present at this meeting was Azione Comunista leader Bruno Fortichiari (1892–1981), who like Damen had been a founder of the PCI in 1921:

> It was interesting, incidentally, that the only time I was interrupted in the speech – in the first few minutes I spoke about how the few here as compared to the 2 million of the CP show us our problem, was a remark by Fortichiari that "but these few are very good, and we have others who did not come because of work, but they too are of the best." I agreed they were of the best, "the *very* best," but reality and totality of crisis only emphasize the task. The fact that they are vanguard, or as they put it even more precisely, "nucleus of vanguard," is important for their morale as for other things. (1959d)

One criticism consistently leveled at Dunayevskaya throughout her revolutionary life was that her refusal to drop or water down the key philosophical/political tenets of Marxist-Humanism in favor of Left "unity" or "regroupment" was "sectarian." It may be surprising then that she had so much admiration and respect for many of those with whom she had disagreements. Damen and Fortichiari, after all, "stood out" all their lives as revolutionaries; having opposed imperialist war in 1914, supported the Russian Revolution, fought against fascism, and opposed Stalinism—all at considerable personal cost. And they were now giving a platform to the new ideas of Marxist-Humanism, itself developed during the McCarthyite repression in the U.S.A.

In the discussion on collaboration between the Italian Left and Marxist-Humanism for the purpose of building a new international movement, Dunayevskaya promised that their role in producing an Italian edition of the book would be reciprocated straightway by throwing the columns of the Detroit-based Marxist-Humanist paper, *News & Letters*, open to contributions from their Italian workers; by building a future conference of Italian groups, U.S. and British Marxist-Humanists, African revolutionaries and others to discuss theoretical and practical developments; and by organizing the sale and distribution of each other's publications. In a later memoir of these events Dunayevskaya recalls:

> I had in my hand for the trip *Marxism and Freedom* as well as our new pamphlet, *Nationalism, Communism, Marxist-Humanism and the Afro-Asian Revolutions*, and I insisted that all those who attended had to focus on the new revolutions in the Third World. I asked that the African comrades be invited (I continued corresponding with Africans until I went to Africa in 1962, and they helped map my trip to Nigeria, Ghana, Senegal, and the Gambia.) The European International Conference itself, while not grounded in philosophy, Marxist-Humanist or otherwise, and not agreeing with my analysis of the very new African Revolutions, did approve my motion to continue discussion on a regular basis in the Italian journal, Prometeo.... Prometeo continued to publish my articles, which included my critique of Luxemburg's *Accumulation of Capital*, as well as one on the Cuban Missile Crisis. (1980a, 1980b)

Unfortunately, none of the groups represented at the September 1959 European International Conference did much to follow up Dunayevskaya's suggestion to work with African revolutionaries.

The British Scene

Dunayevskaya was not unfamiliar with the British Left, having visited London in 1947, but had no real interlocutors there until the publication of *Marxism and Freedom*. On that first visit, she had tried (unsuccessfully) to engage with Tony Cliff on the question of state capitalism. She also tried to meet members of the Trotskyist Revolutionary Communist Party, but was blocked by Gerry Healy, a notorious, dictatorial sectarian, who regarded the organization as his own personal property. Dunayevskaya's letters to Williams express what building an organizational presence in Britain would entail:

What is basic, after all, with these splinter groups with their miserable little mimeographed sheets, is not [to have] yet one more group that is "broad." What is needed is a group that knows where it is going and lays the Marxist foundation for it. Once it does that, it can collaborate with all other groups that it wishes to the extent which is required, etc., etc. Before it does so, on the other hand, it would only add to the confusion, not the clarity. I will leave it in your hands, which should precede which. (1959d)

Dunayevskaya arrived in Britain days after the 8 October 1959 General Election. In Britain's booming post-austerity economy, in which social democrats proclaimed the "End of Ideology," Tory Prime Minister Harold Macmillan's slogan, "You've never had it so good" returned the Conservative Party to office in a near-landslide victory over Hugh Gaitskell's Labour Party. On 11 October a meeting for Dunayevskaya was held in Liverpool at the Stork Hotel, Queens Square, where she found the audience "so broken up" over Labour's election loss that "they could not see beyond 'prosperity' and 'youth' who don't know depression and had voted Tory." This was followed by a lecture at Leeds University 14 October on "Marx's Debt to Hegel," attended by about 40 faculty members and students, then another Leeds meeting which drew a lively 150, mainly "Labour youth" (1959f).

In London, Dunayevskaya sought out various radicals and political tendencies, including the Trotskyist "Pabloites"—"of all things!" she comments. A former leader of the Fourth International, Michel Pablo (also known as Michel Raptis) had abandoned revolutionary politics, "proposing instead that proletarian politics be guided for centuries by the barbarous degradation in Russia and in the buffer states of Eastern Europe" (James, Dunayevskaya, and Lee [1950] 1986: 135). Dunayevskaya also met Michael Kidron of Tony Cliff's *Socialist Review* group ("not without its importance") and *Advance* (edited by Roger Protz of the Labour Young Socialists) (Dunayevskaya 1959d). In a letter to her close colleague in Detroit, Olga Domanski, some days after her arrival, she reports that she has a following of three "handsome lads who had heavy dates they broke to hear me; I think we'll get somewhere" (1959 Archive: 9453, 9465–9466).

Next, she took a train to Glasgow for two meetings organized by Harry McShane. Born in Glasgow in 1891, McShane joined the revolutionary party of John Maclean during World War One and played a leading role in revolt of "Red Clydeside": when a mass strike for a 40-hour week culminated in a pitched battle with police on 31 January 1919 on George Square, Glasgow—after which Prime Minister Lloyd George, fearing Bolshevik revolution in Scotland, sent troops and tanks to control unrest. In 1922, McShane joined the new Communist Party of Great Britain (CPGB). In the 1940s, he became disillusioned with the unprincipled practices of the party and its leaders' mindless subservience to Russian Stalinism. He left the party in the early 1950s (McShane and Smith 1978). Unlike many of those who left the CPGB following the suppression of the Hungarian Revolution in 1956, McShane did not see Trotskyism as representing a truly radical break with the practice and ideology of Stalinism. One reason for this was his memory of "other ways" of thinking and organizing:

> We suffered a long time from the fact that we found it difficult to shake off the "Communist" way of seeing things. Had it not been for the fact that I had been 13 years in the movement before I joined the CP[GB] in 1922, I might never have made it. I certainly would not have made it had it not been for *Marxism and Freedom*. (Hudis 1992: 30)

McShane had been trying to get the *Universities and Left Review* to sponsor the first Glasgow meeting for Dunayevskaya. The *Review* editors had at first been favorable to McShane's suggestion, as Dunayevskaya was "respectably" doing university lectures, but pulled out at the last moment. The meeting went ahead anyway. In Dunayevskaya's description:

> The 2 public meetings in Scotland were so extraordinary that the friend who arranged them, Harry McShane, said: "This is the turning point for us." Here is why: 1) for the first time in a decade all shades of radical view were represented, even dissident communists; that was at the Saturday meeting. 2) It was directly after the Labor Party defeat when too many were bewailing the fact that defeat means "backward step," whereas the meetings revealed that what the workers wanted was something greater than a vote – they wanted a full flag unfurled for a truly new social order. 3) The arrangements were made by that one man [McShane]... with no advertisements, just word of mouth... with a downpour of rain that would have kept all but the hardiest souls at home, 40 showed up for the first meeting on Saturday, and between 75-100 for the second on Sunday, so that *all* present agreed that with any sort of preparation and advertisement they could have a genuine mass meeting which, again, hasn't been

had in years. Harry McShane is a man who has been in the working-class movement and active in every battle from general strike to anti-war, all the way from the end of WW1 when he was a lad till now. A few years ago he broke with the CP and the editor's job he held [on the *Daily Worker*] and returned to the "production line" in the shipyards where he still is – he is 68. It would be hard to find a man half his years with that energy, devotion to the proletarian class and Marxist ideas. (1959d)

As with those Dunayevskaya encountered in Italy, the Scottish Marxists included revolutionary veterans born in the nineteenth century down to the "rock'n'roll youth" of the late-1950s.

Dunayevskaya was very keen to meet Guy Aldred (1886–1963), editor of *The Word*. Aldred, veteran anti-imperialist, Free Love advocate, and brother-in-law of the anarchist Rudolf Rocker, was, according to Ruth Kinna, trying to bridge "the gap between Marxism and Anarchism":

> Believing that his position captured the best of Marxist and anarchist tradi-tions, he argued that socialist factionalism was based on a distortion of Marx's work and that the relationship between Marxism and anarchism was properly understood as one between the head and heart of the movement. (Kinna 2011)

Dunayevskaya, despite her criticisms of anarchism, wanted to meet Aldred. According to a letter from Dunayevskaya to Williams, "[Aldred] wrote enthusiastically about M&F, and had an editorial on it promising a long review but that never was. I wondered why, or if anyone knows about him... He should certainly be informed of my having a meeting in Glasgow and that I personally want to see him" (1959d). The meeting, however, did not take place.

Dunayevskaya records that at one of the Glasgow meetings,

> Present too was the daughter of John Maclean [Nan Milton]... the name which, up to the time of his death in 1923 and even now, stands for the one who got his Socialist Party in World War 1 when the whole 2nd International collapsed, to vote against imperialist war! I spoke on Marxist-Humanism from 1844 through to the Hungarian Revolution of 1956, with a good deal of time on the contribution of American miners in the 1949-50 strike to the question of "What kind of labour should man perform?" At the end Maclean's daughter began to say that since the days of her father she had heard nothing like it – "genuine Marxism"... At the end of

the second, larger, meeting, much of the audience didn't wish to leave at all and since I had to catch a train directly after the meeting they grabbed my bags and began to carry them, and before we knew it something like 25 came with us to see me off on the train. "We could have had hundreds and hundreds at your meetings," everyone bewailed. (1959d)

In London, Dunayevskaya spoke at a meeting organized by Frank Williams at the South London trade union branch of the National Society of Painters, attended by about 50. This was the only meeting in which those attending wanted to hear about American workers, and it was on this topic that she spoke, pointing to how the attitude of technocrats and union bureaucrats, who believed that automation "will bring the millennium," was not shared by American workers. The painters were also very interested in the effects of the U.S. anti-union laws, and the conditions of work and level of wages. Dunayevskaya said,

> When I got to break down that $3.20 an hour for the "lowest" steel workers into the days they work, the price [of goods], etc. they were quite convinced that if there is any gold on the streets of America it is not where the workers live. But most important of all was the interest in News and Letters…and they really do intend to write for the British page – I'm sure of that. (1959d)

After a trip up to Manchester for a University lecture, Dunayevskaya addressed a London meeting of the *Universities and Left Review* (which was about to merge with the *New Reasoner* to form the *New Left Review*). The atmosphere here was in sharp contrast to what she had experienced in Glasgow. The *Review* editors were far from welcoming to Marxist-Humanism, but as they had published Alasdair MacIntyre's positive review of *Marxism and Freedom* they reluctantly agreed to give her a platform. A letter from Dunayevskaya described this meeting, which 250 attended,

> a good crowd of course, but so mixed in attitudes – the student youth are moving away from Marxism, at least in this garbled version of it… every tendency is present and takes time in discussion and helps make Marxism appear mechanical, etc. However some workers followed me here from the trade union branch and I believe it is the first time that group ever had any workers in its audience. The leadership – and they are a worse elite than those of the vanguard parties – almost boycotted the event and

the one editor that did show up walked out after asking a question. This gave me a wonderful opportunity in summation to attack them without gloves and ask the secretaries to take it down: 1) that they complained why was I so "anti-Russian," but the kind of question they asked showed how very necessary it was, not only because they are falling into the CP trap, but because, despite being intellectuals, they read *not* Marx, but what R Palme Dutte says Marx says, with the result that the editor (the future philosopher, Charles Taylor) presented a vulgar materialism against which it was easy to argue, 2) That he had not even read my pamphlet [*Nationalism, Communism, Marxist Humanism and the Afro-Asian Revolutions*] so his concern was that since countries were unindustrialized in Africa "I would not be interested" – and I read out the paragraph "A people mature enough to fight for its freedom is mature enough to take destiny into its own hands." 3) Finally, for Humanists, as they call themselves, not one word was mentioned by *them*, now that I placed *Marxist* humanism as the only 20th century humanism. One of the assistants came up, as did many others, saying that I was "brilliant" and "if I had been in [the] speech as I was in summation" they would have been for me. My reply was: I would never have made the summation as the speech because your approval would have meant nothing… you wouldn't have understood it if you had not first been compelled to understand communism as state-capitalism and as the thing which keeps you imprisoned. (1959d)

The London district forum of the Independent Labour Party (ILP), which Dunayevskaya noted "has long been dead on its feet," (300 members, with 10 branches) normally had "6 – 10" in attendance, but at a meeting the party organized for her at Conway Hall nearly 60 showed up, mainly youth who had no interest in the ILP itself. Dunayevskaya said that while she appreciated being provided with a platform, she thought the ILP's election material made it sound like a "Stalinist Front" in that, while the party was "bravely" against capitalism, it had nothing to say about what that meant in relation to Russian totalitarianism. On 30 October, Dunayevskaya met members of the African Forum, with 25 in attendance, half of them Black. The Forum agreed to sell Marxist-Humanist literature, to write for *News & Letters*, and to invite Dunayevskaya to contribute to their journal, *African Outlook* (Dunayevskaya 1959d).

Referring to her final meeting with contacts in London, Dunayevskaya writes with regard to building international affiliations with News and Letters Committees, the Marxist-Humanist organization she founded in 1955,

Frank Williams is of course magnificent and everyone from friends to enemies (the little radical groups including [Tony] Cliff who are just burning up with jealousy that he was able to secure so many places for me, especially Universities and Left Review that they are always after) recognize what a piece of work he had done in putting Marxist-Humanism on the British map. Around him are 4-6 East Londoners. In my various talks I was able to pick up people who had followed me around from meeting to meeting... All voted for work around News and Letters and an international information bureau – so now there is definitely a group both in Scotland and in England – the rest will depend on themselves and consistent work. (1959d)

After leaving London at the end of October 1959, Dunayevskaya went to Paris for a few days to meet contacts and seek out a publisher. Dunayevskaya met Daniel Mothé, an organizer in the Renault factor at Paris-Billancourt. Although affiliated to Socialisme ou Barbarie, Mothé's ideas about modern capitalism owed more to James and Dunayevskaya than to Castoriadis. Dunayevskaya also met with François Fejtő, Hungarian exile and author of *Behind the Rape of Hungary* (1959d).

In January 1960, following Dunyevskaya's return to Detroit, her monthly paper *News & Letters* began publishing a page on "British Labour News." This section featured reports of industrial labor disputes, debates within the unions, developments in the struggles against British colonialism and South African Apartheid, and a debate (for and against) on Britain's prospective membership of the European Common Market. There was much coverage and correspondence on the ballot-rigging scandal in the Communist Party-controlled Electrical Trades Union, which also warned that the anti-Communist faction, led by the conspiratorial Catholic Action group, showed all the signs of turning the union into an equally authoritarian body, dominated by witch-hunters and class-collaborators. There was extensive coverage of shop floor struggles at the Ford automotive plant at Dagenham, East London, which employed around 40,000 workers. There was little coverage of women's issues, but there is a report on "Plant-Wide Solidarity" from a shop steward at the Plessey engineering plant in Ilford, where there was a one-day protest strike to support equal pay for female plant inspectors,

[s]urely, this stoppage was in some ways unique – in that many men show themselves willing to lose pay, and refuse to accept their own improvements

until a comparatively small number of women can receive benefit also. We
now hope for a settlement without having to resort to further action.
(*News & Letters*, November 1960)

From Glasgow, Harry McShane and his comrade Leslie Forster (1919–
2016) reported on strikes in Scotland, mobilizations by the Campaign
for Nuclear Disarmament, and polemics with the Communist Party,
especially concerning the Glasgow Trades Council.

Frank Williams, in an article for the paper, criticized the depoliticiza-
tion of tendencies that had broken with "vanguardism" in favor of an
economistic syndicalism:

> No genuine workers' movement can be built without politics which are
> more profound than simple opposition to the present bourgeois-reformist
> parties and policies. A hollow advocacy of industrial militancy [a la the
> Syndicalist Workers Federation] begs the questions that workers are asking
> today. They need no lessons from any self-appointed "leadership." Syndi-
> calist economism has nothing to offer the working class. Marxist-Humanist
> answers are urgently needed for the major problems of man's freedom. Can
> the British Marxists not present to the workers the true vision of Marx so
> that the worker recognises it as the inner quality of his own thoughts?
> If capitalism is to be overcome in Britain, something more than a hand-
> to-mouth empirical method is required. The heyday of British imperialism
> drew material strength and intellectual complacency from a vast colonial
> empire. It still is the strong-hold of empiricism. The oppressive grip of this
> slothful outlook has not served the British workers too well. Even in Karl
> Marx's days, it was impossible to find a British publisher for Capital. Offi-
> cial British Labour still pretends it owes more to Methodism than Marxism.
> (Williams 1961)

At the end of 1961 it was decided to end the presentation of British
Labour News as separate from the rest of the paper. Williams, in support
of this move, wrote in an editorial entitled "A New Stage Begins," in
December 1961:

> I think extension of the international content of the paper as a whole with
> regular permeations of co-thinkers' articles and direct news reportage and
> readers' views as a unified editorial whole, and not split into one "British
> page" and seven mainly US, is a very wise decision of the editorial board
> and will result in the international role of the paper, as the medium of a
> total world outlook, being seen much more clearly by all. (Williams 1961)

Shortly afterward, Frank Williams, who had been editorially responsible for most of its English content, dropped out of politics and trade union work. According to Sheila Leslie, a veteran British socialist born in 1927 who knew Williams at the time, his heavy commitment to political and trade union work, as well as problems at work, seriously strained his family life; he found himself having to choose between his political activism and his marriage (personal communication to the author, 2018).

Later British Developments

It took until 1971 for a British publisher, Pluto Press, to take on *Marxism and Freedom*. It appeared with two prefaces: the original one by Herbert Marcuse alongside a new one by Harry McShane. Pluto Press was, at this time, the publishing arm of the International Socialists (IS), led by Tony Cliff. The book's analysis of Russian state capitalism found favor among anti-Stalinists who were unconvinced by the orthodox Trotskyist designation of the USSR as a "degenerated workers' state." Dunayevskaya's theory of state capitalism differed however, from that of Tony Cliff, who held that because of state control and planning the law of value did not operate internally in the Russian economy; its capitalist nature (acting as "one big company") was imposed by the external factor of the world market (Daum 1990).

There were other forces on the revolutionary left—such as the followers of Castoriadis—who could see little in Lenin's legacy other than an authoritarianism that "paved the way" for Stalinism. Add to this the fact that Britain is the ancestral home of empiricism, and many found Lenin's post-1914 Hegelianism hard to digest as well. (The myth of Hegel as the "mystic" who absolutized the Prussian state was prevalent.) Following the youth radicalization of the late-1960s, Tony Cliff's International Socialists recruited thousands of new members— with a very high turnover—while there was no corresponding growth in Marxist-Humanist organization.

Many readers welcomed Dunayevskaya's exposition of what was truly original about Lenin in his study of Hegel and Marx. However, they paid less attention to Dunayevskaya's intimations about what was lacking in "Leninism," which stood increasingly exposed in the aftermath of the Russian Revolution. The attitude was, "Well, if Lenin was so good after all, why would we join a tiny band of Marxist-Humanists, when you can join a growing 'Bolshevik-Leninist,' would-be revolutionary party organized by Tony Cliff?" Both Trotskyism, whether "orthodox" or "Cliffite," and anti-Bolshevik socialist "libertarianism," had (and still have) top down formulas for organizing and recruiting. There is no organizational "formula" as such to be found in *Marxism and Freedom*:

> The working class has not created a new society. But the workers have undermined the old. They have destroyed all the old categories; they have no belief in the rationality either of the economic or political order. The "vanguard," on the other hand, has done nothing. It is stuck in the mud of the old fixed categories, chief of which is "the Party to lead." (Dunayevskaya 1958: 284)

And:

> There is a crying need for a new unity of theory and practice which begins with where the working people are – their thoughts, their struggle, their aspirations. (Dunayevskaya 1958: 284)

Many readers failed to fully appreciate this conclusion—which to some seemed like anarchist practice plus dialectics gleaned through "Lenin's Hegelian conversion." It was often overlooked that Dunayevskaya was actually describing her own attempts to unify theory and practice by drawing intellectuals and workers alike into a worldwide conversation about how to renew the struggle for socialism.

Marxist-Humanist organizational efforts in Britain were not, however, totally without success. In the 1970s, Harry McShane had the brilliant idea of publishing the chapters in *Marxism and Freedom* on the three volumes of Marx's *Capital*, as a separate pamphlet. McShane referred to the success of John Maclean's classes on Marx's *Capital* in Glasgow before the First World War, which were attended by five hundred workers every Sunday afternoon. Dunayevskaya readily agreed, and the pamphlet was published in 1977 with a foreword by McShane; an introduction by Dunayevskaya, entitled "Today's Epigones Who Try to Truncate Marx's Capital," which critiqued Ernest Mandel's introduction to the new Penguin edition of *Capital* Vol. I, and an appendix, also by Dunayevskaya, entitled "Tony Cliff Reduces Lenin's Theory to 'Uncanny Intuition'" (1977). It's hard to imagine now, but back in late-1970s there were hundreds of Left and alternative bookstores in Britain, and there was a national distributor to service them. British Marxist-Humanists managed to convince the distributor to take 500 copies.

UNFINISHED BUSINESS

From Lenin to Hegel (via Marx)

Marxism and Freedom, though a significant theoretical progression for Dunayevskaya, did not contain all that she would have to say on Hegel, Marx, and the revolutionary tradition in the following decades of her life. As late as 1986, writing to the philosopher, Louis Dupré, it is evident that she was still grappling with her 1953 "breakthrough" in the "Letters on Hegel's Absolutes":

> Along with the battle I'm currently having with myself on the Absolutes (and I've been having this battle ever since 1953, when I first "defined" the Absolute as the new society), I am now changing my attitude to Lenin. (Dunayevskaya 2002: 326)

What had changed was that in her 1982 book, *Rosa Luxemburg, Women's Liberation, and Marx's Philosophy of Revolution*, Dunayevskaya had developed the category of "post-Marx Marxism as pejorative." This meant separating Marx's critique of capital from all subsequent interpretations, whether by Engels, Luxemburg, or Lenin. In Lenin's case there had been a failure, despite his own Hegel studies, to connect dialectics to organization. In practical terms, Lenin's concept of the elite vanguard party was, of course, freely adapted by Stalin to validate his single-party totalitarian state.

In philosophical terms, the problem, as she explained it to Dupré, lay "specifically" in the chapter of Cognition, in the Third part of Hegel's *Science of Logic*, the Doctrine of the Notion. In Hegel's writings, "Spirit" is the realization of Reason and the Good in the historical process. Spirit unfolds itself in the world as the Notion transformed by desire and labor, arriving, as it were, in the post-feudal world of industrialization, division of labor, and Adam Smith's political economy. The first form of the Idea in Hegel's Doctrine of the Notion is "Life." Life as Spirit in post-feudalism has a "we-like" character which unifies the "I" with the world, and spirit with nature. The second form of the Idea is Cognition, which is subdivided into pure cognition and volition. Pure cognition has for its object the True; Volition, the active self-universalizing subject, has for its object the Good. How then does the Good become the True, and what is the "objectivity of subjectivity?" As Hegel puts it, no doubt with the French Revolution in mind:

> When external actuality is altered by the activity of the objective notion and its determination therewith sublated, by that very fact the merely phenomenal reality, the external determinability and worthlessness, are removed from that actuality. (Hegel 1998: 465)

In Hegel's terms, this takes the form of an "objective notion": historically, it becomes the General Will that the potential of revolutionary change is actually more real than the merely phenomenal reality, the external determinability, and worthlessness of the crumbling, decadent feudal way of life.

In Lenin's 1914–1915 "materialist" reading of Hegel's *Science of Logic*, "objective truth" can be seen as the subjective-objective conditions for revolution (Dunayevskaya 1989: 27). The Absolute Idea represents the unity of theory and practice, with the emphasis on practice (Lenin never broke from Blanqui's concept of insurrection as an "art" [Lenin 1965]). Lenin conceived of the Russian "workers state" (under the "dictatorship of the proletariat") as a "transitional" society in the first stages of socialism, yet still based economically on wage labor, commodity production, and Taylorist production techniques. Although Lenin's *State and Revolution* of 1917 takes off from Marx's 1875 *Critique of the Gotha Program* in challenging reformism, there is nothing in the latter work to suggest that the "Dictatorship of the Proletariat" is to be identified with a "transitional" society, presided over by a "state," as Lenin wrote.

What was not in *Marxism and Freedom*, but can be gleaned from Dunayevskaya's later writings (including the uncompleted project to write a book on the dialectics of organization and philosophy), is the recognition that the theoretical void, which she said in 1958 had dated from the death of Lenin in 1924, actually began with the death of Karl Marx in 1883. For Dunayevskaya the question was always, "What Happens After" the revolution. Following the catastrophes of the twentieth century, no one seems to know what socialism is, let alone how a revolution might achieve it without recourse to faith in "objective" technological developments. Dunayevskaya interprets Hegel's idea of absolute negativity as tantamount to what Marx expresses in his concept of "revolution in permanence," as well as the argument in the *Critique of the Gotha Program* that the "all-round development of the individual" requires the abolition of the "enslaving subordination" to the division of labor and the antithesis between mental and manual labor (2002: 241). Marx's

Critique of the Gotha Program was of course not itself a program. As Dunayevskaya puts it:

> The whole truth is that even Marx's *Critique of the Gotha Program*, which remains the ground for organization today, was written 112 years ago. What is demanded is not mere "updating," after all the aborted revolutions of the post-World War II world. "Ground" will not suffice alone; we have to finish the building – the roof and its contents. (2002: 9)

The "Changed World"

There is a further challenge to the form of organization which we have worked out as the committee-form rather than the "party-to-lead." But, though committee-form and "party-to-lead" are opposites, they are not absolute opposites. At the point when the theoretic-form reaches philosophy, the challenge demands that we synthesize not only the new relations of theory to practice, and all the forces of revolution, but philosophy's "suffering, patience and labor of the negative," i.e. experiencing absolute negativity. *Then and only then* will we succeed in a revolution that will achieve a classless, non-racist, non-sexist, truly human, truly new society. That which Hegel judged to be the synthesis of the "Self-Thinking Idea" and the "Self-Bringing-Forth of Liberty," Marxist-Humanism holds, is what Marx had called the new society. The many paths to get there are not easy to work out.... (Dunayevskaya [1982] 1991: xxxviii)

When *Marxism and Freedom* was published in 1958, Fordist mass production was reaching its zenith and the Cold War was near its height. But by the time Dunayevskaya died in 1987, neoliberalism was on the rise and state capitalist "communism" was beginning to crumble in what she described as a "changed world."

"Traditional" Leftism, in the forms of vanguardism and Left reformism, was thrown into crisis by the rise of spontaneous rebellions against authoritarian regimes. In both Poland in 1980 and Iran in 1979, for example, the mass movements—which featured women's movements and workers councils—seemed to stand for radical social transformation. But they were soon taken over, in one case by Catholic reactionaries, and in the other by Islamic fundamentalists. In both cases, capitalist neoliberalism ensued. One of Dunayevskaya's very last writings (1987) poses the following questions:

What have the various forms of spontaneity – councils, soviets, committees, associations, communes – achieved? And why when they did come close to power, it wasn't the political organizations that didn't take them over so much, as that they themselves looked to be taken over? (Dunayevskaya Archive: 10955)

Dunayevskaya had long practiced in News and Letters Committees the decentralized "committee-form" of organization in opposition to the centralized vanguard "party-to-lead." It is certainly the case that oppositions within Left activism have manifested themselves in terms of spontaneity versus party control and planning; and more recently, since the "anti-globalization" mobilizations, as "horizontal" versus "vertical" forms of organizing.

However, as Dunayevskaya's *Rosa Luxemburg, Women's Liberation and Marx's Philosophy of Revolution* ([1982] 1991) argues, "though... opposites" the decentralized "committee-form" of organization and centralized vanguard "party-to-lead" are "not absolute opposites." If the "theoretic-form" reaches philosophy, then it is no longer just a question of "new relations of theory and practice" that will somehow unify all the potential forces of revolutionary actuality. Having a revolutionary philosophy demands, as Hegel would put it, "suffering, patience and labor of the negative," i.e., the experiencing of "absolute negativity" as the positive road to a new society along the roads of Marx's "revolution in permanence" (Dunayevskaya [1982] 1991: 91). The "self-development of the idea" (for us, "socialism") is at the same time a materialistic "Self-Bringing Forth of Liberty," in which Hegel's "subjective cognition" is "itself the way to produce it." In this process the new society is itself "the mediating agent in the process" (2002: 29).

REFERENCES

Carr, Edward Hallett. 1959. "Marx's Heirs and Antecedents," Times Literary Supplement, 21 August 1959.
Daum, Walter. 1990. *The Life and Death of Stalinism: A Resurrection of Marxist Theory.* New York: Socialist Voice.
Dunayevskaya, Raya.
1958–1959. *Raya Dunayevskaya Archive.* Wayne State University.
——— a. Raya Dunayevskaya and Jean Malaquais correspondence, May to June, 1958. http://rayadunayevskaya.org/ArchivePDFs/9419.pdf.

———— b. Letter and handwritten notes from Bess and Louis Gogol to Dunayevskaya. July 1958. http://rayadunayevskaya.org/ArchivePDFs/9378. pdf.

1959

———— a. Letters from Dunayevskaya to Onorato Damen. December 1957 to September 1959. http://rayadunayevskaya.org/ArchivePDFs/9410.pdf.

———— b. Raya Dunayevskaya and Maximilien Rubel correspondence July–August 1959. http://rayadunayevskaya.org/ArchivePDFs/9426.pdf.

———— c. Letters from Dunayevskaya to Grandizo Munis. September 1958 to October 1959. http://rayadunayevskaya.org/ArchivePDFs/9429.pdf.

———— d. Letters from Raya Dunayevskaya to Frank Williams; and Dunayevskaya's letters and reports to US colleagues on her trip to Europe. http://rayadunayevskaya.org/ArchivePDFs/9433.pdf.

———— e. Dunayevskaya speech to conference in Milan, September 27, 1959 (typescript). http://rayadunayevskaya.org/ArchivePDFs/9474.pdf.

———— f. Lecture at Leeds University on "Marx's Debt to Hegel." 14 October 1959 (typescript). http://rayadunayevskaya.org/ArchivePDFs/9478.pdf.

Dunayevskaya, Raya. [1958] 1971. Marxism and Freedom: From 1776 until Today. 3rd ed. Preface by Harry McShane and original preface by Herbert Marcuse. London: Pluto Press.

————. [1973] 1989. *Philosophy and Revolution: From Hegel to Sartre, and from Marx to Mao.* Columbia University Press.

————. 1977. *Marx's Capital and Today's Global Crisis.* Preface, Harry McShane. Detroit: News and Letters.

————. 1980a. Overview to Vol, XII of the Raya Dunayevskaya Collection. https://www.marxists.org/archive/dunayevskaya/guide.pdf.

————. 1980b. *25 Years of Marxist Humanism in the U.S.* Detroit: News and Letters.

————. [1982] 1991. *Rosa Luxemburg, Women's Liberation, and Marx's Philosophy of Revolution.* 2nd ed. Foreword by Adrienne Rich. Urbana: University of Illinois Press.

————. 2002. *The Power of Negativity: Selected Writings on the Dialectic in Hegel and Marx.* Edited by Peter Hudis and Kevin Anderson. Lanham: Lexington Books.

Goldner, Loren. 1997. *Communism Is the Material Human Community: Amadeo Bordiga Today.* Baltimore: Collective Action Notes. https://libcom.org/library/communism-is-the-material-human-community-amadeo-bordiga-today.

Hegel, G. W. F. [1910] 1967. *Phenomenology of Mind.* Translated by J. B. *Baillie, with a preface by George Lichtheim.* London: Harper & Row.

————. 1998. *Science of Logic.* Translated by A. V. Miller. New York: Prometheus Books.

Hudis, Peter. 1992. *Harry McShane and the Scottish Roots of Marxist-Humanism.* Glasgow: John Maclean Society Pamphlet.

James, C. L. R. Dunayevskaya, Raya, and Lee, Grace. [1950] 1986. *State Capitalism and World Revolution.* Chicago: Charles H. Kerr. www.marxists.org/archive/jamesclr/works/1950/08/state-capitalism.htm.

Kinna, Ruth. 2011. "Guy Aldred: Bridging the Gap between Marxism and Anarchism." *Journal of Political Ideologies, 16/1.*

Lenin, Vladimir Ilyich. 1965. "Marxism and Insurrection," *Collected Works Vol. 25,* 22–23.

Lichtheim, George. 1964. "From the Finland Station," *New York Review of Books,* December 17, 1964.

MacFarlane, Helen. 2014. *Red Republican: Essays, Articles and Translation of the Communist Manifesto* (ed. David Black). London: Unkant.

MacIntyre, Alasdair. 1958. "The Algebra of Revolution," *Universities and Left Review* (London). Republished in *Alasdair MacIntyre's Engagement with Marxism: Selected Writings 1953–1974.* 2008 Historical Materialism Book Series, Vol. 19. London: Brill.

Marx, Karl and Friedrich Engels. 1982. *Collected Works,* Vol. 57 1844-51. New York: International Publishers.

Mattick, Paul. 1958. "A Marxian Oddity." *Western Socialist,* March–April, 1958. Boston. www.marxists.org/archive/mattick-paul/1958/dunayevskaya.htm.

McShane, Harry and Joan Smith. 1978. Harry McShane: *No Mean Fighter.* London: Pluto Press.

McShane, Harry. 1974. Review of Raya Dunayevskaya's *Philosophy and Revolution,* in *The Scottish Marxist-Humanist* (Glasgow).

News & Letters. 1960–1961. Detroit. https://newsandletters.org/1960s/.

Williams, Frank. 1961. Rank and File Conference—British Labour News. *News & Letters,* January 1961.

PART IV

Freedom and Liberation

CHAPTER 13

Why Marx Is More Relevant Than Ever in the Age of Automation

Paul Mason

The blurry snapshot catches Leon Trotsky in mid-sentence, in Frida Kahlo's house sometime in 1937. To the left of the frame is Natalia Sedova, Trotsky's wife. To the right is Kahlo and, half-hidden behind her, a young woman listening intently: Trotsky's secretary Raya Dunayevskaya.

We don't know what the argument is about but we can be sure of the premise on which it is being conducted: everybody in the photograph is a Marxist. Their ideas about politics, economics, morality and art were shaped by the writings of a man born in Germany 200 years ago.

Trotsky would be assassinated in 1940, and Sedova would rage against the Soviet machine thereafter. Kahlo would become one of the most formidable female artists of the twentieth century. But it is Dunayevskaya who provides the link between classic Marxism and the only form in which it can be relevant today. "Marxism," she would insist, "is radical humanism."

As we pass the 200th anniversary of Marx's birth, the struggle over his ideas shows no sign of stopping. The American alt-right marched

P. Mason (✉)
London, UK

© The Author(s) 2021
K. B. Anderson et al. (eds.), *Raya Dunayevskaya's Intersectional Marxism*, Marx, Engels, and Marxisms,
https://doi.org/10.1007/978-3-030-53717-3_13

through Charlottesville claiming that the town had succumbed to "cultural Marxism." The Bank of England governor Mark Carney has warned that Marxism could make a comeback due to the impacts of automation on jobs and inequality. Meanwhile, in China, a decidedly uncultural form of Marxism has been revived as the new state doctrine of Xi Jinping. To understand what can survive of Marxism and what cannot, we must ask what its teachings might mean in the radically different conditions of today.

By July 1850, Karl Marx was already a theorist of defeat. He had written in *The Communist Manifesto* (1848) that the destiny of the working class was to abolish private property and bring communism, but now he understood it was going to take some time. After two years of trying to push the democratic revolutions in France and Germany in the direction of social justice, Marx had admitted failure and fled to London.

Yet in the upstairs room of a Soho pub, over a pint, Marx assured fellow exile Wilhelm Liebknecht there was hope. He had just seen the prototype of an electric train on display in Regent Street: the age of steam would soon be over and the age of the electric spark would begin. Liebknecht records:

> Marx, all flushed and excited, told me… "Now the problem is solved – the consequences are indefinable. In the wake of the economic revolution the political must necessarily follow, for the latter is only the expression of the former."

Amid the tobacco smoke, Marx had outlined a simple version of the materialist conception of history. A more complicated version would follow. In his preface *to A Contribution to the Critique of Political Economy* (1859) Marx explained social change as the result of a clash between two layers of reality created by human beings: the forces of production—technology and the expertise needed to deploy it—and the social relations of production: the economic model required to bring the technology to life.

Together, said Marx, the technology and the economic model form a "base" on which the "superstructure" of laws, political institutions, cultures, and ideologies are founded in any given system. Revolutions happen when the economic system begins to retard technological progress.

After the 1848 revolutions failed, Marx devoted his life to two comple-mentary projects: forming and educating stable working-class parties to defend workers' interests and prepare them for power; and analyzing the dynamics of industrial capitalism.

Only once, in a notebook that lay unpublished for more than a hundred years, did Marx hazard a guess at the form that the techno-economic revolution might take. In the "Fragment on Machines," written in 1858, he imagined a time when machines do most of the work and in which knowledge becomes "social," embodied in what he called a "gen-eral intellect." Since capitalism is based on profits generated by workers, it could not survive a level of technological advance that eradicated the need for work. The clash between private property and shared social knowl-edge, he said, would blow the foundations of capitalism "sky high." This prophecy, so obviously relevant to our time of robots and networked knowledge, lay in the archives, unread until the 1960s.

* * *

In the 50 years after Marx's death in 1883, his ideas suffered three rein-terpretations. First, his collaborator, Frederick Engels, tried to systematize Marx's ideas into a theory of everything in the universe, encompassing no longer just history but physics, astronomy and ethnography. This was the Marxism that the leaders of the early socialist parties learned; but they added a second revision: claiming that Marx's theories justified peaceful parliamentary socialism, not revolution. Then, starting around 1899, there emerged a Marxism of confrontation and class struggle, elevating human will power and organizational elan above concepts of historical inevitability or fixed stages of development.

This was the Marxism that both Trotsky and Sedova had learned in the Russian underground, and which brought them together as exiles in Paris in 1902. It said: Russia could only become democratic under the leadership of the working class; the task was to organize workers into a party as confrontational, secretive, and hierarchical as the states run by the tsars and kaisers that they were to overthrow. Mass strikes and barricades, not elections and socialist choral societies, were their chosen weapons.

By now Marxism also contained a theory of the working class that was diametrically opposed to that of Marx. For Marx, the revolutions of 1848 had failed because capitalism was not ready to be overthrown. For Lenin, by 1902 it was the workers who were not ready—and never would be without the cattle prod of an elite, underground "vanguard party" to make them move.

The entire skilled workforce of the developed world had been bought off by the proceeds of imperialism, Lenin said: revolution would be a job for the unskilled workers in the West, and for the peoples of the less developed world. From around 1910 the nationalist revolts and land wars unfolding in Mexico, China, Ireland, and ultimately Russia seemed to confirm this prediction.

Trotsky and Sedova had at least seen this new, revolutionary Marxism evolve. For Kahlo and Dunayevskaya's generation it was the only one they had ever known.

Dunayevskaya was born to Jewish parents in today's Ukraine in 1910 and emigrated with them to Chicago in 1922. She joined the Communist Party at the age of 14, during a school strike. She left it four years later, after having been thrown down a staircase for questioning Trotsky's expulsion from the Comintern.

Trotsky had helped to lead the revolution in 1917. He then took part in the abolition of workers' control in factories and the suppression of left-wing opposition movements. But faced with the rise of a new bureaucratic elite he launched, from 1923, his own left opposition. By the 1930s he had concluded that Stalinism and fascism were "twins" separated only by their differing economic basis.

Dunayevskaya's job in the beleaguered Trotskyist movement was to run, from an office in New York, the Russian-language bulletin they were trying to distribute in the USSR. She arrived in Mexico in July 1937 to work as Trotsky's stenographer and translator—just as the Great Purge began to roll up their underground networks.

Kahlo had joined Mexico's communist youth movement in 1928, aged 21. "I am a communist being..." she would write later. For the generation of young intellectuals attracted to Mexican communism, this state of communist being involved not only sexual and artistic experiment, but deep engagement with the indigenous cultures of Mexico and enthusiasm for the peasant wars begun by Emiliano Zapata.

If we list the common assumptions of the people in the photograph, they would be: that revolutions usually happen in backward countries; that they involve mobile warfare, peasant land seizures and ruthless repression of the rich; that a Marxist party has to stand aloof from the conservatism of the Western working class and instead defend indigenous peoples and the racially oppressed; and that the working class is the "revolutionary subject" intrinsically at war with capitalism, though misled.

These were self-sacrificing people, prepared to use manipulation and violence for the greater good. But each was, in their own way, struggling to preserve Marxism with a human face: to resist the organized lying, mass murder, and suppression of artistic freedom that Stalinism had unleashed.

The tragedy is that none of them understood how thoroughly humanist Marxism had been at its conception—and only Dunayevskaya ever would.

Marx disdained philosophy, writing that "philosophers have only interpreted the world; the point is to change it." The *Economic and Philosophic Manuscripts*—written in Paris in 1844 but not published in Moscow until 1927—show how he came to that conclusion: through a critique of Enlightenment philosophy that is thoroughly imbued with humanism and firmly descended from a concept of human nature traceable to Aristotle, via St Augustine and Hegel.

The purpose of human beings, says the Marx of 1844, is to set themselves free. They are enslaved not just by capitalism, nor by any specific form of class society, but by a problem arising from their social nature, which obliges them to work in groups and to collaborate via language, not simply instinct.

When humans make things, or discover a new idea, we tend to embody our concept of "self" in the new object or idea—a process Marx calls self-estrangement or "alienation." We then allow our products, mental and physical, to exercise power over us, whether in the form of religions or superstitions, or by fetishizing consumer goods, or by mindlessly obeying routines and disciplines that we have created for ourselves. To overcome alienation, Marx argued that humanity has to rid itself of all hierarchies and class divisions—which means abolishing both private property and the state.

The 1844 manuscripts contain an idea lost to Marxism: the concept of communism as "radical humanism." Communism, said Marx, is not simply the abolition of private property but the "appropriation of the human essence by and for man... the complete return of man to himself as a social (i.e., human) being." But, says Marx, communism is not the goal of human history. It is simply the form in which society will emerge after 40,000 years of hierarchical organization. The real goal of human history is individual freedom and self-realization.

When they published these notebooks in 1927, Soviet academics treated them as an embarrassing mistake. To do otherwise would be to admit that the whole materialist conception of history—classes, modes of production, technology versus economics—was underpinned by a profound humanism, with moral implications.

Dunayevskaya, who got hold of a Russian version of the *Paris Manuscripts* in the 1940s, spent nearly a decade hawking her English translation around, before publishing them herself in the mid-1950s.

She understood the *Paris Manuscripts* were a challenge to all previous interpretations of Marx. For the Soviet bureaucracy, the contrast between Marx's idea of freedom and their own drab, oppressive reality was obvious. For Western Marxism, which had become obsessed with the study of permanent structures, here was Marx arguing not for impersonal forces but for a clear and almost Aristotelian concept of human nature, autonomy, and well-being. Could it be, Dunayevskaya asked, that all the disasters that had befallen the Marxist left were traceable to the rigid theories propagated by Engels? Could it be that the ruthlessness of the Bolshevik tradition, always justified by the goal of working-class power, was unjustified when compared to the goal of communism outlined by Marx? Could it be that Marxism was not, after all, a break with the philosophical humanism of the Enlightenment, but its most complete expression?

These were the conclusions Dunayevskaya drew. And from them she outlined new practical priorities. All left-wing politics in the future had to be based on the experience of individual human beings and their search for freedom. In 1950s America this meant not only joining the struggle for workers' control on the factory floor, but also advocating feminism, black civil rights, the rights of indigenous people—and supporting anti-imperialist struggles in the global south. It meant, when the revolts against Stalinism began in Germany (1953) and then Hungary (1956), supporting them without equivocation.

When researchers eventually discovered and published Marx's "Fragment on Machines" in the late 1960s, Dunayevskaya understood it was the last piece of the puzzle. This was not an account of capitalist economic breakdown due to the falling profit rate, it was a theory of technological liberation. Freed from work by the advance of automation, Marx had foreseen how humanity would use its leisure time: for the "free development of the individual," not some collectivist utopia.

* * *

Frida Kahlo took a different path. Her last painting shows her seated beneath a portrait of Joseph Stalin. Kahlo had conducted a love affair with Trotsky, seen him assassinated in her own house, and practiced a form of surrealism that Trotsky praised and Moscow labeled degenerate. So why did she end up lionizing the man who had ordered Trotsky's murder?

Kahlo's art was, though she could not know it, a lifelong riff on the Marxist concept of self-estrangement. She clearly regarded the self as the site on which human liberation would be achieved; she explored through her paintings the alienation of her gender, sexuality, disability, and ethnicity. Her unflinching portrayals of unhappiness and isolation have made her, since the 1970s, the artistic patron saint of feminism.

Yet it is clear that she regarded her most famous paintings as un-Marxist and anti-political. She once described them as "small and unimportant, with the same personal subjects that only appeal to myself and nobody else." Political paintings were what her husband, Diego Rivera, did; the concept of the personal as political was alien to her generation.

During the Cold War, as the world divided into "camps," Kahlo made the same choice that many leftists did: she rejoined the Mexican Communist Party and denounced Trotsky. Her paintings changed, too. She began to attempt big social allegories, such as *Marxism Will Give Health to the Sick* (1954), from which the layers of mysticism and metaphor found in her earlier work are stripped. This was not a choice of a political dilettante. In 1952 she wrote in her diary: "I was never a Trotskyite... I understand very clearly the material dialectics of Marx, Engels, Lenin, Stalin and Mao Tse. I love them as the pillars of the new communist world."

Kahlo's political trajectory is a case study of what happens to a Marxism devoid of humanism. She had to keep her artistic engagement with psychological trauma and sexual freedom separate from the ideology she understood as "material dialectics." Her focus on the defenseless self, on the beauty of the oppressed person, on the inescapable power of the natural world, were all products of her engagement with the same idea of freedom that Marx had expressed in 1844. But she just couldn't reconcile it with the Marxism of the Moscow textbooks, and the textbooks won.

* * *

What's left of Marxism in our era of techno-euphoria and environmental doom? Not its class narrative: despite the doubling of the global workforce, the workers of the developing world are as encaged in bourgeois society as their white, male, manual counterparts became in the twentieth century. Workplace unrest will continue but capitalism has worked out how to quarantine it away from revolution.

That's only a tragedy if you have never read the *Paris Manuscripts*. The Marx of 1844 theorized communism first, and the workers' role in bringing it about second. He saw communism not as the end point of history but, as he once put it poetically, the end of prehistory. And for the Marx of these early writings, the workers' role in bringing communism lies in their propensity to self-educate and to create co-operative associations – not as blind automata, driven purely by their material interests.

In the early 1960s the pro-Kremlin French sociologist Louis Althusser "solved" the problem of the *Paris Manuscripts* by declaring them to be un-Marxist. They contained, Althusser argued, the "Marx furthest from Marx"—a humanist philosophy that should be "driven back into the darkness." Yet he recognized their publication as a "theoretical event"—and anybody who calls themselves left-wing is still living with the consequences of that event.

Once the *Paris Manuscripts* were brought to light, the dilemma was clear: either Marxism is about the liberation of individual human beings or it is about impersonal forces and structures, which can be studied but very rarely escaped. Either there is a "human essence," which we can rediscover by abolishing property and class, or we are a sack of bones conditioned by our surroundings and our DNA. Either people make history, as Marx had said, or history makes history.

During the past 50 years, much of left-wing academic thought has followed the anti-humanist path Althusser laid out. Dunayevskaya, like most other people who had embraced humanism in the aftermath of war and genocide, was revered but treated like a crank.

However, the Marx she helped to rediscover is highly relevant to the future we face. If we are to defend human rights against authoritarian populism we must have a concept of humanity to defend—as we must if we insist that human beings should have the power to limit and suppress the activities of thinking machines.

If the Marx of 1844 is correct, the ideal of human liberation and communism can survive the atomization and dispersal of the class that was supposed to bring it. As the revolts of 2011 showed, large masses of people now possess the capacity for autonomous action, self-education, and collaboration that Marx admired in the Parisian working class of the 1840s.

As Dunayevskaya understood, the impulse toward freedom is created by more than just exploitation: it is triggered by alienation, the suppression of desire, the humiliation experienced by people on the receiving end of systemic racism, sexism, and homophobia. Everywhere capitalism follows anti-human priorities it stirs revolt—and it's all around us. In the coming century, just as Marx predicted, it is likely that automation coupled with the socialization of knowledge will present us with the opportunity to liberate ourselves from work. That, as he said, will blow capitalism "sky high." The economic system that replaces it will have to be shaped around the goal he outlined in 1844: ending alienation and liberating the individual.

If I could speak across time to the people frozen in that photograph I would say, after congratulating them for their magnificent lives of resistance and suffering: "That inner desire you are suppressing, for Marxism to be humanistic? That impulse towards individual liberation? It's already there in Marx, just waiting to be discovered. So paint what you want, love whom you want. Fuck the vanguard party. The revolutionary subject is the self."

CHAPTER 14

Raya Dunayevskaya's Emancipatory Marxism

Frédéric Monferrand

Marxism is a theory of liberation or it is nothing.

Raya Dunayevskaya

Raya Dunayevskaya is one of those individuals in whom the historical and the biographical, or—to use the Hegelian vocabulary she so continuously draws on—the universal and particular, tend to coincide.[1] Born Raya Shpigel in 1910 in what is now Ukraine, at that time integrated into the Tsarist Empire, she lived through the great jolts that traversed the history of the twentieth century: the two world wars and the Cold War, the October Revolution and the Chinese Cultural Revolution, as well as the national liberation struggles that spelled the end for the colonial empires. She emigrated to the United States in 1922, where she died in 1987. There, she carried out continuous political and intellectual activity, which led her to participate in the major struggles of the proletariat, the youth, and oppressed minorities, and which led her to cross paths with some of the most important figures in twentieth-century critical Marxism: Leon Trotsky, with whom she collaborated in Mexico in 1937–1938; C. L. R. James, with whom she founded the "Johnson-Forest Tendency" in

F. Monferrand (✉)
University of Namur, Namur, Belgium

© The Author(s) 2021
K. B. Anderson et al. (eds.), *Raya Dunayevskaya's Intersectional Marxism*, Marx, Engels, and Marxisms,
https://doi.org/10.1007/978-3-030-53717-3_14

1941; Cornelius Castoriadis, whose analysis of the USSR she shared to an extent, but whom she would ultimately criticize as a "detractor of Lenin" (Dunayevskaya 1969); and Herbert Marcuse, with whom she engaged in a long correspondence, and who would provide the Preface to *Marxism and Freedom* (Anderson and Rockwell 2012).

According to Dunayevskaya herself (1985: 5–6), *Marxism and Freedom*—which constitutes the first part of a "trilogy of revolution" also comprising *Philosophy and Revolution: from Hegel to Sartre and from Marx to Mao* and *Rosa Luxemburg, Women's Liberation, and Marx's Philosophy of Revolution*—has three main objectives. The first is to establish the "American roots of Marxism" in a context where the American working class, energized from within by Black struggles, represented the best chance of relaunching the communist project. The second is to reconstruct the philosophical coherence of "Marx's Marxism" from the *1844 Manuscripts* to *Capital*, showing it to be animated by the idea that history comprises the efforts undertaken by humanity to realize its freedom. Finally, the third objective is to re-evaluate the centrality of the "Hegelian dialectic" to the constitution of this "new humanism."

This program no doubt seems too ambitious to be carried out in one single text. We are, after all, used to looking at Marxism as a form of academic exercise, detached from all immediate political stakes and treated according to the criteria proper to the division of intellectual labor that characterizes academic research. Now, to read *Marxism and Freedom* is, on the contrary, to experience a rich work that interweaves the analysis of the Soviet economy; philosophical speculation on the "Absolute"; the historical reconstruction of the workers' movement; the sociological study of automation; and a chronicle of the struggles of the global proletariat. This multiplicity of concerns grants to the work a kaleidoscopic twist, where the exploration of a problem is always an occasion to reflect upon another, according to a logic of renewal and variations on the fundamental theme of *the unity of theory and practice*, which for Dunayevskaya is the genuine heart of Marxism. It is therefore the theme of theory and practice that will form the horizon of this chapter. I will try to show that this theme dominates the historical assessments and the philosophical perspective developed in *Marxism and Freedom*. I thus hope to do justice to the main thrust of the work and to account for the contemporary purchase of a text in which Marxism appears as what it must become (again): a theory of liberation.

STATE CAPITALISM AGAINST FREEDOM

Published in 1958, *Marxism and Freedom* represents first of all an intervention in what can be called the central strategic question of the international workers' movement of the period: namely, the question of what attitude to adopt toward "actually existing socialism." Despite the rupture between C. L. R. James and Dunayevskaya in 1955, on this point the book holds to the work they had carried out in common within the "Johnson-Forest Tendency." Named after the respective pseudonyms adopted by these two revolutionaries in the Workers' Party, this Tendency was actually constituted in response to the Trotskyist definition of the Soviet social formation as a "degenerated workers' state." Against this they proposed the thesis that a form of *state capitalism* reigned in the USSR. "The problem of our era," Dunayevskaya explains in the fifth section of *Marxism and Freedom*, is none other than the epochal struggle between freedom and state capitalism.

In order to grasp the importance of this historical assessment, it will be helpful to return briefly to the terms of the debate. For Trotsky, the Soviet state is a "workers' state" because it is the product of a proletarian revolution that has formally instituted the collective ownership of the means of production. But this workers' state in transition toward socialism must be qualified as "degenerated" because the scarcity of goods in circulation allowed for the emergence of a bureaucratic and autonomous caste from within the working class, which parasitically appropriates for itself the social surplus product (Trotsky 1937). Now, as Marcel van der Linden underscores (2009: 314–315), what is unsatisfying about this analysis is that it rests upon a series of inconsistent dualisms (between the economic and the political, between distribution and production). To the extent that the Soviet economy is a planned economy in which production is organized by the state, there is no way of distinguishing the "bad" totalitarian politics from the "good" socialist economy. As Marx writes in the 1857 Introduction to the *Grundrisse*, "The question of the relation between this production-determining distribution, and production, belongs evidently within production itself" (1973: 97). Therefore, we cannot isolate the sphere of the circulation of commodities from the sphere of socialized production: the permanence of bourgeois norms of distribution in the USSR attests rather to the fact that the Stalinist counter-revolution provoked the re-establishment of capitalist relations of production.

For James and Dunayevskaya, Soviet Russia under Lenin could indeed be called socialist, for despite the persistence of capitalist forms such as wage labor, the popular initiatives deployed in the workers' councils guaranteed the exercise of a *proletarian sovereignty* announcing the withering away of the state (James 1941: 56). From this perspective, which sees the intervention of the masses in the dynamics of power as constitutive of the transition toward communism, the members of the Johnson-Forest Tendency present the re-establishment of capitalism in Russia as an essentially political process whose principal moments were the erosion of workers' rights, the police control of the population, the Moscow trials, and the legitimation of the power of state planners in the constitution of 1936. In this regard, we may regret that neither James nor Dunayevskaya proposed an articulated theory of the state, of the class conflicts that it includes and of the different forms (juridical, ideological and repressive) in which it participates in the reproduction of the relations of production. But the principal objective to which the "state capitalism" thesis responds to is nonetheless clear: it is to show that capitalism and communism are not distinguished by the opposition between private and public property, but rather the opposition between exploitation and freedom.

In the various articles she devoted to the "nature of the Russian economy," where we find the main arguments of *Marxism and Freedom* on this issue, Dunayevskaya repeatedly explains, "It is neither titles to property nor motives of individuals that distinguishes different exploitative economic orders, but their method of production, or manner of extracting surplus labor" ([1946–1947] 1992: 73). From this perspective, we can speak of capitalism from the moment that the following take place: the total *separation* between workers and the means of production, the complete *dispossession* of any control exerted by producers upon production, and the *compulsion* to produce for the sake of production under which they find themselves. Now, these three conditions are found together in the Soviet Union, where the means of production are the property of the state which thus oversees the employment of labor power, where the technological and organizational knowledge necessary for production is monopolized by planners and dominates the workers under the objectified form of mechanization, and where the production of the means of industrial production is greater than that of the means of consumption. In the language of the *1844 Manuscripts*, some extracts of which appeared for the first time in English in the first edition of *Marxism and Freedom*, the Soviet Union is thus a capitalist society because in that society labor is totally *alienated*. As the young Marx anticipated, "Even the equality of wages… only changes the relationship of the contemporary worker to his labor into that of all men to labor. Society is then conceived of as an abstract capitalist" ([1844] 2000a: 94–95).

This definition of capitalism in terms of alienation may appear under-determined. Notably, it seems to make little of an essential dimension of the capitalist mode of production: the *competition* that establishes itself between different capitals, and that de facto did not exist in the Soviet Union, where the bureaucracy played the role of "abstract capitalist." Dunayevskaya is conscious of this difficulty, to which she responds with both a doctrinal argument and an economic one. From a doctrinal point of view, she recalls that in the chapter of *Capital* devoted to the "general law of capitalist accumulation," Marx himself envisages the possibility that the centralization of capitals would attain a limit such that "the entire social capital [is] united in the hands of either a single capitalist or a single capitalist company" (1976: 779). From an economic point of view, she strives to show that this unique capitalist—the Soviet state—is in competition with other capitals on the world market. The result of this international competition is that the "law of value," defined as an anonymous constraint pushing firms to produce their commodities in conformity with the "average socially necessary labor time" on the world market, is still in place in the Soviet Union. And it is this resilience of the law of value that will explain the anti-worker politics taken on by the planning intelligentsia raised to the level of a dominant class.

Indeed, for Dunayevskaya, the importation into the USSR of "methods of bourgeois production" such as Taylorism, industrialization on a grand scale, the automation of the labor process and the concomitant development of productive forces must fundamentally be interpreted as so many technologies of power aiming to *discipline* the Russian proletariat. Correlatively, the different forms of "refusal of work"—to use a concept of the Italian workerists that was anticipated by Dunayevskaya in many respects—put in place by proletarians (absenteeism, parallel economy, sabotage, and spontaneous revolts) attest to the fact that the Soviet social formation is always traversed by a class struggle opposing the "despotic plan of capital" to the "cooperation of freely associated labor" (Dunayevskaya 2000: 96). Thus, from the point of view of the mode of production that was dominant there, the Soviet Union, as the "highest stage" of state capitalism, does not differ essentially from a social formation like that found in the United States. It simply reflects the image, like in a trick mirror, of the becoming-totalitarian that animates the whole of the world economy, borne by the tendencies toward more planning, rationalization, and mechanization—in other words, toward greater reification. Far from being limited to the Soviet borders, the opposition between state capitalism and freedom thus sketches the coordinates of a global conjuncture in which the whole of humanity finds itself implicated. And "the totality of the crisis" that is thus announced "compels philosophy, compels a total outlook" (Dunayevskaya 2000: 273), one that *Marxism and Freedom* proposes to outline.

DIALECTIC AND UTOPIA

By "total outlook," Dunayevskaya means at once a method of interpretation of historical phenomena and a utopian horizon—something like a "worldview" with a heuristic and emancipatory scope.

The method in general is none other than "the dialectic," defined as a dynamic means of thinking about contradictions and their historical productivity. In a period when the Hegelian roots of Marxism were still largely repressed, the author of *Marxism and Freedom* was engaged in reintegrating, like the young Marx before her, "negativity as the moving and creative principle" (Marx [1844] 2000b: 109) into revolutionary theory. Qualifying the dialectic as a "method" is not to reduce it to an ensemble of formal laws, such as "the law of the movement from quantity to quality," of "the interpenetration of opposites," or of the "negation of the negation," as Engels attempted in *Dialectics of Nature*. It is rather to present the dialectic as a tool that makes it possible to locate the "labor of the negative" at the heart of positivity—that is, at the heart of the apparently unshakeable character of social relations. The dialectic is, in other words, the logical form of the historical movement by which freedom is engaged in a dynamic of negating the institutions that impede it, and of producing a world that conforms to its essence. It is in this regard that the dialectic represents, as Marx underlined in *Capital*, a "critical and revolutionary" method (1976: 103).

From this point on we can understand the progression of the first chapter of *Marxism and Freedom*, which may at first sight appear puzzling, as the political sociology of the different actors of the French revolution gradually gives way to speculations on "the Absolute." In Hegel's *Science of Logic*, the "absolute idea" designates the movement by which the different oppositions (between being and thought, necessity and freedom, theory and practice), that habitually structure our representations find themselves sublated and articulated in a totality. Now, for Dunayevskaya, this movement of totalization of dichotomies contains "though in abstract form, the full development of the *social* individual" (2000: 39) and, as such, furnishes the most demanding definition of freedom aimed at by the popular masses of Paris in the 1790s. Following Marcuse's *Reason and Revolution*, she interprets Hegel's thought as a sort of philosophical account of the French revolution, but in so doing she does not aim to make it into a relic or an object of historical curiosity. She tasks herself, instead, with drawing its actuality from his thought. As she will indeed specify in *Rosa Luxemburg, Women's Liberation, and Marx's Philosophy of Revolution*, each period must reinvent for itself the revolutionary dialectic understood as a process of the resolution of the inherited contradictions of the past and of the invention of new forms of social life (1982: 194). This in any case is what Lenin had understood when he dove into the *Science of Logic* in order to grasp the paradoxical revolutionary potential contained in the collapse of the Second International and the First World War. And it is this effort to seize "the new society, struggling to be born" (Dunayevskaya 2000: 39) which imposes on revolutionaries the contradictions of state capitalism:

> Our age has seen a successful workers' revolution – the Russian Revolution of November, 1917 – which seemed to open up an entirely new epoch in the free development of humanity only to end in the counter-revolution of state capitalism. It is therefore our age that is preoccupied with the question of man's destiny: What happens *after* a revolution succeeds? (Dunayevskaya 2000: 39)

As we can see, for Dunayevskaya the dialectic not only plays a retrospective role, but also a prospective one.[2] To think dialectically is not only to reconstruct the social, political or cultural processes of the past from the point of view of their contradictory stabilization in the present; it is also to strive to clarify the objectives of emancipatory movements, to ask the question "what comes *after?*," and to be on the lookout for "new beginnings." Now, this movement which leads from method to utopia, from locating contradictions to concretely anticipating their resolution, is exactly that which leads from Hegel to Marx.

To be sure, Marx took from Hegel the idea that "all of history is a series of historical stages in the development of freedom" (Dunayevskaya

2000: 35). But Hegel rested on a class prejudice that prevented him from situating, in the self-activity of the masses, the engine of a history of emancipation that he therefore mystified as a process of the self-development of "Spirit." Marx, on the other hand, conceived the historical trajectory of humanity from the point of view of the revolt of the "living laborer... against the domination of dead labor" (Dunayevskaya 2000: 177). If "Marxism is a theory of liberation," it is thus as a "philosophy of human activity," that it "can be most fittingly called a *New Humanism*" (Dunayevskaya 2000: 148).

Does this then mean that Dunayevskaya's Marxism represents only an avatar of the "theoretical humanism" denounced by Louis Althusser as the last refuge of liberal ideology at the very heart of historical materialism? Yes and no. Yes, if we understand by "theoretical humanism" a philosophy of history written from the point of view of this meta-subject that would be "humanity." No, if we designate with this term a social theory claiming to explain social phenomena from the point of view of certain ahistorical properties of a "human essence." Dunayevskaya does not attribute an explanatory function, but rather a critical and utopian one to this "new humanism": For her, it is not a matter of reducing the forms of social objectivity to the objectification of human nature, but of insisting upon the historically new, which must take the form of the arrival of an emancipated society. As the Soviet counter-example shows, communism cannot be reduced to the collectivization of production; rather, it implies the invention of "new human relations, without classes, in life and in philosophy" (Dunayevskaya 1982: 192) able to assure the individuals involved in building this society of the free development of their capacities. This "new humanism" is, in other words, the materialist translation of the Hegelian "Absolute," the code-name for a freedom conscious of itself because it flourishes in the fabric of social relations. As such, it constitutes the norm in light of which the present is evaluated, and the principle from which the social and political struggles prefiguring the future are oriented. Its theoretical significance thus depends on the power of practical intervention.

THE UNITY OF THEORY AND PRACTICE

For Dunayevskaya, the interpretation of Marxism in terms of a "new humanism" or a "theory of liberation" is not one that intellectuals are free simply to either make their own or to refuse. It is concretely borne by the self-activity of the masses struggling for their freedom, and imposes itself upon whoever conceives of theory as a form of expression and clarification of the political challenges met by practice: "The actions of the proletariat create the possibility for the intellectual to work out theory" (Dunayevskaya 2000: 91). Following this guiding thread, the second section of part five of the book (on state capitalism vs. freedom) opens with various testimonies from workers and accounts of strikes, where workers report on their hostility toward automation as well as their desire to see labor take the form of a free activity, allowing all individuals to develop their capacities. By their opposition to the technological restructuring of the labor process, Dunayevskaya remarks, the workers show that automation does not constitute an objective tendency of the socialization of the productive forces prefiguring a form of communist cooperation, but a supplementary factor of alienation. Thus, the workers discover, on their own, the opposition between alienated labor and creative activity formulated by the young Marx in the "1844 Manuscripts," such that the practice of the class struggle constitutes the strongest way of accessing Marxist theory.

Moreover, it is this movement from practice to theory that Marx himself took on in his most technical writings. The transformations of the plan for the "critique of political economy" between the *Critique of Political Economy* of 1859 and the first volume of *Capital* published in 1867, Dunayevskaya explains, simply cannot be understood if we isolate them from the "great historic events of the 1860s" (2000: 87). Among these "great events" we must count the struggle of Black slaves for their emancipation during the U.S. Civil War, as well as the struggle for the regulation of the working day led by the working class (Marx 1976: 414; Anderson 2010). These two events are indeed at the heart of Chapter 10 of *Capital* on the "Working Day," whose traces we would search for in vain in the *Critique of Political Economy*. And far from figuring as simple illustrations, these two events constitute genuine guides to the truth, making it possible to understand the resurgence and the historical modifications of capitalist accumulation on a global scale. The irruption of social conflicts in the fabric of Marx's argumentation thus marks the passage from a "new political economy" of which the *Critique* was the outline, to a "critique of the very foundations of political economy" in *Capital*, where theory is wed to the dynamic of struggles for emancipation (Dunayevskaya 2000: 106).

The example of the transformations of Marx's project of the "critique of political economy" shows that the movement from practice to theory must be completed by a movement from theory to practice. In response to the thesis that "the actions of the proletariat create the possibility for the intellectual to work out theory" it can indeed be said that "where the workers think their own thoughts, there must be the intellectual to absorb the new impulses" (Dunayevskaya 2000: 286) by integrating them into a general perspective able to orient action. As we previously underlined, it is this function of the theoretical integration of emancipatory struggles that Dunayevskaya attributes to a "new humanism." Despite the heterogeneity of their causes and of their immediate objectives as well as of the subjectivities they mobilize, these struggles must indeed be conceptualized and articulated in a complex fashion, since they share the same historical present, the same global conjuncture. Thus, the wildcat strikes led by American workers in reaction to automation, the revolts against state capitalism carried out in 1953 in East Berlin and then in 1956 in Budapest, as well as the civil rights struggle of Black Americans, all appear in *Marxism and Freedom* as so many proofs of the extension of the totalitarian logic that animates bureaucratic capitalism across the planet. These movements, each in their own way and in an autonomous manner, help to pose in a practical sense "the fundamental problem of true freedom" (Dunayevskaya 2000: 275), and it is on this basis that their convergence can be anticipated.

Here we touch upon what is no doubt the main point of interest of *Marxism and Freedom* for the contemporary reader: the manner in which it envisages the "convergence" of anticapitalist, antiracist, feminist, and "democratic" struggles. From a Dunayevskayan perspective, this convergence will be neither decreed, nor imposed from the outside by an enlightened vanguard, whether the latter takes the form of a collective, a party, or an individual critical intellectual. It rests on the processual unification of theory and practice, whose two political moments are *inquiry* and *organization*.

The attention paid throughout *Marxism and Freedom* to forms of struggle invented by the oppressed across their history responds to the conviction that every revolutionary perspective should be anchored in the concrete knowledge of their conditions of life and labor. Indeed, the practice of worker inquiry not only makes it possible to prevent the risk of substitutionism, of constructing a fantastical subject of emancipation. It also and especially makes possible the production of an alternative form of knowledge of society to that disseminated by the dominant ideology, as well as the circulation of heterogeneous experiences of subalternity, thereby favoring the immanent constitution of an oppositional collectivity. This militant practice of the inquiry, promoted in the same period by the members of *Socialisme ou Barbarie* in France, and later developed by the Italian workerists, represents the necessary condition of every proletarian political composition (Gallo Lassere and Monferrand 2019). But for Dunayevskaya, it is not a sufficient condition. Indeed, whereas in 1955 C. L. R. James called for the abolition of the distinction between party and mass, the author of *Marxism and Freedom* does not seem to have ever truly renounced the necessity of forming a revolutionary organization *relatively* autonomous from social movements.

Insofar as the masses are not constantly in movement, and pursue often contradictory or at least heterogeneous objectives, the relative autonomy of the revolutionary organization appears first of all to be the necessary counterpart to the unequal development of social conflicts. But this autonomy is equally the condition of its functioning as a laboratory where militants can collectively reflect on the meaning and the strategic horizon of their action. The image of the organization that emerges from *Marxism and Freedom* is hence that of a transmission belt linking heterogeneous struggles, valorizing conflict as the motor of its expansion, and supporting all the minoritarian claims capable of radicalizing from within the emancipatory process. It is this permanent valorization of claims made by the most marginalized sections of the proletariat that Dunayevskaya sees at work in Lenin's reflections on the party. And it is equally from this perspective that she studies the role played by Black women in the struggle for the abolition of slavery, as well as the importance of feminist and antiracist struggles for the subversive explosion that marked the 1960s and '70s (Dunayevskaya 1982: 79–88, 192–198). At these different conjunctures, the "convergence of struggles" does not appear as the product of their reduction to the lowest common denominator, as the effect of their subsumption to a monolithic political line, and it is not reduced to the mechanical addition of the different forms of oppression that structure the social world. Rather, this convergence is envisaged as a conflictual dynamic of the continual sublation or overcoming of the tendencies toward stagnation, toward bureaucratization and toward a reactionary turn, which the majoritarian forms of representation of the social movement carry at their core. Ultimately, it is thus the very vocabulary of "convergence" that must be abandoned, to be replaced by that of the "permanent revolution" (Dunayevskaya 1982: 124–133) introduced by the antiracist and feminist movements into the struggle for a truly human society.

Beyond the context of a history now past in which it was written, and whatever we may think of the "humanism" that it defends, *Marxism and Freedom* calls on us to reconnect with the strategic creativity that once belonged to emancipatory movements; to engage ourselves in the historical dialectic that is in any case our destiny; and to supplement the question "what is to be done?" with that around knowing where we want to go. Less than a program, but more than an incantatory call to resistance, this work thus constitutes an invitation to take back the historical initiative that we have abandoned to capital, and to a world that belongs to it only because we have allowed ourselves to be dispossessed of this world.

NOTES

1. This chapter was translated from the French by Conall Cash, whom I would like to thank warmly. It originally appeared as the preface to the 2016 French reprint of *Marxism and Freedom* (*Marxisme et Liberté*, Paris: Éditions Syllepse, pp. 9–23).
2. Hence Dunayevskaya's critique of Theodor Adorno's "negative dialectic," which, she argues, severs the dialectic from its prospective aspect and revolutionary productivity (1980: 173–174).

BIBLIOGRAPHY

Anderson, Kevin B. 2010. *Marx at the Margins. On Nationalism, Ethnicity, and Non-Western Societies*: Chicago: University of Chicago Press.
Anderson, Kevin B. and Russell Rockwell, eds. 2012., *The Dunayevskaya-Marcuse-Fromm Correspondence, 1954–1978: Dialogues on Hegel, Marx, and Critical Theory*. Lanham, MD: Lexington Books.
Dunayevskaya, Raya. 1969. "A Footnote on the Detractors of Lenin." *News & Letters* (December).
———. 1980. "Hegel's Absolute as New Beginning," pp. 162–177 in *Art and Logic in Hegel's Philosophy*, ed. Warren E. Steinkraus and Kenneth L. Schmitz. Atlantic Highlands, NJ: Humanities Press.
———. 1982. *Rosa Luxemburg, Women's Liberation, and Marx's Philosophy of Revolution*. Atlantic Highlands, NJ: Humanities Press.

——. 1985. "Dialectics of Revolution and of Women's Liberation," pp. 1–10 in *Dialectics of Revolution: American Roots and World Humanist Concepts.* Chicago: News and Letters Committees.

——. [1946–1947] 1992. "The Nature of the Russian Economy," pp. 71–87 in *The Marxist-Humanist Theory of State-Capitalism.* With an introduction by Peter Hudis. Chicago: News and Letters Committees.

——. 2000. *Marxism and Freedom: From 1776 until Today.* Amherst, NY: Humanity books.

Gallo Lassere, Davide and Frédéric Monferrand. 2019. "Inquiry: Between Critique and Politics." *South Atlantic Quarterly* 18/2, pp. 444–456.

James, C. L. R. 1941. "Russia—A Fascist State." *New International* VII/3, pp. 54–58.

Marx, Karl. 1973. *Grundrisse*, trans. Martin Nicolaus. New York: Penguin.

——. 1976. *Capital*, Vol. I, trans. B. Fowkes. London: Penguin.

——. [1844] 2000a. "Alienated Labor," pp. 85–95 in McLellan 2000.

——. [1844] 2000b. "Critique of the Hegelian Dialectic and General Philosophy," pp. 104–118 in McLellan 2000.

McLellan, David, ed. 2000. *Karl Marx: Selected Writings.* New York: Oxford University Press.

Trotsky, Leon. 1937. *The Revolution Betrayed*, trans. Max Eastman. New York: Pathfinder.

Van der Linden, Marcel. 2009. *Western Marxism and the Soviet Union*, trans. J. Bendien. Chicago: Haymarket.

CHAPTER 15

Beyond Anti-humanism: Alienation, Praxis, and the Dialectics of Liberation

Kieran Durkin

The publication of *Marxism and Freedom: From 1776 until Today* in 1958 was a landmark event in the history of Marxism. Appearing in the wake of the Montgomery Bus Boycott of 1955–1956, and the Hungarian revolution of 1956, *Marxism and Freedom* contained the first English translations of the central "Private Property and Communism" and "Critique of the Hegelian Dialectic" essays from Marx's *Economic and Philosophical Manuscripts* (1964—hereafter *1844 Manuscripts*).[1] These manuscripts had been circulating in Marxist circles in Central and Western Europe since 1927—when David Ryazanov, Director of the Moscow Marx-Engels Institute, had released them in Russian under the title "Preparatory Work for *The Holy Family*"—so this belated appearance of an English translation of these essays was highly significant.[2] Dunayevskaya's identification of the importance of these essays, and her engagement with them as far back as the early 1940s as part of the Johnson-Forest Tendency, marks her out for inclusion in a select group

K. Durkin (✉)
Department of Politics, University of York, York, UK
e-mail: kieran.durkin@york.ac.uk

© The Author(s) 2021   285
K. B. Anderson et al. (eds.), *Raya Dunayevskaya's Intersectional Marxism*, Marx, Engels, and Marxisms,
https://doi.org/10.1007/978-3-030-53717-3_15

of thinkers in the international Marxist tradition from the period who saw the importance of this insight into Marx's early intellectual development.[3]

Marxism and Freedom is remarkable for more than including English translations of these early writings, however. In the context of the by then incontrovertible evidence of totalitarianism in the Soviet Union, but also of renewed struggles for liberation in Europe and the United States, the book itself spoke to the urgent need to rediscover the essence of Marx's thought, which Dunayevskaya argued was a deep humanism based on a *dialectical relationship between theory and practice*. Since Marxism had been sullied by the development of totalitarianism in Russia—by its co-option into the new Stalinist theory of "dialectical materialism" and the sundering of the working classes under successive Five-Year Plans— Dunayevskaya sought to reclaim it through returning to the basis of Marx's thinking as set against the wider historical context of the period. From the first chapter to the last, Dunayevskaya works out the fundamentals of the dialectical relationship between theory and practice that she argues characterizes the humanism of Marxist thought, mapping the hinterland of its development through the French Revolution, the rise of the Trade Union movement, the workers revolts of the nineteenth century (including the 1848 revolts, and the events of the Paris Commune), right up to the opposition to the twentieth-century automation and state capitalism. Her account of this history is emblematic of the agentic Marxism-Humanism that she maps out in later works, such as *Philosophy and Revolution: From Hegel to Sartre, and From Marx to Mao* and *Women's Liberation and the Dialectics of Revolution: Reaching for the Future*, where we see her marked expansion of the "unchained dialectic" further and further in the direction of the struggles of the Black, anticolonial, women's, and youth movements—an expansion of the dialectic that could be said to outstrip even the capacious understanding of the late Marx.

What I will do in this chapter, then, is explore these various facets of Dunayevskaya's Marxist-Humanism, underlining the centrality of *Marxism and Freedom* to Dunayevskaya's wider emancipatory project, as well as demonstrating how her resurrection and repurposing of the humanism of Marx's thought functions as the essence of her own thinking, which nevertheless has its own individual genesis and trajectory as set against the struggles of her time.

Marx's "New Humanism"

Central to *Marxism and Freedom* is what Dunayevskaya argues is the deep humanism of Marx's thought. This humanism, Dunayevskaya is at pains to stress, is most accurately understood as a *new humanism*—one that can be differentiated from liberal, bourgeois, and Christian humanisms through its unification of idealism and materialism, as well as through its revolutionary underpinnings. Taking her cue from the *1844 Manuscripts*, Dunayevskaya demonstrates that Marx's humanism, as explicated here, transcends not only the abstract, idealistic humanism of Ludwig Feuerbach but also that of G. W. F. Hegel, reaching each beyond the other in an attempt to arrive at the truly human foundation of existence conceived in terms of its *actual life-process*. As part of her analysis, Dunayevskaya notes that in the chapter concerning the "Critique of the Hegelian Dialectic," Marx criticizes Hegel's idealism—which he sees in the form of what appears to be an exclusive concern with ideas and thoughts—but also that he *praises* the dialectical method—what Hegel called "the dialectic of negativity"—as "the moving and creative principle" (Marx in Dunayevskaya [1958] 2000: 57). This focus, in the *1844 Manuscripts*, on the dialectical unity of idealism and materialism—that is to say, the unity of the subjective and the objective—is, for Dunayevskaya, the humanist essence and methodological basis of Marx's thought. Crucially, as these essays also show, it is a humanism that transcends not only the abstract idealism of bourgeois German philosophy but also the abstract materialism of British Political Economy that was at the forefront of economic thought at the time.

Repeatedly, and at different levels of elaboration, Dunayevskaya makes the case for the existence of a fundamental unity across Marx's writings-based precisely on this humanism. Contextualizing the later development of his thought, Dunayevskaya notes that Marx broke with bourgeois society in 1843 and claims that, from this point onwards, his vision was one of "total freedom": the "freedom of humanity" as opposed to "the inevitable misery and waste of life which characterizes contemporary society" ([1958] 2000: 53). Dunayevskaya traces this life-long concern with freedom in Marx through a number of different modalities: from the concern in the *1844 Manuscripts* with the subject-object inversion (and the stress on the alienated worker as a sensuous, organic being estranged from true human needs), to the concern in the *Grundrisse* with the "absolute movement of becoming" and "the development of all human powers as such the end in itself" (Marx 1993: 488), to the concern in *Capital* with "the free individuality of the labourer himself" (Marx 1990: 927). With great precision, and in layered explications, she demonstrates how these concerns are indexed to Marx's identification of the human *need for universality* as the need to be fully human that takes freedom as its condition.

Importantly, Dunayevskaya does not argue for the preference of Marx's earlier over his later writings, as was the case with a number of thinkers from this period; she merely argues that these earlier writings provide the *intellectual biographical basis* for the deep unity that she identifies across Marx's writings as a whole, notwithstanding the successive original developments made over the later years. Of course, in arguing this, Dunayevskaya was working against a dominant trend in Marxist thinking that sought to downplay Marx's earlier writings as "pre-scientific" and "ideological." This trend, which had gathered pace during the 1950s, would find its most high-profile representative in the figure of Louis Althusser. Utilizing Gaston Bachelard's notion of "epistemological rupture" and the fundamental dichotomy between science and ideology (Bachelard 2002), Althusser posited an irreversible break in Marx's thinking between the *1844 Manuscripts* on the one hand and *The German Ideology* and *Theses on Feuerbach*, both of which appeared the following year, on the other. Although Althusser later came to soften his stance on the abruptness of this apparent break (1976), he never relented on his description of the *1844 Manuscripts* as the "Marx furthest from Marx" (1969: 159), containing a humanist philosophy that he insisted Marx came to renounce.

Althusser's critique, so influential in academic circles for the best part of the past fifty years, was opposed not only to the presence of "humanism" and to the Feuerbachian influence imputed therein, but also to the role of Hegel and to the suggestion that Marx ought to be interpreted in *any sense* in philosophical terms. Althusser attributes to Marx, in fact, a "theoretical *anti*-humanism [which is] the absolute (negative) precondition of the (positive) knowledge of the human world itself, and its practical transformation" (1969: 229, emphasis added). In direct contradiction to the argument proffered by Althusser, Dunayevskaya argues in *Marxism and Freedom* (which of course precedes by a few years Althusser's published writings on Marx[4]), that never for a moment did Marx separate his economics from his politics or from his philosophy: "[n]othing from Marx's early Humanism," Dunayevskaya contends, "was

ever jettisoned by [Marx] when, at another period, he called it communism" ([1958] 2000: 64). Broaching the issue of Hegel and of idealism
directly, Dunayevskaya acknowledges that Marx *did* later depart from his
earlier Hegelian language; but while this was so, she demonstrates that
even when Marx utilized Hegelian language in these earlier writings he
was never an idealist in the sense of thinking the that contradictions in
society could be resolved through the machinations of thought alone.
Dunayevskaya makes it abundantly clear that the notion of *the negation
of the negation*, and the whole dialectic of negativity that Marx takes over
from Hegel, is based on real contradictions and on the real transcendence
of those contradictions as an objective (but not solely objective) movement in the world at large. As ought to be clear to anyone who reads
them—and as was certainly clear to Dunayevskaya—what we see in the
1844 Manuscripts, and in the section on the Hegelian dialectic in particular, is what Dunayevskaya calls Marx's demystifying, or "unchaining" of
the dialectic ([1958] 2000: 5), i.e., the placing of it on firmly material
groundings in the sense of explicitly attending to the life practices and
corporeal nature of real, living human beings.

A further, related contribution made by *Marxism and Freedom* in
this regard is the central analytical recognition that is accorded to the
notion of *alienation*. Making the connection once more with *Capital*,
Dunayevskaya draws attention to the commonalities between the later
Marx and the Marx of the *1844 Manuscripts*. In particular, she remarks
upon the similarities between Marx's preoccupation with alienation (i.e.,
estrangement from free, conscious life activity) in his earlier writings
and his later concern with the ways in which under capitalism, all
concrete labors become reduced to one abstract, congealed mass: "dead,
accumulated, materialized labor, that now turns to oppress the living
laborer" ([1958] 2000: 56). As opposed to a thinker such as Althusser,
Dunayevskaya argues that the issue of alienation was not merely a question
of philosophical language which Marx quickly discarded when he worked
out his economic theories. The fact that the term itself *does* appear in
Marx's later works, including *Capital*, although admittedly with much
reduced frequency, provides support for the argument against Marx's
supposed wholesale abandonment of the concept. Moreover, if we move
beyond a merely nominal register, it is clear that a concern with alienation—i.e., the control of living labor by dead labor and the human effects
of this: a concern with the prolongation of the working day, an increase
in the speed of work, its prison-like discipline, and the extent to which

workers have become appendages to the machine—is discernible at the very heart of *Capital*, just as in Marx's earlier writings.

The plausibility of Dunayevskaya's position on this score is further enhanced by her demonstration of the clear underlying similarities that obtain between Marx's account of alienation in the *1844 Manuscripts* and his later account of commodity fetishism. Referring to Marx's observation that under the fetishism of commodities that pervades the surface level of capitalist society social relations between people assume "the fantastic form of the relations between things," Dunayevskaya stresses that this is so not merely because this fetishism conceals the relationship between classes—this is certainly true—but also, and at the same time, because "[i]t is the manifestation of the *perverse* relation of subject and object" (1973: 88, emphasis in original). Under capitalism, Dunayevskaya points out, relations between humans appear as relations between things because *that literally is what they are*. But not only are human relations lived as relations between things: crucially, dead labor, and the machine that mediates it, dictates the lives of real, live human beings who are *reduced to the level of things*. It is this true nature of capitalist production that Marx's analysis of the fetishism of commodities discloses—a disclosure which, while certainly highly significant in itself, nevertheless remains a reconfigured form of the original concern with the subject-object reversal outlined in his theory of alienated labor, albeit significantly expanded and developed.

In a classic case of the disambiguation that characterizes her style, Dunayevskaya cuts to the heart of the matter:

> Marx's primary theory is a theory of what he first called "alienated labour" then "abstract" or "value-producing" labor. Capitalism begins when the capacity to labor becomes a commodity... Hence, it is more correct to call the Marxist theory of capital not a labor theory of value, but a value theory of labor. ([1958] 2000: 138)[5]

It is for this reason that Dunayevskaya was able to say that alienation forms the very *pivot*, not only of the capitalist productive system but of Marx's whole "science" itself.

But Dunayevskaya does not rest here. As yet further evidence for her claim she cites the third volume of *Capital*, where Marx speaks in terms which bear a striking resemblance to her own particular argument presently under consideration: "The way in which surplus value is transformed into profit via the rate of profit is but a continued development of the perversion of subject and object taking place in the process of production" (Marx, in Dunayevskaya [1958] 2000: 130). The clarity of the language here is revealing, taking matters beyond the recognition of strong thematic continuities to a level of explicitness that surely carries significant evidential weight. It would seem to give strong support to Dunayevskaya's claim as to the enduring centrality of the theme of alienation in Marx's critique of capitalism, even where the term itself may not be present. Moreover, the commitment that Marx demonstrates to unmasking the perverted relationship between subject and object at this late stage in his life gives great credence, at the same time, to Dunayevskaya's claim that the humanism of *Capital* "runs like a red thread throughout the work," giving it "both its profundity and its force and direction" ([1958] 2000: 125). So, not only are Marx's economic categories *social categories*; they are also thoroughly permeated with the humanism that arose from his initial engagements with Hegel, Feuerbach, and political economy.

THE CRITIQUE OF STATE CAPITALISM AND "THE NEGATION OF THE NEGATION"

Marxism and Freedom ought to be seen as both the culmination of Dunayevskaya's work as part of the Johnson-Forest Tendency—of which she, alongside C. L. R. James, were titular members—but also as a development beyond this relationship. As has been explored in this volume already (see Hudis and Anderson, Spano, and Hudis), the Johnson-Forest Tendency grew to prominence in the early 1940s,[6] their working union centered on the opposition to the conservatism of the Socialist Workers Party and to Trotsky's defence of the USSR as a "degenerated workers' state" (Trotsky 1965). While this is so, it is important to note that Dunayevskaya had already moved in this direction by 1941, prior to her theoretical and organizational partnership with James, as can be seen in her *The Union of Socialist Republics is a Capitalist Society*. In this pamphlet, which was penned under an earlier iteration of her pseudonym "Freddie James," and which was circulated internally among the Workers Party, Dunayevskaya takes direct issue not only with Trotsky's assertion that the mere existence of statified property was sufficient to warrant the

characterization of the USSR as a workers' state, but also Max Shachtman's designation of the USSR as a form of "bureaucratic state socialism"
(1940). Responding particularly to Shachtman—at the time leader of the
Workers Party—Dunayevskaya contended adamantly that:

> The determining factor in analyzing the class nature of a society is not
> whether the means of production are the *private* property of the capi-
> talist class or are state-owned, but whether the means of production are
> *capitalist*, that is, whether they are monopolized and alienated from the
> direct producers. The Soviet Government occupies in relation to the whole
> economic system the position which a capitalist occupies in relation to a
> single enterprise. (Dunayevskaya [Freddie James] [1941] 1992: 3)

For Dunayevskaya, the fact that state capitalism in the USSR was not
tied to state trustification, as in the West, but to social revolution,
did not obviate the fact that the economic law involved remained the
same: "The *manner* in which the means of production were converted
into state property did not deprive them of their becoming *capitalist*"
(Dunayevskaya [Freddie James] [1941] 1992: 4). Arriving at the heart
of her analysis, she lambasts the exploitative and alienating nature of
productive relations in the USSR:

> To call the piecework system which is best suited to capitalist exploitation
> "socialist working norms" does not lighten the degree of exploitation of
> a bricklayer who has to lay 16,000 bricks per day, or a typist…to type 45
> pages of 30 lines each and 60 strokes in each line per day. (Dunayevskaya
> [Freddie James] [1941] 1992: 4–5)

Dunayevskaya's analysis of Russian state capitalism deepened in the
following years, in a series of pieces written for *The New International*,
including "Labor and Society" (1942), "An Analysis of the Russian
Economy" (1942–1943), "The Nature of the Russian Economy" (1946–
1947).[7] These were followed by the Johnson-Forest Tendency pamphlets
The Invading Socialist Society" (1947) and *The Balance Sheet: Trotskyism
in the United States 1940–1947* (1947). In each of these documents, the
description of the USSR as state capitalist is underlined with reference to
Marx's own interpretation of the defining feature of capitalism—which is
not the sale and purchase of labor but, rather, the repeated *appropriation
of surplus value* that took place in what Marx called "the hidden abode
of production" (Marx 1990: 279).

Dunayevskaya's discussion of state capitalism in *Marxism and Freedom* is a clear development of the concerns outlined in these preceding documents. By this time, however, she is even more explicit in basing her argument not only in Marx's writings but also Hegel's with the additional stress on the humanist nature of her analysis. A classic example of this development can be seen in her repurposing of Marx's demystification of Hegel's account of the *negation of the negation*. Dunayevskaya is clear that the abolition of private property was, for Marx, a means toward the abolition of alienated labor and not an end-in-itself. The abolition of private property, Dunayevskaya notes, leads to a new way of life, or a new social order, "*only if* 'freely associated individuals' and not abstract 'society' become the masters of the socialized means of production" ([1958] 2000: 62). Deepening her argument in this regard, Dunayevskaya draws attention to the importance of Marx's distinction between vulgar and even positive communism on one hand, and his own philosophy of *humanism* on the other:

> another transcendence, *after* the abolition of private property is needed to achieve a truly new, *human* society which differs from private property not alone as an "economic system," but as a different way of *life* altogether. It is as *free* individuals developing all their natural and acquired talents that we first leap from what Marx called the *pre*-history of humanity into its true history, the "leap from necessity to freedom." ([1958] 2000: 58)

This repurposing of Hegel's notion of the negation of the negation, utilized by Marx in the *1844 Manuscripts* in the form of the revolutionary overcoming of real contradictions, allows Dunayevskaya to suggest a level of prescience in Marx, or at least that there exists within Marx's own corpus further conceptual weaponry with which to critique what had clearly become in the USSR a revolution that had failed to progress to its second stage and to thereby realize the kind of society that Marx had envisioned. Quoting Marx in the *1844 Manuscripts*, Dunayevskaya draws attention to his stress on the transcendence of the abolition of private property—which Marx designates as a "mediation"—as needing to move toward a form of "*positive* humanism, beginning from itself" (Marx, in Dunayevskaya [1958] 2000: 58, emphasis added). This positive humanism, as brought into being through the negation of the negation of private property and its replacement by freely associated labor, is a humanism opened to the development of the individual as an end-in-itself. This focus on the individual—which is simultaneously a focus on the individual-social relation, and is so in a way in which the individual is realized in community—Dunayevskaya posits as the "soul" of Marxism. It is for this reason that she emphasizes how Marx warned from the start that "[w]e must above all avoid setting up 'the society' as an abstraction opposed to the individual. The individual," for Marx, "*is* the social entity. The expression of his [or her] life…is therefore the expression and verification of the life of society" (cited in Dunayevskaya [1958] 2000: 65).

Anchoring her analysis consistently in the humanist theme, Dunayevskaya reproaches the Soviet attacks on "humanism" that proliferated in the 1950s. Referring to the hatchet-job provided by V. A. Karpushin and other "Russian totalitarians" ([1958] 2000: 64), Dunayevskaya unveils the interior logic that dictated that the humanism of Marx *must* be destroyed by the Soviet elite in order to prevent the ideological veil being lifted on the tyranny of the Russian state:

> It is that actual world of Russia with its forced labor camps that compels this Russian attack against Marxism. It is not the idealism of Hegel that worries them. It is the revolutionary method of the dialectic and the Humanism of Marx that threatens their existence in theory as the working class does in life. The deeper the crisis in Russia, the greater the need for an ideology to keep the workers at work. (Dunayevskaya [1958] 2000: 63)

Dunayevskaya stresses how this is the *dividing line* between Marxism as a doctrine of liberation and all those who proclaim the names "Marxism," "socialism," or "communism," but who develop at best a truncated form of these theories, or at worst a wholesale abomination of them.

Describing the Russian state in colorful language as an "octopus [that] will gorge itself on what is left of the Revolution and on the workers who dare to resist" ([1958] 2000: 226), Dunayevskaya rails against the enshrined separation between mental and manual labor that characterizes the state bureaucracy, which she describes as "the most deadly, the most insidious, the most dangerous enemy because it springs from the proletariat and cloaks itself in Marxist terminology" ([1958] 2000: 239). Striking at the heart of Stalinist ideology, she pulls apart the proclamation that the perverse form of relations between human beings and machine, where dead labor dominates living labor, had been overcome. On the contrary, she proclaims that "the Plan has perfected it, and become a prisoner of it" (Dunayevskaya [1958] 2000: 239). In fact, so opposed to the fundamental nature of Marx's philosophy had the Russian state become under Stalin that she opines that "[n]ever before has so gigantic a State mobilized itself with such murderous vigilance to keep the proletariat at work while the leaders plan" (Dunayevskaya [1958] 2000: 239). As illustrative of this fact, she singles out the "barrack-like discipline" with which this domination is exercised, which she describes as having assumed, "even in its living visage, a death-like mask" ([1958] 2000: 259).

Of course, Dunayevskaya's elaboration of the theory of state capitalism was not confined to the USSR; she was also at pains to describe its manifestations in the United States, where she ties its development to the response to the economic crash of 1929, the Great Depression, and to Franklin Delano Roosevelt's New Deal that followed. Dunayevskaya is clear as to the prime motivation that lay behind the New Deal: namely, to *save* capitalism, and, as the decades moved on, to compete with a developing Russia. She pays mention to the members of "The Brain Trust" who saw the New Deal as an attempt to move headlong to total planning with some similarities to the Russian model. But what is important to note is that the *basis* of her analysis here once more arises from Marx. For Marx, as Dunayevskaya shows, what happens at a moment of existential crisis—such as the one that gripped the capitalist system in the wake of 1929—is the reversion to the *essence of the system*: namely, to "the despotic plan of capital against the cooperative plan of freely associated labor" ([1958] 2000: 92).

It is this—along with the functioning of the law of value that goes with it—that enables Dunayevskaya to advance this two-pronged critique. The hierarchical structure of control over social labor remains essentially the same, whether in the hands of New Deal Democrats in the United States or of the Stalinist labor bureaucracy in the USSR: "[t]o keep production going on an ever-expanding scale, to extract the greatest amount of surplus or unpaid labor, requires a whole army of foremen, managers, superintendents. These all work for the capitalist, with one aim and purpose: to force labor out of the many laborers" (Dunayevskaya [1958] 2000: 92).

THE DIALECTICS OF PRAXIS

Dunayevskaya's focus on state capitalism—on "the Plan" and on the
the hierarchical control over social labor instantiated in it—is intimately
related to her account of *praxis*. And it is here, in her account of praxis,
that she again makes a signal contribution to Marxism, formalizing and
extending some of Marx's own perhaps insufficiently drawn-out insights
into a distinct theory of her own.

   In contrast to the species of Marxism that has proliferated in most
academic environments since at least the latter half of the twentieth
century, Dunayevskaya's engagement with Marx is one that can claim a
closer connection to his own lived existence. For Dunayevskaya, Marxism
could not be merely a *theory* of liberation; it must also be a *practice* of
liberation. Dunayevskaya expounds upon this connection in *Marxism and
Freedom*, positing a dialectical relationship led by a *movement from practice to theory that also entails a movement from theory to practice*. The
basis for this elaboration is once again Marx, this time the attentiveness
to the wider social and political events of his age which caused him to
significantly modify the structure and content of *Capital*. Dunayevskaya
([1958] 2000: 88) quotes Marx in a letter to Engels in 1866, in which
he explicitly talks about adding a chapter on the working day to *Capital*.
She notes that this decision on Marx's part brought history and theory
together, and that it did so under the development of the class struggle:
showing that the struggles of the workers over the shortening of the
working day not only contributed to the development of capitalism itself,
modifying the very structure and pattern of value extraction and the
relations around it, but also lead to self-wrought improvements in the
conditions of the lives of the workers themselves. In as much as this is the
case, Marx's mature theory is not a narrowly objectivist theory, but one
alive with *subjective resonance*.

   Dunayevskaya saw that what occurred here, in what was a direct
extension of the substance of his original break with bourgeois philosophy and political economy, was that *a new dialectic* flowed out of the
labor process; one that amounted to a revolutionary deepening of Marx's
humanistic historical materialism:

> From start to finish, Marx is concerned with the revolutionary actions
> of the proletariat. The concept of theory is now something unified with
> action. Or, more correctly, theory is not something the intellectual works

out alone. Rather, the actions of the proletariat create the possibility for the intellectual to work out theory. ([1958] 2000: 91)

Dunayevskaya's observation that it was the *actions of the working classes* struggling against the conditions of their labor at the point of production that helped Marx break free from the bourgeois concept of theory is instructive, as is her sharp criticism of "professional Marxists" who operate with "too sophisticated an attitude to the revolts which have raged throughout the history of capitalism" ([1958] 2000: 116). Contrary to this approach, Dunayevskaya details Marx's engagement with the working class and their struggles—an engagement that she argues led to the creation of an entirely *new intellectual dimension* and *new philosophy of labor*, "an intellectual whose whole intellectual, social, political activity and creativity [became] the expression of precise social forces" ([1958] 2000: 65).

This characteristic attentiveness to the fullness of Marx—to his concern with the changing nature of the struggle for freedom—is revealed in magnified form in Dunayevskaya's own work. In the period following the horrors of the Second World War and Nikita Khrushchev's denunciation of Stalin, after which many other supposedly radical intellectuals retreated into various forms of pessimism and abandonment of struggle, Dunayevskaya remained attentive to the progressiveness of not only the international working class in general, but also to that of the U.S. working class, so often maligned as lacking in militancy and class consciousness. Once again, Dunayevskaya elaborates her argument here as a form of humanism. Influenced by her intimate knowledge of the strikes that punctuated the late 1940s and early 1950s (she had deliberately moved to Pittsburgh and West Virginia during this period to be closer to the strikers), Dunayevskaya saw the response of U.S. workers to the length of the working day but also—and crucially—to the very *mode of labor* they were forced to engage in as extending and making explicit Marx's theory of alienation. Moreover, she noted that this engagement had taken place *before* any such similar widespread engagement on the part of the Russian workers ([1958] 2000: 276).

Importantly, the struggles of the working classes are seen by Dunayevskaya not only in the negative, but also in the *positive*, as pointing to the way *forward* toward freedom. Summing up this faith in a typically dialectical manner, Dunayevskaya announced with striking conviction that "[t]he elements of the new society present in the old are everywhere in evidence in the thoughts and lives of the working class" ([1958] 2000: 286). This retained stress on the centrality and radicality of the working classes marks Dunayevskaya out during a period in which many thinkers turned away from them almost entirely.[8] For Dunayevskaya, writing in *Marxism and Freedom*, "No theoretician, today more than ever before, can write out of his [sic] own head. Theory requires a constant shaping and reshaping of ideas on the basis of what the workers themselves are doing and thinking" ([1958] 2000: 24). Dunayevskaya, in fact, explicitly salutes the contributions of autoworkers, miners, steelworkers, with whom she conducted dialogues, in *Marxism and Freedom*, declaring them its "coauthors" ([1958] 2000: 24).

Having lived as an activist-intellectual since a young age, this was no grand gesture on Dunayevskaya's part. In fact, in *Marxism and Freedom* we see at first hand Dunayevskaya's undiminished faith in what she also termed the "voices from below." Her commitment is particularly evident in chapter sixteen. Here, Dunayevskaya explicitly confronts the issue of automation and the effects of the introduction of the automated continuous miner—dubbed "the man killer" by the mineworkers—which she notes brought about the longest strike in mine workers' history. She also takes up the 1955 Westinghouse strike over automation and against the "time study." Elaborating this discussion of enhanced dehumanization at the hands of the machine through reference to Marx's own writings—particularly his stress on how the instrument of labor in automation confronts the laborer during the labor process as dead labor that dominates and sucks dry their living labor power—Dunayevskaya conveys an illustrative parallel between the constant tendency toward the breakdown of the machines on the one hand and the related mental breakdown of the nervous systems of the workers on the other.

Through extensive use of direct quotations from the mineworkers themselves, Dunayevskaya is able to bring to the surface in a very direct way the real fears over work, alienation, and daily survival at the hands of the machine. Quoting a young Los Angeles worker in a manner that supports her thesis concerning the maturity of the working classes and its new stage of consciousness, Dunayevskaya reveals the humanism striving to break free: "What skill do you need in this day of Automation? What pride can you have in your work if everything is done electronically and you are there—if you are lucky to get a job—just to blow the whistle when the machine breaks down? What about the human being?" ([1958] 2000: 272). This is followed by the words of an electrical worker, remarking on the false panacea of the separation of work and leisure time: "Under a new society work will have to be something completely new, not just work to get money to buy food and things. It will have to be completely tied up with life" (in Dunayevskaya [1958] 2000: 256). Quoting yet another miner—"[w]hat has to be different is the *way* we have to work" (in Dunayevskaya [1958] 2000: 276, emphasis added)—she underlines with justification, the extent to which the real essence of Marx's thought (i.e., the quest for universality) was evidenced here, in the revolt against automation, as a new form of humanism.

Dunayevskaya's commitment to the subjectivity of the working class at a time at which she discerned its maturity is evident also in her work with News and Letters Committees—the group that she started in 1955, after her split with C. L. R. James and the Correspondence Committees. The first edition of the new group's newspaper, *News & Letters*, appeared in June of 1955. The editorial and writing staff was mostly comprised of workers, such as Johnny Zupan and Charles Denby (the latter of whom became sole editor) and contained a whole section specially devoted to detailing "Reader's Views." In her own column, "Notes from a Diary," August 5, 1955, Dunayevskaya is clear on the need to transcend "the most monstrous division of all—the division between mental and manual labor." The intellectual, she tells us, "must be attuned to hear the movement from practice to theory. This is the nub...Theoreticians cannot be bystanders to a paper that mirrors the workers' thoughts and activities as they happen" (1955: 5).

Importantly, this stress on the activity of theoreticians during the course of struggle hints at a further unique aspect of Dunayevskaya's position relative to other Marxists, including other leaders of the Johnson-Forest Tendency. While it is true that it was a theoretical and practical commitment to the creative agency of the proletariat that helped distinguish the early work of the Johnson-Forest Tendency, it was also precisely this relationship between theory and practice in relation to the proletariat that was to form the substance of Dunayevskaya's break with James and Grace Lee (later Lee Boggs). As Spano has expounded earlier in this volume, what distinguishes Dunayevskaya's position from that of James and Lee, besides their difference over the issue of humanism,[9] was a difference concerning the notion of *praxis*. This difference had its genesis in two related developments. The first concerns the developments in terms of the consciousness of the proletariat already noted: the U.S. miners strikes in the late 1940s and early 1950s, along with the wave of revolts in Eastern Germany and Russia following Stalin's death in 1953. The second, related development concerns Dunayevskaya's studies of Hegel, which had gathered pace during the Johnson-Forest Tendency studies in late 1940s and particularly the early 1950s.

What is important here is the differential approach to the study of Hegel that had developed between the two camps. Whereas the Johnson-Forest Tendency's engagement with Hegel—initially led by James—had focused heavily on the issue of contradiction (seen most clearly in *State Capitalism and World Revolution*), Dunayevskaya's focus during the early 1950s was increasingly on the notions "second negativity" and the Absolute Idea. Dunayevskaya's work on Hegel during this period reached its early high point—what she considered a "breakthrough"—in two letters on Hegel's Absolutes on May 12 and 20, 1953.[10] In these letters, Dunayevskaya posits that the drive for freedom evident in the struggles of the age must be realized through the unity of subjective and objective— theory and practice—as a single, indivisible unit ([1984] 1992: 9). The need for a second revolution (a revolution *within* a revolution), as was made clear by developments in the USSR, was intimately connected to the unity of subjective and objective considered not only in terms of class consciousness but also the relationship of theory and practice, as the only way in which a successful second revolution worthy of the name could come about.

Dunayevskaya's position here self-consciously avoided the failure, as she saw it, on the part of James and Lee to sufficiently engage with the world situation in these terms. James and Lee, despite agreeing as to the need for a second revolution, and to the need for this revolution to be led by the workers themselves, were moving toward a more spontaneist position in which the difference between theory and practice ought to be resolved toward the latter, to the point whereby theory almost evaporates in favor of the unmediated valorization of practice. The divergence between the two sides of the tendency on this issue can be seen first of all in James' refusal to devote the first issue of *Correspondence*—the new paper that was set up following their final split from the Socialist Workers Party in 1951—to the 1949–1950 Miners' strike. James and Lee were also moving further from Marxism as an explanatory device and political strategy. The fruits of this shift are evident most clearly in the book *Facing Reality*, written primarily by James and Lee after the break-up of the Johnson-Forest Tendency, in which the opening line proclaims that "[t]he whole world today lives in the shadow of the state power" (1958: 5). Dunayevskaya rightly accused James and Lee of abandoning Marxism here, noting that "now statism has become the evil—not state capitalism" (1972: 11). Although *Facing Reality* did emphasize the importance of the Hungarian Revolution and the workers councils that had sprung up during this movement, the book is strikingly devoid of Marxian terminology, with "capitalism" replaced by terms such as "official society" and a prominent declaration that philosophy—including Marxist philosophy—had reached its end.

In contrast to James and Lee, Dunayevskaya, on leaving the Correspondence group, set up News and Letters Committees, which was structured by a marked retention of their previous Marxist approach as well as the foregrounding of a newly formulated Marxist-Humanist philosophy that was to be announced in *Marxism and Freedom*. Opposed not only to James and Lee, but also aspects of the later New Left and various forms of hyper-militant radicalism that proliferated in the 1960s and 1970s, Dunayevskaya was presciently aware of the dangers contained in thinking that theory could be picked-up "en route." As she was to put it toward the end of her life: "Activists by themselves are as one-sided as theory by itself. Only in their unity—in a new relationship that is rooted where the action is—can we rise to the challenge of the times" (1984: 41). The Marxist-Humanist philosophy that came to stand as her signal contribution remained tied to the resurrection of Marx's humanist praxis—first evidenced in the *1844 Manuscripts* in the insistence on the unity of idealism and materialism—as well as to her reinterpretation of Hegel's Absolutes in the context of new world situation, in which Marx's notion of a "revolution in permanence"[11] took on a new meaning.

EXPANDING THE DIALECTIC

The concern with praxis that Dunayevskaya unearths in her account of Marx's attentiveness to the struggles of the working classes, and that she herself extends in her own engagements, is deepened further in her expansion of the dialectic to the struggles of women, Black Americans, youth, and to the colonized peoples of the earth. Once more, the original source for this engagement is Marx's humanism—particularly his early engagement with Hegel in the *1844 Manuscripts*, but also the humanism that marks his subsequent writings, including the *Grundrisse*, *Capital*, and the *Ethnological Notebooks*.[12]

Following the pattern outlined in her account of praxis, it is once again in *Marxism and Freedom* that Dunayevskaya first stakes out the ground for this expansion—although it should be noted that she first engages with the issue of Black struggles some years earlier (Dunayevskaya 1944). In her discussion of *Capital* here she identifies the transfigured form of Hegel's Absolutes in terms of what she describes as Marx's identification of the "new passions and forces" striving toward the new society ([1958] 2000: 37). Commenting on Marx's evocation of the Abolitionist movement in the United States in *Capital*, Dunayevskaya notes that Marx speaks passionately here about the end of slavery and of its connections with the struggle for an eight-hour day. More radically, Dunayevskaya identifies Marx's own crystal-clear enunciation on the humanistic relationship that by this stage in his life[13] he saw as obtaining between the universal and the particular in terms of racism and capitalism: "Labor cannot emancipate itself in the white skin where in the Black it is branded" (Marx, in Dunayevskaya [1958] 2000: 84). Dunayevskaya's concern here is at once historical and contemporary, and ought to be seen as an extension of her recognition of the "new stage of consciousness" that she identified in the working class struggles against state capitalism in the U.S. and the USSR.

This extension is evident particularly in chapter sixteen of *Marxism and Freedom* where she discusses the school desegregation struggle in Little Rock, Arkansas, and the Montgomery bus boycott in 1956. Describing these events as "a new stage in the Negro struggle for freedom" ([1958] 2000: 279),[14] Dunayevskaya praises the spontaneity of the boycott's organization in its demand for a new form of humanism that, as well as being truly historic, "contains our future" ([1958] 2000: 281). What we see here, then, although perhaps in somewhat germinal form, is the sense in which, for Dunayevskaya, the Black dimension in the United States was opening the future toward a new form of humanism premised on the development of new forms of subjectivity that would help usher in the "new society." As she was to opine some years later, "[the] Black masses in motion have always been the touchstone [in U.S. history]" (1984: 41).

Dunayevskaya's engagement here, although admittedly more attenuated than in her subsequent writings, ought not to be seen as tangential. As noted, she had written on Black struggles in the United States since the 1940s along with James and others in the Johnson-Forest tendency, under the name Freddie Forest. It is also striking to note that *News & Letters* was edited by Charles Denby, a Black auto worker from Detroit (the first time that a U.S. Black production worker had been editor of *any* Marxist paper). Of further note is the fact that a Black woman, Ethel Dunbar, authored the regular *News & Letters* column "We Are Somebody;" and that the very first edition carried an article and picture of Njeri, a Kenyan woman and a central figure in the Mau Mau struggle against British colonialism in Keyna.[15] Nevertheless, it is certainly the case that her writings after *Marxism and Freedom* demonstrate a renewed— and deeper—engagement with the issue of the Black struggle in a world setting.

What is evident in these writings is the dual recognition that the Black struggle mattered, first of all, in and of itself, but also, that it had a significance that went *beyond* itself. This relationship is first expressed in *Marxism and Freedom* where Dunayevskaya stresses the issue of the alignment of the liberatory actions of Black school children breaking down segregation in Little Rock, Arkansas, the wildcat strikes in auto-mobile plants in Detroit, and other struggles for freedom the world over, including, as becomes evident in her work in the subsequent years, the African anti-colonial revolutions and worldwide women's liberation movement. And it was these latter two struggles, two new sets of passions and forces unleashed upon the world—the African anti-colonial struggle, and the struggle of women—that can be considered the two main extensions in her work from the 1960s onwards in terms of revolutionary subjectivity.

The first of these concerns is expanded most significantly in *Philosophy and Revolution: From Hegel to Sartre and from Marx to Mao* (1973), in which Dunayevskaya proclaims that "[t]he African revolutions opened a new page in the dialectic of thought as well as in world history" (1973: 13). Noting how the United Nations had decreed 1960 the "Africa Year" (1973: 215), Dunayevskaya rails against white leftist arrogance toward Africa and the fact that many Marxists did not see the African anti-colonial struggles as real revolutions. To this end, she approvingly cites the humanist Marxist proclamations of figures such as Léopold Sédar Senghor[16] and Frantz Fanon, praising their deep and avowed commit-ment to universal as well as particular freedom. Of Fanon, who she was most impressed with, the more revolutionary of the two, she stresses that "it is not true that he has only the Black in mind," but that this new humanism "is global as well as revolutionary; it is total as well as historically continuous" (1973: 284).

The African struggles are seen by Dunayevskaya, then, as consequen-tial in and of themselves—as imperative struggles against colonialism and racialized disfigurement—but also as part of the wider dialectics of liberation of the era. As noted above, Dunayevskaya drew attention to the ways in which the Black struggle in the United States had influenced the African revolutionaries, but she also pointed out the extent to which the African revolutions had helped to influence the revolts in Black America and even in Eastern Europe. As she was to put it some years later, highlighting the fact that the dialectic is alive and connected as part of the wider striving for self-realization: "[w]hen a new revolution erupts, the tendency is to immediately try to box it in as if it were a question of France/Algeria; or of the West in general/the African revolutions; or in the Middle East, of Arab/Israel" (1986: 20). This "confining of the new within old categories" (1986: 20–21) represented a significant conceptual problem for Marxism, according to Dunayevskaya. "Post-Marx Marxists, she maintained, have disregarded too many revolutions, successful or aborted; disregarded too many philosophies underlying those revolutions. They just allow intellectual sloth to accumulate and accumulate" (1986: 21).

If this notion of a living, connected dialectic can be revealed in the African anti-colonial revolutions, it can be revealed no less in the women's liberation movement of the period. Once more, the expansion of the dialectic to the liberation of women was hardly a new concern on the part of Dunayevskaya. Her writings on women stretch back beyond the period of 1949–1950 Miners' General Strike, in which she spoke to and praised the militant efforts of miner's wives ([1950] 1985). This said, reference to women's issues were restricted to a few instances in *Marxism and Freedom*. By the time of *Philosophy and Revolution*, however, the concern had begun to shift to a more central position, following the bursting forth of the women's liberation movement in the late 1960s, as influenced by the struggles of U.S. Blacks and antiwar activists. Here Dunayevskaya describes the "Women's Revolution," as she called it, as "one of the most anti-elitist new forces and new passions that had come on the historic stage and that [was] raising altogether new questions" (1973: 278). What was particularly important—and unique—about this movement was that it sought to challenge male chauvinism not only under capitalism itself but also within the revolutionary movement. Dunayevskaya was once again able to set the relationship between universal and particular into a healthy arrangement: "the fact that it will not be possible to fully overcome male chauvinism as long as class society exists does not invalidate the movement any more than any struggle for freedom is invalidated" (1973: 280–281).

The high point in Dunayevskaya's work on women's liberation, however, came in the 1980s. *Rosa Luxemburg, Women's Liberation and Marx's Philosophy of Revolution*, an analysis of the hitherto all-too-often overlooked Marxist theorist and activist, appeared in 1982, charting Luxemburg's important contribution to Marxian theory and practice as well as to feminism. But it was in 1985, toward the very end of her life, with *Women's Liberation and the Dialectics of Revolution: A 35-Year Collection of Essays*, that the zenith of her engagement was reached. Here, Dunayevskaya deepens her excavation of Marx's humanism, noting that a concern with what she terms the "Man/Woman" relationship is evident as far back as his *1844 Manuscripts*, where Marx speaks of the alienating subordination of women to men (1985: 53–54). There is interpretative recourse here also to Marx's vision of human development, outlined in the *Grundrisse* as "an absolute movement of becoming," and to his notion of a "revolution in permanence." On the basis of these interpretative excurses, Dunayevskaya calls for her own "total revolution" built on the "passion for a total uprooting of this exploitative, racist, sexist society, stretching from the anti-Vietnam War movement and the beginnings of a New Left within socialism to the present search for a philosophy of revolution to meet the challenge of the ongoing revolutions of our day" (1985: 3).

CONCLUSION: TOWARD AN ABSOLUTE HUMANISM

The humanism that characterizes Dunayevskaya's account of the dialectics of liberation is the lynchpin of her central contribution to Marxism. It should be clear from the foregoing that this humanism was neither a static nor an abstract humanism, but one turned to human agency, subjectivity, and to the unity (and uniting) of idealism and materialism in the social forces of her time. Dunayevksaya discerns the basis of this "new philosophy," as she terms it, in Marx's *1844 Manuscripts*, as well as in his later writings, and, together with a re-engagement with the Hegelian texts that Marx confessed shaped his thinking, devises her own, unique form of humanism that speaks to the movement from practice to theory (and from theory to practice) in the processes of realizing the *whole human dimension*.

Although Dunayevskaya is robust in defending production as her "point of departure...because to see the crisis in production is to understand it everywhere else" ([1958] 2000: 281–282), hers is an account shorn of economic or class reductionism. Whether the struggle concerns issues of class, race, gender, or sexuality,[17] or a combination of these aspects, the dialectic between universal and particular is never sundered in an exclusionary concern for the one over the other. In as much as they are humanist struggles for self-realization—struggles pushing back against domination and fighting for the expansion of the space for freedom at all levels of society—they are *connected and mutually reinforcing*, possessing the potential to lead to the kind of progression that would usher in a true humanism instantiated in both production *and* social relations. We can, in fact, see her engagement here—in this *intersectional* Marxism— as a form of "absolute humanism,"[18] which is nothing other than "the articulation needed to sum up a class*less*, *non*-racist, *non*-sexist society, where truly new human relations self-develop" (1992: 11). In this way, Dunayevskaya was able to articulate Marxism for her age in a manner that few others have done, and with a seriousness that is finally beginning to find the level of recognition that it deserves.

NOTES

1. The essays, which appeared as an appendix to the book, were dropped from subsequent editions (after publication of Erich Fromm's *Marx's Concept of Man*, which contained a translated version of the entirely of the *1844 Manuscripts*).
2. Dunayevskaya had, along with C. L. R. James and Grace Lee, been engaging with these manuscripts as far back as the early 1940s, their translations being used as pamphlets circulated among Socialist Workers Party and Worker Party circles and among workers.
3. Included in, but not exhaustive of this group are Herbert Marcuse, Henri Lefebvre, Erich Fromm, Iring Fetscher, and the Yugoslav Praxis philosophers, as well, of course, as C. L. R. James and Grace Lee, her then collaborators.
4. Althusser had, however, been working on Marx since early 1950s, in a way which directly prefigures his writings of the 1960s (Kelly 1982: 86–87).
5. As Dunayevskaya was to say some years later, "[t]he supreme example of this alienation is that even living labor takes the form of a commodity" (1973: 88).
6. The group was led by J. R. Johnson (C. L. R. James), "Freddie Forest" (Raya Dunayevskaya), and "Ria Stone" (Grace Lee).
7. These, and a further analysis—"Is Russia Part of the Collectivist Epoch of Society?" (1942)—which was unpublished during her lifetime, can be found in *The Marxist-Humanist Theory of State Capitalism*.

8. A case in point, especially given their correspondence (see Anderson and Rockwell 2012), and the fact that he wrote the preface to *Marxism and Freedom*, is Herbert Marcuse. See Dunayevskaya's "Intellectuals in the Age of State Capitalism" where she explicitly takes Marcuse to task for his account of the "backwardness" of the working class, as well as his related elision of Lenin and Stalin. It is also worth noting that Trotsky continued to speak of the immaturity of the proletariat, something Dunayevskaya herself commented on (1973: 147).

9. This difference can be seen in *State Capitalism and World Revolution*, authored primarily by C. L. R. James, with some parts by Raya Dunayevskaya and Grace Lee. Here, in the philosophical section, mostly written by Grace Lee, humanism is considered as either Christian or Existentialist, and as such as reactionary and unsuited to the issue of class struggle (James, with Dunayevskaya and Lee [1950] 1986: 126–130). Although Lee wrote the section, it is inconceivable that James would have signed off on it without approval.

10. These letters are included in *The Power of Negativity: Selected Writings on the Dialectic in Hegel and Marx* (2002).

11. Marx speaks of the need for a revolution in permanence against the bourgeoise in his 1850 "Address to the Communist League," in the aftermath of the failed revolutions of 1848 (2000: 311).

12. Dunayevskaya was one of the first thinkers to seriously study Marx's *Ethnological Notebooks*, written late in his life and published only in the 1970s, and discussing colonized and indigenous peoples across the world.

13. See Anderson (2016) for a detailed account of the shifts in Marx's thinking on this score.

14. Dunayevskaya elsewhere referred to Civil Rights Movement as the "Freedom Now" struggles, or as the "Black Revolution," and was one of the key voices in the Marxist tradition that saw something more than a liberal struggle for rights taking place here.

15. *News & Letters* also had a youth column written by Robert Ellery called "Thinking it Out."

16. Dunayevskaya also critiqued Senghor's later ties to French neo-colonialism.

17. Dunayevskaya wrote little on sexuality, although from what she does say about Marx and "gay liberation" it is clear that this is an area in which her concern with the dialectics of liberation also applies: "People want to have a conclusion on the question of love – what is love, whether it's physical, whether it's emotional, whether it's total, and all that sort of thing. But I don't think it's correct for us to try and solve it for others. I think what we have to do is to create the conditions for everyone to be able to experiment with choices, in love, in the family – and I don't think we'll really have those choices until we get rid of capitalism" (1985: 180).

18. Dunayevskaya here is self-consciously referencing Gramsci's notion of the same name, which she develops in her own direction, as is evident here.

Bibliography

Anderson, Kevin. 2016. *Marx at the Margins: On Nationalism, Ethnicity, and Non-Western Societies*. Chicago: University of Chicago Press.

Anderson, Kevin, and Russell Rockwell (eds.) 2012. *The Dunayevskaya-Marcuse-Fromm Correspondence, 1954–1978: Dialogues on Hegel, Marx, and Critical Theory*. Lanham: Lexington Books.

Althusser, Louis. 1976. *Essays in Self-Criticism*. London: NLB.

Althusser, Louis. 1969. *For Marx*. London: Verso.

Bachelard, Gaston. 2002. *The Formation of the Scientific Mind: A Contribution to a Psychoanalysis of Objective Knowledge*. Manchester: Clinamen.

Dunayevskaya, Raya. 1944. "Negro Intellectuals in Dilemma: Myrdal's Study of a Crucial Problem." *The New International*, Vol. 10, No. 11, November, pp. 369–372.

Dunayevskaya, Raya. 1955. "Notes From a Diary." *News & Letters*, August 5. Detroit: News and Letters.

Dunayevskaya, Raya. 1972. *For the Record. The Johnson-Forest Tendency, or the Theory of State-Capitalism, 1941–51; Its Vicissitudes and Ramifications*. Detroit: News and Letters.

Dunayevskaya, Raya. 1973. *Philosophy and Revolution: From Hegel to Sartre, and from Marx to Mao*. New York: Delta.

Dunayevskaya, Raya. 1982. *Rosa Luxemburg, Women's Liberation, and Marx's Philosophy of Revolution*. Chicago: University of Illinois Press.

Dunayevskaya, Raya. 1984. With Andy Philips. *A 1980s View: The Coal Miners' General Strike of 1949–50 and the Birth of Marxist Humanism*. Chicago: News and Letters.

Dunayevskaya, Raya. 1985. *Women's Liberation and the Dialectics of Revolution: Reaching for the Future. A 35-Year Collection of Essays—Historic, Philosophical, Global*. Atlantic Highlands, NJ: Humanities Press.

Dunayevskaya, Raya. 1986. *The Myriad Global Crises of the 1980s and the Nuclear War World Since World War II*. Chicago: News and Letters.

Dunayevskaya, Raya. 1992. "Intellectuals in the Age of State Capitalism." *The Marxist-Humanist Theory of State Capitalism: Selected Writings*. Edited by Peter Hudis. Chicago. News and Letters.

Dunayevskaya, Raya. [1958] 2000. *Marxism and Freedom: From 1776 Until Today*. New York: Humanity Books.

Dunayevskaya, Raya. 2002. *The Power of Negativity: Selected Writings on the Dialectic in Hegel and Marx*. Edited by Peter Hudis and Kevin B. Anderson. Lanham: Lexington Books.

Dunayevskaya, Raya [Freddie James]. [1941] 1992. "The Union of Soviet Socialist Republics is a Capitalist Society." Chicago: News and Letters.

Fromm, Erich. [1961] 2004. *Marx's Concept of Man*. London: Continuum.

James, C. L. R., Grace Lee Boggs, et al. 1958. *Facing Reality*. Detroit: Correspondence Publishing Company.

James. C. L. R., Raya Dunayevskaya, and Grace Lee. 1947. *The Balance Sheet: Trotskyism in the United States 1940–1947*. Johnson-Forest Tendency.

James. C. L. R., Raya Dunayevskaya, and Grace Lee. [1947] 1972. *The Invading Socialist Society*. Detroit: Bewick Editions.

James. C. L. R., Raya Dunayevskaya, and Grace Lee. [1950] 1986. *State Capitalism and World Revolution*. Chicago. Charles H. Kerr.

Kelly, Michael. 1982. *Modern French Marxism*. Baltimore: The John Hopkins University Press.

Marx, Karl. 1964. "Economic and Philosophical Manuscripts." *Karl Marx: Early Writings*. Edited by Tom Bottomore. New York: McGraw-Hill.

Marx, Karl. 1993. *Grundrisse: Foundations of the Critique of Political Economy (Rough Draft)*. Translated with a Foreword by Martin Nicolaus. London: Penguin.

Marx, Karl. 1990. *Capital: A Critique of Political Economy. Volume I*. Introduction by Ernest Mandel, translated by Ben Fowkes. London: Penguin.

Marx, Karl. 2000. "Address of the Central Committee to the Communist League." *Karl Marx: Selected Writings*. By David McLellan. Oxford: Oxford University Press.

Shachtman, Max. 1940. "Is Russia a Workers' State?" *New International*, Vol. 6, No. 10 (Whole No. 49), December, pp. 195–205.

Trotsky, Leon. 1965. *The Revolution Betrayed*. New York: Merit Publishers.

CHAPTER 16

Two Kinds of Subjectivity in *Marxism and Freedom*: Hegel, Marx, and the Maoist Detour

Kevin B. Anderson

It is over six decades since the publication of Raya Dunayevskaya's *Marxism and Freedom*, a work both of its time and out of joint with its time, in the sense that it was ahead of its time. First published in 1958, at the height of the Cold War, but also not long after the Hungarian Revolution of 1956, it was one of a number of writings in the period that put forth a democratic, humanist, and revolutionary Marxism, both against the Russian Stalinist system and against the "liberal democratic" capitalism of the U.S. and Western Europe. This was the same period when E. P. Thompson broke away from the British Communist Party over Hungary, and when Edgar Morin and others formed the *Arguments* group in France, both of them reacting against the brutal Russian intervention in Hungary.

K. B. Anderson (✉)
Department of Sociology, University of California, Santa Barbara, CA, USA
e-mail: kanderson@soc.ucsb.edu

© The Author(s) 2021
K. B. Anderson et al. (eds.), *Raya Dunayevskaya's Intersectional Marxism*, Marx, Engels, and Marxisms,
https://doi.org/10.1007/978-3-030-53717-3_16

REVOLUTIONARY HUMANIST SUBJECTIVITY

Dunayevskaya had long since broken with Stalinism, some thirty years earlier, and had gone on to write economic analyses in the 1940s of the USSR as a totalitarian state-capitalist society. For her, therefore, the newness of Hungary 1956 lay not so much in any proof of the reactionary, anti-worker character of the Russian and East European Stalinist regimes, as in the proof it offered that (1) contra Orwell and Arendt, totalitarianism could never extinguish the struggle for human liberation, and (2) contra the Hungarian revolution's liberal supporters, the emergence of workers' councils and the Marxist intellectuals of the Petofi circle showed that a third way was possible—a socialist humanism that was entirely different from both Stalinism and Western liberalism. As she wrote with respect to the workers' councils: "When all said that everything was over, the Hungarian Workers' Councils sprung up....They began to fight in the factories, which they were using as their places of refuge....The workers evolved new ways of fighting, both on the job and when they walked out on strike" (1988: 256).

Another mass movement of the period, the Montgomery Bus Boycott of 1955–1956 in Alabama, also figured prominently in *Marxism and Freedom*. In her treatment of what is now seen as an epochal event that launched the Civil Rights Movement, Dunayevskaya stressed its grassroots character, rather than the role of the leadership of the newly prominent Martin Luther King. She noted that the movement had no visible hierarchy. Rather, it was governed through mass meetings held as often as three times per week. She also singled out the fact that in boycotting the buses for over a year, the Black working class had to arrange its own informal transportation networks in the face of threats and repression from the state and the Ku Klux Klan. In declaring, "Clearly, the greatest thing of all in this... spontaneous organization was its own working existence," she was pointing to its revolutionary potential (Dunayevskaya 1988: 281). For that phrase, "its own working existence," would have been known to any serious Marxist as the one Marx had employed in *The Civil War in France*, his epochal analysis of the Paris Commune of 1871: "The great social measure of the Commune was its own working existence" (1986: 339). So too for the Montgomery Bus Boycott, the movement that launched over a decade of revolutionary activity on the part of African Americans and their allies, much of it based upon grass-roots political activism and organizing rather than hierarchical forms of organization. Concerning the period just before the book appeared, Dunayevskaya also singled out the new stage reached by the U.S. labor movement. On the one hand, workers were increasingly distancing themselves from the newly powerful labor bureaucracy, which undercut union democracy and had tied labor to the state ever since the Second World War. On the other hand, at a time of Fordist high wages in some major industries, the new stage of production represented by automation became a dividing line between rank-and-file workers and the political and economic establishment. Importantly, as Dunayevskaya saw it, that establishment included not only the corporations, the government, and the liberal social scientists who advised capital and the state from the universities, but also the trade union bureaucracy itself. For their part, rank-and-file workers feared and opposed automation, both because it was creating mass unemployment and because it was heightening the alienated labor in their workplaces. Workers, Dunayevskaya held, were demanding nothing less than the end of the division between mental and manual labor. She summed this up with a reference to the young Marx: "Thus, the workers, the American workers, made concrete and thereby extended Marx's most abstract theories of alienated labor and the quest for universality" (1988: 276).

These three movements and upheavals—the Hungarian workers' councils, the Montgomery Bus Boycott, and the stirrings of rank-and-file labor against both automation and the labor bureaucracy—could be considered to be examples of collective, emancipatory subjectivity, in contrast to the way most Marxist and radical analysis usually focuses on the objective, structural side of social relations. The two most prominent examples of these kinds of objectivism could be found in (1) mainstream sociology, which gave little space to social movements or to resistance, and (2) Russian Stalinist orthodoxy, which stressed the economic base over everything else, pointing to the rapid industrialization of the USSR as a success story despite the terrible human price it enacted on the population.

To Dunayevskaya, the emergence of these three new forms of collective subjectivity in the 1950s revealed a new stage of opposition to the rule of capital. This new opposition was emerging not from organized parties of the Left, nor was it inspired by leftist intellectuals; rather, it came from the grassroots participants' own life experience, from their own organization and practice. Implicitly referencing not only Stalinism, social democracy, and liberalism, but also orthodox Trotskyism, Dunayevskaya was incisive in outlining the actions and the thinking of the new, alternative types of social movements that had emerged in the 1950s: "In truth, while the intellectual void today is so great that the movement from theory to practice has nearly come to a standstill, *the movement from practice to theory, and with it, a new unity of manual and mental labor in the worker, are in evidence everywhere*" (1988: 276, emphasis in original). This "movement from practice to theory" was the underlying theme of *Marxism and Freedom*. It captured the spirit of an era that was to see mass social movements, many of them marked by spontaneity, in the 1960s and after. It was obviously a repudiation of the top-down politics of both social democracy and what is usually termed the Leninist "vanguard party." In this sense, it anticipated not only the 1960s, but also events like the wave of revolutions and protests that have impacted so many countries since the Arab revolutions of 2011, from the Indignados in Spain to Occupy Wall Street in the U.S., and from Gezi Park in Turkey to Nuit Debout in Paris, as well as more recent uprisings in Sudan, Hong Kong, Chile, Algeria, and Puerto Rico, among others.

However, while Dunayevskaya believed firmly in the creativity of spontaneous, sometimes leaderless movements, she did not, either in *Marxism and Freedom* or in her writings afterward, ever argue that the Marxist theoretician was therefore irrelevant, or a mere bystander. What was emerging, she held, was a movement from practice to theory, not a spontaneous movement that had no need for Marxist theory. What she did argue was that the greatest revolutionary thinkers had absorbed into their philosophical perspectives the creativity of the movements from below of their times, while at the same time offering those movements some theoretical and political direction.

And this had organizational implications as well. This commitment to theory differentiated Dunayevskaya from her erstwhile U.S. colleague, the great Afro-Caribbean Marxist, C. L. R. James. Despite many commonalities with Dunayevskaya, James hewed to a more spontaneist position. So did other contemporary groups that also exhibited commonalities with Dunayevskaya's position, like *Socialisme ou Barbarie* in France, and later, the Italian *operaïstes*. As Frédéric Monferrand notes in his well-researched new preface to the 2016 French edition: "Thus, where C. L. R. James called after 1955 for the abolition of 'the distinction between party and mass,' the author of *Marxism and Freedom never seems to have really renounced the need to form a revolutionary organization relatively autonomous from the social movements"* (2016: 22).

It is also important to note that Dunayevskaya's movement from practice was not a transhistorical concept. This movement from practice was linked to a specific form of capitalism, the stage of state capitalism that she saw as having arisen out of the crisis of monopoly capitalism, which had, in turn, been brought about by the Great Depression and the transformation of the Russian revolution into its opposite. This generated three basic forms of state capitalism: those found in Nazi Germany, Stalinist Russia, and Roosevelt's New Deal. In all three instances, a central stress was placed on a planned economy as the solution to the "anarchy" of the market, as well as on the promised of greater economic security and an increase in the standard of living of the masses. All three versions of state capitalism increased the power and size of the state apparatus, including its security and military side. All three strove for world domination in forms that fused the political and the economic. All three incorporated science, technology, and a new type of scientific and social scientific intellectual into their quest capital accumulation and military strength through centralized planning.

Such commonalities did not exclude differences, however. Stalinist Russia more thoroughly eliminated private economic ownership, whereas the New Deal and Nazism evidenced more hybrid structures that allowed many aspects of the older monopoly capitalism to continue. Nazi party officials exercised considerable power inside the corporate apparatus, as did Roosevelt's wartime government planning agencies, but each left plenty of room for private profit. Stalinist Russia and Nazi Germany each had a far more extensive network of secret police and concentration camp systems, but these were by no means absent in Roosevelt's U.S., which saw the rise of the FBI and the OSS (later renamed the CIA) to great prominence within the state and the mass internment of Japanese Americans in concentration camps.

Dunayevskaya also noted that certain technological developments that accompanied state capitalism led to an increased questioning of and even revolutionary opposition to the system by sectors beyond the industrial proletariat. Thus, World War II and its nuclear weapons endangered the very survival of the human race, something that called forth new social movements on the part of youth, such movements later also including opposition to environmental destruction as well. The genocidal anti-Semitism and racism of Nazism, and the war's weakening of the old colonial powers, helped to spark anti-racist, Black liberation, and anti-colonial liberation movements in its wake. The mass mobilization of women for the war effort and the targeting of civilian populations, including women, especially by the Nazis, helped to bring about a new women's movement. Other developments, such as the move by industrial capital into automation, led to still newer forms of resistance. As Dunayevskaya pointed out in a later recollection on the birth of her distinctive form of Marxist-Humanism, the postwar era was characterized by a "new stage of production, new stage of cognition, new kind of organization" (1980: 1).

With these kinds of questions in mind, let us look briefly at some of the key theoretical junctures in *Marxism and Freedom*.

Dunayevskaya's Hegel: The Power of Abstraction as Revolutionary

The opening chapter on Hegel and the French Revolution is heavily indebted to the anarchist thinker Daniel Guérin for its account of the *sans-culottes* as part of a creative movement from below that was to the left of the Jacobins and that conceptualized and fought for a popular democracy:

> *Democracy, thus, was not invented by philosophic theory nor by the bourgeois leadership. It was discovered by the masses in their method of action.* There is a double rhythm in destroying the old and creating the new which bears the unmistakable stamp of the *self-activity which is the truly working class way of knowing*. This, in fact, was the greatest of all the achievements of the great French Revolution—the workers' discovery of their own way of knowing. (1988: 30–31, emphasis in original)

Dunayevskaya's brief account of Hegel, which was in part the product of a dialog with Herbert Marcuse (Anderson and Rockwell 2012), is an impressive summation that illuminates the truly revolutionary aspects of his philosophy. Dunayevskaya stresses the impact of the French Revolution—and its aftermath—on the German creator of the modern form of dialectics.

She also notes how the young Hegel singled out the phenomenon of *alienated labor*, writing that "the consciousness of the factory worker is degraded to the lowest level of dullness" (cited in Dunayevskaya 1988:

33). An important limitation of Hegel's treatment of alienation is seen in the fact that the worker was here a passive, even ignorant object, rather than a creative subject. Thus, despite his insight into the conditions suffered by the workers, Hegel could not yet discern the yearning for a creative and non-exploitative form of labor that was to imbue the modern working-class movement in its most revolutionary moments. That would have to wait for Marx. In this sense, Hegel revealed a gap in his thinking concerning the industrial worker when he brought his dialectic down to the circumstances of his own society and became trapped in his own class prejudices.

But at a more abstract level, in his famous dialectic of lordship and bondage (master and slave) in the *Phenomenology of Spirit*, "labor remained integral to his philosophy" (Dunayevskaya 1988: 34). Here, writes Dunayevskaya, Hegel "shows that the bondsman 'gains a mind of his own' and stands higher than the lord who lives in luxury, does not labor, and therefore cannot really gain true freedom" (1988: 34). Over a decade later, in *Philosophy and Revolution*, Dunayevskaya made a similar argument, but at a more general level. Hegel's thought, she wrote, became more revolutionary the further it drifted from the socio-political reality of his own time: "Precisely where Hegel sounds most abstract, seems to close the shutters tight against the whole movement of history, there he lets the lifeblood of the dialectic, absolute negativity – pour in" (Dunayevskaya 1989: 32). This was what she was to call the "power of abstraction" in dialectics, a phrase Marx used in the preface to *Capital* (2002: 310).

What Hegel *did* discern in his published work—and here the influence of the French Revolution was obvious—was that the quest for freedom and emancipation marked the entire course of human history. Additionally, in seeing the social world not only as substance, but also as subject, Hegel paved the way for the Marxian concept of the collective revolutionary subject. Dunayevskaya singles this out as a central contribution of Hegel's. But it was in his notion of the Absolute Idea, above all, especially its aspect of the unity of theory and practice, that she found of the greatest significance.

In his later writings, where he takes up Absolute Spirit or Mind, Dunayevskaya concludes that Hegel stressed the dialectical relationship between the social and the individual:

For in Hegel's Absolute there is embedded, though in abstract form, the full development of the *social* individual, or what Hegel would call individuality 'purified of all that interferes with its universalism, i.e., freedom itself.' Here are the objective and subjective means whereby a new society is going to be born. That new society, struggling to be born, is the concern of our age. (1988: 39)

For Dunayevskaya, the key here was not so much the rather banal notion that individuals must become social to fully realize themselves as individuals. Her real point centered on something slightly different, how the quest for individual self-development and freedom could link up with broader epochal movements for human emancipation in such a way that both were deepened, in a truly dialectical relationship. Thus, when Rosa Parks sat down on that bus in Montgomery, Alabama and defied the system of racial segregation, her quest for individual emancipation managed to link up with the universal in such a way that it helped touch off a whole era of revolutionary radicalism.

Importantly, Dunayevskaya noted as well that Marx drew his concept of the negation of the negation from Hegel, whom he extolled in 1844 for having uncovered "the dialectic of negativity as the moving and creative principle" (cited in Dunayevskaya 1988: 34). At the same time, she critiques the retrogression into statism in the later Hegel, while also arguing for the enduring influence of the German idealist on Marx. Finally, the discussion of Hegel turns toward the Stalinist rejection of Hegel, especially his concept of negativity.

Marx as a Revolutionary Humanist Who Concretized the Dialectics of Race, Class, and the State

With Marx, Dunayevskaya stresses the fundamental continuity of the young Marx of 1844 with *Capital*, not only in Vol. I, but also in Vols. 2 and 3. I know of no other serious analyst of Marx who swam so easily in both the humanist/dialectical aspect—alienation, fetishism, dialectic, etc., and in concepts like the tendential decline in the rate of profit as the foundation of Marx's theory of economic crises and depressions.

In its original 1958 edition, *Marxism and Freedom* contained as an appendix the first published English translations of two of the most important of Marx's *1844 Essays*, "Private Property and Communism" and "Critique of the Hegelian Dialectic." The theme of Marx's revolutionary humanism continues into one of the four chapters devoted to his *magnum opus*, "The Humanism and Dialectic of *Capital*, Vol. I." In the *1844 Essays*, Marx is seen as having put forth his own version of the dialectic, as having not only "stood [Hegel] on his feet," but also as having separated himself from "vulgar communism" (Dunayevskaya 1988: 85), which Dunayevskaya traces back to some of the communist sects of Marx's own time, albeit with a clear contemporary target, the vulgate of Soviet Marxist-Leninism. Here she connects philosophy and economics in the sense that vulgar communism sought to change property relations but not production relations, not the actual daily life of the worker: Marx was strongly "opposed to anyone who thinks that the ills of capitalism can be overcome by changes in the sphere of distribution" (59). As for the Russian Stalinist ideologists, they focused on the merits of state property and therefore devoted "incredible time and energy and vigilance to imprison Marx within the bounds of the private property vs. State property concept" (Dunayevskaya 1988: 63). This was also an implicit critique of classical Trotskyism, with its focus on nationalized property as the dividing line between capitalism and a workers' state, albeit bureaucratically deformed.

Throughout, Marx is presented as a revolutionary activist as well as a thinker, even during his supposedly cloistered British Museum years when he immersed himself in the study of political economy. Not only was he an activist as well as a thinker, but world events and his engagement with them decisively shaped his greatest theoretical work, *Capital*. Here the kinds of themes alluded to at the beginning of this essay—the new forms of emancipatory struggle found during the 1950s in the Hungarian revolutionaries, Alabama Black activists, and the rank-and-file workers—emerge as central to the book's underlying theoretical premises.

Thus, the decisive impact of the U.S. Civil War on *Capital* I is elaborated not just as political background, but as having had core theoretical importance. Dunayevskaya's chapter covering these issues begins with Marx's applauding from afar the incipient slave insurrection he was hoping for in the wake of John Brown's attack on Harper's Ferry. Marx not only differed with Engels on the potentially revolutionary character of the Civil War, but he also strongly attacked Lincoln's non-revolutionary reluctance to issue an emancipation proclamation. In addition, Dunayevskaya stresses Marx's strong support in his letters and journalism for the British workers who sided with the North even as the

British establishment took the opposite position. In a remarkable display of proletarian internationalism, those workers maintained their support even when told that a British intervention on the side of the South might quickly end the war and the cotton blockade that had led to mass unemployment in the manufacturing districts. She also notes how language about race, class, and the fight for the eight-hour day found its way into Marx's text, as in this often-overlooked passage from *Capital*:

> In the United States of America, every independent movement of the workers was paralyzed as long as slavery disfigured a part of the Republic. Labor cannot emancipate itself in the white skin where in the Black it is branded. But out of the death of slavery a new life again arose. The first fruit of the Civil War was the eight hours agitation, that ran with the seven-leagued boots of the locomotive from the Atlantic to the Pacific, from New York to California. (cited in Dunayevskaya 1988: 84)

Thus, the dialectics of race and class was no mere sideshow, but a crucial aspect of the struggle for the emancipation of labor.

But there were other theoretical stakes here as well. Dunayevskaya also makes the argument that the very structure of *Capital* changed as a result of Marx's engagement with the Civil War in the U.S. Based upon a study of the early drafts of *Capital*, she concludes that it was only after he became engaged with the Civil War that Marx added an entire chapter on "The Working Day," apparently completed as late as 1866, just after the war's end. This chapter is one of the book's most crucial, not because it exposes the oppression resulting from a brutally long working day, which many had done before, but because it shows how the dramatic lengthening of the working day constituted the breaking point that produced the modern labor movement. This chapter on the working day contains the most detailed treatment of working-class resistance to capital of the entire book, as it chronicles the struggle for a shorter working day, first in Britain, and then in France and the U.S., where it became intertwined with the dialectics of race and class.

Importantly, Marx is not only describing here but also prescribing. What he is suggesting in this chapter on the working day is that, short of actual proletarian revolution, the fight for a reduced working day challenges capital in a fundamental way, more, for example, than that for higher wages. In dialectical terms, this struggle constituted a particularization, at a specific historical juncture, of the universal aspiration on the part of the working class for a total change, for a communist society of free and associated labor. The revolutionary importance of this fight for a shorter working day was something that Marx advocated in the First International, helping to place it on the agenda of the working class across Western Europe and North America. Turning to our own times, it could be noted that in recent decades the French working classes have been carrying out the fight for a shorter working day, but in isolation from other highly developed economies like Britain or the U.S., where the issue has lain dormant.

Dunayevskaya conceptualizes a similar process concerning the relationship of the Paris Commune to *Capital*. Following the argument of Marx's *Civil War in France*, she outlines what he saw as the Commune's most salient revolutionary features: its grassroots democratic character, its destruction of a modern bureaucratic state, and its development of worker self-rule in some of the factories. Dunayevskaya added a point not stated explicitly by Marx concerning the leading role of female workers, milkmaids, in touching off the insurrection early in the morning of March 18, 1871: "As in every real people's revolution, new strata of the population were awakened" (1988: 95).

Next, Dunayevskaya argues that several important formulations in *Capital* were added only after the Commune. She notes that the last version of *Capital* I that Marx personally vetted before it was published was the French edition, issued in serial form from 1872–1875. Although it was translated by Joseph Roy, Marx's correspondence shows that he went over every page and reworked many parts of the text. Few, except specialist scholars, are aware that the 1867 version of *Capital* was quite different from the text we know today (Anderson 2010). Most importantly, the first chapter did not exist in 1867 in anything like its present form. Only after the events of the Paris Commune did Marx reorganize the book, creating for the first time a separate first chapter ending with a discussion of commodity fetishism. Some of the material on fetishism was already there in 1867, but additional material was incorporated after Commune, which, as Dunayevskaya points out, had illustrated in concrete form what Marx for years had been referring to as free and associated labor. Dunayevskaya also argues that after 1867, Marx moves his focus in the discussion of commodity fetishism from "the fantastic form of appearance," wherein human relations took the form of relations between things, to "the *necessity* of that form of appearance," given that the reification of human relations was "in *truth*," the form taken under capitalism of "what relations between people *are* at the point of production" (1988: 100).

This is not only an example of revolutionary events influencing and deepening Marx's theorization of capitalism, but it also shows Marx carrying out some of his most original theoretical labor under the impact of the Commune. In carrying out this reworking of *Capital*, he developed further a book that aimed not only to reflect but also to shape the consciousness of the working class, in order for it to carry out the struggle for its self-emancipation more effectively. To be sure, it was not Marx's fault that post-Marx Marxists, beginning with Engels, virtually ignored the crucial section on commodity fetishism until the 1920s.

LENIN AS A DIALECTICAL THINKER WHO SAW ANTI-COLONIAL MOVEMENTS AS A NEW FORM OF SUBJECTIVITY IN THE ERA OF IMPERIALISM

Dunayevskaya's discussion of Lenin as a thinker and as revolutionary takes a similar form. The early Lenin's notion of the vanguard party as elaborated in 1902 in *What Is to Be Done?* is seen as undergoing modifications under the impact of the creativity and self-organization displayed by the Russian working class in 1905 and 1917. Moreover, in anticipation of many recent discussions by Lars Lih (Lenin 2006) and others, that early form of vanguardism is shown to have been not that different from the prevailing concept of organization in the Second International. However, in contrast to Lih, Dunayevskaya does not view this as something positive in Lenin. As she sees it, Lenin in 1902 "merely brought to its logical conclusion Karl Kautsky's formulation" to the effect that workers on their own could achieve trade union but not socialist consciousness. The latter was seen by Lenin, erroneously in Dunayevskaya's eyes, as something that could only be brought to the workers by radical intellectuals (Dunayevskaya 1988: 179).

The First World War served to undermine Lenin's support for Kautsky and the other chief theoreticians of the Second International, leading him to embark upon the formulation of Marxist perspectives aimed at a general and global audience rather than only Russian one. Was this a result of a steadfast adherence to earlier revolutionary principles or a new departure for Lenin? Dunayevskaya holds more to the second possibility, underlining Lenin's in-depth study of Hegel and dialectics, imperialism, and the state and revolution, issues he had largely avoided up until this point. One major departure, still controversial even today, is Dunayevskaya's elaboration of a philosophical break in Lenin's thought. This break, she contended, was a result of his 1914–1915 notebooks on Hegel's *Science of Logic*, written after the Second (or Socialist) International collapsed in the wake of World War I, when its main constituent parties violated their principles by supporting their respective governments in what Lenin saw as an imperialist war. These Notebooks implicitly repudiated his crudely materialist and reductionist 1908 treatise in Marxist philosophy, *Materialism and Empirio-Criticism*. Singling out revolutionary Hegelian concepts like self-movement and contradiction, Lenin also embraces aspects of Hegel's philosophical idealism as superior to crude materialism, writing: "Intelligent idealism is nearer to intelligent materialism than is stupid materialism" (cited in Dunayevskaya 1988: 207). Moreover, in an implicit self-critique, Lenin holds that one cannot understand *Capital* without having studied Hegel's *Logic*, and that "Consequently, none of the Marxists for the past half-century have understood Marx!" (cited in Dunayevskaya 1988: 171). While Henri Lefebvre translated and introduced Lenin's notebooks on Hegel to the French public over two decades before they appeared in English in *Marxism and Freedom*, he did not, until 1959, acknowledge a break in Lenin's philosophical thought after 1914. In contrast, Dunayevskaya had developed her concept of such a break in a dialog with C. L. R. James and Grace Lee Boggs in the 1940s.[1]

As Dunayevskaya saw it, Lenin theorized the development of the capitalist economy into its monopoly stage and the concomitant emergence of imperialism soon after his study of Hegel, in part on the basis of the new dialectical insights he gained from his study of the German philosopher. At this point, Lenin became dissatisfied with what he regarded as Rudolf Hilferding's non-dialectical theorization of monopoly capitalism. First, this was because Hilferding underplayed how a radical transformation took place within competitive capitalism, seeing the change toward monopoly as a more or less incremental, evolutionary development. Dunayevskaya writes that for Lenin, monopoly capital was instead the result of a "development through contradiction, through *transformation into opposite*" (1988: 208, emphasis in original).

Second, Lenin taxed Hilferding and even some of his Bolshevik comrades, such as Nikolai Bukharin, for not addressing changes brought about by imperialism at the subjective level, that is, of the experience and struggles of the working people in both the imperialist lands and the colonies. One aspect of this was that a deep internal contradiction appeared inside the working class of the imperialist metropoles, with a small portion of the workers transforming into an aristocracy of labor that benefitted from and supported imperialist exploitation. As Lenin saw it, that stratum also formed the core of those elements of the working class that supported the First World War. Dunayevskaya connected the concept of a labor aristocracy to racial segmentation within the U.S. working class, wherein whiter, native-born, and more skilled workers, along with trade union bureaucrats, formed such a labor aristocracy with particularly American characteristics.

Another aspect of Lenin's dialectical theory of imperialism was that in the colonies, anti-imperialism was leading to the creation of modern, progressive nationalist movements. Here Lenin singled out the Easter Uprising in Ireland of 1916, in the middle of World War I, and up to that point the most serious blow against imperialism and the war anywhere in the world. Ireland was for Lenin the harbinger of new forms of consciousness and struggle that later came to be called "national liberation movements." In supporting the Irish uprising, and in polemicizing with hostile class-reductionist perspectives from Karl Radek and more ambivalent ones from Leon Trotsky, Lenin underlined the dialectical underpinnings of his position, referring to the Irish events as part of the "dialectics of history," wherein colonized nations fighting for their national emancipation can take the lead, moving ahead of the international working class in the struggle against imperialism, and ultimately, capitalism itself (Dunayevskaya 1988: 174).

For Dunayevskaya, Lenin's originality lay not only in grasping new subjective developments like the emergence of the labor aristocracy and of the national liberation movements but also in conceptualizing the relationship of those forces to the overall working-class movement. Additionally, Lenin incorporated the peasantry into his analysis, especially in his discussions of major countries in the Global South like colonial India and semi-colonial China.

Whatever his flaws as a Marxist thinker and revolutionary leader, especially on the one-party state, flaws that have been pointed out by other revolutionary thinkers ever since Rosa Luxemburg, Lenin's two major insights—on Hegel and dialectics, and on imperialism and national liberation—remain fruitful theoretical resources for us today. For

Dunayevskaya, Lenin's Hegelian Marxism was more salient than that of Lukács or Marcuse because he made political and economic conclusions on the basis of his dialectical investigations. He was therefore able to elaborate a fully dialectical theory of the emergence of imperialism and of its internal contradictions, seen most prominently in the national liberation movements and self-determination struggles to which it gave impetus across the colonial and semi-colonial world. Lenin's great sensitivity as well to national and ethnic oppression inside large countries like Russia was an important and related insight that he was to develop in terms of groups like African Americans in the years following the Hegel notebooks and his book on imperialism.

Dunayevskaya took from Hegel, Marx, and Lenin two conceptual threads: on the one hand, a certain type of dialectics of revolution, and, on the other hand, a sensitivity to new social forces and movements with revolutionary potential. These two threads of analysis enabled her to conceptualize a new form of capitalism—automated state capitalism—in which workers faced the state, capital, and their own union bureaucracy, and where new social movements like the Black movement in the U.S. were emerging. At the same time, events like Hungary 1956 showed not only the bankruptcy of the Stalinist regimes, but also that the working people and youth under those regimes shared similar aspirations with those in radical social movements across the world.

MAO ZEDONG: AN ALIENATED FORM OF SUBJECTIVITY

When it came off the press in 1958, *Marxism and Freedom* caught something of the spirit of the times, developing an audience far beyond what remained of the socialist and Marxist left, much reduced as it was after nearly a decade of McCarthyism. Its impact was amplified by the fact that the book made available for the first time in English two of Marx's essays from the *1844 Manuscripts*. It was published on the eve of, and caught much of the spirit of, the flowering in the 1960s of grassroots social movements for civil rights and Black liberation, for peace and against imperialism, for women's liberation, and for environmental protection. Dunayevskaya's Marxist-Humanism had weathered the McCarthyite 1950s, not only because it was always liberationist and opposed to all forms of state capitalism and totalitarianism, and thus could not easily be linked to Stalinism, but also because it aligned with the *zeitgeist* in skewering elitist, top-down forms of radical and revolutionary

326 K. B. ANDERSON

organization, in favor of extolling creativity from below. As we have seen, Dunayevskaya's concept of a movement from practice that was itself a form of theory credited ordinary working people and Black grassroots activists not only with creativity of action, but also with a certain creativity of thought, especially with respect to critiquing and resisting the new type of alienated labor that arose with automated capitalism, a mutation still in progress over six decades later.

On the issue of revolutionary subjectivity, Dunayevskaya liked to quote Lenin's Hegel Notebooks at the point where he wrote that "the world does not satisfy man and man decides to change it by his activity" (Lenin 1961: 212–213). Lenin wrote those lines in response to Hegel's evocation of the power of human subjectivity: "the subject possesses... a certainty of its own actuality and the non-actuality of the world" (Hegel 1969: 818).

But what if the power of the subject took an alienated, non-emancipatory form, as in the Maoist detour from humanism and the dialectics of revolution?

For just as *Marxism and Freedom* was coming off the press in 1958, Mao Zedong was beginning to put forth China as an independent pole of Marxist revolution, and one which was soon to enter into competition with the reigning form of Stalinist orthodoxy emanating from Nikita Khrushchev's Soviet Union. As is well known, Khrushchev, like his mentor Stalin, stressed objective economic growth and raising the standard of living through economic planning by a centralized, still largely totalitarian state apparatus. He also sought a degree of great power equilibrium with the U.S., as exemplified by his slogan of peaceful coexistence. For his part, Mao in the 1950s and 1960s stressed confrontation, disruption, and revolutionary will, in what amounted to an alienated, state-capitalist form of subjectivity. He zigzagged from the liberalizing Hundred Flowers Campaign of 1957 to the repression of the students and intellectuals who had taken up his invitation to speak out, and from the massive famine created by his 1958 Great Leap Forward in the countryside to his equally destructive Cultural Revolution of 1966. In so doing, Mao, again and again, experimented with forms of what he considered to be "revolutionary will" in order to make China leap ahead of other developing countries. This was a truly alienated form of subjectivity.[2]

For a time, the spirit of Maoist resistance and subjectivity attracted many young people, this writer included, as could be seen in groups like Students for a Democratic Society or the Black Panther Party in the U.S., or the Maoist-influenced intellectuals, especially numerous in France, like Louis Althusser, Michel Foucault, Jean-Paul Sartre, and Simone de Beauvoir.[3]

The turn toward Maoism did help to make anti-colonialism and anti-racism more central to the concerns of Western intellectuals. It also helped to undermine the deterministic objectivism of Russian Stalinism, which had little room for the human subject, collective or individual. But Maoism's form of subjectivism also harmed the left in decisive ways, as Barbara Epstein (2014) has noted:

> Maoism was... taken to mean that it was incumbent upon Maoists to orga-nize revolutions, which did not require populations already oriented in that direction, but could be brought about, more or less regardless of circumstances, by sufficiently disciplined, dedicated and skilled groups of revolutionaries.... Anarchism and Maoism shared an orientation toward cultural politics, the view that transforming people's ideas, and the ideas governing society as a whole, was a major, if not the major, component of revolutionary politics.... The rhetoric of violence and the threat of actual violence drove many, especially women, out of the movement, and the expectation of imminent revolution led to widespread disappointment.

Outside Western Europe and North America, Mao strongly influenced movements and parties with substantially larger mass followings—especially in India, Indonesia, and Peru—almost always with negative effects on the possibilities for radical change.[4] The espousal of voluntarist Maoist slogans like "Dare to struggle, dare to win" was not merely youthful enthusiasm during the 1960s, but something that was deeply rooted in the theory and practice of Maoism. As a result, its wide influence played no small part in the eventual defeat of some of the most radical parts of the movements of the 1960s.

An added dimension of this defeat was a certain disillusionment on the left with China by the early 1970s for betraying the anti-imperialist cause it had seemed to champion. By now, Mao's opposition to "revisionist" Russia resulted in a 1972 rapprochement with Nixon's America at the height of the U.S. bombing of Vietnam. A few years later, in 1975–1976, China tacitly supported South Africa, Zaire (as Congo was then known), and the U.S. against the African liberation fighters of Angola, who beat back the apartheid South African forces with the aid of Cuban troops sent there with Russian support.[5]

While to be sure subjectivist, Maoism was also imbued with a deep anti-humanism, as it dismissed all humanism as at best hypocritical humanitarianism on the part of the dominant classes and nations. At a philosophical level, this can be seen in the crude dismissal of the young Marx by Mao's chief philosopher for a time, Zhou Yang, writing here in 1963 at the height of the Sino-Soviet rift:

> In the early stages of the development of their thought, Marx and Engels were, indeed, somewhat influenced by Humanist ideas... But, when they formulated the materialist concept of history and discovered the class struggle as the motive force of social development, they got rid of this bourgeois influence. (cited in Dunayevskaya 1989: 182)

What is new here theoretically is the vehement rejection of humanism, comparable to that of Althusser and published during the same period as his anti-humanist screed, *For Marx*. At a more general level, the spirit of extreme self-sacrifice associated with Maoist voluntarism constituted a polar opposite to life-affirming notions of Marx as revolutionary humanist.

To be sure, the 1949 Maoist revolution in China was one of history's great national revolutions, one that finally cast out a vicious form of Western imperialism that had dominated the country since the First Opium War of 1839–1842, defeating the newer Japanese imperialism in the process. Domestically, the 1949 revolution undermined much of the old patriarchal domination of women and destroyed the old landlord classes. But Maoism also established, from the first, a totalitarian apparatus that ruled over the population from above, all the while stifling any real political debate or popular initiative. At the same time, the regime's numerous mass campaigns, also orchestrated from the top, gave the regime the aura, at least at the international level, of revolutionary participation. This was most notable during the Cultural Revolution of the 1960s, which drew in many who should have known better. Besides naïve liberals and Stalinists, these included some anarchists and independent socialists, among the latter Dunayevskaya's erstwhile colleague from the 1940s, Grace Lee Boggs, and, to an extent, C. L. R. James as well, her other important theoretical interlocutor from that time.

Throughout the 1960s and 1970s, when enthusiasm for Maoism reached its zenith, Dunayevskaya took a principled stand that cost her supporters among some of the very parts of the revolutionary youth that she was trying to win over. Despite this, as *Marxism and Freedom* was successively reprinted during this period, she added appendixes on Mao's

China in 1964 and 1971, also making a critique of his thought central to her 1973 book, *Philosophy and Revolution*.

In *Philosophy and Revolution*, Dunayevskaya also expanded the horizons of *Marxism and Freedom* with a substantial discussion of African liberation movements and the imperialist world economy they faced. In the early 1960s, she visited West Africa and from then on tended to see Africa's more democratic and humanist form of anti-imperialism as something of a counterweight to Maoism and other varieties of 1960s Third Worldism. As part of this effort, she took up Frantz Fanon as a revolutionary humanist thinker.

While Dunayevskaya's critique of Mao included economic and political aspects, its core was philosophical, not least because, as she wrote, Mao's independent version of Stalinism itself exhibited a philosophical bent. As she maintained in *Philosophy and Revolution*, "It is no accident that, where Stalin embarked on the transformation of the Marxist philosophy of liberation into its opposite on the economic plane, Mao, before and after he gained state power, concentrated mainly on the philosophical sphere, very nearly pre-empting the category 'Contradiction'" (1989: 161).

Two Kinds of Subjectivity: Maoist and Revolutionary Humanist

For her first substantial critique of Mao, in the 1964 appendix to *Marxism and Freedom*, Dunayevskaya developed a concept of "two kinds of subjectivity" (1988: 326). The first form of subjectivity, exemplified by Mao, "has no regard for objective conditions" and believes that it can carry out something like the Great Leap Forward on the backs of the masses (Dunayevskaya 1988: 327). Moreover, if revolt or dissension appears, this form of subjectivity can deal with that as well, by remolding minds through forced re-education programs.[6] Here we are confronted with voluntarist leaps in the direction of radical change coupled with Mao's notion of reconciliation that, as Dunayevskaya later argued, "was hardly distinguishable from [that of] a Confucian" and the accompanying notions of a harmonious society (1989: 164).[7]

While at one level Maoism's voluntarist and harmonizing/remolding attitudes are opposed to each other, what unites them is a belief that if states of mind can be changed, material transformation is sure to follow. To work this out in Marxist terms, Mao advocated the outright inversion of superstructure and base in light of the situation of revolutionary

China, intoning: "When the superstructure of politics, culture, and so on hinders the development of the economic base, political and cultural reforms become the principal and decisive factors" (cited in Dunayevskaya 1989: 163).[8] While Dunayevskaya retorted that Mao's thought was at this juncture running "counter... to the revolutionary materialism of Marx" (1989: 163), this kind of thinking lay at the center of the Cultural Revolution and of Maoist thought reform more generally.

Dunayevskaya regarded this type of subjectivism as a form of outright retrogression in a period that, unlike that of the ancient moral idealists, was already familiar with modern political economy and with Marx's critique of it as he developed a materialist interpretation of history and society.

In casting Maoist subjectivity as retrogressionist, Dunayevskaya drew on Hegel's tripartite categorization of three attitudes toward objectivity: simple faith, early modern European rationalism, and a third attitude—characterized as retrogressive by Hegel—that arose after the French revolution and amalgamated elements of Romanticism with an intuitionist philosophy of immediacy. This third attitude was often linked to rejections of reason in favor of feeling and intuition, and to the primacy of the will as against objective reality. (Hegel also implied a fourth attitude, modern dialectics, which critically appropriated aspects of the three previous attitudes, while also transcending [*Aufheben*] them.)

Dunayevskaya connected Hegel's third attitude to Mao's thought, wherein "the modern version of the intuitionist and voluntarist alternative to dialectics has indeed led down a retrogressionist path of primitive accumulation of capital" (1989: 162). The reference to primitive accumulation referred to the notion, central to the state-capitalist theory she and C. L. R. James originated in the early 1940s, that the Stalinist forced industrialization drives are animated by a form of accumulation strikingly similar to early capitalism's expropriation of the English peasantry from their smallholder land allotments and its creation of the modern slave plantation, all at a terrible human cost. It is likely that Dunayevskaya was also referencing, at a more specific level, the counter-productive gyrations of Mao's Great Leap Forward, where peasants were pushed into collective living spaces termed "People's Communes." There, the Chinese peasants were also enjoined to produce steel in backyard furnaces without proper technology or training, with predictably adverse results. The disruption of agriculture led in turn to a famine that killed over 20 million people.

As against Maoist subjectivism, Dunayevskaya's "second" form of subjectivity centers on the kinds of issues discussed in the beginning section of this chapter on revolutionary humanist subjectivity, where I considered the Hungarian revolution, the Montgomery Bus Boycott, and the wildcat strikes of rank-and-file labor, as well as the dialectical notions of subjectivity that emerged from her consideration of Hegel and Marx. This second form of subjectivity, she writes, "is the subjectivity that has absorbed objectivity, that is, through its struggle for freedom it gets to know and cope with the objectively real" (Dunayevskaya 1988: 327). Here she again offers the Hungarian revolutionaries of 1956 and the Paris Communards as examples. In this type of subjectivity, the collective revolutionary subject expresses something that is objective—that the situation has changed and that the old ways cannot go on any longer. Here the revolutionary subject is not voluntarist, for it is in tune with its epoch and its material situation, while at the same time reaching beyond both toward a positive future.

This subjectivity is of the same type that Dunayevskaya finds evidenced at a theoretical level in the revolutionary thought of Marx, who wrote that he had no abstract ideals to realize but was instead responding to and theorizing the real movement of self-emancipation of labor. Thus, it is important to note that a subjectivity that has absorbed objectivity is also found in the best philosophical and revolutionary thinkers, above all Marx. These thinkers theorized with acuity the social conditions and the aspirations of actually existing social forces like the working class.

Of course, it is not always easy, in the heat of the moment, to discern which kind of subjectivity is emerging—whether that of a subjectivism disconnected to the collective human subject and to its epoch, or one that has made those connections, and thus a subjectivity that has absorbed objectivity. But Dunayevskaya enjoins us to make such an effort as part of the concretization of Marxism in one's era, as she did in her analysis in real time of the Hungarian revolution and the Montgomery Bus Boycott. These revolutionary dialectical analyses have, I would argue, stood the test of time.

While diametrically opposed to one another, the voluntarist subjectivity of Maoism and the Marxist-Humanist notion of a subjectivity rooted in objectivity do, nevertheless, share something in common. Neither are deterministic in the crudely materialist sense of the "scientific" Marxism that dominated socialist thought during the Second International of the early twentieth century and was found in Russian Stalinist ideology.

However, Maoism is an aberrant form of the attempt to go beyond this kind of determinism—one that ends badly. And as we have seen in recent years, the excesses of the 1960s, in which Maoism played no small part, have pushed some youth and intellectuals who are rediscovering socialist thought back toward the mechanical materialism of the Second International.

Dunayevskaya's dialectical critique of Maoism is important today, not least because it helps us to sharpen our understanding of the Marxist-Humanist concept of the subject. Moreover, aspects of Maoist voluntarism continue to exist all around us. This can be seen in voluntarist political forms like insurrectionist anarchism or the black bloc. It can also be seen in academicized forms of cultural Marxism devoid of any connection to the material reality faced by working people or oppressed minorities, even when these radical intellectuals take a militant, confrontational stance toward liberalism and the capitalist order.

While *Marxism and Freedom* was published six decades ago, it and related writings of Dunayevskaya from the period still speak to us today, at a time when grassroots social movements for radical change have covered the globe in ways not seen since the 1960s. While this is so, it is also true that, with the growth of rightwing populism, the economic and political contradictions of capitalism are more glaring—and ominous—than at any time since the 1930s. This unprecedented situation compels Marxists of the twenty-first century to rethink our old categories, especially those inherited from either social democracy or Stalinism, whether in its Russian or Chinese varieties. In carrying out for today the needed creative engagement with Marx and Marxism, one that is rooted in both dialectics and material reality, the Marxist-Humanism of Raya Dunayevskaya is indispensable.

[Parts of this chapter first appeared in my article, "Marxism and Freedom After Sixty Years, for Yesterday and Today," *New Politics* XVII:1 (Summer 2018), pp. 45–52.]

NOTES

1. I discuss Lefebvre, Althusser, James, Dunayevskaya, Lukács, and other commentators on Lenin's relation to Hegel in Anderson (1995).
2. Dunayevskaya also criticized at length Sartrean subjectivity, which she saw as too individualized and as ultimately nihilistic, in her *Philosophy and*

Revolution (1989). And she obviously repudiated the subjectivism of mainstream economic reason, with its assumption of an acquisitive individual exercising rational choice.

3. On French Maoist intellectuals, see Richard Wolin (2010).
4. Lovell (2019) has carried out the most comprehensive survey to date of Maoism as an international phenomenon.
5. As someone who felt that disillusionment personally, I would like to mention that this confrontation was the subject of my first full-length published article, written—with considerable advice and help from Dunayevskaya—under the pseudonym Kevin A. Barry (1976).
6. In the 1950s, the U.S. government and media sensationalized Maoist re-education as "brainwashing" when it was applied U.S. soldiers captured in the Korean War, and the term came into common usage as a result.
7. Interestingly, Chinas current ruler, Xi Jinping, the only one since Mao to harbor philosophical ambitions, has openly evoked the Confucian ideal of a harmonious society. Of course, this means that Chinese society is to be harmonious in the sense that the powerless and exploited, as well as the intellectuals, need to renounce their negativity in relation to the apparatus. However, Xi has given up any pretense of a revolutionary stance, replacing Mao's "uninterrupted revolution" with the evocation of China's 3000 years of "uninterrupted civilization that still continues today," something he has declared to be "unique" in the world (Lemaître and Pedroletti 2019).
8. While space does not permit a discussion here, the Maoist notion of base and superstructure changing places has deeply impacted the Western intellectual left, most notably Louis Althusser's structuralist concept of the ideological state apparatus and continuing in poststructuralism. For recent critiques from Marxist humanist standpoints, see Alderson and Spencer (2017).

REFERENCES

Alderson, David and Robert Spencer. 2017. *For Humanism: Explorations in Theory and Politics.* London: Pluto Press.

Althusser, Louis. [1965] 1969. *For Marx,* trans. Ben Brewster. New York: Pantheon.

Anderson, Kevin B. 1995. *Lenin, Hegel, and Western Marxism: A Critical Study.* Urbana: University of Illinois Press.

———. 2010. *Marx at the Margins: On Nationalism, Ethnicity, and Non-Western Societies.* Chicago: University of Chicago Press.

——— and Russell Rockwell, eds. 2012. *The Dunayevskaya-Marcuse-Fromm Correspondence, 1954–1978: Dialogues on Hegel, Marx, and Critical Theory.* Lanham MD: Lexington Books.

Barry, Kevin A. [Kevin B. Anderson]. 1976. "U.S. Imperialism Seeks New Ways to Stifle True Angolan Revolution." *News & Letters* 21:4 (May).

Dunayevskaya, Raya. 1980. *25 Years of Marxist-Humanism in the U.S.* Detroit: News & Letters.

———. [1973] 1989. *Philosophy and Revolution: From Hegel to Sartre and From Marx to Mao.* With a preface by Louis Dupré. New York: Columbia University Press.

———. 1988. *Marxism and Freedom: From 1776 Until Today.* New York: Columbia University Press. First published in 1958.

———. 2002. "The Power of Abstraction," pp. 311–314 in *The Power of Negativity: Selected Writings on the Dialectic in Hegel and Marx*, ed. by Peter Hudis and Kevin B. Anderson, Lanham, MD: Lexington Books.

Epstein, Barbara. 2014. "On the Disappearance of Socialist Humanism." *International Marxist-Humanist* (Feb. 24).

Hegel, G.W.F. 1969. *Science of Logic*, trans. A.V. Miller. New Jersey: Humanities Press.

Lemaître, Frédéric and Brice Pedroletti. 2019. "Xi Jinping, le nouveau timonier." *Le Monde* (July 30).

Lenin, V.I. 1961. "Conspectus of Hegel's Book *The Science of Logic*," pp. 85–238 in *Collected Works*, Vol. 38. Moscow: Progress Publishers.

———. 2006. *Lenin Rediscovered: What Is to Be Done? In Context*, edited, translated, and annotated by Lars Lih. Leiden: Brill.

Lovell, Julia. 2019. *Maoism: A Global History.* New York: Knopf.

Marx, Karl. 1986. "The Civil War in France," pp. 309–355 in Marx and Engels, *Collected Works*, Vol. 22. New York: International Publishers.

Monferrand, Frédéric. 2016. "Un Marxisme de la liberation: Préface à l'édition française," pp. 9–23 in Raya Dunayevskaya, *Marxisme et liberté*. Paris: Éditions Syllepse.

Wolin, Richard. 2010. *The Wind from the East: French Intellectuals, the Cultural Revolution, and the Legacy of the 1960s.* Princeton: Princeton University Press.

INDEX

© The Editor(s) (if applicable) and The Author(s), under exclusive
license to Springer Nature Switzerland AG 2021
K. B. Anderson et al. (eds.), *Raya Dunayevskaya's Intersectional
Marxism*, Marx, Engels, and Marxisms,
https://doi.org/10.1007/978-3-030-53717-3

Mao Zedong, 11, 151, 326, 328–330, 333. *See also* "Great Leap Forward"; Cultural Revolution

"revolutionary will", 17, 326

subjectivism, 327, 331

voluntarism, 11, 17, 327–332

Marcuse, Herbert, 8, 9, 13, 17, 26, 29, 30, 41, 49, 66, 67, 84, 170, 182, 186, 194–196, 198, 203, 213, 214, 216, 217, 219, 224, 233, 237, 239, 251, 272, 277, 306, 307, 316, 325

Marcuse, Herbert (works)

One-Dimensional Man, 9, 194

Reason and Revolution, 29, 49, 170, 182, 277

Marxism, 4, 5, 7, 8, 10–13, 15–18, 24, 25, 34, 40, 49, 52, 53, 55, 65–68, 70, 72, 73, 77–79, 81, 84–86, 91, 93, 96, 97, 99–101, 110, 135–137, 174, 185–189, 191–199, 201–204, 210, 213, 216–218, 223, 234, 235, 237, 239, 246, 247, 250, 261–268, 271, 272, 278, 285, 286, 294, 296, 300, 301, 304–306, 311, 325, 331, 332. *See also* Post-Marx Marxism

American roots, of, 213, 216, 218, 272

Marxist-Humanism, 4–7, 10, 12, 13, 16, 17, 25, 26, 35, 39, 40, 45, 46, 51–53, 59, 60, 76, 82, 92, 121, 122, 129, 137, 141, 163, 164, 211, 214, 238, 242, 243, 246–252, 255, 286, 301, 316, 325, 331–333

Marx, Karl.

"absolute general law" of capitalist accumulation, 32, 72

accumulation of capital, on, 74, 211, 212, 218, 222, 223, 226–228

alienated labor, on, 10, 13, 30, 70, 72, 95, 146, 170, 182, 190, 220, 279, 290, 293, 313, 326

automation, on, 15, 72, 205, 215, 219, 262, 266, 269, 286, 298

Black dimension, and, 4, 8, 17, 95, 122, 137, 156

capitalist crisis and collapse, theory of, 15

Civil War (U.S.), 95, 155, 156, 172, 213, 218, 279, 319, 320

fetishism of commodities, 36, 72, 190, 290, 321, 322

fetishism of commodities, on, 36, 72, 107, 190, 290, 321, 322

freedom, on, 13–15, 55, 61, 68, 92, 93, 97, 112, 142–145, 150, 170, 179, 190, 237, 239, 250, 265–267, 272, 276, 277, 287, 288, 293, 297

Hegel, relationship to, 4, 11, 15, 253, 288

humanism of, 10, 15, 17, 67, 72, 77, 96, 145, 151, 154, 169, 170, 172, 186, 188, 190, 193, 212–215, 217, 225, 229, 239, 265, 267–269, 278, 286–288, 294, 296, 301, 305, 328

man/woman relationship, on, 108, 116, 135, 305

pre-capitalist societies, on, 199, 223

"revolution in permanence," on, 12, 14, 41, 79, 93, 96, 101, 105, 108, 115, 137, 254, 256, 301, 307

tendential decline in rate of profit, 15, 209–211, 214, 216, 218, 227, 228, 318

Pre-capitalist societies, 199, 206, 223
Primitive communism. *See*
   Communism
Prison Industrial Slavery Complex
   (PISC), 133, 134
Private property. *See* Property, private
Production, 30–32, 37, 47, 48,
   53, 55, 57–59, 66, 69, 79,
   96, 98, 109, 111, 112, 122,
   136, 146–148, 151–154, 160,
   171–174, 176–182, 199–204,
   210–216, 220, 222–229, 254,
   255, 262, 266, 273–275, 278,
   280, 290–293, 295, 297, 303,
   305, 306, 313, 316, 319, 322
Proletariat. *See* Working class
Property, 32, 46, 108, 109, 153, 157,
   158, 187, 193, 195, 199, 203,
   204, 243, 268, 274, 278, 291,
   319
   communal, 99, 108
   private, 32, 33, 57, 79, 108–111,
      172, 189, 190, 193, 200, 262,
      263, 265, 274, 285, 292, 293,
      318, 319
   state, 292, 319
Proudhon, Pierre-Joseph, 152,
   170–172

R

Raimondi, Luciano, 240
Reagan, Ronald, 7, 34, 131
Reason
   Black masses as, 158
   forces of revolution as, 105
   Hegel, in, 29–31, 34, 40, 71, 143,
      221, 234, 253, 330
   Marx, in, 40, 82, 105, 143,
      172–174, 198, 234, 290, 294
   proletariat as, 187
   women as, 94, 104, 113, 114, 156,
      161, 164

Reification, 29, 276, 321
Revolution
   African, 4, 11, 33, 240, 243, 303,
      304
   American (1776), 4, 131, 171
   French (1790), 8, 143, 171, 238,
      253, 276, 277, 286, 316, 317,
      330
   Hungarian (1956), 8, 9, 38, 60, 95,
      126, 196, 245, 246, 285, 301,
      311, 312, 319, 331
   Iran (1979), 7, 11
   Irish (1916 Uprising), 324
   Middle East and North Africa
      (MENA) (2011-13), 3
   Russian (1905), 67, 77, 95, 96,
      177, 210, 241, 242, 251, 315
   Russian (1917), 26, 159, 277
   two-stages theory, 81
   Women's, 304
Revolutionary Subject. *See* Subject
Revolution in permanence, 12, 14,
   41, 79, 93, 95, 96, 98, 101, 105,
   108, 115, 137, 233, 254, 256,
   301, 305, 307. *See also* Marx,
   Karl; Organization
Ricardo, David, 172
Rich, Adrienne, 4, 14, 40, 62, 102,
   151
Roberts, Michael, 209, 210, 227, 229
Rojava, 15, 161, 162
Rorty, Richard, 6
Rousseau, Jean-Jacques, 15, 170, 180,
   181
Roy, Manabendra Nath, 185, 186,
   203, 204, 321
Rubel, Maximilien, 239, 240
Russia, 3, 10, 15, 25, 26, 35, 38,
   47, 49, 67–70, 81, 91, 92, 103,
   175–179, 215, 218, 219, 223,
   240, 241, 244, 245, 248, 251,
   254, 263, 264, 266, 274, 275,

285, 286, 292, 294, 295, 297,
300, 311–313, 315, 319, 322,
325, 327, 332
Ryazanov, David, 285

S

Sans-culottes (France, 1789-93), 316
Sartre, Jean-Paul, 11, 327
Schapiro, Meyer, 25
Science/Technology, 51, 188, 200,
201, 205, 262, 266, 275, 315,
330
Scotland, 16, 238, 245, 249, 250
Second International, 15, 49, 77, 78,
83, 84, 174, 175, 186, 217, 218,
221, 235, 277, 322, 331, 332
Second negativity. *See* Dialectic,
negation of the negation
Sedova, Natalia, 16, 261, 263, 264
Self-determination of nations, 229
Self-determination of the Idea. *See*
Hegel, Georg Wilhelm Friedrich
Self-determination struggles. *See*
Anti-colonialism
Senegal, 243
Senghor, Léopold Sédar, 303, 307
Shachtman, Max, 46, 84, 292
Slavery, 47, 53, 95, 99, 106, 113,
133, 155, 156, 173, 204, 219,
281, 302, 320
Smith, Adam, 118, 172, 245, 253
Social democracy, 6, 313, 314,
332. *See also* German Social
Democratic Party
Socialism, 3, 6, 10, 25, 34, 46, 47,
50, 55, 57, 60, 65, 66, 68, 69,
77–80, 86, 110, 118, 121, 132,
142, 153, 158, 160, 163, 169,
174–177, 188, 192, 193, 212,
223, 233–236, 246, 251, 252,
254, 256, 263, 273, 274, 292,

294, 305, 322, 323, 325, 328,
331, 332
Socialisme ou Barbarie (SoB), 240,
249, 281, 314
Socialist Labor Party (USA), 49, 246
Socialist Workers Party, 9, 46, 84, 95,
291, 300, 306
Solidarnosc (Solidarity), 81
South Africa, 81, 129, 131, 135, 327
South African Communist Party, 81,
131
Soviets, 1, 4, 6, 10, 13, 33, 46, 50,
58, 60, 61, 69, 80, 86, 118,
151, 174–177, 183, 186, 193,
198, 234–236, 256, 261, 266,
272–276, 278, 286, 292, 294,
319, 326
Spinoza, Baruch, 27
Stalinism, 8, 10, 11, 25, 35, 46, 47,
49, 50, 52–55, 58, 67–69, 74,
80, 84, 95, 186, 194, 197–199,
240–242, 245, 251, 264–266,
273, 286, 294, 295, 311–313,
315, 318, 319, 325–330, 332
Stalin, Joseph, 25, 37, 38, 46, 47, 52,
53, 60, 67, 69, 94, 151, 178,
215, 236, 253, 267, 295, 297,
300, 307, 326, 329
State capitalism, 4, 8, 13, 16, 34,
45–49, 51, 52, 54–56, 58,
118, 151, 177–179, 183, 194,
234, 240, 241, 243, 251, 255,
273–277, 279, 280, 286, 292,
295, 296, 301, 302, 307, 315,
325
State-Capitalist Tendency, 8, 35, 46,
214, 215
State, One Party totalitarian, 35, 47,
67, 94, 178, 253, 312, 326
Stirner, Max, 189, 190, 203–205
Stone, Ria. *See* Boggs, Grace Lee
Subject, Black, as, 14, 76, 125

revolutionary, 14, 55, 60, 61, 104, 122, 127, 137, 142, 145, 146, 148, 150, 151, 197, 205, 221, 265, 269, 303, 317, 326, 331
women as, 15, 60, 104, 105, 108, 109, 111, 122, 157
Subjectivism, Maoist. *See* Mao Zedong
Subjectivity/Objectivity, 15, 51, 61, 82, 123, 253, 280, 331
Sudan, 3, 80, 314
Surplus value, 68, 69, 147, 173, 178, 201, 202, 211–213, 222, 224, 228, 291

T
Tanzania, 128
Taylor, Keeanga-Yamahtta, 125, 161
Thatcher, Margaret, 7, 34
Theory, movement from (as form of philosophy), 14, 38, 59–61, 75, 95, 114, 123, 126, 137, 151, 153, 158, 160, 280, 314. *See also* Practice, movement from
Thompson, Edward Palmer, 198, 204, 311
Totalitarianism, 26, 68, 179, 248, 286, 312, 325
Totality, 28, 30, 53, 72, 76, 122, 137, 214, 229, 242, 277
Tronti, Mario, 202, 203
Trotskyism, 37, 45, 46, 72, 73, 245, 251, 314, 319
Trotsky, Leon, 4, 11–13, 16, 25, 35, 46, 47, 49, 68, 76, 92, 94, 98, 177, 178, 185, 192, 214, 261, 263, 264, 267, 271, 273, 291, 307, 324
Trump, Donald, 2, 7, 149, 162
Truth, Sojourner, 5, 106, 157
Tubman, Harriet, 5, 106, 134

U
United States, 2–4, 9, 11, 14, 25, 26, 35–37, 47, 48, 60, 67, 68, 72, 76, 95, 106, 115, 117, 118, 121, 123, 125, 126, 129–131, 133–135, 138, 141, 149, 150, 155–159, 161, 213, 215, 219, 242, 243, 247, 271, 275, 286, 295, 297, 299, 302–304, 313–315, 320, 321, 324–327, 333
Universality, 49, 107, 118, 220, 299, 313
Universities and Left Review, 234, 245, 247, 249
Use value, 201
Utopian socialism, 171, 191, 205

V
Value, 16, 35, 53, 66, 68–70, 73, 79, 99, 106, 117, 148, 153, 156, 170, 171, 187, 200, 203, 211–213, 226, 228, 235, 251, 275, 290, 295, 296. *See also* Exchange value; Surplus value; Use-value
form of, 72, 233
history of theory, 172, 219
labor theory of, 290
Vanguard Party. *See* Organization
Vietnam, 9, 305, 327
Vogel, Lise, 111
Voluntarism. *See* Mao Zedong

W
Wildcat strikes, 37, 48, 72, 125, 280, 303, 331
Williams, Frank, 16, 237–239, 243, 246, 247, 249–251
Women/Women's Liberation, 4, 5, 10, 11, 14, 17, 26, 31, 34,

CPSIA information can be obtained
at www.ICGtesting.com
Printed in the USA
LVHW061301230821
695899LV00002B/46